WRITING FROM A TO Z

The Easy-to-Use Reference Handbook

Fourth Edition

Sally Barr Ebest
University of Missouri–St. Louis

Gerald J. Alred
University of Wisconsin–Milwaukee

Charles T. Brusaw
NCR Corporation (retired)

Walter E. Oliu
U.S. Nuclear Regulatory Commission

Boston   Burr Ridge, IL   Dubuque, IA   Madison, WI   New York
San Francisco   St. Louis   Bangkok   Bogotá   Caracas   Kuala Lumpur
Lisbon   London   Madrid   Mexico City   Milan   Montreal   New Delhi
Santiago   Seoul   Singapore   Sydney   Taipei   Toronto

McGraw-Hill Higher Education

A Division of The **McGraw-Hill** Companies

1 2 3 4 5 6 7 8 9 0 DOC/DOC 0 9 8 7 6 5 4 3

Library of Congress Cataloging-in-Publication Data
Writing from A to Z : the easy-to-use reference handbook / Sally Barr Ebest . . . [et al.].—4th ed.
   p. cm.
   Includes index.
   ISBN 0-07-294774-8
   1. English language—Rhetoric—Handbooks, manuals, etc. 2. English language—Grammar—Handbooks, manuals, etc. 3. Report writing—Handbooks, manuals, etc. I. Ebest, Sally Barr.

PE1408.W773 2002
808'.042—dc21   2002075370

Executive editor, Lisa Moore; *senior development editor,* Renée Deljon; *development editor,* Barbara Armentrout; *production editor,* April Wells-Hayes; *manuscript editor,* Zipporah Collins; *design manager,* Jean Mailander; *art editor,* Emma Ghiselli; *text designers,* Linda Robertson and Glenda King; *illustrators,* Robin Mouat and Natalie Hill; *production supervisor,* Rich DeVitto. The text was set in 10/12 Berkeley Medium by Thompson Type and printed on 45# New Era Matte in black and Pantone Reflex Blue by R. R. Donnelley & Sons Company.

www.mhhe.com

To the Instructor

Through three editions, increasing numbers of students and instructors across the country have discovered the advantages of *Writing from A to Z*'s alphabetical organization. Although this organization is nontraditional for an English handbook, its familiarity makes the book easier than most other handbooks for students to use. Why? Students using this text do not need to crack a specialized "code" of organization that requires them to know established categories of writing information and instruction such as usage, grammar, and style. Instead, because the entries in *A to Z* are familiar and intuitive, students need only turn to a letter of the alphabet to find the appropriate entry that will answer their questions and provide examples. Easy-to-use cross-references also direct students to additional information.

Another advantage of this book's organization is that it makes plastic-coated, tabbed section dividers unnecessary and so eliminates this sometimes cumbersome feature. This truly is a handbook that allows students to flip through the pages easily and find the information they need quickly. For these reasons, students at all levels and across the disciplines actually use *Writing from A to Z* and use it comfortably, which helps to build their confidence and independence as writers. After they've completed their writing classes, they have a reliable writer's tool for the rest of their college coursework.

Key Features

The most distinctive feature of *Writing from A to Z* is the alphabetical organization of its core section, but an abundance of other notable features make it a handbook that students consistently use.

- **The most straightforward alphabetizing system available in a handbook.** The A to Z entries are organized by the letter-by-letter system, so users can ignore punctuation marks (such as slashes, hyphens, and commas) and spaces between words. This nontechnical alphabetizing system ensures ease of use.

- **Separate composing and research processes guides.** These concise guides precede the alphabetical entries and are identified with thumb tabs along the edges of their pages. For additional ease of use, each section opens with its own table of contents.

- **Extensive, integrated coverage of Internet research and writing with computers.** The up-to-date, detailed coverage of online writing and research, flagged with a computer icon , helps students use computers effectively throughout their writing and research processes. Extensive guidelines for finding, evaluating, and using online sources are set off with a new thumb tab (Internet Searches) within the larger research section.

- **Coverage of the four most common documentation styles.** The MLA (Modern Language Association), APA (American Psychological Association), CSE (Council of Science Editors, formerly the Council of Biology Editors [CBE]), and Chicago (CMS) styles are covered in detail. Model student papers are provided for the MLA and APA formats, as are sample pages from student papers for the CSE and CMS formats, making *Writing from A to Z* especially effective for writing-intensive courses across the disciplines.

- **Coverage of graphics and document design.** In addition to a separate **document design** entry, *Writing from A to Z* provides entries such as **graphics**, **lists**, **manuscript form**, **tables**, and **typefaces** to help students produce papers that meet today's visual standards and use the design capabilities of computers appropriately.

- **Coverage of argumentation, informal logic, and critical thinking.** Principally located within the **logic** entry, this material includes discussions of topics such as deductive and inductive reasoning, the Toulmin method, and logical fallacies.

- **Integrated usage entries.** In traditional handbooks, students must locate a separate glossary of usage (containing word pairs and brief explanations of standard usage) and then find the information they need. In *Writing from A to Z*, usage entries such as *imply/infer* appear in the text's alphabetical section. The headings for these entries are italicized for ready recognition. For instance, on pages 314–15 students will find the following sequence:

  hanged/hung

  hasty generalization

  headings

  healthful/healthy

  helping verbs

  he/she, his/her

- **ESL entries throughout and a separate ESL index.** An ESL (English as a Second Language) icon used throughout the book makes it easy for non-native speakers of English to find the help they need. This coverage is also listed in a separate ESL index, beginning on page E-1, that precedes the book's full subject index.

- **A fail-safe general index.** The exceptionally student-friendly index, beginning on page I-1, provides an alternative way for students to locate appropriate alphabetical entries. *A to Z*'s index provides a comprehensive listing of the handbook's contents, identified not only by standard terms but also by the commonsense, intuitive terms students might think of instead—for example, *dots* for *ellipsis points.*

- **Contents by Topic Area.** This listing, located on the inside front cover, provides a general overview of the book's contents by topic area. Not only does the topical contents offer an additional means of access, it also gives students and instructors a way to see *A to Z*'s contents arranged in the traditional categories, making it easier to pair the book with traditionally organized writing guides and readers and helping students pull together information on broad subjects covered in multiple entries.

- **Examples with handwritten changes wherever appropriate.** Unlike "correct" and "incorrect" examples, the handwritten changes make corrections and improvements easy to see and also reinforce the editing and proofreading processes.

New to the Fourth Edition

In addition to fresh examples and general improvements throughout, this edition of *Writing from A to Z* offers several major changes that increase its value for today's students.

- **Expanded coverage of online research.** Appearing within the Research Processes section, a new tab, Internet Searches, marks seven pages of up-to-date information on topics such as evaluating the reliability of Internet sources and experimenting with keywords and other search engine strategies.

- **Directory of MLA documentation models for Internet sources.** Another new tab, Electronic Sources, highlights this new listing of thirty-one documentation models (the most available in any handbook) for online sources within the MLA section. With guidance from the Modern Language Association (MLA), Ellen Strenski prepared these models based on her research at the University of California, Irvine, examining the kinds of electronic sources student writers really use.

- **Increased coverage of plagiarism.** Now covered in the research section and an expanded alphabetical entry, this increasingly important topic is discussed from various perspectives, including that of ethics.

- **More quick-reference aids.** In addition to the new Contents by Topic Area provided on the inside front cover and new computer and ESL icons throughout the book, the fourth edition includes numerous new boxes, charts, and checklists that further improve its visual appeal and ease of use.

- **Updated APA coverage.** Thoroughly revised to reflect the many changes in the fifth edition of the APA's *Publication Manual*, this section now also provides expanded coverage of documenting electronic sources.

- **New A-to-Z entries.** New entries in this edition include **academic writing, audiovisuals, credibility, database, I,** and **rhetoric.**

McGraw-Hill Resources for Online Instruction and Distance Learning

- **Web site.** The *Writing from A to Z* Web site provides an array of interactive exercises, research activities, and links. The contents of the Web site are compatible with most electronic classroom management systems, including WebCT and Blackboard.

- **E-text.** *Writing from A to Z* is available in electronic format both online and on CD-ROM.

- **PageOut.** McGraw-Hill's own PageOut service is available to help you get your course up and running online in a matter of hours—at no cost. Additional information about the service is available online at <www.pageout.net>.

- **Webwrite.** This online product, available through our partner company Meta-Text, makes it possible for writing teachers and students to—among other things—comment on and share papers online.

- **AllWrite!** Available online or on CD-ROM, *AllWrite!* offers over 3,000 exercises for practice in basic grammar, usage, punctuation, spelling, and techniques for effective writing. The popular program is richly illustrated with graphics, animations, video, and Help screens.

- **Teaching Composition Faculty Listserv at** <www.mhhe.com/tcomp>. Moderated by Chris Anson at North Carolina State University and offered by McGraw-Hill as a service to the composition community, this listserv brings together senior members of the college composition community with newer members—junior faculty, adjuncts, and teaching assistants—through an online newsletter and accompanying discussion group to address issues of pedagogy in theory and practice.

Print Supplements for Students

- *Research across the Disciplines,* **Second Edition.** This resource expands the contents of the handbook's research section by offering tips on researching and writing in more than forty disciplines, as well as model student papers.

- *The Mayfield Quick View Guide to the Internet for Students of English,* **Version 2.0.** This concise, information-packed guide is free when shrink-wrapped with *Writing from A to Z.*

For further information about these and other supplemental resources, contact your local McGraw-Hill representative, visit the English pages on the McGraw-Hill Higher Education Web site at **<www.mhhe.com/catalogs/hss/english>**, or visit McGraw-Hill's Digital Solutions pages at **<www.mhhe.com/catalogs/solutions>**.

Acknowledgments

We continue to be indebted to Catharine D. Slawson, Solano Community College, for help with the ESL material so crucial to serving the needs of an increasingly diverse student population.

We are grateful to many users of the previous editions for their suggestions and especially to Ellen Strenski and her colleagues at the University of California, Irvine, and Les Perelman at the Massachusetts Institute of Technology. Again we also thank the manuscript reviewers who helped us create the first edition: Kathy Evertz, University of Wyoming; Kathryn Harris, Arizona State University; Peggy Mulvihill, University of Missouri, St. Louis; Patricia Y. Murray, California State University, Northridge; and Holly Zaitchik, Boston University.

For allowing us to use words and ideas from their McGraw-Hill (formerly Mayfield) books, we are grateful to G. Scott Cawelti, University of Northern Iowa, and Jeffrey L. Duncan, Eastern Michigan University, authors of *The Inventive Writer: A Discovery-Based Rhetoric*; Robert Keith Miller, University of St. Thomas, author of *Motives for Writing*; W. Ross Winterowd and Geoffrey R. Winterowd, University of Southern California, authors of *The Critical Reader, Thinker, and Writer*; and David W. Chapman, Samford University, and Preston Lynn Waller, McLennan Community College, authors of *The Power of Writing*.

We deeply appreciate the helpful comments of this edition's reviewers: William M. Carroll III, Abilene Christian University; Linda Cullum, Kutztown University; Caley O'Dwyer Feagin, University of California, Irvine; Susan Ghiaciuc, University of Louisville; Tim Gustafson, University of Minnesota; Anita Guynn, Beloit College; Jan Hardy, Spoon River College; Sylvia Ballard Huete, Dillard University; John Hyman, American University; Mary Kramer, University of Massachusetts at Lowell; Bryan Moore, Arkansas State University; Mark Rollins, Ohio University; Jack Shreve, Allegheny College; Phillip Sipiora, University of South Florida; and Deborah Coxwell Teague, Florida State University.

We also wish to again thank the reviewers of the second and third editions: Adrienne R. Ackra, Old Dominion; Margarethe Ahlschwede, University of Tennessee at Martin; Akua Duku Anokye, University of Toledo; Valerie Balester, Texas A & M; Larry Beason, University of South Alabama; Kathy Boardman, University of Nevada at Reno; Joseph Colavito, Northwestern State University; Joseph F. Dunne, St. Louis Community College at Meramec; Susan Fitzgerald, University of Memphis; Jose Flores, Austin Community College; Gretchen Fox, University of California at Irvine; Shawn Fullmer, University of Nevada at Reno; Celia Gilmore-Hezekiah, South Carolina State; Lucy Gonzalez, Del Mar Community College; Joan Griffin, Metro State College; Karyn Hollis, Villanova University; Janis Butler

Holm, Ohio University; John Hyman, American University; Teresa Johnson, University of Memphis; James Kastely, University of Houston; Paul Kleinpoppen, Florida Community College; Mike Little, Texas A & M; Joe Lostracco, Austin Community College; Anne Maxham, Washington State University; Michael Moghtader, University of New Mexico at Albuquerque; Jean Nienkamp, University of Massachusetts at Amherst; Douglas L. Okey, Spoon River College; Mona Oliver, Northeast Louisiana; Nancy Prosenjak, Metro State College; Kris Ratcliffe, Marquette University; Denise Rogers, University of Southwestern Louisiana; Paul Sanchez, University of Utah; John Schaeffer, Northern Illinois University; Tim Schell, Clackamas Community College; Marcia Smith, University of Arkansas at Little Rock; Deborah Coxwell Teague, Florida State University; Ray Wallace, Northwestern State University; Jackie Walsh, McNeese State University; Marian Wernicke, Pensacola Junior College; Lisa Williams, Jacksonville State; Liz Wright, University of New Mexico at Albuquerque; and Dede Yow, Keenesaw State University.

Finally, we must again extend special thanks to Ellen Strenski at the University of California, Irvine, for her work that appears in the Internet Searches section and for her tireless commitment to developing this edition's catalog of MLA documentation models for electronic sources. Her work and that of her colleagues with whom she collaborated contributes not only to this text but to the field of composition.

Finally, we salute the dedicated, highly professional people at and working with McGraw-Hill Higher Education: Lisa Moore, our executive editor; Renée Deljon, senior development editor; Linda Toy, production director; April Wells-Hayes, production editor; Zipporah Collins, manuscript editor; Jean Mailander, design manager; Emma Ghiselli, art editor; David Patterson, marketing manager; and all the others, especially Barbara Armentrout, who have helped to make this book.

To the Student:
How to Use This Book

Organized alphabetically like a dictionary, with key words at the tops of the pages and with the letters of the alphabet along the margins for easy access, *Writing from A to Z* enables you to turn directly to the information you need without first having to figure out what broader category your writing problem belongs to (usage? grammar? style? something else?) as you would in a topically organized handbook.

Please take the time to read the introductory sections, **Composing Processes** (beginning on page 1) and **Research Processes** (beginning on page 25). They provide a framework for all the other material in the book.

Alphabetizing System

You may not be aware that there are different systems of alphabetizing. All alphabetizing in this book is letter by letter, which simply means that punctuation marks and spaces between words are ignored. For example, on pages 506–08 you will find this sequence of entries:

verbals

verb errors

verb phrases

verbs

Notice that the order after the letters *v-e-r-b* is *a, e, p, s*. Just remember to ignore punctuation marks and spaces between words when searching for an alphabetical entry, and you will have no trouble finding what you need.

Cross-References within Entries

One of the most important features of *Writing from A to Z* is the network of cross-references within the entries. Every term that has an entry of its own is printed in bold type wherever it appears in other entries. Using these bold-type references, you can pursue a topic as extensively as you wish or quickly find only the information you require to continue with a particular writing task.

For example, suppose you felt (or a classmate or your instructor suggested) that something you had written would be more effective if certain points were given stronger emphasis. Flipping to the alphabetical entry for **emphasis**, you would find an opening paragraph that defines *emphasis* and lists various ways of achieving it, followed by three subsections headed IN PARAGRAPHS, IN SENTENCES, and WITH WORDS. This **emphasis** entry alone might very well give you all the help you need, but in reading the entry you would also encounter bold-type references to the following additional entries, all of which have something to do with emphasis:

repetition	balanced sentences
sentence types	parallel structure
punctuation	sentence fragment
intensifiers	dash
italics	exclamation point
compound sentences	word choice
complex sentences	verbs
simple sentences	active voice
cumulative sentences	sentence variety
periodic sentences	hyperbole

Many of these entries, in turn, contain further bold-type references. Which topics to pursue and how far to pursue them are entirely up to you.

Composing Processes

The first section of the book provides detailed guidance that will help you adapt your composing processes to suit the various writing situations you encounter. It covers topics such as identifying purpose, analyzing audience, drafting, revising, and proofreading. At the end of the section, on pages 22–23, you'll find a Checklist for Composing, which highlights the primary concerns of successful composition.

Research Processes:
Finding, Using, and Documenting Sources

The second section of the book will guide you through the processes of gathering information from a wide variety of primary and secondary sources, print and electronic, and using it effectively in documented papers. **Research Processes** explains four styles for citing sources: Modern Language Association (MLA), American Psychological Association (APA), *Chicago Manual of Style* (CMS), and Council of Science Editors (CSE). The section on MLA style concludes with a complete sample research paper, and the other three sections each end with an array of sample pages.

Fail-Safe General Index and ESL Index

If going straight to an alphabetical entry in the book should fail to solve your problem, turn to the index. It provides an exhaustive listing of the topics covered in *Writing from A to Z,* not only by the terms used in the entries but also by commonsense terms you might think of instead—for example, *dots, spaced* or *periods, spaced* for *ellipsis points* (the three dots used to show an omission in a quotation or occasionally to signal a pause or hesitation in dialogue).

If English is not your native language, you will find English as a Second Language (ESL) listings not only throughout the general index but also collected for your convenience in a special ESL index beginning on page E-1.

Information for Writers of English as a
Second Language (ESL)

Throughout the book you will notice ( ) symbols. These icons mark information of particular importance for writers whose native language is not English. An index for ESL writers begins on page E-1.

Contents by Topic Area

The Contents by Topic Area can help you pull together information on broad subjects covered by multiple entries. You'll find this handy listing on the inside of the book's front cover.

Internet Coverage Identified with an Icon

Writing from A to Z has extensive, up-to-date coverage of the Internet, including particularly helpful guidelines for evaluating and documenting

Internet sources. This icon identifies all Internet-related coverage so that you can find it as quickly as possible.

Word-Usage Entries

In *Writing from A to Z,* word-usage entries (such as ***imply/infer***) appear right along with other kinds of entries in alphabetical order. Thus, on pages 314–16 you will find the following sequence:

> **headings**
> *healthful/healthy*
> **helping verbs**
> *he/she, his/her*
> *himself/hisself*

Just look up whatever word you are wondering about as you would look it up in a dictionary. Headings for word-usage entries are in italics, as shown in the list above; other headings are not italicized. A complete list of word-usage entries appears under the entry **usage.**

Mini Tables of Contents in Long Entries

Composing Processes and **Research Processes** as well as long or complex alphabetical entries have their own mini tables of contents or directories (as on page 158) to help you locate the specific information you need.

Revision Chart

Inside the back cover, you will find a chart of revision symbols commonly used by instructors in marking papers. The chart gives the meaning of each symbol and lists the number of the page that explains how to make the needed revision.

COMPOSING PROCESSES

1

Overview of Composing Processes

(Note: Throughout this book, words printed in **bold type** refer to alphabetical entries that give you more detailed information. Those entries may, in turn, contain other references in bold type. Thus, you can investigate any topic as quickly or as thoroughly as you wish.)

When we say that writers have gone through the composing processes, we mean that they have taken a piece of writing from the point at which they develop ideas and consider ways of organizing them, through drafting, revising, editing, and proofreading. The process is not as neat and straightforward as it sounds, nor does every writer follow the same pattern. Writers sometimes jump ahead, sometimes loop back, sometimes draw arrows and stars, and sometimes hit the delete key. (The flowchart on page 4 illustrates the process.) Nevertheless, most writing—and all successful academic writing—is the result of the writer's attention to all phases of the composing process. This section describes each phase, moving from prewriting through proofreading; however, the order in which they are done depends upon each writer's personal process.

ASSESSING THE RHETORICAL SITUATION

Every act of writing is done in a particular context, called *the rhetorical situation*. Different kinds of writing may emphasize different elements of the rhetorical situation, but five elements are always present: writer, occasion, audience, topic, and purpose.

Occasion

Occasion is the occurrence that prompts you to write. You may need to answer a letter from a friend, leave instructions for your child's caregiver, or write a paper for a class. Obviously, these three occasions would lead to quite different decisions about a number of matters—for instance, the length and

3

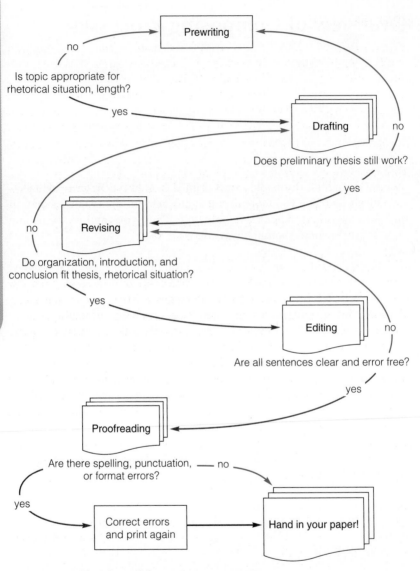

Figure CP-1. Flowchart of the composing processes.

the formality of the **tone.** In most letters, use of the second-person pronoun *you* is permissible, whereas in academic writing, *you* should be avoided. In instructions—such as those in this book—using *you* personalizes the tone. Pay attention to the occasion, and adjust your tone accordingly.

Audience

Just as you speak in different ways to different people—friends and strangers, adults and children, family members and colleagues at school or work—your **audience** also affects how and what you write. For instance, terms that are clear to one audience need to be defined for another. A writing course presents a special audience problem: Your instructor is part of your audience, but not all writing instructors want you to write just for them. Some instructors want you to write for a more general audience consisting of intelligent, well-intentioned readers. A useful technique for doing so is to imagine one specific reader who is typical of the audience and write to that person. If your course includes **peer response** sessions in which students read and comment on one another's drafts, you may know your readers personally, be able to write for them, and benefit from their feedback.

Topic

In a writing course, the instructor may assign a **topic** or allow you to choose your own. If the topic is assigned, unless it is one that already interests you, the challenge is to discover some aspect of it, some way of focusing, or narrowing, it, that does interest you. Even when you have the luxury of picking a topic, you may still have the problem of focusing it so that you can do it justice in a paper of the expected length. In addition to considering your **audience** and **purpose**, take into account your knowledge of the subject. If your area of expertise is already highly specialized, the problem is solved. However, if you know, or find, a great deal of information about a general topic, try breaking it into subcategories and writing about the area of most interest. Even the best writers find it difficult to write about something they know or care little about, so whenever possible try to narrow the topic to something that interests you.

Purpose

At the outset or during the writing process, try to decide on your **purpose**, and then make sure as you draft, revise, and edit that everything in your paper works toward accomplishing that goal. Depending on the purpose, you will emphasize some elements of the rhetorical situation more than others. Some writing—usually called **expressive**—emphasizes the writer almost to the exclusion of other elements. Examples of expressive writing include personal response **journals**, in which the writer can express feelings and explore ideas, and **narrative** essays that recount and reflect on personal experiences.

Other writing—certainly most writing done for college courses—emphasizes the **topic**. What you know about a topic is far more important in such

COMPOSING PROCESSES

ELEMENTS OF THE RHETORICAL SITUATION

- **The Writer:** What do I already know about this subject? What interests me about it? What is my attitude toward it? What image, or persona, do I want to project (for example, irate customer, friend, or job applicant)?
- **The Occasion:** What is the context for writing? How long should this piece be? How much time should I allot for planning, organizing, drafting, and revising a piece of this length? How formal should my tone be?
- **The Audience:** Who is my audience? Are audience members likely to have some knowledge of my subject, or do I need to define basic terms? Can I get feedback from a representative member of my audience?
- **The Topic:** Do I need to narrow the topic so that it can be effectively covered in a paper of the required length? What sources of information are available to me (such as personal experience, direct observation, books and periodicals in the library, documents on the Internet)? What kinds of new information will I need to seek?
- **The Purpose:** Why am I writing? Do I want to express my feelings and explore my ideas? Do I want to inform the audience? Or do I want to persuade the audience to accept my position?

---

expository writing than what you feel. Still other writing, such as newspaper editorials, aims to be **persuasive**, to move the audience to some belief or course of action. (For more on persuasive writing, see the entries about **argument** and **logic**.) In analytical writing, you are also being persuasive, trying to convince the audience that your thesis or opinion is valid by using examples. When writing a **literary analysis**, for example, you might try to persuade the reader that the **characterization** is unrealistic or that the **setting** helps to establish the mood. Finally, some writing is done for its own sake, as art. The writing itself, rather than the writer, topic, or audience, is foremost in the writer's mind. Most poems, stories, and plays, as well as many essays, fall into this category of creative writing.

PREWRITING

All the planning you do, including assessment of the rhetorical situation, belongs to the prewriting stage of composing. Finding a suitable topic and deciding how to approach it are often the most difficult prewriting tasks. Several unstructured techniques may prove helpful at the outset; try them and see which ones work best for you. Brainstorming (which also lends itself to a collaborative, or group, approach), listing, clustering, and freewriting are all ways of drawing on the unconscious mind to bring ideas to the surface. (As the bold type indicates, each technique is treated at more length in an alphabetical entry in this handbook.) The key to making these techniques productive is not to edit or critique prematurely but to work as quickly and freely as possible.

Brainstorming the topic of education might yield the following items:

parochial schools	required uniforms
busing	computer-aided instruction
delaying college	college versus trade school
parents' role	required education for new parents
driver's education	banking versus transmission methods
use of small groups	need for better teacher training
affirmative action	advantages of community colleges

Here is an example of **freewriting** on education resulting from the use of brainstorming, listing, or clustering ideas first:

EDUCATION

When I think of education, the first thing which comes to mind is hot, boring classrooms, trying to stay awake while Dr. Martin droned on and on. Lots of things follow that image, like his angry tirades when we did poorly on tests or didn't understand how to write the papers he wanted. The fact that once I got out of Poli Sci, or even the day after a test, I couldn't remember a thing. The belief that Poli Sci apparently had nothing to do with real-world events, and my disappointment that what I thought would be an interesting class, especially in an election year, was yet one more dreary recital of names, dates, faces, and terms. Who cares? This guy was a walking advertisement for the "banking concept of education."

Listing as a follow-up to brainstorming on the topic of education might yield these examples:

BANKING VERSUS TRANSMISSION METHODS OF TEACHING

boredom of lectures

necessity of coverage

fear of chaos

ADVANTAGES OF ACTIVE LEARNING

interest

involvement

accountability

application of theory

Figure CP-2. Example of clustering.

USE OF SMALL GROUPS

active learning or anarchy?

need for teacher training re: use of small groups

need for student instruction re: small group behavior and responsibility

need for tasks, direction, supervision, and accountability

The example of **clustering** on the topic of education (Figure CP-2, above) is a follow-up to brainstorming or an alternative to listing.

TIPS FOR PREWRITING ON THE COMPUTER

For some writers, the computer makes prewriting easier. Later, they can copy and paste any of their prewriting notes into the rough draft.

- To avoid the temptation to edit while **freewriting** or **brainstorming**, you might turn down the contrast on the screen or use a dark gray background so that you can't easily read what you are typing. You may also want to create separate files for ideas that you discover during freewriting or brainstorming.

- Some word-processing programs allow you to turn a **list** into an **outline**. Then you can change the levels of headings and move them to different places easily. For directions about outlining with your word-processing program, consult its Help files.
- You can use a drawing or painting program to do **clustering** if this kind of spatial planning works best for you. However, clustering your ideas may be just as easy with a pencil and paper.

Development Strategies

Once you have decided on a tentative topic, or at least a general subject, one or more of the following structured processes can help you focus and develop it.

Journalists' Questions If the assignment is to write about an event, one of the simplest techniques for exploring it is to ask the journalists' questions: *Who? What? When? Where? Why? How?* Not all the questions will be equally productive with every topic, but asking them will nearly always reveal something.

Burke's Pentad A more powerful variation on the journalists' questions is rhetorician Kenneth Burke's pentad. Burke points out that every event has a dramatic structure, like a play. Something happens; hence, there is an *act*. The act takes place at some time and some place; hence, it has a *scene*. Something—human or otherwise—performs the act; hence, it has an *agent*. The agent commits the act by some means or other; hence, the act requires *agency*. To perform the act, the agent must have a motive; hence, the act involves *purpose*. Notice how the five parts of Burke's pentad correspond to the journalists' questions:

act = what?

scene = where and when?

agent = who?

agency = how?

purpose = why?

The real power of Burke's pentad, however, comes from considering the various elements in pairs—which Burke calls *ratios*—to discover how each element affects the others. For example, how does the scene affect the agent?

Would the agent have behaved differently at night than during the day? If it were summer rather than winter? If he or she had been in a small rural town rather than a city neighborhood?

If you were asked to write about a significant personal experience—a common assignment in writing courses—you would first select an experience (or act, in Burke's terms). Then you would have to decide how to focus the essay: where to begin your account, how much to include, and what point to emphasize. If applying the pentad led you to discover the importance of the scene, for example, you would probably decide to devote much of your essay to the ways in which the scene contributed to the act.

Methods of Development Another set of questions that can help focus and develop a subject was devised by the Greek philosopher Aristotle. Aristotle's questions, which he called *topoi* (Greek for "place"), were designed to discover proofs in persuasive writing, but they can also help shape your composition. (Each **method of development** named in bold type is described and illustrated in an alphabetical entry in this book.)

- **Analysis:** Should I *divide* my subject into parts and then discuss each part separately or perhaps focus on a single part?
- **Cause and effect:** Should I explain what *caused* this event or describe its *effects*?
- **Classification:** Can I *classify* this subject by putting it in a group of similar items?
- **Comparison and contrast:** Should I *compare* my subject to a similar one or *contrast* it with something different in order to make my point?
- **Definition:** Should I *define* my subject's source and meaning?
- **Description:** Should I *describe* the features of my subject?
- **Examples:** Should I provide an *example* of what I mean?
- **Narration:** Should I tell a story? (See also **anecdote**.)
- **Process:** Can I present this subject as a series of steps and explain how it works?

Organization The methods of development you choose play a key role in the organization of the paper. Selecting **cause and effect** or **comparison and contrast** more or less determines the organization, whereas choosing other methods broadens the organization options. For example, if the method of development is **analysis, classification,** or **definition,** you might decide to organize your paper following the principles of **general to specific** or **increasing order of importance.** If your paper relies on **examples, narration,** or **process** as the method of development, you could organize it chronologically. With **description,** you could use either **chronological** or **spatial** organization. And if the paper is to be persuasive, you may use a variety of methods to make your **argument** convincing. In sum, decisions regarding methods of development and organization go hand in hand. But they are also determined by the paper's thesis.

The Thesis

Some kinds of writing—for example, writing to explore an idea or to describe a scene—may be unified by a search for meanings or simply by some dominant impression or mood rather than by a central idea that can be stated in a sentence or two. For most writing, however, you will need to develop a **thesis** at some point in the composing process. The thesis is also sometimes referred to as the focus, or the point. None of these terms should be confused with the **topic**. The difference between a topic and a thesis is important. The topic is the subject narrowed to a manageable scope; it can simply be named. "Equality for women in military service" is a topic. The thesis is the position you take on the subject; it should be stated in a declarative sentence or two. "Women should be allowed in combat" is a thesis.

All the techniques described earlier for finding and focusing a topic can also help you formulate a thesis. Some writers have a thesis before they begin writing a draft; other writers may not know their position on the topic until they see what they have to say. Become aware of your writing process, and develop strategies that help you make the most of it. One final word about the thesis: Be prepared to change it if you find it is not workable or if you no longer believe it. Writing at its best is always a process of discovery.

DRAFTING

A **first draft** should be just that. Your instructor may require you to turn in several drafts, but, even if this is not a requirement, make a habit of writing at least two or three drafts. Rereading and rewriting are closely related, mutually reinforcing processes. When rereading a draft, you are likely to discover a word, phrase, or idea that can be stated better. When rewriting, you may come up with words and ideas you did not think of before. Whether you are changing a few words, adding a section, or rearranging paragraphs, rereading and rewriting can only improve your compositions. Drafting does not mean writing the paper; it is just the first step. Focusing on perfection during drafting can shut down the creative side of your mind and lead to writer's block. Draft first, then edit.

As noted earlier, some kinds of writing do not include a thesis. Careful assessment of the rhetorical situation will guide you in deciding whether a thesis is called for. But thesis or no thesis, if a clear **purpose** is not evident, the audience will be confused or bored or both. If you have not started out with a clear purpose, writing a first draft should help you find one. Some writers compose a speedy "discovery draft" for the sole purpose of discovering what they have to say before they give any thought to **organization** or **methods of development**.

Different writers follow different processes, but most focus in the drafting stage on large-scale or fundamental matters of content, purpose, and thesis, leaving issues of organization, style, and correctness for the revising, editing, and proofreading stages. As you begin the first draft, remember that this is merely a version of the paper that no one else will read. Write quickly. If a good **introduction** does not come immediately, don't worry. Start with the section that seems easiest; your audience will not know or care which part you wrote first. Likewise, don't worry at this stage about writing a **conclusion**. It will be difficult to develop until you know what the rest of the paper contains. Finally, don't bother with **transitions** at this stage unless they come easily. And don't try to polish or revise before finishing at least one complete draft. Concentrate on developing your ideas.

Stop writing before you are completely exhausted. If you need to stop before finishing a draft, you might try Ernest Hemingway's trick of stopping in the middle of a sentence that you will remember how to complete when you return. Before resuming, reread what you have written so far; often this reading process will trigger the frame of mind that was productive.

TIPS FOR DRAFTING ON THE COMPUTER

- To avoid unintentional **plagiarism**, keep your draft in a separate file from your source notes. Whenever you copy a quotation or a paraphrase from your source notes, be sure to identify the source in your draft at the same time, and be sure to insert quotation marks around any direct quotation.
- Each time you revise a draft, save it in a separate file, in case you want to go back and retrieve some material from a previous version. Give each draft file a different name (such as "Draft 1," "Draft 2," and so on) so that you can tell which is the most recent version.
- Use the click-and-drag function to move paragraphs and sentences around and experiment with the **organization** of your draft.
- If you are using Word for Macintosh or for Windows, use the split-screen function to view your draft and your prewriting, outline, or source note files at the same time. You can also copy and paste between files.
- When you write notes to yourself as you are drafting, use a bold font or change the font color so that the notes stand out.
- Print out a hard copy of each draft, because revising is easier when the entire text is in front of you.
- To protect yourself against computer crashes, save your changes often while you are drafting, and make backup copies of everything on a floppy disk.

REVISING

Revising is not just another name for editing or proofreading. Those are the final stages in which you polish the style and fix grammar, spelling, and punctuation errors. *Revising* means, literally, seeing again—as if with new eyes. It is concerned with fundamental matters of meaning and structure (if in the course of revising you happen to notice an error of spelling or grammar, of course, you should feel free to correct it). Good writers do not expect to get any piece of writing right the first time. They know they need to look again, from the perspective of their intended **audience**.

Revising requires getting enough distance from your writing to see it afresh. The best way to achieve this objectivity is to take a break after preparing the previous draft—ideally a day or two, but at least a few hours. Whether you reread the paper alone or listen while someone else reads and responds to it, a little distance makes it easier to tell the difference between what you actually wrote and what you thought you wrote.

As a rule, the best way to revise is to work from large-scale concerns, such as organization, to those on a smaller scale, such as paragraph development and word choice. Following this order will help you avoid the frustration of throwing out or drastically revising material that you have already fine-tuned.

Large-Scale Concerns

Keeping in mind all the elements of the rhetorical situation discussed earlier, first evaluate whether the piece of writing reflects your original **purpose** and supports your **thesis**. If your writing has begun to wander, cut out the irrelevant material—unless you have wandered in a more interesting direction, in which case you may wish to reconsider your purpose and begin again.

The same strategy applies to your thesis, or central position. If some **paragraphs** are not clearly related to it, either directly or indirectly, this lack of **unity** may be caused either by the paragraphs or by the thesis itself. If the process of writing has changed your views, consider rethinking the thesis and reworking the paper. However, if the thesis still seems valid and clearly stated, the unrelated paragraphs may need to be rewritten or deleted.

Once you have determined that the focus is clear, consider drafting the **introduction**. Although some writers feel they must have their introduction before they can proceed with the rest of the draft, others find such pressure frustrating. If you fall into the latter category, now is the time to decide how to begin your paper.

Introductions may take a variety of forms: They can consist of a **definition, question, quotation,** or **analogy;** a **characterization, description, example,** or **anecdote;** or facts, statistics, or background information. The type of introduction should be determined by the paper's purpose, but it should also take into account the needs of the **audience**. If you want people to read the paper or agree with the ideas, you first have to get their attention. So take some time to experiment with different types of introductions; pick two or three to freewrite, and then decide which one is most appropriate.

When the introduction seems suitably developed, see how it fits with the **body** of the paper by reading through the entire manuscript. If the introduction and body feel cohesive, then move on to examine the organization.

Outlining the paper can be helpful in revealing shortcomings in structure and logic. Skipping over any purely transitional paragraphs, write down, in order, the **topic sentences** or central ideas of all the other paragraphs, indenting the subordinate ones under those they support. This outline is the skeleton of your paper. Look at it closely. Do any points need to be supported with more information or **examples** in order to be clear to your audience? Do any problems of **logic** need to be corrected?

Next, consider the sequence of the paragraphs. The **coherence** of a piece of writing depends on the ease with which readers can move from idea to idea and grasp the relationships among them. Coherence is achieved in a number of ways, especially by establishing a natural, logical sequence of ideas; by choosing appropriate **methods of development** for the whole paper and for individual paragraphs; by providing **transitions** that help readers move easily from one idea to the next; by eliminating material that interrupts the flow of ideas (see **conciseness/wordiness**); by supplying necessary information that the readers could not be expected to know; and by avoiding distracting **shifts** in **tense**, **mood**, or **point of view**.

Small-Scale Concerns

Take a close look at the first **paragraph** or two. These paragraphs—or first few sentences—may be nothing more than "throat clearing"; the paper may really start farther down the page. Also consider whether the **introduction** captures the reader's interest and sets the stage for what follows—and whether the paper's **conclusion** is consistent with your purpose and will leave the **audience** with a satisfying sense of completion. If you have not already done so, start thinking about a **title**. Even a working title (like everything else in the paper, subject to further revision) will help you maintain a clear focus and a consistent **tone**.

Read each paragraph to assess whether its central idea is either clearly stated in a **topic sentence** or so clearly implied that no explicit statement is necessary. Does each paragraph have **unity**? That is, is everything in the paragraph related to the central idea? Is each paragraph coherent and well developed? (See **coherence** and **methods of development**.)

COMPOSING PROCESSES

TIPS FOR REVISING ON THE COMPUTER

- You may find it easier to see your draft "with new eyes" if you change it to a different, or a larger, font. Use the "select all" command (Command or Control + A in Word for Macintosh or Windows), and then choose a new font (but not a fancy one that will be difficult to read).
- Do your revising on a hard copy of the most recent draft so that you can see the entire text rather than having to scroll through the document on the screen.
- To quickly check for overly long or short paragraphs, use the page or print view and "zoom out" to reduce the image so that you can see an entire page on the screen at once.
- If you decide to cut paragraphs or sentences as you revise, paste them into a "scrap" file rather than deleting them, in case you change your mind or find a better place for them.

Getting Feedback

Because being objective about your own writing is difficult, **peer response—** the reading and constructive criticism of your draft by a fellow student, a friend, or a colleague—is one of the best aids to revision. Some guidelines for critical and constructive reading follow. The first list applies to most kinds of writing. The others are specific to personal, expository, argumentative, analytical, or researched writing.

GENERAL GUIDELINES FOR PEER RESPONSE

1. Describe the introduction. How does it engage the reader's interest?
2. What is the best part of this essay? Be specific—it might be the subject, the organization, particular paragraphs, or certain details.
3. Does the essay introduce issues that it does not develop? If so, what are they?
4. Describe the organizational pattern. What paragraphs, if any, need to be moved or omitted?
5. What, if anything, damages the writer's credibility? Look for errors of fact or logic, mistakes in grammar or punctuation, misspellings, and problems in citations of sources. List the problems and the pages on which they occur.
6. What else would you like to know?

PEER RESPONSE GUIDELINES FOR SPECIFIC KINDS OF WRITING

Peer Response for Personal, Exploratory Writing

1. What is the author's purpose in this essay?
2. Describe the author's voice, and list examples of it. Where is the voice inappropriate to the subject?
3. What paragraphs are best developed? What paragraphs, if any, need further clarification?
4. Which details best show what's going on? Which details merely tell?
5. How is the paper organized? Were any paragraphs or details distracting? If so, what should be moved or omitted?

Peer Response For Expository, Thesis-Oriented Writing

1. What is the thesis? Restate it in your own words.
2. List the main points. Which points include enough specific facts and details to be convincing? Which points need more facts or details?
3. Describe the organization. Do any paragraphs detract from the thesis? Note those that should be moved or omitted.
4. Does the documentation (if any) provide all the necessary information— author, source, date, pages? Put a D by any citation needing additional information. Put a question mark by information that appears to need documentation.
5. How does the essay conclude? Is the thesis restated? Are main points summarized? Describe what the author needs to do to end conclusively.

Peer Response for Argumentation

1. Is the thesis arguable (for example, are there two sides to the issue)? If not, suggest ways to sharpen the thesis.
2. Using three columns, list each main point, its counterarguments, and the author's refutations. Which points are not addressed?
3. Where are the facts used effectively? Where are more needed?
4. Are the sources (if any) credible? Where should there be more?
5. Does the author's argument convince you? What else do you need to know or have addressed?

Peer Response for Literary Analysis

1. What is the author's focus (for example, character, setting, tone, theme)?
2. Does the introduction identify the work and its author and summarize it briefly to establish a context? Note omitted elements.

3. How is the paper organized—chronologically or in increasing order of importance? Which method is more appropriate?

4. Is each assertion illustrated with an example or a quotation? Are they followed by page numbers? Note statements in need of support and documentation.

5. Is there an even balance between analysis and support? If the writer relies too heavily on quotations, note those that could be paraphrased or omitted.

Peer Response for Researched Papers

1. Are headings necessary in this paper? If so, where should they be placed?

2. Is the documentation sufficient? Is it correct? Note places where citations or additional information is necessary.

3. What documentation style is used? Is it appropriate to the assignment or the discipline?

4. What areas are well developed? What areas need additional supporting material?

5. What is the author's focus? Note any places where the focus seems to vary.

6. Describe the organization. What needs to be changed or moved?

7. How does the author conclude the paper?

8. Look at the Works Cited page, and circle and compare its citations to those within the paper. What, if anything, is missing?

EDITING

Once you are satisfied that revising has solved the large- and small-scale problems of structure and meaning—development, unity, coherence, logical structure—print out or retype a clean copy of the draft, and begin editing for more specific matters. Just as having a hard copy to examine the whole essay helps in adding or rearranging large chunks of material, working from a hard copy also makes editing and polishing easier.

While editing, look not only for errors but also for ways to make the paper as effective as possible in fulfilling its **purpose** and to make it a pleasure to read rather than a chore. However, if further large-scale revisions are obviously needed, go ahead and make them. One aspect of revising will almost certainly need further attention: Be sure to include effective **transitions** to improve **coherence**. If you have not already chosen a satisfactory title, try to come up with one as you edit. Look through the paper again for problems of **logic**, especially for those errors of reasoning called *fallacies,* which may creep into writing at any level—in a sentence, paragraph, or whole composition. Mark all changes on your hard copy, and then transfer them to the computer file. If you are not using a computer, wait to retype until later.

Sentence Structure

Read each sentence for **ambiguity**. There are many possible causes, especially **squinting, misplaced,** and **dangling modifiers.** Awkward or confusing **shifts** of **tone, person,** or verb **tense** can occur in the paper as a whole, in paragraphs, or in individual sentences. Certain kinds of **sentence faults** are particularly annoying to writing instructors, who expect their students to understand the conventions of **grammar.** Unless you are writing a stream-of-consciousness story or novel, avoid **run-on sentences.** Find and correct **sentence fragments** and **comma splices;** they can be justified only in special circumstances. Check for **agreement of subjects and verbs** and **agreement of pronouns and antecedents,** for correct **case** of **pronouns,** and for **verb errors,** especially problems with verb tenses. If you need to review any of the **parts of speech** to determine correct usage, now is the time to do so.

Word Choice

One of the principal obstacles to **clarity** is unwise **word choice,** especially **vague words, clichés** and other **trite language,** and words that are beyond the vocabulary of your **audience.** For example, **jargon** may be an efficient means of communication among workers in a particular field, but it will leave other readers mystified. The same is true of **allusions,** which may be clear to one reader but baffling to another.

Choose appropriately between **abstract and concrete words** and between **general and specific words.** Abstract and general terms allow you to express large ideas with great economy, but they may need to be supported with more concrete and specific terms or **examples** in order to be clear.

Avoid language that discriminates or appears to discriminate against members of either sex. You will find useful advice in this book under both **nonsexist language** and **agreement of pronouns and antecedents.**

A **dictionary** and the many **usage** entries in this handbook can help you find the right word to express your meaning. A thesaurus can also be helpful with **synonyms;** however, since it gives no information about **connotations,** it can lead you to use an unfamiliar word inappropriately if you do not check the meaning in a dictionary.

Especially if English is not your native language, check for correct use of definite and indefinite **articles** and of **idioms** and for the appropriate order of descriptive **adjectives.** Throughout the alphabetical entries in this handbook, an icon marks points of special interest to people for whom English is a second language.

Clarity and Conciseness

Clarity is enhanced by effective **subordination** and **emphasis, sentence variety, balanced sentences, parallel structure**, and avoidance of vague or ambiguous **pronoun reference. Choppy writing** can be eliminated by combining **simple sentences** into **compound, complex**, or **compound-complex sentences**. Sometimes an **analogy** or one of the other **figures of speech** can help explain an unfamiliar concept or clarify a vague one.

Look through your paper for ways of making it more concise (see **conciseness/wordiness**). One of the surest ways to tighten your writing and give it more life is to substitute **active** for **passive voice**—unless the passive voice is preferable for reasons of emphasis, tact, or **audience.**

Documentation

If you have used ideas or language from any source other than your own knowledge and invention, make sure that in every instance you have given proper credit with appropriate **documentation.** To fail to give such credit is to commit **plagiarism**, a very serious offense (even if it is unintentional). Read the alphabetical entries on documentation, plagiarism, **quotations, paraphrasing**, and **summarizing** to decide when such credit is needed.

If you are editing a research paper, make certain that it conforms in every respect to the documentation style you are supposed to follow—whether that of the Modern Language Association (MLA), the American Psychological Association (APA), the *Chicago Manual of Style* (CMS), or some other. (See **Research Processes.**)

Mechanics

Before turning to some final mechanical matters that are more efficiently addressed when everything else is in place, read the paper through aloud— or, better still, have someone read it to you—and pay special attention to the consistency and appropriateness of the tone for the **audience** you have in mind. Listen for anything that sounds "off key," especially for **contractions** and other **informal** or **colloquial** usages that may be inappropriate in this rhetorical situation.

Next, go through the paper to check all **punctuation.** Attention to this detail is important because lapses will hurt your credibility. Check **commas, periods**, and **semicolons**, as well as closing **parentheses** and **quotation marks.**

Check any **abbreviations** and any **numbers and symbols.** Look for proper and consistent use of **capital letters** and **italics** (or underlining). Check all **dates, proper nouns**, and **proper adjectives** for accuracy and correct form.

Finally, go through the paper—with a dictionary in hand if necessary—to check all spelling. Both the handbook entry on **spelling** and "Tips for Proofreading" on page 21 offer help.

When you have completed all these editing steps, print out or type your paper in the appropriate **manuscript form.** (See also **Research Processes.**) Be sure to proofread it carefully before handing it in.

TIPS FOR EDITING ON THE COMPUTER

- Editing is easier on a hard copy than on screen, and your pencil corrections will be easier to spot on a paper that is double-spaced.

- If your word-processing program has a grammar or style checker, you might turn on that function to see what "errors" it flags. Be aware, however, that these checkers look for only a few kinds of errors, apply the "rules" mechanically, and sometimes suggest "corrections" that make no sense.

- The thesaurus in word-processing programs can be a useful tool, but it does not define the words it offers, so you should check the meaning of unfamiliar words in a dictionary to avoid using ones that are inappropriate.

- In some fonts, punctuation marks may be barely visible on screen, so checking your punctuation may be easier if you "zoom in" and enlarge the type to 150 percent.

- If your word-processing program has a "sort" function, you can use it to alphabetize your works cited list. However, you still need to double-check the list, because the "sort" function is not programmed for exceptions such as ignoring **articles** at the beginning of titles when alphabetizing.

PROOFREADING

Proofreading is the final stage in the composing process. It should be done after printing out or typing your final draft. To proofread well, you must be critical and stay alert; accurate proofreading is easier if you can let the paper sit for a day, or at least a few hours, after editing. If you are **writing on a computer,** proofread a printed copy. Make the necessary corrections on the paper copy, and then enter them on the computer and print the final version.

Proofreading should include rechecking all **punctuation, abbreviations, numbers and symbols, capital letters, italics** (or underlining), and **spelling.** When you have finished proofreading, if your instructor accepts handwritten corrections and yours are neatly written and amount to no more than one or two on each page, you are ready to hand in your paper. Otherwise, print out or retype a clean copy that incorporates all corrections and follows the appropriate **manuscript form.**

TIPS FOR PROOFREADING

- You will spot more of the typographical errors if you read the paper aloud either from beginning to end or backward, word for word. If you are **writing on a computer**, increase the font size by two points, and print the paper out; the errors in both spelling and punctuation should be more visible.

- If you are writing on a computer, the spell checker will alert you to anything that is not a correctly spelled word. But it cannot tell you if you have typed one word in place of another. Make a list of pairs of words you tend to confuse—for instance, *its/it's*, *affect/effect*, and *advice/advise*—and quickly review it before you proofread.

- Check a **dictionary** for all words of which you are not certain. Is it *privilege* or *privelege*, *gauge* or *guage*, *friend* or *freind*? Words with double letters—such as *accommodation* and *occurrence*—are especially difficult to remember. Check whether a **compound word** should be written as one word, as two words, or hyphenated.

- Watch closely for omissions of *-ed* or *-s*. Watch for silent letters, as in *rhythm* and *ghost*.

- Mentally repeat each syllable of long words with many vowels, such as *evacuation, responsibility, continuously,* and *individual*.

- After a first check for spelling and punctuation, double-check your final draft. Remember, you are responsible for correct spelling.

CHECKLIST FOR COMPOSING

Prewriting   (6–11)

❑ Who is the **audience**?   (5, 203)

❑ What is your **purpose**?   (5–6, 436)

❑ What is your **topic**?   (5, 6, 11, 28, 29, 495)

❑ How long should the piece be? How much time do you have to write it?   (3–6)

❑ What is your preliminary **thesis**?   (11, 29, 491–92)

Drafting   (11–12)

❑ What **methods of development** could you use?   (10, 372–73, 400–03)

❑ What kind of **introduction** might you use?   (12, 13–14, 336–38)

❑ What might the **title** be?   (14, 493–94)

❑ What is your **conclusion**—or do you need to find more information or rethink your **thesis**?   (14, 254–55)

Revising   (13–17)

❑ Have you received **peer response** on your draft?   (5, 15–17, 413)

❑ Does the draft reflect your original **purpose**?   (13, 436)

❑ Is your **thesis** still appropriate, or does it need altering? (13, 491–492)

❑ Does the draft meet the needs of your **audience**?   (13, 203)

❑ Does an **outline** of the **topic sentences** of your draft show a logical organization?   (14, 397)

❑ Do you need to provide additional **examples** to support your claims?   (14, 293)

❑ Are the **methods of development** effective?   (10, 372–73, 400–03)

❑ Are there **transitions** from one idea to the next?   (14, 496–99)

❑ Are all the **paragraphs** to the point and about the same length? (14, 398–405, 495–96)

❑ Does the **introduction** capture the reader's interest?   (14, 336–38)

❑ Is the **conclusion** consistent with your **purpose**?   (14, 254–55)

❑ Does the **title** indicate the paper's **thesis** and interest the reader? (14, 493–94)

Editing and Proofreading (17–21, 259)

❑ Can you spot any fallacies in **logic**? (17, 362–66)

❑ Are the **transitions** between ideas effective? (17, 496–99)

❑ Are all sentences free of **ambiguity**? (18, 190–91)

❑ Have you checked for **nonsexist language**? (18, 381–84)

❑ Is the **word choice** concrete, specific, and free of **clichés**? (18, 227–28, 515)

❑ Are the **connotations** of words appropriate? (If you are not sure, check a **dictionary**.) (18, 259, 272–75)

❑ Are there any awkward **shifts** of tone, **person**, or the **tense** of **verbs**? (18, 415–16, 487–89, 494–95)

❑ Is **passive voice** used appropriately and not excessively? (19, 169, 411–12)

❑ Is there **sentence variety**? (19, 459–61)

❑ Have you eliminated **wordiness** and needless **repetition**? (19, 250–55)

❑ Have you corrected **sentence faults**? (18, 239–40, 451–52, 455–57)

❑ Have you ensured **agreement of subjects and verbs** and **agreement of pronouns and antecedents**? (18, 180–83, 184–88)

❑ Is **pronoun reference** clear? (18, 221, 431–35)

❑ Is all **punctuation** used correctly? (19, 436)

❑ Have you made sure that there are no **spelling** errors? (20, 467–77)

❑ Are **capital letters** and **italics** (or underlining) used correctly? (19, 211–18, 343)

❑ Are **numbers and symbols** used correctly? (19, 390–92)

❑ Are **abbreviations** correct? (19, 158–67)

❑ Is the **manuscript form** correct? (20, 368–69)

COMPOSING PROCESSES

RESEARCH PROCESSES
Finding, Using, and Documenting Sources

Overview of Research Writing

Many students enter composition courses with the misperception that writing a research paper is a tedious and unnecessary process required only by the English department. But researched writing need not be long and tedious, nor is it necessary only in composition courses. Outside the English department—indeed, outside the university—research is used to strengthen an argument, to demonstrate the need for change, to provide additional information and verification, to trace a pattern or trend, to validate ideas (using statistics), to discover a process or a remedy, or to add spice to an otherwise unpersuasive or uninteresting piece of writing.

Research is not confined to hushed libraries or lonely online searches. Depending on the topic, research may include **interviews** and observations, surveys and questionnaires; it may involve reading novels, conducting experiments, or examining historical documents such as letters and original manuscripts. All of these **primary sources** are considered valid and reliable research materials. They can be supplemented with **secondary sources** such as analyses, assessments, and evaluations of primary sources. For example, if you were writing a paper about a character in a novel, you might use material not only from the novel itself (a primary source) but also from a literary critic's analysis or from biographies of the author (secondary sources).

The type of research methodology selected depends on the context for writing. Some composition courses require a paper based on **interviews**, such as an oral history; business courses might include a paper based on surveys; and a literature course could assign a **literary analysis**. All would necessitate research and would have requirements about length, style for documenting sources, and mode of development (argumentative, expository, or analytical). You must consider all these factors when deciding on a **topic**. A topic such as "the demise of the rainforest" would be too broad for most assignments at the undergraduate level. If the paper had to be argumentative and the thesis was that the rainforest is disappearing, or that its disappearance is bad, this topic would be a poor choice because both statements are true and, hence, not arguable.

RESEARCH AND COMPOSING PROCESSES

Whether your instructor assigns a **topic** for a research paper or gives you free rein, you need to go through the same composing processes entailed in any other type of writing, as well as researching sources and integrating them into your writing. First, to zero in on a topic and identify what you know and what interests you about it, **brainstorm, freewrite, list, cluster,** or explore ideas in your **journal.** If the topic seems quite broad, consider how you might narrow it to fit the required length and type of paper (argumentation, exposition, or analysis) and the **audience.** To fill the gaps in your background knowledge of the topic, such as key dates, people, places, and definitions, it may be helpful to check dictionaries, encyclopedias, atlases, and other basic reference works. As you read, pay attention to terms used to discuss important concepts; they may be useful later for keyword searches.

Maybe at this point you have a preliminary **thesis,** or maybe you need to look for potential **primary** and **secondary sources.** Even after you have both a topic and a thesis, however, keep in mind that they are only tentative until you have confirmed that they are appropriate from the information you gather. As you learn more about your topic, you will be able to refine your keywords for more efficient searching. Be prepared to adjust your thesis or even to abandon it in favor of another if your research suggests that you are on the wrong track.

Search for potential sources, and take careful notes from the ones that look most promising. Before you begin your **first draft,** review your notes and consider the **methods of development** and the organization of your paper. Integrate the relevant **summaries, paraphrases,** and **quotations** from your notes, and make sure you have complete and accurate **documentation** for all of them. Read your draft, and ask whether it fits your **purpose,** your thesis, and your audience. If there are holes in your argument, you may want to do additional research to fill them and redo your draft.

Once you are satisfied that your draft covers all the bases, create a list of works cited from your working bibliography. To avoid **plagiarism,** make sure that every summary, paraphrase, and quotation has an in-text citation and that each citation has a corresponding entry in the works cited list. Finally, proofread your paper for typos and correct formatting.

The checklist on page 34 is provided to help you through these processes.

The Research Writer's Responsibilities

When you write from sources, you have three additional responsibilities: (1) to choose sources that strengthen your credibility, (2) to use material from your sources appropriately and effectively, and (3) to avoid both intentional and unintentional **plagiarism.**

Use Sources That Strengthen Your Credibility   Once you have a topic, consider the kinds of information you might use. Will you need historical documents, newspaper articles, motion picture reviews, scientific research, firsthand interviews? Don't start by randomly surfing the **Internet** or scrolling through the library catalog; create and use specific keywords.

Use the best available information by experts in the field. These are authors who are often cited in other writings on the topic and whose works are listed in topic bibliographies. They may also be ones whom your instructor has mentioned. If you find a good source by an unfamiliar author, try to locate his or her credentials. If they are not given in the book or article, look in a biographical reference, such as *Contemporary Authors* or *Who's Who;* look in a periodical database, such as InfoTrac or LexisNexis, for other articles written by the person; or do an Internet search.

Use sources that are appropriate to your **thesis.** For example, you can find the same statistical information about immigration on two Web sites. One site <http://www.nnirr.org> is sponsored by the National Network for Immigrant and Refugee Rights, a public interest group that works "to defend and expand the rights of all immigrants and refugees, regardless of immigration status." The other site <http://www.fairus.org> is sponsored by the Federation for American Immigration Reform, which aims "to end illegal immigration" and "to set legal immigration at the lowest feasible levels." These sites have very different agendas. Unless you state otherwise, when you cite information from a source, you give the impression that you are also endorsing it.

Tip: To find out about the sponsor of a Web site, look for a page labeled "Home," "About Us," or "Mission Statement." If you can't find such a link, try trimming back the URL to the first single slash (/). For example, trimming back the URL <http://www.nnirr.org/news/archived_netnews/immigrants economyhtm.htm> would take you to the home page of the National Network for Immigrant and Refugee Rights.

Use Sources Appropriately and Effectively   Your paper should reflect *your* thinking and not simply string together **quotations, paraphrases,** and **summaries** from your sources. Reasons to use sources include

- providing specific facts as evidence for your argument or interpretation,
- giving examples of different points of view on a subject, and
- emphasizing a particularly striking phrase, sentence, or passage.

Be especially careful not to overuse direct quotations.

Your task is to integrate into your draft information from the sources and to credit your sources every time you use material from them, whether it is a quotation, a paraphrase, or a summary. Careful note taking (discussed later in this chapter on pages 46–48) will help ensure that your sources receive proper credit. A smooth way to integrate source information in your paper is with a **signal phrase** at the beginning, middle, or end of a direct quotation, paraphrase, or summary. In parentheses, add the page number or date, depending on the citation style you are using. Note, however, that if the author is a journalist or freelance writer rather than an expert in the field, you may decide to include the author's name in the parenthetical citation rather than to emphasize it in a signal phrase. Here are examples of signal phrases and parenthetical citations in MLA style.

SIGNAL PHRASE INTRODUCING QUOTATION
According to Sylvia Nasar in *A Beautiful Mind,* "An individual's vulnerability to schizophrenia [. . .] lies in his genes. But psychological stresses are thought to be catalysts" (188).

SIGNAL PHRASE INTERRUPTING QUESTION
"A significant number of teenage boys are now drinking five or more cans of soda every day," reports Eric Schlosser in *Fast Food Nation.* "Each can contains the equivalent of about ten teaspoons of sugar" (54).

SIGNAL PHRASE INTRODUCING AND PARENTHETICAL CITATION
FOLLOWING PARAPHRASE
A recent issue of *Smithsonian* reported that Hawaii's fish are disappearing not only because of overfishing, ocean warming, and pollution but also because of aquarium collectors (Wuethrich 26–28).

VERBS USED IN SIGNAL PHRASES

acknowledges	comments	disagrees	lists	remarks
adds	concludes	discusses	maintains	replies
admits	concurs	disputes	notes	reports
agrees	confirms	emphasizes	objects	responds
argues	considers	explains	observes	says
asks	contends	holds	opposes	shows
asserts	criticizes	illustrates	points out	suggests
believes	declares	insists	reasons	thinks
claims	describes	interprets	refutes	writes

Each source cited in your paper must be represented by an entry in the **works cited** list at the end of the paper. This list gives your readers a way to identify and check your sources for the existence and accuracy of the information borrowed from them. As you **revise** and **edit** your draft, make sure that each use of source material is identified in the text and has a corresponding entry in the works cited or reference list. The section "Documentation and Research Paper Formats" at the end of this chapter describes in detail in-text citations and works cited or reference lists in MLA, APA, CMS, and CSE/CBE styles.

Avoid Plagiarism **Plagiarism** is using someone else's words, graphics, or ideas without giving credit. It can be intentional, such as cutting and pasting from an online document. Or it can be unintentional, such as failing to credit sources that you **paraphrase** or **summarize** or neglecting to put quotation marks around a direct **quotation**. The penalties for the first kind of plagiarism can include suspension, expulsion, and even denial of a degree. The penalties for the second kind of plagiarism are usually less severe— perhaps a conference with the instructor and some extra scrutiny of your work afterward.

Students may deliberately plagiarize because they had put off doing a paper until it was too late to do any research or because they lack confidence in their writing ability. If they copy a paper from an Internet "paper mill" or cut and paste passages from source documents, they are cheating not only the original authors but also their fellow students (who put in the time and effort to do the work) and themselves (by losing an opportunity to exercise their minds, acquire new knowledge, and learn new skills). Most instructors can spot this kind of wholesale plagiarizing. They are as familiar as students are with the online term-paper mills, they have a good idea of their students' writing abilities, and they can tell when all or part of a paper has probably been written by someone else.

Unintentional plagiarism is much more common, because many students are not familiar with the conventions of crediting sources. Common misconceptions and mistakes include

- failing to take careful notes that clearly indicate direct quotations and identify the source of every passage;
- assuming that only direct quotations, not paraphrases or summaries, need to be attributed;
- failing to indicate clearly with the use of **signal phrases** and **quotation marks** how much of a sentence or paragraph comes from the source;

- using a **paraphrase** that is too similar in wording and structure to the original passage;
- being unsure of which information must be documented and which is **common knowledge**;
- failing to recognize turns of phrase that are unique to the author and using them without quotation marks; and
- assuming that simply listing sources in the bibliography is sufficient.

TIPS FOR AVOIDING PLAGIARISM

In Your Notes

1. Enclose every direct quotation in large, dark quotation marks.
2. Label every note as a **quotation**, a **paraphrase**, a **summary**, or your comments. (See "Taking Notes" on pages 46–48.)
3. For every quotation, paraphrase, and summary, identify the source, including the page number. You can use a short form, such as the author's last name, but be sure that you can match it to the complete source identification in your working bibliography.
4. When you are paraphrasing or summarizing, read the original carefully, and then put it aside. Write the paraphrase or summary in your own words. Afterward, check your paraphrase or summary against the original for accuracy and for accidentally borrowed phrases.
5. If you make your notes on a computer, keep them in a separate file from your drafts so that you do not accidentally confuse them. You might also use different fonts for your notes and your drafts so that you can tell them apart at a glance.

In Your Paper

6. If you paste a direct quotation from your notes into your paper, do not forget to put quotation marks around it or, if the quotation is longer than four lines, to indent it as a **block quotation.** In both cases, immediately add the source citation; if you put that off, you might forget to do it.
7. If you are not sure whether a piece of information might be **common knowledge,** be safe and cite a source for it.

In General

8. Value academic honesty, and uphold its standards.
9. Value the contributions research makes to your overall education.

CHECKLIST FOR WRITING A RESEARCH PAPER

❏ Based on the assignment and on your interests, have you **brainstormed** for ideas and keywords, done **freewriting**, made a **list** or **cluster**, or explored ideas in your **journal**?   (6–9)

❏ Have you considered how to narrow the **topic** to fit the required length and type of paper (argumentation, exposition, or analysis) and the **audience**?   (5–6)

❏ Have you done background reading in dictionaries, encyclopedias, atlases, and other basic reference works?   (38–41)

❏ Have you made a list of keywords and subject headings?   (41–42)

❏ Have you explored and evaluated primary and secondary sources (36) and compiled your **working bibliography**?   (42–44)

❏ Have you narrowed or redefined your topic, if necessary, and formulated a preliminary **thesis**?   (11, 491–92)

❏ Have you taken careful notes from your sources, identifying them as **summaries**, **paraphrases**, or **quotations** so that you will avoid **plagiarism**?   (46–48, 420)

❏ Have you considered the **methods of development** you can use to organize your paper?   (10, 372–73, 400–03)

❏ Have you written a **draft** (11–12), integrating the summaries, paraphrases, and quotations from your notes? (46–48, 406–408, 440–43, 483–84)

❏ Have you made sure you have complete and accurate **documentation** in your working bibliography for all the material you are incorporating from your research notes?   (60–153)

❏ Have you revised your draft, reconsidering your **purpose**, your **thesis**, your **audience**, and your **methods of development** and structure, and rewritten as necessary?   (13–17)

❏ Have you created a list of **works cited** from your **working bibliography**? (42–44, 60–152)

❏ Have you edited your paper, checking for **transitions** (17), **signal phrases** (31), **logic** (17), **clarity** (19), and **sentence faults** (17–21)?

❏ Have you checked that all **summaries**, **paraphrases**, and **quotations** have an in-text citation (63–66), and that all in-text citations have a corresponding entry in the **works cited** list (67–86)?

❏ Have you proofread your paper (20–21), and made sure that it is correctly formatted (86–98)?

GATHERING INFORMATION FROM SOURCES

To begin your research, do a bit of background reading. Then make a list of keywords and subject headings, and start gathering information, taking notes, and compiling your working bibliography. Except for information gathered firsthand, such as observation, personal experience, and **interviews**, most of the information you need for a research paper can be found in the library—and some can be found on the Internet. The key to successful research is knowing what resources are available and how to use them. Because resources and procedures differ from library to library, you need to read your library's introductory materials on the resources available in the reference room and on the campus computer network. Consult a reference librarian whenever you have questions.

LIBRARIES AND LIBRARIANS

The library contains more than books. It also houses collections of periodicals in print, on microfilm, and in electronic archives. Its holdings probably also include maps, videos, sound recordings, music scores, dissertations, and government documents. The library's electronic and CD-ROM databases contain specialized indexes and subject guides, which are available only to library users. Through interlibrary loans, the library can access the holdings of a vast network of other libraries. Because libraries also offer Internet access and make the online services they subscribe to available to their users, it's increasingly common to hear libraries referred to as "information portals"—that is, gateways to vast resources. Until you become an experienced researcher, ask a reference librarian for help navigating the library's resources. They are highly trained information professionals, available specifically to guide you through the world of sources. Your library may also have tutorials and handouts describing its resources. Read them!

The World of Sources

The kinds of information that you might use (or that your assignment requires) might be found in historical documents, newspaper articles, motion picture reviews, scientific research, firsthand interviews, and a wide variety of other materials. Before wading in, you may find it helpful to ask a reference librarian, your instructor, or a writing-center tutor to suggest places to start researching your topic. Will you need primary or secondary sources? Popular or scholarly resources? And are they most likely to be found in the library or online?

RESEARCH PROCESSES

Primary Sources **Primary sources** are firsthand accounts, such as historical documents (letters, speeches, diaries, and eyewitness reports), literary works, works of art, musical compositions, statistics, and experiments. They also can include your own experience, interviews, observation, and correspondence. Primary sources include

- books in the library for historical documents, such as letters, diaries, and eyewitness reports;
- books in the library or the bookstore for literary works (some older ones may be available online);
- U.S. Census Bureau reports in the library or online at <www.census.gov> for statistics; and
- art books in the library or sites on the Internet for works of art.

Secondary Sources **Secondary sources** report and analyze information from other sources. Biographies, reviews, op-ed columns about controversial issues, analyses of scientific studies or historical events, and critical readings of a literary work are secondary sources. Such sources include

- general references (such as encyclopedias), biographies, and autobiographies about the person for biographical information;
- op-ed articles in reliable newspapers, such as the *New York Times,* and in news periodicals for opinions about current controversies (Internet searches are also likely to turn up a variety of opinions, but some may not be credible);
- scholarly journals in the field, specialized databases, such as Medline, and the Web sites of government agencies, such as the Centers for Disease Control and Prevention (CDC) <http://www.cdc.gov>, and of professional organizations, such as the American Psychological Association <www.apa.org>, for reports of experiments and research findings;
- books and periodicals that publish essays about historical events (such as the magazine *Smithsonian* and scholarly history journals) for historical analyses; and
- books and scholarly journals for critical readings of a literary work.

Popular and Scholarly Sources As implied in the previous discussion, some sources are scholarly and some are not. Scholarly sources—books, articles, and Internet documents—are written by academics and researchers for an audience of their peers. Popular sources are written by journalists or other professional writers for a general audience. They range from publications written for an educated audience, such as *Scientific American* and *Atlantic Monthly,* to general-interest magazines, such as *Time* and *O.* Scholarly sources are more likely to add to your paper's credibility, but some of them, such as specialized scientific reports, may be too technical for your **topic** or your **audience.** The box on page 37 compares characteristics of two kinds of sources to help you recognize them.

COMPARISON OF SCHOLARLY AND POPULAR SOURCES

	SCHOLARLY SOURCES	POPULAR SOURCES
Audience	Academics and researchers	General public
Author	Expert in the field or researcher	Journalist or freelance writer
Illustrations	Graphs, charts	Photographs, drawings
Reading level	High, using terminology of the discipline	Low to medium, using nontechnical language
Advertisements (in periodicals and online)	Few or none	Many
Primary/secondary source	Firsthand reports of research experiments	Second- or thirdhand reporting of information
Source citations, bibliography	Yes	Rarely
Publisher	University press, professional association, government agency	Commercial publisher

Print and Electronic Sources Print and electronic media each have strengths and limitations. Keep them in mind as you build your collection of potential sources. Use both types of sources for the advantages they offer.

1. **Reliability.** Printed books and periodicals (including those available through electronic databases such as InfoTrac) have gone through a screening process for accuracy and reliability. The publisher decided that they were worth buying. On the Internet, anyone can publish anything. Only some online scholarly journals, government documents, and subject directories are monitored for credibility and accuracy. If you use a **Web site** as a source, you must take extra care in evaluating it.

2. **Scope versus currency.** Because electronic documents can be updated much more quickly than books, the Internet and online periodical databases are usually better sources than print documents for up-to-the-minute information. However, most electronic documents do not contain the breadth of information and the amount of specific detail that books do. In addition, libraries contain millions of documents that predate the Internet and will probably never be available online. If you are researching a current event, you might go to the Web site of a reliable newspaper, such as the *New York Times* <http://www.nytimes.com> or search a periodical database in the library. However, if you are looking for historical in-depth information or analysis, turn to books.

3. **Searchability versus readability.** The printed page is static; hypertext Web documents are interactive and searchable. Sometimes a book will fit your needs, and sometimes the Internet is the answer. For example, searching for a particular word or phrase in an Internet document (say in one of Shakespeare's plays at <http://www.theplays.org/>) is much faster and more efficient than searching through a book line by line; but reading an entire book or play on screen is much more difficult than reading a print version. Use the Internet to locate a particular piece of information in a large document; use a book when you need to study an entire work.

Reference Works for Background Reading

After you have chosen a topic or had one assigned, write down what you already know about it (try **brainstorming, clustering,** or **freewriting**), and then make a list of the things you would like to learn. A good place to begin assembling background information is in general reference books: dictionaries, encyclopedias, almanacs, biographical dictionaries, and atlases. Some of these resources are available online (through the campus network or the Internet) and on CD-ROM as well as in print. General reference works provide definitions and overviews that can help fill gaps in your knowledge, and they can direct you to related topics and other sources of information. After doing some background reading, you may decide to change the scope of your topic to make it more appropriate for the length of the paper and the time you have to write it. For example, suppose you began with the tentative topic "the effectiveness of advertising." After reading the general articles on advertising in general encyclopedias and the relevant entries in the *Encyclopedia of Advertising,* you might decide to narrow the topic to focus on differences in the advertising of a particular product to different audiences.

A variety of basic references, such as the *Oxford English Dictionary* and the *Encyclopaedia Britannica,* may be available through your campus computer network as well as in the library reference room. (**Tip:** Check the encyclopedia's index first to increase your chance of finding the relevant information.) Searchable general dictionaries and encyclopedias available free on the Internet include the following:

American Heritage Dictionary (4th ed.) <http://bartleby.com/61/>

Merriam-Webster's Collegiate Dictionary (10th ed.) <http://www.m-w.com/dictionary>

Columbia Encyclopedia (6th ed.) <http://www.bartleby.com/65/>

For links to other general references, see My Virtual Reference Desk <http://www.refdesk.com/essentl.html> and Bartleby.com <http://www.bartleby.com>.

Specialized Encyclopedias and Dictionaries In addition to general encyclopedias such as *Encyclopedia Americana* and *Encyclopaedia Britannica,* the library has specialized encyclopedias and dictionaries for a variety of fields, including literature (from classical to twentieth century), music (from opera to rock), economics, business, U.S. and world history, art, philosophy, physical education, science (from chemistry to computers), and the social sciences (from anthropology to sociology). The entries in these works not only provide a detailed overview of the topic but also usually end with a bibliography of authoritative sources. Some libraries keep these books in the reference section; others keep them in the appropriate subject area in the main stacks. Many of these references are also available online on the campus network or on CD-ROM.

Biographical Dictionaries and Indexes   If you come across an unfamiliar name, look it up in a biographical reference, such as one of the following works, which may be available in print, on CD-ROM, or online in the library. In addition to general references, such as those listed, the library also has biographical dictionaries specialized by profession or country.

> *Contemporary Authors*
>
> *Current Biography* (biographies of people of many nationalities and professions; includes short bibliographies and addresses)
>
> *International Who's Who*
>
> *Who's Who*
>
> *Who's Who in America*

You can often find biographical information on the Internet by typing the name in the text box of a search engine (you may need to enclose the name in quotation marks or parentheses—read the search instructions). Some biographical databases are also available on the Internet, including the following:

> Biographical Dictionary <http://www.s9.com/biography>
>
> Biography.com <http://www.biography.com/search/index.html>
>
> Biography section of Michigan Electronic Library <http://mel.lib.mi.us/reference/REF-biog.html>

Almanacs and Yearbooks   For information about recent developments and up-to-date statistical data, consult the annual yearbook supplements of general encyclopedias, almanacs (such as *Information Please Almanac* <http://www.infoplease.com/almanacs.html> and *World Almanac and Book of Facts*), and the following annual publications in the reference section of your library. Some are available in print and some on CD-ROM.

> *Budget in Brief* (summary of U.S. federal budget)
>
> *Demographic Yearbook* (United Nations information on world economics and trade)

Facts on File Yearbook (weekly digest of world news)

Political Handbook of the World (Council on Foreign Affairs publication)

Statistical Abstract of the United States (U.S. Bureau of Census summary of industrial, political, social, and economic data)

Statistical Yearbook (United Nations publication)

Government documents and other sources for statistics are also available free on the Internet at the following sites (you may need to download an Adobe Acrobat Reader if they are pdf files):

FedStats (statistics from more than seventy federal agencies) <http://www.fedstats.gov>

FirstGov (official U.S. gateway to resources and services—all government information) <http://www.firstgov.gov>

GPO Access (U.S. government documents, including the federal budget and the *Congressional Record*) <http://www.access.gpo.gov/su_docs>

InfoNation (statistics about UN member nations) <http://www.un.org/Pubs/CyberSchoolBus/infonation/e_infonation.htm>

Statistical Abstract of the United States (pdf files) <http://www.census.gov/statab/www/>

United Nations Statistics Division (international statistics) <http://www.un.org/Depts/unsd/>

University of Michigan Documents Center (extensive directory of links to statistical resources) <http://www.lib.umich.edu/govdocs/stats.html>

U.S. Census Bureau <http://www.census.gov>

World Factbook (annual CIA publication with statistics and maps for every nation in the world) <http://www.odci.gov/cia/publications/factbook>

Atlases   As you do background reading, consult an atlas to locate unfamiliar places. Your library contains not only general atlases of today's world (check the publication date, because the names and boundaries of countries change) but also historical atlases and specialized atlases, such as atlases of the oceans and of the universe.

The Internet is the ideal medium for locating a particular place or mapping a route between two locations (see, for example, Mapquest at <http://www.mapquest.com>). But studying a map in pieces, one computer screen at a time, is less satisfactory than having the entire map spread out before you. Here are some sources for **Internet** atlases and maps:

INFOMINE Maps (searchable collection) <http://infomine.ucr.edu/cgi-bin/search?maps>

Perry-Castañeda Library Map Collection <http://www.lib.Utexas.edu/maps>

National Geographic's Maps and Geography <http://www.nationalgeographic. com/maps>

Making a List of Keywords or Subject Headings

Once you have specified a preliminary topic, start a list of **subject headings** or **keywords** and phrases to use in your search for research sources. This list will help you find information in the library catalog, in periodical indexes, and on the Internet. As you search, you will undoubtedly refine your list and add new terms to it.

To categorize their books, most library catalogs use the Library of Congress's subject headings, which may be different from the keywords that first occur to you. For example, the Library of Congress heading is *Afro-American* rather than *African American* or *Black American.* If your search is not turning up the expected number of hits, consult the *Library of Congress Subject Headings* (*LCSH*) directory, which is usually located near the reference or information desk. Or go to the catalog entry for a book you know is on your subject and look at its list of subjects or topics (for an example of a catalog entry, see Figure RP-8 on page 52). Usually, those subject headings are links that will take you to a list of other library holdings on that subject.

Your library probably has a variety of online, CD-ROM, and print indexes of general-interest and specialized periodical articles. These periodical indexes may not use Library of Congress subject headings; look for their thesaurus or list of topics, descriptors, or subject headings. Their search results, like the library catalog entries, may also include a list of subjects. In addition, you may want to consult the *Readers' Guide to Periodical Literature,* one of the standard sources for periodical subject headings. It is usually located near the library's reference desk.

For Internet search tools, there is no standard source for subject headings. Instead, you must create your own keywords. Most search engines will try to match up your keywords with words in online documents in their databases. They will then retrieve for you any document that contains your search term. Create and combine keywords to find what you need. Brainstorm and free-associate terms so that you start with a group of keywords. Some keywords are synonyms, like *Ecstasy, MDMA,* and *3,4-methylenedioxymethamphetamine.* Other keywords are more distantly related, like *war on drugs* and *crack cocaine.* You can also combine a keyword identifying your topic with an additional keyword specifying the kind of information you want about this topic, for example, the keywords *Elian Gonzalez* with the keyword *picture,* or the keywords *basic facts* with the keywords *war on*

RESEARCH PROCESSES

drugs. Enclose groups of keywords with quotation marks in order to search for the whole phrase: *"war on drugs."* Be prepared to create and search with new keywords as you learn more about your topic.

Creating a Working Bibliography

After you have defined your topic, begin to search for books and articles about it. As you look, create a **working bibliography**—a list of all the sources that may possibly be relevant to your topic. Because not all sources are as good as they first appear and not all may be available in your library, a working bibliography will be longer than your final list of works cited.

For each source, write the title, author, publication information (city, publisher, year), and call number (if the source is a book) in a "working bibli-

---

WHAT TO INCLUDE IN A WORKING BIBLIOGRAPHY

For books, record

- author (last name first)
- title
- publication information (city, publisher, year)
- call number

For periodical articles, record

- author (last name first)
- title of article
- title of periodical
- date
- volume and issue numbers
- page numbers
- call number (for bound periodicals)

For Internet and other electronic documents, record

- author (last name first)
- title of document
- name of database
- name of site's sponsor
- date of site's most recent revision
- date of access
- **URL** (Internet address)

Q
125
.H62
1986
c.1

Hiskes, Ann L., and Richard I. Hiskes.
<u>Science, Technology, and Policy Decisions.</u>
Boulder, CO: Westview, 1986

Figure RP-1. Working bibliography entry for a book.

Kalette, Denise.
"Voice Mail Taps Wrath of Callers."
<u>USA Today</u> 2 Mar. 1992: 2A-2B

Figure RP-2. Working bibliography entry for a periodical.

ography" file on your computer, on a three-by-five-inch card, or on paper—the important thing is to record all pertinent information. (Figures RP-1 and RP-2 illustrate sample bibliography cards.) When you are ready to compile the list of works cited in your paper, alphabetize the cards for the sources you used or number the entries in your list in alphabetical order and type the list. If you made a file on your computer, copy it, delete the sources you did not use, and alphabetically sort the sources you used. Whatever method you use, if you record the information according to the documentation style you need to follow for your list of works cited, creating the final list is even simpler. (Four documentation styles are discussed in detail at the end of this chapter; see pages 60–152.)

A convenient way to keep bibliographic information for Internet documents is to print them out with the **URL**, title, and date of access as a header or footer (see the example in Figure RP-3). You may also want to **bookmark** the Web pages you are likely to revisit. It may be helpful to give the bookmarks titles that clearly identify the contents (especially if they are graphics files labeled with only jpeg or gif numbers). If you share a networked computer with other students, you may want to copy your bookmarks on a floppy disk so that they do not get lost. (See your browser's online help manual or FAQ for information about copying bookmarks.)

Evaluating Sources

A quick survey can help you decide whether a book, magazine, or online source has information that may be useful to your research and—especially for an online source—whether it is credible.

- Note the publication date. Is it current or several years old? Does your topic require up-to-date information? On most reliable Web pages, the revision date will appear at the beginning or the end. If not, it may be given in the Document Information. A Web page that has not been updated for a year or more may be a "zombie" page—abandoned by its creator and containing links that have become dead ends.

- Evaluate whether the publication is an overview for a general audience or a technical discussion for experts. For a Web page as well as a print document, the source can tell you something about the intended audience. For example, medical research findings would likely be reported more thoroughly and accurately in the *Journal of the American Medical Association* <http://www.ama-assn. org/public/journals/jama/jamahome.htm> than in *USA Today* <http://www. usatoday.com>.

- Check whether the author is an expert in the field—someone who is cited in other works on the subject or who has been mentioned by your instructor.

- To assess the usefulness of a book, look at the table of contents and then skim the introduction and the index.

- To assess the usefulness of a magazine article or an online document, scan the headings or the paragraphs to get an idea of the major topics.

- To assess the usefulness of an online document, scan the home page and check at least some of the internal links.

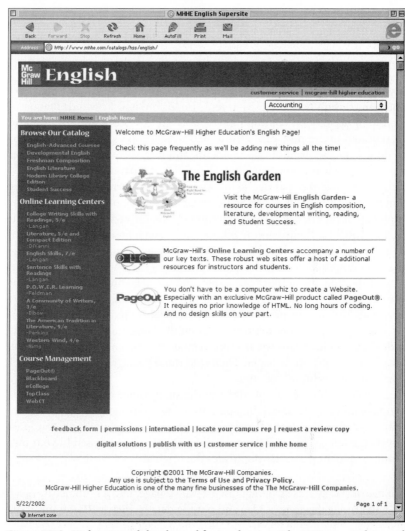

Figure RP-3. Web page with header and footer showing title, URL, access date, and page number.

For more ways to evaluate the reliability of an Internet source, see the box on pages 55–56.

After you have selected a number of potentially useful sources, you need to evaluate them critically as you read them.

- Is the treatment of the topic evenhanded, or does the author have a strong bias? Is the author credible? (Credibility is especially important for online sources.)

RESEARCH PROCESSES

- Are the conclusions solidly backed up? Are facts and statistics documented?
- Are any logical fallacies apparent? (See **logic**.)

Taking Notes

As you read through the most likely sources for your research paper, take notes on relevant points and passages. Also, record new keywords that occur to you for use in your continuing search for good sources. You may want or be required to use note cards. However, some people prefer to photocopy or download and print out passages and annotate them, or type their notes directly into a word-processing document). Use a separate card, or the equivalent, for each idea or passage so that you can easily rearrange the cards when you begin writing your paper. Some researchers take notes on three-by-five-inch cards; others use four-by-six-inch cards for content notes and the smaller cards for their working bibliography. Some prefer computer files. If you do too, be sure to keep your notes files separate from your draft files so that you don't accidentally mix them up. Label each note with a brief version of the title, the author's last name, and the page number so that, if you use the idea in your paper, you can document its source. Presenting someone else's idea in your paper without giving proper credit is **plagiarism**.

The first step in note taking is to skim the book (table of contents and index) or article (headings or topic sentences) to locate the passages that may be relevant to your paper. Then read those passages, and decide which ones contain useful information.

Depending on the complexity and the significance of the passages, you can take notes by **summarizing, paraphrasing**, or using **quotations**. A summary records only the main point and eliminates the details; a paraphrase covers the same ground as the original passage but is expressed in your own words; a quotation exactly duplicates the original.

Summaries   Condense a paragraph, or even a page, into a sentence or two if all you need is the general idea and not the details. Figure RP-4 is an example of a summary note about the following passage.

> Human actions bring about scarcities of renewable resources in three principal ways. First, people can reduce the quantity or degrade the quality of these resources faster than they are renewed. This phenomenon is often referred to as the consumption of the resource's "capital": the capital generates "income" that can be tapped for human consumption. A sustainable economy can therefore be defined as one that leaves the capital intact and undamaged so that future generations can enjoy undiminished income. Thus, if topsoil creation in a region of farmland is 0.25 millimeter per year, then average soil loss should not exceed that amount.

"Environmental Change," Homer-Dixon,
Boutwell, and Rathjens, 40

The major human causes of shortages of renewable
resources are (1) overconsumption, (2) overpopulation,
and (3) unequal distribution.

Figure RP-4. Summary note.

The second source of scarcity is population growth. Over time, for instance, a given flow of water might have to be divided among a greater number of people. The final cause is change in the distribution of a resource within a society. Such a shift can concentrate supply in the hands of a few, subjecting the rest to extreme scarcity.

—THOMAS HOMER-DIXON, JEFFREY BOUTWELL, and GEORGE RATHJENS, "Environmental Change and Violent Conflict"

Paraphrases   Use a paraphrase to simplify a complex concept or to highlight details that are especially relevant to your topic. The challenge of paraphrasing is to use your own words to record the author's ideas faithfully. Because it is easy to plagiarize unintentionally instead of paraphrasing, consciously search for different words and sentence structure. If a particular phrase or sentence is so well worded that it cannot be paraphrased, enclose it in quotation marks to indicate that it is in the author's words rather than yours. Figure RP-5 (page 48) is an example of a paraphrase note.

Quotations   Quote directly from a source only when you need the author's exact words. Direct quotations should be as brief as possible. As a rule, do not use direct quotations that are longer than a paragraph, and use those sparingly. Your paper should present what *you* think or know, not merely stitch together other people's words.

Direct quotations must be accurate. Double-check your note against the source to make sure you have copied the passage exactly, including its

"Environmental Change," Homer-Dixon,
Boutwell, and Rathjens, 40

There are three major human causes of shortages of
renewable resources. (1) People consume the resources or
dilute their quality faster than the resource can regenerate.
(In this regard, a "sustainable economy" is one that uses
resources only as fast as they can be renewed.) (2) Population
increases put excessive demand on the supply of resources.
(3) A few people take control of the resources and restrict
distribution of them.

Figure RP-5. Paraphrase note.

punctuation, spelling, and capitalization. In your notes, be sure to put **quotation marks** around all direct quotations so that you will not mistake them for paraphrases when you incorporate the notes into the paper. Figure RP-6 is an example of a quotation note card.

Periodicals

To locate current information about your topic published in magazine, journal, and newspaper articles, look in periodical indexes and check databases. Your library probably has general-interest and specialized indexes in print form, on CD-ROM, and online. Most major daily newspapers are also indexed, and libraries usually have at least the *New York Times Index* and the *Wall Street Journal Index* as well as local newspapers. Full-text articles are available from some index databases, such as InfoTrac, Lexis-Nexis, and FirstSearch. The articles listed in other indexes may need to be retrieved from an electronic archive, such as ProQuest, JSTOR, or igenta (formerly UnCover); the library stacks; or microfilm or microfiche. Figure RP-7 shows a sample search result from the *America: History and Life* index. Copy all the bibliographical information for each promising article into your working bibliography so that you can retrieve it. If you have trouble locating an article, ask a reference librarian for help. If your library does not have some of the articles you need, you may be able to get photocopies through an interlibrary loan. Most loans take at least two weeks, however, so choose this alternative only if you have plenty of time to complete your research.

"Environmental Change," Homer-Dixon,
Boutwell, and Rathjens, 40

Homer-Dixon, Boutwell, and Rathjens use financial terms to describe resource consumption. Depleting resources faster than they can be renewed is "the consumption of the resource's 'capital.'" Accordingly, a "sustainable economy" is one that "leaves the capital intact and undamaged so that future generations can enjoy undiminished income."

Figure RP-6. Quotation note.

Type:	Book Review
Author:	Sale, Kirkpatrick.
Title:	The Green Revolution: The American Environmental Movement, 1962–1992.
Publication:	New York: Hill & Wang, 1993. 124 pp.
Citation:	*Journal of American History 1995 81(4): 1832–1833.* **Reviewer:** Schrepfer, Susan R.
Period:	1962–92.
Subject:	Social Movements. Politics. Environmentalism.

Figure RP-7. Sample search result from *America: History and Life* index.

Newspaper and Magazine Indexes on the Internet Most major daily newspapers and many general-interest magazines index their archives on the Internet, but free Internet access to full-text articles is generally possible for only the most recent issue. (Your library is likely to have electronic or print archives of older articles, which you can access for free.) Here are the online archive-search pages for a sampling of popular newspapers and magazines:

Atlantic Monthly <http://pqasb.pqarchiver.com/theatlantic/>

Boston Globe <http://www.globe.com/globe/search/>

Christian Science Monitor <http://www.csmonitor.com/archive/index.html>

RESEARCH PROCESSES

Los Angeles Times <http://pqasb.pqarchiver.com/latimes/>

New York Times on the Web <http://www.nytimes.com/search/>

Newsweek <http://archives1.newsbank.com/ar-search/we/Archives?>

Scientific American <http://www.sciam.com/?section=search>

U.S. News & World Report <http://www.usnews.com/usnews/search/ magazine_search.htm>

Washington Post <http://www.washingtonpost.com/wp-adv/archives/>

Directories of links to online news sources, both U.S. and international, include

Abyz News Links <http://www.abyznewslinks.com/index.html>

HeadlineSpot.com <http://www.headlinespot.com/>

Newspapers.com (includes college newspapers) <http://www.newspapers. com/index.htm>

The Paperboy <http://www.thepaperboy.com/welcome.html>

Current-news search engines include

Lycos News (newswires) <http://news.lycos.com/>

Northern Light Current News Search (two-week archive of newswire news) <http://www.northernlight.com/news.html>

Pandia Newsfinder (search and directory) <http://www.pandia.com/news/ index.html>

Total News (print, television, radio, and electronic sources) <http://www. totalnews.com>

Specialized Indexes and Databases If you need more specific or more technical information than that contained in general-interest periodicals, consult a database or index of journals and other publications in a specific field. Most of these are available online or on CD-ROM at your library; a few may be available only in print. To make sure the index will meet your needs, check its home page or introduction for a list of the publications indexed, the years covered, and a key to abbreviations used in the entries. The following list is a sampling of special-subject indexes, collections of abstracts, and bibliographies. The citation indexes listed here can be especially helpful if you want to track the discussion of a controversial topic or find reviewers' opinions of a particular book.

ABI/Inform: citations, abstracts, and some full-text articles about business, management, finance, and economics

America: History and Life: citations for articles on U.S. and Canadian history

Anthropological Literature

Art Abstracts

Arts & Humanities Citation Index: citations for articles in twenty-five disciplines in the arts and humanities, listed by subject and author and by cited author and article

Bibliography of Native North Americans: citations for works from the sixteenth century to the present

BIOSIS: index to literature in all areas of the life sciences and biology

Book Review Digest: reviews of fiction and nonfiction books

Computer Articles: citations and some abstracts and full-text articles from computer magazines

Congressional Universe: full text of U.S. legislative information

ERIC: index of education literature

Handbook of Latin American Studies: annotated bibliography of scholarly works on Latin America in the social sciences and humanities

Historical Abstracts: index to works in world history, *except* the United States and Canada, from 1450 on

Index Islamicus: bibliography of publications on Islam and the Muslim world since 1906

Index to Black Periodicals (or *Black Studies on Disc* on CD-ROM)

MEDLINE: citations and abstracts for articles in medicine, life science, and health administration

MLA Bibliography: index for literature, languages, and folklore

PAIS International: index of books, documents, and articles on contemporary public issues

Philosopher's Index: abstracts of journal articles and books in fifteen fields of philosophy

PsychInfo: index of books and articles in psychology

Science Citation Index: lists of articles in all branches of the sciences by subject and author and by cited author or article

Social Sciences Citation Index: lists of articles in the social sciences by subject and author and by cited author or article

Sociological Abstracts: citations and abstracts for sociology and related disciplines

Women's Studies Index (or *Women's Studies on Disc* on CD-ROM)

Because scholarly publishing online is a relatively recent development, to date not all online journals are included in specialized indexes. Some electronic databases that may be available through your library, such as ECO (Electronic Collections Online from OCLC) and JSTOR, index some scholarly electronic journals. A collection of scholarly electronic journals (mainly in medicine and life sciences but some in physical and social sciences) is also indexed by HighWire Press <http://highwire.stanford.edu/searchall/>. If you want to include electronic journals in your search for sources, ask a reference librarian for help.

❑ **1.**

Author:	Nasar, Sylvia
Title:	**A beautiful mind :** a biography of John Forbes Nash, Jr., winner of the Nobel Prize in economics, 1994/Sylvia Nasar.
Publisher:	New York, NY : Simon & Schuster, c 1998.
Description:	459 p. : ill. ; 25 cm.
Notes:	Includes bibliographical references (p. [435]-437) and index.
ISBN:	0684819066
Language:	English
Subjects:	Nash, John F.,--1928-
	Mathematicians--United States--Biography

Holdings:

Library		Call Number	Other Information
UCD	Shields	QA29.N25 N37 1998 c.1	
		Circ Status: checked out; due 6/30/2002	

Figure RP-8. Online entry, library catalog.

The Library Catalog

The library lists each book and periodical series in a central catalog, which usually can be accessed on computer terminals near the reference or circulation section. The catalog may also be accessible to students and faculty through Internet or Telnet connections to the campus computer network.

You can search the catalog by subject, title, or author. Unless you do a title search, you will first see a list of all holdings by the same author or about the same subject; skim through these for other potential sources.

Figure RP-8 shows a typical catalog listing for a book. You can use the links to see other works by the author or about the same subject. The subject headings may provide additional keywords for your list. The entry notes special features, such as an index, a bibliography, and illustrations—all of which may prove useful in your research.

Library Classification Systems Each book's location is identified by a call number; the same number is written on the book's spine. To find books about a particular topic, either you can browse through the shelves housing books with the appropriate call number or you can look through the central catalog entries with that subject heading. Call numbers are usually assigned according to the Library of Congress system or the Dewey decimal system. Ask a librarian for a list of your library's classifications.

The Library of Congress system, usually used by college libraries, uses letters to identify twenty major subject categories.

A	general works	L	education
B	philosophy and religion	M	music
C	history and auxiliary sciences	N	fine arts
		P	language and literature
D	universal history and topography	Q	science
		R	medicine
E/F	American history	S	agriculture
G	geography, anthropology, folklore	T	technology
		U	military service
H	social sciences	V	naval service
J	political science	Z	library science and bibliography
K	law		

Subcategories are represented by a second letter. For example, TL in the technology category (T) represents books about motor vehicles, aeronautics, and astronautics, and TT marks books about handicrafts and arts and crafts.

The Dewey decimal system, often used by public libraries, uses numbers to identify ten major subject categories.

000–099	general works
100–199	philosophy
200–299	religion
300–399	social sciences
400–499	language
500–599	pure sciences
600–699	technology (applied sciences)
700–799	fine arts
800–899	literature
900–999	history

Each of these general categories is divided into ten subcategories. For example, 610–619 in the technology category (600–699) is for books in medical sciences, and 640–649 is for books about home economics.

Interlibrary Loans and Publishing Bibliographies   If you cannot find a particular book or periodical in your library catalog, ask a reference librarian about interlibrary loans. Most college and university libraries have interlibrary loan arrangements, and you can usually access the catalogs of participating institutions online. To identify specific books or articles or to verify that your source's information about a particular book or article is correct, you can consult a publishing bibliography, such as the following:

Books in Print (U.S. books indexed by author, title, and subject; issued annually, with supplements)

Cumulative Book Index (all books published in English indexed by author, title, and subject; issued annually, with supplements)

Catalog of U.S. Government Publications (nonclassified publications of all federal agencies by subject, author, title, report number, and ordering instructions)

Ulrich's Periodicals Directory (serial publications throughout the world; issued annually, with supplements)

An Internet site that is useful for finding publication information (and often, brief reviews) about specific books is amazon.com (an online bookstore with a huge database) <http://www.amazon.com>.

Finding Good Sources on the Web

The **World Wide Web** contains billions of pages of information. The challenge is to find reliable information that will be relevant to your paper. For that, you need a list of keywords and a search engine. This section offers an introduction to basic Internet research techniques. Your library, computer center, or writing lab may provide more extensive information, or you can visit an online Internet tutorial, such as

<http://www.lib.berkeley.edu/TeachingLib/Guides/Internet/FindInfo.html> from the University of California at Berkeley, or

<http://www.ouc.bc.ca/libr/connect96/search.htm> from Okanagan University College in Canada.

Because no two search engines search exactly the same databases and because they index keywords in different ways, different search engines may come up with different results. (For a concise list, with links, describing which search engines are best for which kinds of information, go to the Nueva School Library <http://www.nueva.pvt.k12.ca.us/~debbie/library/research/adviceengine.html>.) Many people choose Google <http://www.google.com> because it searches the largest number of pages and lists its sites according to page popularity—or the number of other sites linked to them. To check that no important Web sites have been missed, a thorough researcher may scan results from more than one search engine or from a metasearch engine, which superficially searches many search engines at once. Search engines recommended by the Librarians' Index to the Internet <http://www.lii.org> include

Google <http://www.google.com>

AllTheWeb <http://www.alltheweb.com>

Alta Vista <http://www.altavista.com>

Excite <http://www.excite.com>

HotBot <http://www.hotbot.lycos.com>

NorthernLight <http://www.northernlight.com>

Recommended metasearch engines include

Ixquick <http://www.ixquick.com>

MetaCrawler <http://www.metacrawler.com>

HOW TO EVALUATE THE RELIABILITY OF INTERNET SOURCES

Reliable Web sources usually include the following information:

- the author's name
- the author's credentials
- the date the page was created or last revised
- the name of the database or a link to the sponsoring institution
- accurate, documented information
- an objective, well-reasoned presentation

Signs of unreliable Web sources include

- anonymity
- no date of creation or revision
- no documentation for facts or statistics
- exaggerated claims and one-sided arguments
- typos, misspellings, and poor grammar

Tips for Evaluating Internet Sources

First, examine the **URL** (Uniform Resource Locator), the address of the Web site. Its abbreviations often provide clues about the source of the site—for example:

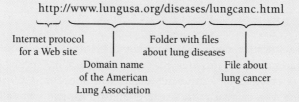

http://www.lungusa.org/diseases/lungcanc.html

Internet protocol for a Web site

Domain name of the American Lung Association

Folder with files about lung diseases

File about lung cancer

The last segment of the domain name indicates the type of institution sponsoring the site: *.com* and *.biz* are used by commercial businesses, *.edu* by colleges and universities, *.gov* by government agencies, *.mil* by the military, *.net* by network organizations, *.org* by nonprofit organizations, and *.k12* by elementary and high schools. Web sites outside the United States are usually identified with a two-letter abbreviation, such as *.uk* for the United Kingdom and *.ca* for Canada.

(continued)

(For a complete list of country abbreviations, see <http://www.din.de/gremien/nas/nabd/iso3166ma/codlstp1/en_listpl.html>. A tilde (~) in a folder name indicates a personal page; try to ascertain the qualifications of the author.

If the author's or creator's name does not appear at the top or bottom of the page, try to find out who is responsible for the site by going to a "home" or "about us" link. If there is no link, try deleting everything after the domain name; the shortened version may be the URL of the sponsor's home page.

Look for information about the author's or sponsor's qualifications as an authority on the topic. For additional information, use the author's or sponsor's name as a search term in your favorite search engine. If the document is on an academic Web site (.edu), look for an internal directory on the home page, and use it to search for the author.

If the Web site does not include the date of creation or latest revision at the top or bottom of the document, you might

- use the "Document Information" feature in Netscape's View menu,
- look for the directory or subdirectory containing your page by trimming the URL to the last slash (and trimming again if the URL has a lot of slashes), or
- use the title of the page (enclosed in quotation marks) as a search term in a search engine whose results show dates, such as HotBot <http://hotbot.lycos.com/>.

Another way to check the reliability of an Internet source is to click on a few of its links. If many of them are no longer live, the document is probably dated. If they lead to sites that seem to have an obvious bias, your source probably shares it.

For additional hints about evaluating Web pages critically, see the checklist "Thinking Critically about World Wide Web Resources," from the UCLA library <http://www.library.ucla.edu/libraries/college/help/critical/index.htm> and the list of links, "Resources for Evaluating Information on the Internet," from the University of Iowa libraries <http://twist.lib.uiowa.edu/resources/evaluate.html>.

Because each search engine has somewhat different features, go to its Help link if you have not used the engine before. Find out what special features the engine offers, and look at its **advanced search** options. With an advanced search, you can use more search tool features, and you will be less likely to get irrelevant documents.

Experiment with Keywords The first step in researching a topic on the Internet is to create a list of **keywords** and phrases. (See the box that follows for advice about searching for phrases or combinations of keywords.) As you start searching, you will probably find that some keywords are more effective than others in getting to relevant sources and reliable information, and you will undoubtedly discover additional keywords as you learn more about your topic. Some search engines—such as AltaVista, AllTheWeb, Excite, and HotBot—even suggest possible keywords or phrases with a related-searches feature (usually near the top of a results page).

SEARCH TERMS

Most search engines use some or all of the following features, but read the instructions for each search engine before starting your search:

- To search for a proper name or a specific phrase, enclose it in quotation marks: "Victorian literature".
- To make sure all the keywords are in retrieved documents, use AND: cloning AND sheep. Some search engines use + (with no space after) instead: cloning +sheep.
- To avoid getting documents you do not want, use AND NOT: cloning AND NOT mice. Some search engines use - (with no space after) instead: cloning -mice.
- If there are common synonyms for some of your terms, use OR: (women OR females) AND architects.
- To search for all the variations of a keyword, some search engines let you use "truncation" and add an asterisk or other symbol to the root of the word: child* will retrieve "child," "children," and other words beginning with "child."

For a more detailed discussion of how to tailor search terms to your search, see <http://www.lib.berkeley.edu/TeachingLib/Guides/Internet/ Strategies. html#FeaturesTable> from the University of California at Berkeley Internet tutorial.

If a keyword or phrase retrieves too many sources, try keywords that are more specific; for example, instead of *school violence,* try *school shootings* or even *Columbine.* Some search engines, such as Google and AltaVista, allow you to search for another keyword within your results. In other search engines, such as NorthernLight and AllTheWeb, you need to add new keywords to your search terms and do a new search.

Search Engine Strategies Start at the top of your list of results and examine the URL and the brief description of the site to see if it is likely to be the kind of information you need. When you find a promising link, do one or more of the following things to make sure you are able to retrieve the information later:

- Bookmark the site or add it to your Favorites (or e-mail it to yourself if you are working on a library computer).
- Copy and paste the URL into your working bibliography.
- Copy and paste all or part of the text into your file of promising sources. (Be sure to add the URL and the day's date.)
- Print out the text. (Be sure to configure your browser's page setup to print the URL and the date in a header or footer.)

Before returning to the next site in your search results, make sure you have recorded all the identifying information for the promising link so that you can cite it properly if you end up using it as a source for your paper. If you copy the document into a file of potential sources, be sure to keep it separate from the files of your own writing. If these two files get mixed up, you may accidentally commit **plagiarism.**

When you find a quality site, you may want to follow its links in search of other potentially valuable sources. For example, a search for *global warming* may take you to the Environmental Protection Agency's Global Warming Site <http://www.epa.gov/globalwarming>. This site can be a takeoff point for an extensive search of many valuable links. When you have exhausted the trails leading from the takeoff site, return to your search results via your brower's History or Go path, or start a new search based on what you learned from your exploration.

Subject Directories If you are looking for an overview of your topic or for additional quality sites, you might consult subject directories. These tools have smaller and more selective databases than do general search engines, and their links are selected by librarians or experts in the field rather than by computers.

The largest general-interest subject directories are:

Yahoo! <http://www.yahoo.com>

Google's directory <http://www.google.com/dirhp?hl=en>

For links to single-subject directories, go to that subject in Yahoo! or Google's directory, and click on the link for Web directories (Yahoo!) or directories (Google's directory).

Searchable academic multiple-subject directories include:

Academic Info <http://www.academicinfo.net/index.html>

Argus Clearinghouse <http://www.clearinghouse.net/>

BUBL Link <http://bubl.ac.uk/link/index.html>

Digital Librarian <http://www.digital-librarian.com>

INFOMINE: Scholarly Internet Resource Collection
<http://infomine.ucr.edu>

Librarian's Index to the Internet <http://www.lii.org>

Browsable multiple-subject directories include:

The Internet Public Library Reference Center <http://www.ipl.org/ref/>

UC Berkeley & Internet Resources by Academic Discipline
<http://www.lib.berkeley.edu/Collections/acadtarg.html>

World Wide Web Virtual Library <http://vlib.org>

If you are looking for very specific information, such as a piece of legislation or a database of toxic chemicals, you may want to search the "invisible Web"—searchable databases that general-purpose search engines can't or don't index. Two search engines for the invisible Web are:

Direct Search <http://gwis2.circ.gwu.edu/%7Eprice/direct.htm>

InvisibleWeb.com <http://www.invisibleweb.com/>

You can find some of these databases by adding the word "database" to your search term in Google and Yahoo!

Electronic Newsgroups and Mailing Lists Newsgroups (sometimes called Usenet or discussion forums) and mailing lists (listservs) are ways for groups of people to exchange information and opinions about a particular topic via e-mail. Because the content of a newsgroup or a mailing list depends on what the participants wish to discuss, these e-mail exchanges are not usually a good resource for basic research about a topic. Their primary value for researchers is that the discussions may be about current "hot" topics in a field, and some of the participants may be subject experts who can give advice about tracking down an obscure piece of information. It may not be easy to tell which participants are the true experts, however. Before deciding to use one of these postings as a source in your paper, try to learn the author's credentials—perhaps by doing an Internet search.

Most newsgroup discussions are archived and available to the public on the Internet, although you must be a subscriber if you want to send or receive postings. Google Groups <http://www.google.com/grphp?hl=en> is the best source for locating Usenet archives. Newsgroups are divided into discussion categories and subcategories. Top-level categories include *biz.* for business products and reviews; *comp.* for computer hardware and software; *humanities.* for fine art, literature, and philosophy; *sci.* for applied and social sciences; *soc.* for social issues and culture; and *talk.* for current issues and debates. These categories are subdivided, and the name for each subcategory is also followed by a period. You can follow the subdivisions until you get to a specific subcategory, such as *soc.history.early-modern.*

Fewer mailing lists than newsgroups are archived; to access most lists, you need to subscribe so that you can receive e-mail from the list. To locate a mailing list about a particular topic, you can search Topica <http://www.liszt.com> or Publicly Accessible Mailing Lists (PAML) <http://paml.net>. Tile.Net <http://tile.net> has links to both mailing lists and newsgroups. Mailing lists are housed on listservers—central computers (usually at universities) that automatically receive and distribute the messages. When you subscribe, you receive instructions about where to post messages and how to unsubscribe. Be sure to save these instructions. Note: Mailing lists have two addresses: the address you subscribe to (the list manager) and the address you use to post messages. Don't sent your "subscribe" message to the posting address, or it will appear in the e-mails of all the list's members.

NETIQUETTE FOR NEWSGROUPS AND MAILING LISTS

If you are thinking about posting a message to a newsgroup or mailing list, remember some basic rules of netiquette:

1. Read the group's FAQ (frequently asked questions) or browse its archive before posting a message. If you ask a question that has already been answered dozens of times or if the group is not appropriate for your topic, you will probably be ignored. To find the FAQ for Google newsgroups, enter "faq" and the name of the group in the search box.
2. Write with care, and reread your message before posting it. The people reading your posting will know you only by what you write.
3. Be brief.
4. Use a descriptive subject line.
5. Do not send your message indiscriminately to multiple groups or lists.

DOCUMENTATION AND RESEARCH PAPER FORMATS

Documentation is the credit given to sources used or quoted in a research paper, journal article, book, or other document. Full and accurate documentation prevents **plagiarism** and allows readers to locate and consult the sources cited. All facts and ideas that are not common knowledge should be documented, as should all direct **quotations**. When you edit your paper, make sure that quotations and ideas from other sources are documented and that the in-text citations correspond to entries in the list of references or works cited.

The following pages provide examples of the four styles of documentation most frequently used in undergraduate courses: MLA (Modern Language Association of America) style for arts and humanities courses, APA (American Psychological Association) style for social science courses, CMS (*Chicago Manual of Style*) style for history and humanities courses, and CSE (Council of Science Editors; formerly Council of Biology Editors, or CBE) style for life sciences. A complete sample research paper in MLA style appears on pages 90–98. The manuscript form for the other three styles is illustrated with sample pages.

Many other professional organizations and journals also publish style manuals that describe documentation formats used in other disciplines. A list of such style manuals appears on page 153. Ask your instructor which style to use, and follow it consistently, in every detail of order, punctuation, and capitalization.

MLA Style

The *MLA Handbook for Writers of Research Papers*, 5th ed. (New York: MLA, 1999), recommends a system of brief in-text citations that refer to a list of works cited (with full publication information) at the end of the paper.

continued

MLA

MLA In-Text Citations

Parenthetical in-text citations should not distract the reader, but they must be complete enough to allow the reader to locate the corresponding entry easily in the list of works cited. The best place for a citation is just before the final punctuation of the sentence. If that is not appropriate, put the citation before a comma or other internal punctuation or, if nothing else is possible, before a natural pause in the sentence. The following examples illustrate the MLA style of in-text citation.

1. *Author named in text.* In parentheses, provide the page number of the source. (With block quotations, enclose the page number in parentheses one space after the last punctuation mark.) If you are citing a source that uses paragraph numbers rather than page numbers, such as an electronic journal, precede the number with the abbreviation "par." or "pars."

According to Tompkins, critics who admire Cooper find themselves in a

bind: They must attempt to diminish the embarrassing (and major)

features of the novels, or they must alter their standards for evaluating

works of literature (98).

MLA

If the list of works cited contains two authors with the same last name, include the first initial or, if that too is the same, the first name of each one in the in-text citations.

2. *Author not named in text.* In parentheses, give both the author's last name and the page number, separated by one space. (With block quotations, place the parenthetical citation one space after the last punctuation mark.) If you are citing a source that uses paragraph numbers rather than page numbers, place a comma after the author's name and use the abbreviation "par." or "pars."

> The Last of the Mohicans presents a dilemma for literary critics; even
>
> when they are sympathetic, they "have been hard put to explain why
>
> they should continue to be fascinated by a novel which, by their own
>
> accounts, is replete with sensationalism and cliché" (Tompkins 95).

3. *More than one author.* If the source has no more than three authors, name them all in the text or the parenthetical citation. If the source has more than three authors, list them all or use only the first author's name followed by "et al." (the abbreviation for the Latin phrase meaning "and others").

> McCrum, Cran, and MacNeil call the development of the English language
>
> "the story of three invasions and a cultural revolution" (51).

4. *Author of two or more works cited.* If the list of works cited includes more than one work by the same author, the source must be identified by both the author's name and a short version of the title. (The full title of the work in this example is *Sensational Designs: The Cultural Work of American Fiction 1790–1860.*)

> Certain nineteenth-century American novels, despite critical consensus
>
> that they are short on literary merit, played an important role by
>
> "providing society with a means of thinking about itself" (Tompkins,
>
> Sensational 200).

5. *Corporate author or government agency.* The corporate or agency name should match the entry in the list of works cited. For example, if the works cited entry begins with "United States. Department of Commerce," the in-text citation should be "U.S. Department of Commerce" rather than "Commerce Department."

> Chicago Women in Publishing recommends that workers' titles "be
>
> described in a way that indicates the job could be filled by a member of
>
> either sex" (10).

6. *Unknown author.* If the source is not signed (a brief article in a newspaper or magazine, for example), use its full title in the text or a shortened version in the citation. A short title should begin with the same word (excluding articles) as the full

title so that the work can be located in the list of works cited; the full title in this example, "Can Your Mind Heal Your Body?" could be shortened to "Can Your Mind Heal?" but not to "Mind/Body."

> Both physicians and entrepreneurs have recently become interested
>
> in how the mind can affect physical health ("Can Your Mind Heal Your
>
> Body?" 107).

7. *Entire work.* If you are referring to an entire work rather than to a specific passage, no page number is necessary in the in-text citation.

> Tompkins's eloquent argument is this: American literature gives its
>
> readers nothing less than a means of comprehending their history and
>
> constructing their social consciences.

8. *Multivolume work.* If you consulted a multivolume work in your research, the in-text citation must include the volume number (followed by a colon) as well as the page number.

> Like the paintings of Braque, Dali, and Picasso, the compositions of
>
> Stravinsky and Schoenberg come from the intellect, not the emotions
>
> (Hauser 4: 230).

9. *Literary work.* When you are quoting from a literary work that has been published in many editions, include information that will enable the reader to locate the passage in any edition.

For novels, give the page number followed by a semicolon and the chapter or part number.

> Fifty years ago, Richard Wright wrote, "Who knows when some slight
>
> shock, disturbing the delicate balance between social order and thirsty
>
> aspiration, shall send the skyscrapers in our cities tumbling?" (Native
>
> Son 25; bk. 1).

For poems, cite only the line number (or numbers); a page number is unnecessary. Use a hyphen to indicate inclusive lines.

> In earlier parts of "In Just-" e. e. cummings's darker references to
>
> "the little/lame balloonman" (4-5) and to "the queer/old balloonman"
>
> (11-12) have prepared us for the perhaps not-so-innocent "goat-footed/
>
> balloonMan" of the poem's conclusion (20-21).

MLA

For prose plays, give the page number followed by a semicolon, the number of the act, a comma, and the number of the scene (43; 1, 3). Use Arabic numerals unless your instructor specifies a preference for Roman numerals. For verse plays, omit the page number but include the line number (or numbers), and separate the act, scene, and line number with periods.

> The 1970s musical Hair turned Hamlet's musings--"What a piece of work
>
> is man! How noble in reason!" (2.2.320)--into a song.

10. *Indirect source.* To show that a quotation in your paper was also a quotation in your source (rather than written by the source's author), use the abbreviation "qtd. in" ("quoted in"). In the list of works cited, include only the source you consulted (which would be Trimbur in the following example).

> Kenneth Bruffee observed, "While students often forget much of the
>
> subject matter shortly after class is over, they do not easily forget
>
> the values implicit in the conventions by which it was taught" (qtd. in
>
> Trimbur 95).

11. *More than one source.* If a point has two or more sources, separate them with a semicolon.

> Critics have long had difficulty justifying serious consideration of the
>
> works of James Fenimore Cooper (Reynolds 102; Tompkins 98).

12. *Electronic source.* If you name the author in the text and are citing an electronic source that uses screen, section, or paragraph numbers rather than page numbers, precede the number with "screen," "sec.," "par.," or "pars." If you did not name the author in the text, place a comma between the author's name and "screen," "sec.," "par.," or "pars." If you are referring to an entire electronic work or to a part of one that has no numbered screens, sections, or paragraphs, you need not give screen, section, or paragraph numbers in the in-text citation.

> In "Petruchio's Horse: Equine and Household Mismanagement in The
>
> Taming of the Shrew," Peter Heaney describes glanders, mose in the
>
> chine, the lampass, and several other equine disorders that affect
>
> Petruchio's poor animal (par. 3).

MLA Information Notes

You may use a few brief numbered notes in addition to the parenthetical citations if you need to comment on a source or to include information that is necessary but would interrupt the flow of the text. Use an Arabic numeral raised above the line after the final punctuation of a sentence, and number the notes consecutively throughout the paper. Place the notes themselves, with the centered title "Notes," on a separate page before the list of works cited (or, if your instructor so specifies, as footnotes at the bottoms of the pages on which the corresponding raised numbers appear in the text). Indent the first line of each note half an inch (or five spaces if you are using a typewriter), and begin it with a raised number without punctuation. If the note is longer than one line, the second and subsequent lines begin at the left margin. Double-space within and between the notes. (Footnotes are single-spaced, with double spaces between notes, and begin four lines—two double spaces—below the text.)

TEXT   Critics have long had difficulty justifying serious con-

sideration of the works of James Fenimore Cooper.[1]

NOTE   [1]Scholarly studies of Cooper are reportedly

planned by several university presses, however.

MLA List of Works Cited

Beginning on a separate page at the end of your paper, list in alphabetical order all the sources you cite, and give full publishing information for them. Title the list "Works Cited," and center this heading an inch from the top of the paper. Double-space both within and between entries, and indent the second and subsequent lines of each entry half an inch (or five spaces on a typewriter). Note that MLA style requires underlining rather than italics.

BOOKS   Book entries have three parts, and each one ends with a period. The first part is the author's name; the second is the title and subtitle (which are underlined); and the third is the publishing information (place of publication, publisher, and year). You will find all this information on the book's title page and copyright page.

Use a short version of the publisher's name (Harcourt for Harcourt Brace and Company and Beacon for Beacon Press, Inc., for example). If an abbreviation for the publisher's name is familiar to your audience, use it (such as GPO for Government Printing Office and ALA for American Library Association). Use the abbreviation UP for University Press. For other abbreviations acceptable in documentation, see **abbreviations**, pages 134–43.

1. *Book with one author.*

Boorstin, Daniel J. The Discoverers. New York: Random, 1983.

2. *Book with two or three authors.* List authors' names in the order in which they appear on the title page. Invert the first author's name (to alphabetize); enter the

MLA

BASIC FORM FOR NONPERIODICAL REFERENCES IN MLA STYLE

Book:

> Author, Anna A., and Barney B. Author. Title of Work. Location:
>
> Publisher, 2002.

Chapter or part of a book:

> Author, Anna A. "Title of Chapter." Title of Book. Ed. Enid E. Editor
>
> and Edward E. Editor. Location: Publisher, 2002. xx-xx.

---

coauthors' names in regular order (first name, last name), and separate them with commas. (Write out "and" before the name of the last author rather than using an **ampersand.**)

> Gilbert, Sandra, and Susan Gubar. The Madwoman in the Attic: The
>
> Woman Writer and the Nineteenth-Century Literary Imagination.
>
> New Haven: Yale UP, 1979.

3. *Book with more than three authors.* Give all the authors' (or editors') names (with only the first one inverted), or include only the name of the first author followed by the abbreviation "et al." (for the Latin phrase meaning "and others").

> Malson, Micheline R., et al., eds. Black Women in America: Social Science
>
> Perspectives. Chicago: U of Chicago P, 1990.

4. *Two or more books by the same author.* List the author's name in the first reference only. For succeeding references, instead of the author's name, enter three hyphens (---) followed by a period and one space, and then enter the title of the work. Alphabetize works by the same author by the first significant word in the title (ignore the articles "a," "an," and "the").

> Brophy, Brigid. Beardsley and His World. New York: Harmony, 1976.
>
> ---. Black and White: A Portrait of Aubrey Beardsley. New York: Stein and
>
> Day, 1969.

5. *Book by a corporate author.* Alphabetize the entry by the name of the corporation or institution, even if the corporate author is the publisher.

> CompuServe. CompuServe Information Service: User's Guide. Columbus,
>
> OH: CompuServe, 1985.

MLA

6. *Book with an editor.* Follow the first name with a comma and the abbreviation "ed." (for "editor").

Van Thal, Herbert, ed. The Mammoth Book of Great Detective Stories.

London: Robinson, 1985.

7. *Book with an author and an editor.* Give the author's name (in inverted order) before the title; give the editor's name (in normal order) after it, preceded by the abbreviation "Ed." (for "Edited by").

James, Henry. Selected Fiction. Ed. Leon Edel. New York: Dutton, 1953.

8. *Translated work.* Give the author's name (in inverted order) before the title; give the translator's name (in normal order) after it, preceded by the abbreviation "Trans." (for "Translated by").

García Márquez, Gabriel. One Hundred Years of Solitude. Trans. Gregory

Rabassa. New York: Harper, 1970.

9. *Book without a listed author.* Alphabetize the book by the first significant word in the title (omit the articles "a," "an," and "the").

Waterstone's Guide to Books. London: Waterstone, 1981.

10. *Book edition, if not the first.* Place the abbreviated edition number ("Rev. ed." or "2nd ed.," for example) after the period following the title.

Kiniry, Malcolm, and Mike Rose. Critical Strategies for Academic Thinking

and Writing. 2nd ed. Boston: Bedford, 1993.

11. *Republished book.* Place the original publication date after the title. Separate it from the publication information with a period.

Faulkner, William. The Sound and the Fury. 1929. New York: Vintage-

Random, 1946.

12. *Multivolume series.* List the total number of volumes after the title of the work. Use Arabic numerals. If you used only one volume of the series in your research, identify that volume after the title. You may add the complete number of volumes at the end of the entry.

Sewall, Richard B. The Life of Emily Dickinson. Vol. 1. New York: Farrar,

1974. 2 vols.

13. *Selection in an anthology or edited book.* Give the author and title of the selection in quotation marks with the period inside them and then the title of the collection or anthology in which it appears and the editor of the volume (preceded by "Ed." for "Edited by"). Include the page numbers of the selection at the end of the entry.

MLA

Gordimer, Nadine. "The Bridegroom." African Short Stories. Ed. Chinua

Achebe and C. L. Innes. London: Heinemann, 1985. 155-63.

14. *Article in a reference work.* If the article is signed, begin with the author's name; if it is unsigned, begin with its title, followed by the title of the work. If the articles in the reference work are listed alphabetically, omit the volume number (if any) and page numbers.

Levison, Sanford. "Supreme Court." The Reader's Guide to American

History. Ed. Eric Foner and John A. Garraty. Boston: Houghton, 1991.

15. *Foreword, introduction, preface, or afterword.* If you quote or use information from one of these elements, cite the name of the author of that element, followed by the name of the element (do not underline it or put it in quotation marks). The names of the author, editor, and translator (if any) follow the title. The page numbers of the element go after the publication information.

Weir, Charles I., Jr. Introduction. Madame Bovary. By Gustave Flaubert.

Trans. Eleanor Marx Aveling. New York: Holt, 1948. vii-xii.

16. *Dissertation.* For an unpublished dissertation, enclose the title in quotation marks. Follow with the name of the degree-granting institution and the date. For a published dissertation, underline the title, and add publishing information (place of publication, publisher's name, and year) at the end of the entry.

Marks, Barry Alan. "The Idea of Propaganda in America." Diss. U of

Minnesota, 1957.

PERIODICALS   Entries for articles from periodicals have three parts, and each one ends with a period. The first part is the author's name; the second is the title of the article (which is enclosed in quotation marks); and the third is the title of the periodical (which is underlined), the publication informa-

---

BASIC FORM FOR PERIODICAL REFERENCES IN MLA STYLE

Magazines paginated by issue:

Author, Anna A., Barney B. Author, and Clarice C. Author. "Title of

Article." Title of Periodical Aug. 2002: xx-xx.

Periodicals paginated by volume:

Author, Anna. "Title of Article." Title of Periodical 4 (2002): xxx-xx.

tion—such as the volume number and the date of publication (followed by a colon and a space)—and the page numbers.

17. *Article in a monthly magazine.* Abbreviate all months except May, June, and July; for the abbreviations of months, see **abbreviations**. (Note that, when the title ends with a question mark or exclamation point, it is not followed by a period.) If an article is continued from its first page to a nonconsecutive page, give only the first page followed (without a space) by a + sign.

Johnson, Fenton. "Beyond Belief: A Skeptic Searches for an American

Faith." Harper's Sept. 1998: 39-54.

18. *Article in a weekly magazine.* The format is the same as that for a monthly magazine, except that the publication information includes the day as well as the month and the year.

Franzen, Jonathan. "Imperial Bedroom." New Yorker 12 Oct. 1998: 48-53.

19. *Article in a journal paginated by annual volume.* For journals whose pagination is continuous throughout each annual volume, follow the journal name with the volume number, the year (in parentheses followed by a colon), and the page numbers.

Boettcher, Bonna J., and William L. Schurk. "From Games to Grunge:

Popular Culture Research Collections at Bowling Green State

University." Notes 54 (1998): 849-59.

20. *Article in a journal paginated by issue.* For journals that begin each issue with page 1, give the volume number (followed by a period), the issue number, the year (in parentheses followed by a colon), and the page numbers.

Sloan, Jacob. "Days of Our Years." Commentary 106.4 (1998): 51-54.

21. *Article in a newspaper.* The entry follows the format of an entry for a weekly magazine (see example 18), with the addition of the number or letter, if any, of the section in which the article is found. If an edition is given on the newspaper's masthead, specify the edition, preceded by a comma, after the date.

Sack, Kevin. "A Literary Sherman in Pastels, Tom Wolfe Takes Atlanta."

New York Times 2 Nov. 1998: A7.

When the section is identified by number rather than letter, use the following format:

Austin, Elizabeth. "The Truth Is Not There: Conspiracy-Laden Series

'The X-Files' Is Bad for America." Chicago Tribune 8 Nov. 1998,

sec. 2: 1.

MLA

22. *Unsigned article.* Use the form for the appropriate kind of periodical, but begin with the article title, and alphabetize the entry according to the first main word in the title. Use a shortened form of the title in the in-text citation.

"The Master of Ambiguity." <u>Maclean's</u> 30 Nov. 1998: 2.

23. *Review.* List the reviewer's name, followed by the abbreviation "Rev. of" (for "Review of") and the title of the reviewed work. Separate the title from the author of the work with a comma and the word "by."

Barnes, Julian. Rev. of <u>Birds of America</u>, by Lorrie Moore. <u>New York</u>

<u>Review of Books</u> 45.16 (1998): 15.

24. *Editorial.* Begin with the title of the editorial (if it is signed, begin with the author's name). Follow the title with a period, the word "Editorial," and another period. Give the day, month, and year of the newspaper, followed by the section and page number on which the editorial appears.

"The Clout Is Out There." Editorial. <u>Los Angeles Times</u> 30 Nov. 1998: A14.

25. *Letter to the editor.* Follow the writer's name with a period and the word "Letter," followed by a period.

Aronson, Michael A. Letter. <u>Chronicle of Higher Education</u> 16 Oct. 1998: B11.

ELECTRONIC SOURCES In general, documentation for electronic publications is similar to that for publications in print, but some additional information must be included so that the electronic data can be retrieved. For more examples, see the MLA style FAQ at <http://www.mla.org/>.

26. *Article from a library database, project, or service.* To cite a newspaper, magazine, or journal article that is available only through a library subscription, such as *Expanded Academic ASAP* or *Project Muse* in the California Digital Library, identify the sponsoring library and the URL. Instead of the very long URL of a search trail, use the URL of the database's search page.

Fetto, John. "Candy for Cookies." <u>American Demographics</u> Aug. 2000.

<u>Infotrac General Reference Center</u>. Santa Monica Public Lib., Santa

Monica, CA. 4 June 2001 <http://infotrac.galegroup.com>.

Schwindt, Richard, and Aidan Vining. "Proposal for a Mutual Insurance

Pool for Transplant Organs." <u>Journal of Health Politics, Policy</u>

<u>and Law</u> 23.5 (1998): 725-41. <u>ABI/Inform</u>. California Digital Lib.,

U of California, Irvine. 16 Feb. 2001 <http://www.cdlib.org/

collections>.

BASIC FORM FOR ELECTRONIC REFERENCES IN MLA STYLE

Article in an online journal:

> Author, Anna A. "Title of Article." Title of Periodical Date of article's
>
> publication. Page range or number of paragraphs. Date of
>
> access and <URL>.

Article republished in an online commercial or library database:

> Author, Anna A. "Title of Article." Title of Periodical 28 Aug. 2001.
>
> xx–xx. Name of Database. Name and Location of Library.
>
> 1 Dec. 2002 <URL of database's search page>.

Online document:

> Author, Archibald A. Title of Document. 28 Aug. 2001. Publisher.
>
> 1 Dec. 2002 <URL>.

An expanded discussion of these basic forms appears on this book's Web site at <www.mhhe.com/ebest>, along with additional models for online sources.

> Thomson, Judith Jarvis. "The Right to Privacy." Philosophy and
>
> Public Affairs 4.4 (Summer 1975): 295-314. JSTOR. UCI Libs.,
>
> U of California, Irvine. 6 Nov. 2000 <http://www.jstor.org>.

27. *Article from a public database, project, or service.* To cite a newspaper, magazine, or journal article from a freely available, commercial or public database, project, or service, for example, *FindArticles.com* or the *Perseus Project,* identify the source in the URL. If the URL is a search trail, trim back the URL to a page with a search capacity.

> Atkins, Scott. "The American Sense of Puritan." Capitol Project. 31 July
>
> 1998. American Studies Group, U of Virginia. 4 Mar. 2000 <http://
>
> xroads.virginia.edu/~CAP/puritan/purmain.html>.

> Barnett, A. H., and David L. Kaserman. "Comment on 'The Shortage in
>
> Market-Inalienable Human Organs': Faulty Analysis of a Failed
>
> Policy." American Journal of Economics and Sociology Apr. 2000.
>
> FindArticles.com. 6 Mar. 2001 <http://www.findarticles.com>.

Electronic Sources

MLA

Burns, Margo. "Arthur Miller's The Crucible: Fact & Fiction." 14 July

  2000. 17th Century Colonial New England. 6 Aug. 2001 <http://

  www.ogram.org/17thc/crucible.shtml>.

MacFayden, Lynn, Gerard Hastings, and Anne Marie MacKintosh.

  "Cross Sectional Study of Young People's Awareness of and

  Involvement with Tobacco Marketing." BMJ 3 Mar. 2001. British

  Medical Association. PubMedCentral. 2 June 2001 <http://www.

  pubmedcentral.nih.gov/new/#search>.

28. *Article from an online journal or online version of a periodical.*

Reaves, Jessica. "Case for Man-Made Global Warming Gets Stronger.

  Time Online 17 May 2000. 26 Oct. 2000 <http://www.time.com>.

"Safety First on the Playground." Healthy Child Care America

  Newsletter 1.2 (Sept. 1997). National Child Care Information Center.

  17 Oct. 2000 <http://nccic.org/hcca/n1/sep97/playgnd.html>.

Taber, Andrew. "'Roid Rage." Salon 18 Nov. 1999. 9 Apr. 2001 <http://

  salon.com/health/feature/1999/11/18/steroids/print.html>.

29. *Report from an online newspaper archive.*

O'Harrow, Robert. "Opinion Split on Web Privacy." Washington Post

  Online 3 Apr. 2000: E12. 22 May 2001 <http://washingtonpost.com/

  wp-dyn/articles/A28560-2001Apr2.html>.

Phillips, Heather Fleming. "Congress Faces Taxing Questions over

  E-Commerce." Orange County Register 20 May 2001. OCRegister.

  com. 4 June 2001 <http://www.ocregister.com/sitearchives/2001/

  5/20/business/nettax19cci.shtml>.

Powers, Mary. "Face Off: Teenagers and Plastic Surgery May Not Be

  the Greatest Mix." Abilene Reporter-News 15 Sept. 2000. 24 Dec.

  2001 <http://www.reporternews.com/2000/features/face0915.

  html>.

"The Taliban Should Be Condemned." Editorial. New University Spring

    2001. 11 June 2001 <http://www.newu.uci.edu/archive/2000-2001/

    spring/010604/o-010604-editorial.html>.

30. *Article from an online news network or service.*

"'Cookiegate' Alarms Watchdogs." Wired News 22 June 2000. Wired.com.

    12 Oct. 2000 <http://www.wired.com/news/politics/>.

Crary, Dick. "Old and On the Road." 22 Nov. 1999. ABCNews.com. 28 Jan.

    2001 <http://www.abcnews.go.com/sections/living/DailyNews/

    elderlydrivers991122.html>.

Crouch, Cameron. "Will Big Brother Track You by Cell Phone?"

    PCWorld.Com. 20 Apr. 2001. CNN.com. 26 Apr. 2001 <http://

    www.cnn.com/2001/TECH/ptech/04/20/location.services.idg/

    index.html>.

Kranhold, Kathryn, and Michael Moss. "Companies Fight to Protect

    Cookies." Wall Street Journal Interactive Edition 20 Mar. 2000.

    ZDNN. 24 Oct. 2000 <http://www.zdnet.com/filters/printerfriendly/

    0,6061,2470654-2,00.html>.

31. *Entry in an online encyclopedia or dictionary.*

"Cookie." ZDWebopedia. n.d. ZDNet. 12 Oct. 2000 <http://www.

    zdwebopedia.com>.

"Privacy." Encarta. n.d. Microsoft. 1 July 2000 <http://encarta.msn.com>.

Rosen, Jeffrey. "Invasion of Privacy on the Internet." Encyclopaedia

    Britannica. n.d. 10 Oct. 2000 <http://www.britannica.com>.

32. *Information from a government site.* Treat a government site like any other
Web site, identifying the sponsoring agency or organization.

Daley, Richard M. "Federal Agenda 2001." 2001. Office of the Mayor,

    City of Chicago. 5 Feb. 2001 <http://w4.ci.chi.il/us/daley/

    2001federalagenda/Environment.html>.

California's "Emerging Renewables Buy-Down Program." n.d. California

   Energy Commission. 4 June 2001 <http://www.ca.gov/greengrid/

   index.html>.

Leman, Christopher K., Preston L. Schiller, and Kristin Pauley.

   "Re-Thinking HOV: High Occupancy Facilities and the Public

   Interest." 1 Aug. 1994. Report by the Chesapeake Bay Foundation.

   Federal Transit Administration, US Dept. of Transportation. 7 Feb.

   2001 <http://www.fta.dot.gov/library/planning/RETK/retk.html>.

"State Fiscal Picture." 21 Feb. 2001. Legislative Analyst's Office, State

   of California. 5 Mar. 2001 <http://www.lao.ca.gov/analysis_2001/

   highlights_01-02anal.html>.

33. *Information from an organization, association, or institute.* Identify the organization, for example, the Coalition to Stop Gun Violence, the Union of Concerned Scientists, the Entertainment Software Ratings Board, the American Academy of Pediatrics, or the National Institute of Diabetes and Digestive and Kidney Diseases.

Ad-Hoc Working Group on Unsolicited Commercial Email. "Report to the

   Federal Trade Commission." 17 June 1997. Center for Democracy

   and Technology. 20 Nov. 1999 <http://www.cdt.org/spam/>.

Culnan, Mary J. "Georgetown Internet Privacy Policy Study." 11 Aug.

   2000. Technology Center, McDonough School of Business,

   Georgetown U. 25 Aug. 2000 <http://www.msb.edu/faculty/

   culnanm/gippshome.html>.

"Sample Scenario." n.d. Online Ethics Center for Engineering and Science.

   25 Aug. 2000 <http://www.onlineethics.org/privacy/scene.html>.

State of the Beach. 2001. Surfrider Foundation. 1 June 2001 <http://

   www.surfrider.org/stateofthebeach>.

34. *E-mail message.*

Kay, David. "Re: College student/researcher needs some of your valuable

   time." E-mail to the author. 2 Dec. 2000.

35. *Course or class material.*

Student paper.

> Chuang, Chris. "Minorities and the Television." 1 June 1999. Student
>
> > paper. Prof. Bruce Lusignan. Seminar: Ethics of Development in a
> >
> > Global Environment. Stanford U. 3 Feb. 2001 <http://www.stanford.
> >
> > edu/class/e297/poverty_prejudice/mediarace/minorities.html>.
>
> Kolln, Lonny. "MP3 Technology and the Evolving Law around It." Spring
>
> > 2001. Student paper. Prof. Nicholas Johnson. Cyberspace Law
> >
> > Seminar. U of Iowa College of Law. 29 May 2001 <http://www.
> >
> > uiowa.edu/~cyberlaw/cls01/kolln1.html>.

Lecture notes.

> Zimmerer, Karl. "Purpose of the Endangered Species Act." Lecture notes.
>
> > Geography/IES 399. Spring 2001. U of Wisconsin. 16 Dec. 2001
> >
> > <http://www.geography.wisc.edu/classes/geog339/339outlinespart1/
> >
> > ESAoverheads.html>.

Reading notes.

> Landow, George P. "Snowcrash: Reading Notes on Theme and Subject."
>
> > Eng 111: Cyberspace to Critical Theory. n.d. Brown U. 21 June
> >
> > 2001 <http://landow.stg.brown.edu/cspace/scifi/ns/themenotes.
> >
> > html>.
>
> Mitchell-Boyask, Robin. "Study Guide for Sophocles' Antigone." n.d.
>
> > Dept. of Greek, Hebrew, and Roman Classics, Temple U. 28 Mar.
> >
> > 2001 <http://www.temple.edu/classics/antigone.html>.

Assigned reading.

> Cannatella, David. "Chapter 2: Trees and Taxa." ZOO 384L (Systematics).
>
> > Spring 2000. U of Texas. 29 Jan. 2001 <http://www.lifesci.utexas.
> >
> > edu/courses/systematics/handouts/Chapter_2.pdf>.

Electronic Sources

MLA

Mailing list message.

> Thuotte, Stephanie. "The Salem Witch Trials: Rhetorical Aspects."
>
> > Online posting. 21 May 2001. COM 446: Final Projects. Cal. State U
> >
> > Northridge. 28 May 2001 <http://hyper.vcsun.org/HyperNews/
> >
> > battias/get/cs446/project/1.html>.
>
> Hutchinson, Kim. "Snow Crash." Online posting. 23 Jan. 2001. Engl 15:
>
> > Cyberspace. DeVry College of Technology. 3 Apr. 2001 <http://
> >
> > www.nj.devry.edu/wcb/schools/001/001/arosu/40/forums/forum1/
> >
> > messages/98.html>.

36. *Online discussion/newsgroup message.*

> Hypo. "CGI cookie to identify repeat visitors." Online posting. 19 May
>
> > 2001. Message Board. Cookie Central. 22 May 2001 <http://www.
> >
> > cookiecentral.com/board>.
>
> Shostak, Adam. "Hobsian interpretations of Snow Crash (was No matter
>
> > where you go . . .)." Online posting. 14 Apr. 1996. Cypherpunks.
> >
> > 27 Sept. 2000 <http://cypherpunks.venona.com/date/1996/04/
> >
> > msg00838.html>.
>
> Warewolf. "Re: Neil Stephenson: Great SF writer?" Online posting.
>
> > 11 Aug. 2000. Science Fiction and Fantasy Discussion Board.
> >
> > Amazon.com. 4 Oct. 2000 <http://amazon.remarq.com/read/35132>.

37. *Online graphic illustration.*

> Congressional Internet Caucus Advisory Committee. "Internet Economy
>
> > Growing at an Astounding Rate." Graph. 1999. 23 Oct. 2000
> >
> > <http://www.netcaucus.org/statistics/1999/growth.jpg>.
>
> "Napster Timeline." Chart. n.d. CBSNews.com. 24 Jan. 2001
>
> > <http://www.cbsnews.com/htdocs/napster/timeline.html>.
>
> Kauffman, Robert J., and Loan Nguyen. "Observations on 'cookie.txt.'"
>
> > Slide 57 of 85. Applications of Emerging Technologies for Electronic

Commerce–Internet Cookies. n.d. Carlson School of Management,
U of Minnesota. 17 Oct. 2000 <http://webfoot.csom.umn.edu/
faculty/wanninger/ldsc3460/Mcnair1/sld057.htm>.

"The Number of Prisoners on Death Row Has Been Increasing." Graphic
illustration. Bureau of Justice Statistics, US Dept. of Justice.
29 Jan. 2002 <http://www.ojp.usdoj.gov/bjs/glance/dr.htm>.

38. *Online cartoon.*

Nash, Ken. "Parent's Cookies." Cartoon. n.d. 4 June 2000 <http://www.
nashken.com/techniks/techniks_promo/0099.html>.

39. *Online map.*

"A Map of Cholera Deaths in London, 1840s." Geography 43:
Cartography. 6 Jan. 1999. Dartmouth College. 7 May 2001 <http://
www.dartmouth.edu/~geog43/lectures/09_dotmaps/snow.html>.

Upham, W. P. "Map of Salem Village in 1692." Witchcraft in Salem Village.
2000. 27 July 2001 <http://etext.lib.virginia.edu/salem/witchcraft/
maps/uphamsmall.jpg>.

40. *Online painting, sculpture, or photograph.*

Vermeer, Jan. Girl with a Pearl Earring. 1665. Mauritshuis, The Hague.
Paintings of Vermeer. Ed. Roy Williams Clickery. n.d. California Inst.
of Technology. 2 June 2001 <http://www.cacr.caltech.edu/~roy/
vermeer/xce.jpg>.

41. *Online interview.*

Francis, Mike. "Interview with Mike Francis." Downhome Computing
with the PC Dads. KUIK Radio. 12 Feb. 1998. 21 Feb. 2001 <http://
i01vd003.easystreetnet.com/realdads/feb12_98.ram>.

"The Last Yankee: An Interview with Arthur Miller." Interview by
Steven R. Centola. 1996. 27 May 2001 <http://uc.edu/www.
amdrama/millerint.html>.

Electronic Sources

McCollum, Bill. Interview. <u>Frontline</u>. WGBH, Boston. 1 Dec. 1999. <u>PBS

> Online</u>. 12 Jan. 2001 <http://www.pbs.org/wgbh/pages/frontline/

> shows/snitch/procon/mccollum.html>.

Vastag, Brian. "Talking with Alan I. Leshner, Ph.D., National Institute

> on Drug Abuse Director." <u>JAMA</u> 7 Mar. 2001. American Medical

> Association. 15 Mar. 2001 <jama.ama-assn.org/issues/v285n9/

> ffull/jmn0307-1.html>.

42. *Document on a TV or radio program's Web site.*

"First Successful Kidney Transplant Performed: 1954." <u>People and

> Discoveries</u>. Companion Web site to <u>A Science Odyssey</u>. WGBH,

> Boston. 1998. <u>PBS Online</u>. 25 Feb. 2001 <http://www.pbs.org/

> wgbh/aso/databank/entries/dm54ki.html>.

Hahn, Robert, and Paul Tatlock. "Driving and Talking Do Mix." 12 Nov.

> 1999. Letter. <u>Car Talk's Time Kill Central</u>. 6 Dec. 2000 <http://cartalk.

> cars.com/About/Cell-Update/hahn-letter.html>.

"Senior Drivers: A CBS 2 Special Assignment." 17 Feb. 1998. Transcript.

> <u>Channel 2000</u>. 3 Mar. 2001 <http://www.channel2000.com/

> news/specialssign/news-specialassignment-980218-002712.

> html>.

43. *Online report.*

Fox, James Alan, and Marianne W. Zawitz. <u>Homicide Trends in the United

> States</u>. 15 Mar. 2001. Bureau of Justice Statistics, US Department

> of Justice. 6 June 2001 <http://www.ojp.usdoj.gov/bjs/homicide/

> homtrnd.htm>.

<u>Trust and Privacy Online: Why Americans Want to Rewrite the Rules</u>.

> 20 Aug. 2000. <u>Pew Internet and American Life Project</u>. Pew

> Research Center. 6 Feb. 2001 <http://www.pewinternet.org/

> reports/toc.asp?Report=19>.

MLA

44. *Online book or part of a book.*

Edwards, Mark J. "Firewall Basics." Internet Security with Windows NT.

By Edwards. Durham, NC: Duke UP, 1997. smartbooks.com. 13 Nov.

2000 <http://www.smartbooks.com/b9801/bw901inetsecwinntchp.

htm>.

Mitchell, William J. City of Bits: Space, Place, and the Infobahn. MIT P.

14 July 2001 <http://mitpress.mit.edu/e-books/City_of_Bits/>.

Sophocles. Antigone. Ed. Sir Richard Jeb. Cambridge: Cambridge UP,

1891. Perseus Project. 25 Apr. 2001 <http://www.perseus.tufts.

edu>.

45. *Law online.*

Children's Online Privacy Protection Act of 1998. Final Rule. USC 6501-

6505. Federal Trade Commission. 21 May 2001 <http://www.ftc.

gov/os/1999/9910/64fr59888.htm>.

Privacy Act of 1974. Pub. L. 93-5795. USC 552a. 88 Stat. 1896. 24 Oct. 2000

<http://www4.law.cornell.edu/uscode/5/552a.html>.

46. *Court case online.*

Quill Corp. v. North Dakota. 91-0194. 504 U.S. 298. 1992. 28 Sept. 2000

<http://supct.law.cornell.edu/supct/html/91_0194.ZO.html>.

Steve Jackson Games v. United States Secret Service. 36 F3d 457. 1994.

Lexis-Nexis. California Digital Lib., U of California, Irvine. 13 Oct.

2000 <http://www.lexisnexis.com>.

47. *Press release or press conference online.*

"EPIC Files FOIA Requests to Evaluate President Bush's First 100 Days

on Privacy." 30 Apr. 2001. Electronic Privacy Information Center.

4 May 2001 <http://EPIC.org/open_gov/bushadmin/foiapr.html>.

"Coca-Cola Announces New Education Advisory Council: Major Changes

in Its Public/Private Partnerships with the Nation's Schools."

Electronic Sources

MLA

13 Mar. 2001. Coca-Cola Company. 18 Mar. 2001 <http://www2.

coca-cola.com/business/presscenter/release_3.html>.

Lieberman, Joe. "Video Game Report Card Press Conference." 1 Dec.

1998. 21 Apr. 2001 <http://www.senate.gov/member/ct/lieberman/

general/r120198a.html>.

48. *Review online.*

Frye, Curtis. Rev. of Persuasion and Privacy in Cyberspace, by Laura

Gurak. Dr. Dobb's Electronic Review of Computer Books 21 Aug.

1997. 22 May 2001 <http://www.ercb.com/brief/brief.0039.html>.

Garisso, Larry. Rev. of Snow Crash, by Neal Stephenson. Oct. 1999. POSC

388i: Cyberspace Citizenship. Cal State U Long Beach. 19 Oct. 2000

<http://www.csulb.edu/~lgarriso/cybernovelreview.html>.

49. *Abstract online.*

Berinato, Scott, and Dennis Callaghan. "Will Tool Crumble Cookies?

Feature Puts Microsoft in Middle of Privacy-vs.-Advertising Debate."

eWeek 7 Aug. 2000: 36. Abstract. Magazine and Journal Articles.

California Digital Lib., U of California, Irvine. 12 Oct. 2000 <http://

www.cdlib.org/collections>.

50. *Speech online.*

Lodge, Henry Cabot. "League of Nations." American Leaders Speak:

Recordings from World War I and the 1920 Election. 1996. American

Memory. Lib. of Congress, Washington. 4 May 2000 <http://lcweb2.

loc.gov/mbrs/nforum/90000004.ram>.

Love, Courtney. "Love's Manifesto." Transcript. 14 June 2000. 29 Jan.

2001 <http://www.holemusic.com/speech>.

51. *Sound recording online.*

Pinsky, Robert. "To Television." The Internet Poetry Archive. U of North

Carolina P and Office of Information Technology at the U of North

Electronic Sources

MLA

Carolina at Chapel Hill. 17 May 2001 <http://www.ibiblio.org/ipa/
pinsky/sound/television.ram>.

Subcommittee on Commerce, Trade, and Consumer Protection.

"Opinion Survey: What Consumers Have to Say about Information

Privacy." Committee hearing. 8 May 2001. US House of

Representatives. 20 May 2001 <http://energycommerce.house.

gov/107/ram/0508200ctcp.ram>.

52. *Musical or theatrical recording online.*

"Pirate Jenny." By Kurt Weill and Marc Blitzstein. Three Penny Opera.

1954. Broadway Midi. 30 June 2001 <http://www.broadwaymidi.

com/down/ThreePennyOpera-PirateJenny.mid>.

53. *Film online.*

Don Quixote. Dir. Georg Wilhelm Pabst. Perf. George Robey, Sidney Fox,

and Fyodor Chaliapin. 1933. movieflix.com. 2 May 2000 <http://

www.movieflix.com/movie_info.mfx?movie_id=1938>.

54. *Ad online.*

Cookie Crusher Vers. 2.6. Advertisement. The Limit Software. 4 June 2001

<http://www.thelimitsoft.com/cookie.html>.

55. *Commercial product description online.*

"Solar-Tec Systems All-Climate Solar Hot Water System." 1999. Solar-Tec

Systems. 4 June 2001 <http://www.solar-tec.com/SolarHotWater.

htm>.

56. *CD-ROM or other portable database.* Give the author's name; title of the work
(underlined); publication medium ("CD-ROM," "Diskette," or "Magnetic tape"); edition, release, or version (if relevant); place of publication; name of publisher; and date
of publication. The first example is a citation for an entire CD-ROM database; the
second is a citation for a poem on that database.

The English Poetry Full-Text Database. CD-ROM. Rel. 2. Cambridge, Eng.:

Chadwyck-Healey, 1993.

Blunt, Wilfrid Scawen. "Gibraltar." The Poetical Works: A Complete Edition.

London: Macmillan, 1914. 234-35. The English Poetry Full-Text

Database. CD-ROM. Rel. 2. Cambridge, Eng.: Chadwyck-Healey, 1993.

OTHER SOURCES

57. *Government document.* If an author is not listed, name the government (followed by a period) and then the name of the agency (which may be abbreviated).

United States. Dept. of State. Foreign Relations of the United States:

Diplomatic Papers--the Conferences of Cairo and Tehran 1943.

Washington: GPO, 1961.

58. *Pamphlet.* Cite a pamphlet as you would a book. If the pamphlet has no listed author, begin with the title.

This Is Apartheid: A Pictorial Introduction. London: Intl. Defence and Aid

Fund, 1978.

59. *Interview, published or broadcast.* Begin with the name of the person interviewed, followed by the title of the interview (if it is untitled, use "Interview"). Give the name of the interviewer after the title of the interview.

Sanchez, David. "Gimme 5: David Sanchez." By Michael Bourne. Down

Beat 65.12 (1998): 15.

For a broadcast interview, include the name of the program and information about the broadcast.

Smith, Anna Deavere. Interview with Terry Gross. Fresh Air. Natl. Public

Radio. KQED, San Francisco. 6 Aug. 1992.

60. *Interview, unpublished.* Give the name of the person interviewed and the date.

Huber, Joy. Personal interview. 5 Aug. 1999.

61. *Letter, published.* Follow the writer's name with the words "Letter to" and the name of the recipient. Give the date on which the letter was written, and identify the source in which it was published.

William, Rose. Letter to Allettie Mosher. 27 Sept. 1885. In To All Inquiring

Friends: Letters, Diaries and Essays in North Dakota. Ed. Elizabeth

Hampsten. Grand Forks, ND: Dept. of English, U of North Dakota,

1979.

62. *Letter or e-mail, unpublished.* To cite a letter or e-mail message written to you, begin with the writer's name, followed by the phrase "Letter (or e-mail) to the author" and the date. End each element with a period.

Parnell, George. E-mail to the author. 21 Sept. 1999.

63. *Lecture or public address.* In addition to the speaker's name and the title of the address (in quotation marks), give the title of the meeting, the name of the sponsoring organization, the location, and the date.

Somerville, Richard. "Viable, Virtual, or Vanished? The Future of the

University." Eighty-First Annual Convention. Assn. for Educ. in

Journalism and Mass Communication. Baltimore, 6 Aug. 1998.

64. *Film or video recording.* Give the title, the director, the distributor, and the year of release. You may add other information, such as the names of leading cast members. If you are citing the contribution of a particular person, begin the entry with his or her name.
For a video recording, add the original release date (if pertinent) and the medium before the distributor.

Howard's End. Dir. James Ivory. Perf. Emma Thompson, Anthony Hopkins,

and Vanessa Redgrave. Videocassette. Merchant Ivory, 1992.

65. *Television or radio program.* Give the title, network, producer, location, and date. The title of an episode or segment is enclosed in quotation marks; the title of the program is underlined; and the title of the series (if any) is neither underlined nor enclosed in quotation marks. You may add other relevant information, such as performers or director. If the reference is to the work of a particular individual, cite that person's name before the title.

Frank Lloyd Wright. Prod. Ken Burns and Lynn Novick. PBS. KQED, San

Francisco. 10 Nov. 1998.

66. *Recording.* List either the composer, the conductor, or the performer first, depending on the desired emphasis. Include the title of the piece, the performer, the title of the recording, the manufacturer, and the year of issue. If you are not citing a compact disc, indicate the medium ("Audiocassette," "Audiotape," or "LP") before the manufacturer's name. Underline the titles of records, tapes, or CDs; enclose the names of songs in quotation marks.

Mellencamp, John. "Just Another Day." Perf. John Mellencamp. Mr.

Happy Go Lucky. Mercury, 1996.

67. *Live performance.* To cite a performance of a play, concert, ballet, or opera, usually begin with the title and include information similar to that for a film (see

MLA

example 64), plus the place and date of the performance. If you are citing the contribution of a particular person—such as an actor, director, or choreographer—begin with that person's name instead.

> La Virgen de Tepeyac. Adap. Luis Valdez. Dir. Rosa Maria Escalante. El
>
>> Teatro Campesino. Cowell Theater, San Francisco. 20 Dec. 1992.

68. *Work of art or artist.* Underline the title of a work of art, and include the institution and city where the work is located; if the work is privately owned, include the owner's name, followed by the city.

> Nevelson, Louise. Cathedral. Museum of Modern Art, New York.

69. *Advertisement.* Give the name of the product or company that is the subject of the advertisement, followed by the descriptive label "Advertisement." Conclude with the publication or broadcast information.

> Apple Power Macintosh. Advertisement. Newsweek 27 Feb. 1995: 4-5.

70. *Map or other illustration.* Follow the title of the illustration (italicized or underlined) with a descriptive label, such as "Map" or "Graph." Then give the source of the illustration, including the page number (if there is one). If the creator of the illustration is credited, begin the entry with that name.

> Cambodia 1972. Map. Sideshow: Kissinger, Nixon and the Destruction of
>
>> Cambodia. By William Shawcross. New York: Simon, 1979. 254.

71. *Legal source.* For a court decision, include the names of the plaintiff and defendant (any word after the first one may be abbreviated); the volume, name (abbreviated and not underlined), and page of the law report cited; the name of the court that decided the case (if it was the U.S. Supreme Court, no name is necessary); and the year of the decision.

> Brown v. Board of Ed. 347 U.S. 483. 1954.

In the in-text citation, the name of the case is underlined.

> Brown v. Board of Ed.

For a law or statute, include its name, its Public Law number, the date it was enacted, and its *Statutes at Large* cataloging number (if it has been codified).

> Atomic Energy Act of 1946. Pub. L. 585. 1 Aug. 1946. Stat. 60.767.

Names of laws are not underlined in in-text citations.

For papers with many legal citations, consult *The Bluebook: A Uniform System of Citation,* 17th ed. (Harvard Law Review Assn., 2000).

MLA Manuscript Form

In addition to the conventions under the alphabetical entry **manuscript form,** MLA style covers other aspects of the appearance of the finished manuscript. (See Figure RP-9.) Note that MLA style requires underlining rather than italics.

MARGINS Leave one inch at the top, bottom, and sides.

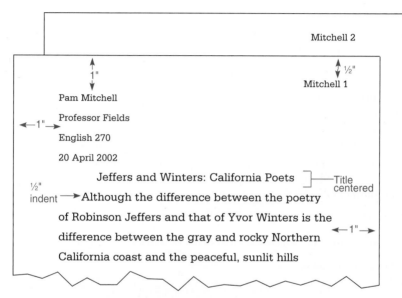

Mitchell 2

½"
Mitchell 1

Pam Mitchell

←1"→ Professor Fields

English 270

20 April 2002

Jeffers and Winters: California Poets ⎤—Title centered

½" indent →Although the difference between the poetry

of Robinson Jeffers and that of Yvor Winters is the

←1"→

difference between the gray and rocky Northern

California coast and the peaceful, sunlit hills

Figure RP-9. MLA manuscript format, first page.

MLA

FIRST PAGE: HEADING AND TITLE Put the heading and the title of the paper at the top of the first page rather than making a separate title page. Starting one inch from the top of the page and flush with the left margin, type your name, the instructor's name, the course name and number, and the date, double-spaced on separate lines.

Double-space again, and center the title. Do not underline the title (except for words you would underline in the text, such as book titles), enclose it in quotation marks, or type it in all capital letters. Follow MLA's conventions of capitalization for titles: Capitalize the first and last words, the first word after a colon, and all principal words (including those following the hyphen in **compound words**); do not capitalize **articles, prepositions, coordinating conjunctions,** or the *to* marking **infinitives.**

Double-space between the title and the first line of text.

PAGE NUMBERS Starting with the first page, number all pages consecutively in the upper right-hand corner, half an inch from the top of the page and flush with the right margin. Type your last name before the page number so that a mislaid page can be easily identified.

CORRECTIONS AND INSERTIONS If you are using a word processor, proofread the final draft carefully, and reprint the corrected pages. If you are not using a computer and your instructor permits minor corrections, type them (or write them neatly in ink) directly above the line, and use **carets** (∧) to indicate where they go. Do not write corrections in the margins or below the line. Retype pages that have more than a few corrections.

BLOCK QUOTATIONS A prose quotation longer than four typed lines should be set off from the rest of the text. Indent it one inch (or ten spaces) from the left margin, and double-space it. Do not add quotation marks. If the quotation is only one paragraph or part of one, do not indent the first line. If the quotation is two or more paragraphs, indent the first line of each paragraph an additional quarter inch (or three spaces), unless the first sentence quoted is not the beginning of a paragraph. The in-text citation (often only the page number) is added after the final punctuation mark of the quotation.

> The high-minded Plutarch, who knew little if anything about the real
>
> character of Archimedes, assigned him a personality so esoteric that it
>
> became laughable:
>
> > Thus, one cannot doubt what has been said about Archimedes,
> >
> > that he was always bewitched by some familiar and domestic
> >
> > siren so that he would forget to eat his food and neglect the
> >
> > care of his person, that when forcibly dragged to be bathed
> >
> > and to have his body anointed and perfumed he would draw
> >
> > geometric figures in the ashes of the fire, and that when his
> >
> > body was oiled he would trace diagrams on it with his finger,
> >
> > for he was truly possessed by the Muses. (Marcellus 17.3-7)

A verse quotation longer than three lines should be set off from the text. Indent the lines one inch (or ten spaces) from the margin, and double-space them. (If the lines are too long to permit a one-inch indention, reduce the indention or continue on the next line and indent the continuation an additional quarter inch, or three spaces.) If the lines are indented irregularly (as in the example that follows), reproduce the indention of the original as closely as possible. If the quotation begins in the middle of a line of verse, do not shift it to the left margin.

Add the in-text citation (usually the line numbers of the poem) after the final punctuation mark of the quotation. If the last line of verse is too long to allow for the parenthetical reference, put the reference on the next line, flush with the right margin.

> Among images of childlike innocence in the earlier parts of the poem--
>
> such as "mud-luscious" and "puddle-wonderful"--the darker references to
>
> "the little/lame balloonman" (lines 3-4) and "the queer/old balloonman"
>
> (lines 11-12) have prepared us for the perhaps not-so-innocent "goat-
>
> footed/balloonMan" of the poem's conclusion:

>> it's
>>
>> spring
>>
>> and
>>
>>   the
>>
>>
>>   goat-footed
>>
>> balloonMan   whistles
>>
>> far
>>
>> and
>>
>> wee (16-24)

Sample MLA Research Paper

On the following pages is a sample research paper that uses MLA manuscript form and documentation style.

- The author's name, the class information, and the date are at the top of the first page above the title.
- The title is centered on the page.
- The paper is double-spaced throughout.
- All pages are numbered, starting with the first page, and the author's last name appears before the page number.

This sample paper also illustrates the form for in-text citations, block quotations, and a list of works cited. To see another sample paper in MLA style, visit this book's Web site at <http://www.mhhe.com/ebest>, and follow the links to "Poisoned Cookies" in the research section of the site.

MLA

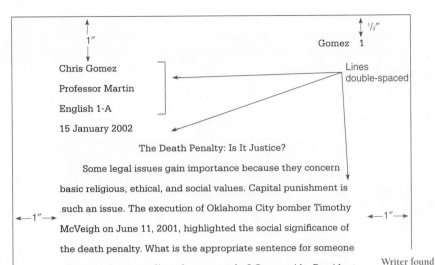

Gomez 1

Chris Gomez

Professor Martin

English 1-A

15 January 2002

The Death Penalty: Is It Justice?

Some legal issues gain importance because they concern basic religious, ethical, and social values. Capital punishment is such an issue. The execution of Oklahoma City bomber Timothy McVeigh on June 11, 2001, highlighted the social significance of the death penalty. What is the appropriate sentence for someone who commits premeditated mass murder? On one side, President George W. Bush declared that McVeigh "met the fate he chose for himself six years ago" (qtd. in Shapiro, "McVeigh"). On the other side, Bruce Shapiro argues:

> The notion of "fate"--a predetermined outcome-- sanitizes state-sponsored killing even as it fulfills McVeigh's megalomaniacal delusions. But fate had nothing to do with it. Death sentences are a matter of caprice rather than legal predetermination, as evinced by the twenty-one of twenty-three federal death-row inmates remaining in Terre Haute whose "fate" was to be born nonwhite. ("McVeigh")

Justice is supposed to be blind. But at the beginning of 2002, in the whole country there were 3,711 prisoners on Death Row (Death Row USA). Of this number, 1,691 (45.57%) were white and 1,595 (42.98%) were black. This proportion alone suggests that something is wrong with our legal system. Moreover, as Figure 1 demonstrates, this overall number has increased dramatically in the last half century. Obviously, the execution of Timothy McVeigh

Writer found quotation from Bush in Shapiro, so uses "qtd. in" in the citation. Because writer cites two works by Shapiro, the citations here use a brief version of the title.

Figure RP-10 Sample paper.

Gomez 2

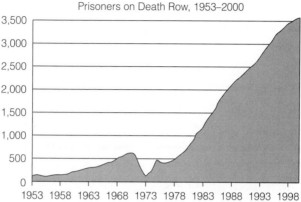

Fig. 1. "The Number of Prisoners on Death Row Has Been Increasing." 11 Dec. 2001. Bureau of Justice Statistics, US Dept. of Justice. 26 Jan. 2002 <http://www.ojp.usdoj.gov/bjs/glance/dr.htm>.

is not some kind of lone example that can be easily dismissed. Almost four thousand prisoners on Death Row, and almost half of them black, demand our attention.

> Arguments for death penalty come from writer's own general knowledge. If drawn from other source, they would require citation.

 Arguments favoring the death penalty hold that it (1) is moral, (2) deters potential murderers, (3) saves the state money, (4) fulfills the concept of justice, and (5) is more humane than life imprisonment.

 Is the death penalty moral? Expert opinion is divided. For example, Ernest van den Haag, professor of jurisprudence and public policy at Fordham University, argues, "His crime morally sets the murderer apart from his victim. The victim did, and therefore the murderer does not, deserve to live. His life cannot be sacred if that of his victim was" (Death Penalty 61). However, Michael E. Endres,

MLA

Gomez   3

professor of criminal justice at Xavier University, says that capital

punishment is immoral because

Quotation
more than
four lines long
is indented
ten spaces
and appears
without
quotation
marks.
Citation comes
after final
punctuation,
separated by
one space.

> the death penalty serves no rehabilitative purpose; it
> exceeds the requirements of justice and social unity;
> alternatives to it may serve the same purpose as well;
> finally, the incapacitation or special deterrence of a
> given offender is insured by execution, but there are
> other effective ways to inhibit reoffending. (67)

Author being
quoted,
Michael E.
Endres, is
identified in
lead-in to
quotation;
thus his name
is omitted from
parenthetical
citation at end.
Full source is
found under
"Endres" in
"Works Cited."

If it is moral to execute convicted, responsible adults, is it also

moral to execute children or mentally incompetent adults? Is a

sixteen-year-old a responsible adult? If not, should an offender this

young be executed? Currently, seventy-three death-row inmates

in the United States committed their crimes before they were

eighteen years old, and in the last decade nine such offenders

have been executed (Amnesty International, sec. 4). Since 1990,

only five other nations have executed juvenile offenders: Iran, Nigeria,

Pakistan, Saudi Arabia, and Yemen (Amnesty International, sec. 4).

Source of both
pieces of
information
about
execution
of minors
is section 4
of Web
publication
by corporate
author.

Diminished mental capacity is a mitigating factor in capital

offenses, and psychiatric evidence must be considered (Hood 63-64).

However, psychiatrists who assess the defendant's mental state

are often in a double bind, for the very condition that mitigates the

crime may also make the defendant a danger to society (Hood 64).

Furthermore, psychiatry is more an art than a science and thus does

not provide conclusive evidence for a decision regarding life or death.

Hood is cited
twice, for
different
kinds of
information:
first for fact
and second for
his opinion.
Both citations
are required.

The moral questions regarding capital punishment are open

to so much controversy that it is difficult for an informed person to

take a definitive stand one way or the other on moral grounds.

Paragraph 6
states
writer's own
conclusion,
not that of
any source.

Does the death penalty deter potential murderers? Roger Hood

is clear on this question: "The evidence as a whole gives no positive

MLA

Gomez   4

support to the deterrent hypothesis" (167). One might argue, of course, that the death penalty is a deterrent only if executions are actually carried out. Thus, as the number of executions increases, the frequency of murder should decline. However, according to Hood (117-48), no evidence indicates that more frequent executions lead to lower homicide rates. For example, the last executions in Australia took place in the mid-1960s, but "the reported homicide rate per 100,000 of population has fallen, and the murder rate has remained constant" (Hood 124-25); in the United States, when the first execution took place after a decade-long moratorium, the homicide rate almost doubled, from 4.8 per 100,000 to 8.8 (Hood 126). Some admittedly inconclusive evidence suggests that executions may actually bring about more murders. One study, reported by Horgan, indicates that in the month after each execution in New York State between 1907 and 1963, the number of murders rose by an average of a bit more than two (17).

Dividing murderers into two categories is useful when one considers the deterrence argument: what Adam Hugo Bedau terms "'carefully contemplated murders,' such as 'murder for hire'" (172), and so-called crimes of passion. As Bedau points out, those who carefully plan murders do so with a view to avoiding detection and punishment; hence, the threat of the death penalty plays little or no role in the decision to commit the crime. No threat would deter the killer who is carried away by uncontrollable rage or hatred.

If capital punishment is a deterrent, then painful methods of execution should have more effect than painless ones, yet Texas, Georgia, and other states have adopted lethal injection as the method of execution--ameliorating the severity of the death penalty, supposedly for "humanitarian" reasons. States that use lethal

---

Exact quotation is from Hood, page 167. Since Hood's name is mentioned in lead-in to quotation, it is not repeated in parenthetical citation.

Citations indicate writer is summarizing pages 117–48 of Hood and using facts from pages 124–25 and 126 of Hood and page 17 of Horgan.

Idea of dividing murderers into two types is writer's own, but quotation from Bedau provides information about one type. Citation points to discussion on page 172 of Bedau.

MLA

gas as a means of execution do not make the agony of death by

asphyxiation a matter of public knowledge. If the death penalty is

a deterrent, the agonies of execution should not be reduced, as in

Texas, or kept hidden from the public, as in California.

  Since no one has been able to show that the threat of the

death penalty reduces the number of murders, the argument for

capital punishment on the basis of its deterrent value crumbles.

  Does capital punishment save the state money? Robert L.

Spangenberg, an attorney who directs the Boston Legal Assistance

Project, points out that "states spend anywhere from $1.6 million

to $3.2 million to obtain and carry out a capital sentence; states

could incarcerate someone for 100 years or more for less money"

(qtd. in Horgan 18). Of course, a cost/benefit analysis might reveal

that the death penalty is economically sound because it provides

social benefits such as protection from potential murderers.

However, as Bedau says, "we cannot have such an analysis without

already establishing in some way or other the relative value of

innocent lives versus guilty lives (38)."

  It appears, then, that economic arguments in favor of capital

punishment have no solid basis.

  Does the death penalty fulfill the requirements of justice?

Immanuel Kant argued that justice demands complete equality;

thus, if one murders, the commensurate punishment is death.

Bedau (17) quotes from <u>The Metaphysical Elements of Justice</u>:

> Only the law of retribution . . . can determine exactly
>
> the kind and degree of punishment. . . . All other
>
> standards fluctuate back and forth and, because
>
> extraneous considerations are mixed with them, they
>
> cannot be compatible with the principle of pure and
>
> strict legal justice. (Kant 101)

Marginal notes:

Citation shows that Horgan (page 18) presents information from Spangenberg.

MLA

Writer found quotation from Kant on page 17 of Bedau. Quotation, however, is from page 101 of Kant's book, as indicated in parentheses at end of quotation. Writer knows Bedau's source because Bedau documented carefully.

Gomez 6

As Bedau points out, the principle of equality applies to murderers who are intrinsically vicious and have rationally willed to kill another. "If modern criminologists and psychologists are correct, however," says Bedau, "most murders are not committed by persons whose state of mind can be described as Kant implies" (17). Even if we accept Kant's principle of justice, we find that it is inapplicable in the real world.

Quotation marks show that writer has used an exact quotation from Bedau's book (from page 17, as citation indicates).

Finally, is it more humane to execute a convicted murderer than to require him or her to spend years, or life, in prison? It is, of course, impossible to make such a judgment for the condemned. Lifers in prison do commit suicide, and convicted murderers do ask for death rather than life imprisonment. As Bedau says, however, it is impossible to determine which is more severe, life in prison or death, for there is no way to compare the two alternatives (27). We do know, however, that death makes it impossible to correct errors in judgment. In any case, society does not base its penalties on the preferences of the convicted.

From Bedau (page 27) writer gained idea that it is impossible to determine whether life in prison or death is more severe punishment; because Bedau's idea is paraphrased (that is, restated in writer's own words), quotation marks are not used. However, Bedau must still be given credit.

There is, then, no agreement about the morality, deterrent value, economic effectiveness, justice, or humaneness of the death penalty--and there is always a possibility that an innocent person will be put to death.

Ernest van den Haag asserts that "miscarriages of justice are offset by the moral benefits and the usefulness of doing justice" ("Ultimate Punishment"). However, an increasing number of public officials charged with life-and-death decisions about capital punishment appear to be questioning this stance. In 2000, the governor of Illinois, George Ryan, invoked a moratorium on executions in the state after thirteen convicts were released from Death Row when evidence showed that they had been wrongfully

MLA

convicted (Shapiro, "Talk"). A year later, twenty of the thirty-eight

states with a death penalty were considering moratoriums, and

members of Congress were considering legislation to set minimum

standards for court-appointed lawyers in capital cases and access

to DNA tests for capital defendants (Novak). Supreme Court

Justice Sandra Day O'Connor, usually a swing vote on capital

punishment cases, now is questioning whether the death penalty

is administered fairly. "If statistics are any indication," she said,

"the system may well be allowing some innocent defendants to be

executed" (Associated Press).

     The death penalty should be abolished. I believe that it

dehumanizes my society and hence robs me of part of my humanity.

The Declaration of Independence sets the standard:

> We hold these Truths to be self-evident, that all Men
>
> are created equal, that they are endowed by their
>
> Creator with certain unalienable rights, that among
>
> these are Life, Liberty, and the Pursuit of Happiness.

Individuals or the state can take life only when no alternative exists,

and quite obviously alternatives to capital punishment do exist.

     Writing just a few days after the tragedy of September 11,

Sister Helen Prejean, well-known death penalty opponent and

author of <u>Dead Man Walking</u>, asked:

> What are the root causes of violence in our country,
>
> and is the use of violence by government powers--the
>
> execution of criminals--the only solution we know to
>
> contain and prevent that violence? The Catholic
>
> bishops of this country have given us a good spiritual
>
> motto: "If we want peace, we must work for justice."

MLA

Works Cited

Amnesty International. Juveniles and the Death Pena.

Worldwide Since 1990. Nov. 1998. AIUSA. 12 Jan. 1999

<http://www.amnesty-usa.org/abolish/act501198.html>.

Associated Press. "O'Connor Questions Death Penalty." 3 July

2001. CBSNews.com. 11 Jan. 2002 <http://www.cbsnews.

com/2001/07/03/supremecourt/main.shtml299592>.

Bedau, Adam Hugo. Death Is Different: Studies in the Morality,

Law, and Politics of Capital Punishment. Boston: Northeastern

UP, 1987.

Death Row USA. Winter 2002. Criminal Justice Project of the NAACP

Legal Defense and Educational Fund. 29 Jan. 2002 <http://www.

deathpenaltyinfo.org/DeathRowUSA1.html>.

Endres, Michael E. "The Morality of Capital Punishment." The Death

Penalty: Opposing Viewpoints. Ed. Bonnie Szumski, Lynn Hall,

and Susan Bursell. St. Paul: Greenhaven Press, 1986. 62-67.

Hood, Roger. The Death Penalty: A World-Wide Perspective; A

Report to the United Nations Committee on Crime Prevention

and Control. Oxford: Oxford UP, 1989.

Horgan, John. "The Death Penalty." Scientific American July 1990:

17-19.

Kant, Immanuel. The Metaphysical Elements of Justice. 1797.

Trans. John Ladd. Indianapolis: Bobbs, 1965.

Novak, Viveca. "A Change in the Weather on the Way?" Time 57.20

(21 May 2001): 40. Expanded Academic ASAP. California

Digital Lib., U of California, Irvine. 10 Jan. 2002 <http://www.

dbs.cdlib.org>.

"The Number of Prisoners on Death Row Has Been Increasing."

11. Dec. 2001. Graphic illustration. Bureau of Justice Statistics,

MLA

Gomez   9

US Dept. of Justice. 26 Jan. 2002 <http://www.ojp.usdoj.gov/

bjs/glance/dr.htm>.

"O'Connor Questions Death Penalty." 3 July 2001. CBSNews.com.

11 Jan. 2002 <http://www.cbsnews.com/stories/2001/07/03/

supremecourt/main299592.shtml>.

Prejean, Helen. "Terrorist Attacks Affirm Need for a Paradigm

Shift." 17 Sep. 2001. The Moratorium Campaign. 11 Jan. 2002

<http://www.moratorium2000.org/>.

Shapiro, Bruce. "McVeigh: Done to Death." The Nation 2 July 2001.

11 Jan. 2002 <http://www.thenation.com/doc.

mhtml?i=20010702&s=shapiro>.

---. "A Talk with Governor George Ryan." The Nation 8 Jan. 2001.

11 Jan. 2002 <http://www.thenation.com/doc.

mhtml?i=20010108&s=shapiro.>.

van den Haag, Ernest. The Death Penalty: A Debate. New York:

Plenum, 1983. Excerpt rpt. in The Death Penalty: Opposing

Viewpoints. Ed. Bonnie Szumski, Lynn Hall, and Susan Bursell.

St. Paul: Greenhaven Press, 1986. 58-61.

---. "The Ultimate Punishment: A Defense." Companion Web site to

Angel on Death Row. WGBH, Boston, 1998. PBS Online and

WGBH/Frontline. 10 Jan. 2002 <http://www.pbs.org/ogbh/

pages/frontline/angel/procon/haagarticle.html>.

Use three hyphens in place of author name for second and subsequent entries by same author, alphabetized by title.

MLA

APA Style

The *Publication Manual of the American Psychological Association,* 5th ed. (2001), recommends a system of brief in-text citations that refer to an alphabetical list of references (with full publication information) at the end of the paper. APA style is also covered in detail online at <http://www.apastyle.org>.

**KEY CHANGES IN THE 5TH EDITION OF THE
APA *PUBLICATION MANUAL* (2001)**

1. The hanging indent is now the preferred form for reference lists. The first line of each entry should be flush left, and second and subsequent lines should be indented. However, if it is difficult to create hanging indents with your word-processing program, paragraph indents (first line indented and subsequent lines flush left) are permissible.

2. The section on documenting electronic media has been greatly expanded and revised. The essentials of those changes are reflected in the guidelines here. A fuller summary of the changes is available from the APA Web site at <http://www.apastyle.org/elecref.html>. For a fee, the complete guidelines for electronic resources from the 5th edition of the *Publication Manual* can be downloaded as a pdf file <http://www.apastyle. org/styleelecref.html>.

3. In the reference list, italics are now preferred to underlining, unless you are not using a word processor with font-formatting capacities.

A chapter-by-chapter list of changes in the 5th edition of the *Publication Manual* is available online at <http://www.apastyle.org/fifthchanges.html>.

GUIDE TO APA STYLE

APA

continued

APA In-Text Citations

Parenthetical in-text citations should not distract the reader, but they must be complete enough to allow the reader to locate the corresponding entry easily in the reference list. If a specific passage is being quoted or referred to, include the page number (or numbers) in the citation; if the whole work is being referred to, page numbers are not necessary. The following examples illustrate the APA style of in-text citation.

1. *Author named in text.* Include the year and, if necessary, the page number (or numbers) of the citation (preceded by "p." or "pp."). Separate the elements with a comma. If a work is cited more than once in a paragraph, only the first mention needs to include the year.

According to Inose and Pierce (1994, p. 157), the term *artificial intelligence*

may be a misnomer.

If the reference list contains two authors with the same last name, include the first initials of each one in the in-text citations.

2. *Author not named in text.* Separate the author's name, date of publication, and page numbers (if needed) with commas.

The scarcity of daycare is an obstacle to employment for many women

with young children (Sidel, 1986, p. 344).

3. *More than one author.* For a work with two authors, cite both names every time. When the names are in parentheses, use an ampersand (&) instead of writing out "and."

Edward A. Feigenbaum, an artificial intelligence researcher, has produced

a program that "analyzes mass spectra and produces highly probable

molecular structures" (Inose & Pierce, 1994, p. 142).

For a work with three to five authors, cite all the names in the first reference to the work; in subsequent references, give only the first author's name followed by "et al." (the abbreviation for the Latin phrase meaning "and others").

The inherited aspects of intelligence cannot be considered separately

from environmental influences (Conley, Bennett, Alling, Sherwin, &

Reid, 1992).

For a work with six or more authors, give only the first author's name followed by "et al." in the first as well as all subsequent citations.

E. Jones et al. (1995) summarize a 37-nation study of adolescent

pregnancy.

4. *Author of two or more works in one year.* If you cite two books or articles by the same author published in the same year, the reference list should show the date of the first followed by an "a" and the date of the second followed by a "b." The

APA

order is determined by the alphabetical order of the titles. The in-text citations should also show "a" and "b."

> More women--224,000 of them--serve in the United States armed forces
>
> than in any other military forces in the world (Moore, 1989a).

5. *Group author or government agency.* If the name of the agency or institution is long, write it out in full for the first reference and abbreviate it (if the abbreviation is familiar) in second and subsequent citations.

> Over ten thousand respondents to a survey of Pacific Bell customers (Field
>
> Research Corporation, 1995, p. 42) estimated that 74 percent of their calls
>
> were "personal or social."

6. *Unknown author.* If the source is not signed (a brief article in a newspaper or magazine, for example), use the first few words of the title in the citation. Enclose the title of an article or chapter in quotation marks; italicize the title of a periodical, book, brochure, or report. (The full title for the article cited in the example is "Can Your Mind Heal Your Body?")

> Both physicians and entrepreneurs have recently become interested in
>
> how the mind can affect physical health ("Can Your Mind Heal?" 1993).

7. *Indirect source.* To cite a quotation by someone else in your source, identify the source being quoted, and then precede the name of your source with the phrase "as cited in." The reference list should include only your source.

> Kenneth Bruffee observed, "While students often forget much of the
>
> subject matter shortly after class is over, they do not easily forget the
>
> values implicit in the conventions by which it was taught" (as cited in
>
> Trimbur, 1992, p. 95).

8. *More than one source.* If a statement has more than one source by the same author (or authors), list the years of publication after the author's name.

> This conclusion is repeated in the more recent issues of her work
>
> (Vanderbilt, 1987, 1996).

If a statement has more than one source by different authors, list the sources in alphabetical order, and separate them with a semicolon.

> Most advanced industrial countries in the West--except the United States--
>
> have a universal program of national health insurance or a national health
>
> service (Leichter, 1989; Roemer, 1997; Simanis & Coleman, 1998).

APA

9. *Personal communication.* Letters, e-mail, telephone conversations, personal interviews, and other personal communications that are not publicly available are cited in the text but not included in the reference list. Give the initials and the last name of the source, and follow it with the phrase "personal communication" and the date.

> The study was originally commissioned by North Carolina (T. R. Purefoy,
>
> personal communication, November 11, 1998).

10. *Electronic source.* If you name the author in the text and are citing a specific part of a source that does not use page numbers, list the section or paragraph number after the date, where you ordinarily include the page number. Use the abbreviation "para." or the symbol "¶."

> According to Fitch and Denenberg (1995, para. 6), ovarian hormones play
>
> a significant role in the sexual differentiation of the brain.

If the author is not named in the text and the source does not use page numbers, the parenthetical citation should include the author's name, the date, and the section or paragraph number of the cited information.

> Ovarian hormones play a significant role in the sexual differentiation of
>
> the brain (Fitch & Denenberg, 1995, para. 6).

If pages or paragraphs are not numbered, cite the nearest preceding heading and the paragraph number (count the paragraphs).

> (Malloy, 2000, Introduction, para. 2)

If you are referring to an entire work, no page, section, or paragraph numbers are necessary in the in-text citation.

APA Reference List

Beginning on a separate page at the end of your paper, list in alphabetical order all the references you cite, and give full publishing information for them. Title the list "References," and center this heading at the top of the page.

Alphabetize the entries according to the last name of the author or the first important word in the title if the author is not identified. Entries for an author writing alone precede entries in which that author has coauthors. Arrange works by the same author (or authors) according to the publication date, starting with the earliest. If two or more works by the same author were published in the same year, arrange them alphabetically by the first main word in the title, and add "a" after the year of the first one, "b" after the year of the second one, and so on. Use both the year and the letter in the in-text citation.

APA

Double-space both within and between entries. Format each entry with a hanging indent, starting the first line at the left margin and indenting subsequent lines half an inch. Hanging indents are a paragraph formatting option in many newer word-processing programs. If hanging indents are difficult to create with your word-processing program, paragraph-style indents for reference list entries are acceptable according to the 5th edition of the APA *Publication Manual*—but discuss this option with your instructor.

BOOKS Book entries have four parts, and each one ends with a period. The first part is the author's name (if no author is listed, put the title first). The second part is the year of publication in parentheses. The third part is the title and subtitle, italicized; only proper nouns and the first word of the title and the subtitle are capitalized. The fourth part is the place of publication (with the two-letter postal abbreviation for the state if the city's location is not common knowledge) and the name of the publisher in as brief a form as is intelligible.

BASIC FORM FOR NONPERIODICAL REFERENCES IN APA STYLE, 5TH EDITION

Book:

Author, A. A. (2002). *Title of work.* Location: Publisher.

Chapter or part of a book:

Author, A. A., & Author, B. B. (2002). Title of chapter. In A. Editor &

B. Editor (Eds.), *Title of book* (pp. xxx–xxx). Location: Publisher.

Other types of print nonperiodicals, such as brochures and pamphlets:

Author, A. A. (2002). *Title of work* [Type of work]. Location: Publisher.

---

1. *Book with one author.* Give the author's initials, not the full first name, after the last name.

Bromwich, D. (1992). *Politics by other means: Higher education and group*

thinking. New Haven: Yale University Press.

2. *Book with two or more authors.* Invert the names of the first six authors (last name followed by a comma and the initials), and separate them with commas. Use

an ampersand (&) instead of the word "and" before the name of the last author. If there are seven or more authors, use the abbreviation "et al." (Latin for "and others") in place of the names of the seventh and subsequent authors.

Barr, R., & Dreeban, R. (1983). *How schools work.* Chicago: University of

Chicago Press.

3. *Book with a group author.* Alphabetize group-author entries by the first main word in the name (omit the articles "a," "an," and "the"). If the group author is also the publisher, use the word "Author" (not italicized) as the name of the publisher.

United Nations Children's Fund. (1990). *The state of the world's children*

1990. New York: Oxford University Press.

4. *Book with an editor.* Begin with the name of the editor (or editors). Enter the abbreviation "Ed." for "Editor" (or "Eds." for "Editors"), enclosed in parentheses, following the name of the last editor. For a book with an author and an editor, give the author's name as the first element, and put the editor's name in parentheses after the title, as a translator's name is treated (see example 5).

Zigler, E., & Valentine, J. (Eds.). (1979). *Project Head Start: A legacy of the*

war on poverty. New York: Free Press.

5. *Book with a translator.* In parentheses after the title of the work, insert the name of the translator (or translators) followed by a comma and the abbreviation "Trans." (for "Translator" or "Translators").

Durkheim, E. (1938). *The rules of sociological method* (8th ed.) (S. A.

Solovay & J. H. Mueller, Trans.). New York: Free Press.

6. *Book with an unknown author.* Alphabetize the entry by the first significant word in the title (omit the articles "a," "an," and "the").

American Heritage Larousse Spanish dictionary. (1986). Boston: Houghton

Mifflin.

7. *Book edition.* Give information about the edition immediately following the title, before the period. Abbreviate it ("Rev. ed." for "revised edition," "2nd ed." for "second edition," and so on), and enclose it in parentheses.

Goodall, J. (1988). *In the shadow of man* (Rev. ed.). Boston: Houghton

Mifflin.

8. *Selection in an edited book.* Begin with the name of the author of the selection, followed by the title of the selection (do not italicize the title or enclose it in

APA

quotation marks). Next, identify the edited volume: After the word "In," give the editor's name in normal order, followed by "Ed." in parentheses. After a comma, give the book title (italicized) and, enclosed in parentheses, the volume number (if any) and the page numbers of the selection.

> Freud, S. (1959). Analysis of a phobia in a five-year-old boy. In A. Strachey
>
> & J. Strachey (Eds. & Trans.), *Sigmund Freud: Collected papers*
>
> (Vol. 3, pp. 78–94). London: Hogarth Press. (Original work published
>
> 1909)

This entry also shows the format for a *republished work*. The date of republication goes after the author's name; the original date of publication is indicated at the end of the entry in parentheses after the phrase "Original work published." The in-text citation should read "(Freud 1909/1959)."

9. *Multivolume series*. After the title, enclose in parentheses the number of the volume (or volumes) consulted (see example 8). If all the volumes in the set were consulted, use inclusive numbers (such as "Vols. 1–4"). If each volume has a different title and editor, use the following format:

> Mussen, P. H. (Series Ed.), & Hetherington, E. M. (Vol. Ed.). (1983).
>
> *Handbook of child psychology: Vol. 4. Socialization, personality,*
>
> *and social development* (4th ed.). New York: Wiley.

PERIODICALS   Entries for articles from periodicals have four parts, and each one ends with a period. The first part is the author's name. The second part is the date of publication, in parentheses. The third part is the title of the article, which is not enclosed in quotation marks or italicized; only proper nouns and the first word of the title and subtitle are capitalized. The fourth part is the title of the periodical, italicized, with all significant words capitalized, followed by numbers identifying the volume (italicized), issue (if needed), and pages.

APA

BASIC FORM FOR PERIODICAL REFERENCES
IN APA STYLE, 5TH EDITION

Author, A. A., Author, B. B., & Author, C. C. (2002). Title of article.

Title of Periodical, xx(xx), xxx–xxx.

10. *Article in a magazine.* For a nonacademic magazine, give the month of publication (and the day, if the magazine is published weekly) after the year. The month is not abbreviated. After the title, in italics, include the volume number, in italics, and then the page numbers. Give all page numbers, including discontinuous pages.

Colapinto, J. (1997, December 11). The true story of John/Joan. *Rolling*

Stone, 775, 54–73, 92–97.

11. *Article in a daily newspaper.* Give the date of the issue along with the year of publication. List the section and page number (or numbers) at the end of the entry, using the abbreviation "p." (or "pp."). (Newspapers are the only kind of periodical whose page numbers are preceded by "p.")

Marano, H. E. (1998, August 4). Debunking the marriage myth: It works for

women, too. *New York Times,* p. B8.

12. *Article in a journal paginated by annual volume.* For a scholarly journal, follow the journal title with a comma and the volume number (italicized). After another comma, give the page numbers.

Rustine, G. L., & Nolen-Hoeksema, S. (1998). Regulating responses to

anger: Effects of rumination and distraction on angry mood. *Journal*

of Personality and Social Psychology, 74, 790–803.

13. *Article in a journal paginated by issue.* For a scholarly journal, follow the journal title with a comma, the volume number (italicized), and the issue number (in parentheses). After another comma, give the page numbers.

Wechsler, H., Dowdall, G. W., Maenner, G., Gledhill-Hoyt, T., & Lee, H.

(1998). Changes in binge drinking and related problems among

American college students between 1993 and 1997. *Journal of*

American College Health, 47(3), 57–68.

14. *Unsigned article.* Use the form for the appropriate kind of periodical, but begin with the article title, and alphabetize the entry according to the first main word in the title. Use a shortened version of the title (such as "Cost") in the in-text citation.

The cost of coping. (1998, November/December). *Psychology Today,*

31(6), 12.

APA

15. *Interview, published.* Begin with the interviewer's name, and use the form for the appropriate kind of periodical. After the interview title (if any), insert a bracketed description that includes the interviewee's name.

Thomson, B. (1998, November/December). The second act of Dean Ornish.

[Interview with Dean Ornish]. *Natural Health, 113*–115, 173–175.

16. *Review.* If the review has a title, insert it in front of the bracketed description (as in example 15). Identify the medium (such as book, motion picture, television program) in brackets along with the title of the work being reviewed.

Gottfried, P. (1998, November/December). [Review of the book *Why race*

matters: Race differences and what they mean]. *Society, 36*(1), 91–93.

17. *Letter to the editor.* If the letter has a title, insert it before the bracketed description, as in example 15.

Shulman, T. (1997, November/December). [Letter to the editor]. *Health,*

11(8), 14.

GOVERNMENTAL AND LEGAL PRINT SOURCES

18. *Government report.* If an author is not listed, begin with the name of the agency. If there is a report number, include it in parentheses immediately after the title, before the period. If the agency is both author and publisher, use the word "Author" (not italicized) in place of the publisher's name.

U.S. Department of State. (1961). *Foreign relations of the United States:*

Diplomatic papers--The conferences at Cairo and Tehran 1943.

Washington, DC: U.S. Government Printing Office.

19. *Legal source.* For a court decision, include the name of the case (plaintiff v. defendant); the volume number, the abbreviated name of the source where the case is published, and the page number; and the court jurisdiction (if it was the U.S. Supreme Court, no name is necessary) and date of decision in parentheses. In the example below, "U.S." stands for *United States Supreme Court Reports.*

Brown v. Board of Educ., 347 U.S. 483 (1954).

In in-text citations, the names of cases are italicized and not abbreviated.

Brown v. Board of Education (1954)

For a law or statute, include the name of the act, the volume and page or section number of the source, and the year in parentheses.

Atomic Energy Act of 1946, Pub. L. No. 585, 60 Stat. 767 (1947).

APA

In in-text citations, the names of laws or statutes are not italicized.

> Atomic Energy Act (1946)

If your paper has many legal citations, consult the *Publication Manual of the American Psychological Association,* 5th ed., or *The Bluebook: A Uniform System of Citation,* 17th ed. (Harvard Law Review Assn., 2000).

ELECTRONIC SOURCES A reference to an electronic source should include, at a minimum, a document title or description, a date (either the date of publication or update or the date of retrieval), and an address (uniform resource locator, URL). If possible, identify the authors as well. Omit the final period of the reference when it ends with a URL.

Tip: If you are using a word-processing program, select the URL in the address bar in your browser, use the copy command, and paste it into your paper, to avoid typos. If the URL is too long to fit on one line, break it after a slash or before a period. Do not add a hyphen to break the URL between lines.

For examples of references to electronic sources in addition to the ones shown below, see APA's Web page <http://www.apastyle.org/elecmedia.html>.

BASIC FORM FOR ELECTRONIC REFERENCES IN APA STYLE

Online periodical article:

> Author, A. A., Author, B. B., & Author, C. C. (2002). Title of article.
>
> > *Title of Periodical, xx,* xxx–xxx. Retrieved month, day, year,
> >
> > from URL

Online document:

> Author, A. A. (2002). *Title of work.* Retrieved month, day, year, from
>
> > URL

---

20. *Internet article based on a print source.*

Kraut, R., Lundmark, V., Patterson, M., Kiesler, S., Mukopadhyay, T., &

> Scherlis, W. (1998). Internet paradox: A social technology that
>
> reduces social involvement and psychological well-being? *American*

Psychologist, 53, 1017–1031. Retrieved November 1, 2001, from

http://www.apa.org/journals/amp/amp5391017.html

21. *Article in an Internet-only journal.*

Dublin, T., & Doak, M. (2000). Miner's son, miners' photographer: The

life and work of George Harvan. *Journal for MultiMedia History, 3.*

Retrieved November 1, 2001, from http://www.albany.edu/jmmh/

vol3/harvan/index.html

22. *Electronic daily newspaper article available by search.* For the URL, use only that of the home page instead of the entire search string, which is only a temporary URL.

Gallagher, W. (2001, November 13). Young love: The good, the bad, the

educational. *New York Times.* Retrieved November 17, 2001, from

http://www.nytimes.com

23. *Copy of a journal article from a periodical database.* Note that no URL is necessary.

McNeill, B. W. (2001, October). An exercise in ethnic identity awareness.

Journal of Multicultural Counseling and Development, 29(4), 274.

Retrieved November 6, 2001, from InfoTrac Expanded Academic

ASAP database.

24. *Report from a private organization.*

Howard Hughes Medical Institute. (1995). *Seeing, hearing, and smelling*

the world. Retrieved November 17, 2001, from the Howard

Hughes Medical Institute Web site: http://www.hhmi.org/senses/

senses.pdf

25. *Section in an Internet document.*

Pines, M. (1997). Illusions reveal the brain's assumptions. In *It's all in the*

brain. Retrieved November 17, 2001, from http://www.hhmi.org/

senses/a/a110.htm

Tip: If the publication date is not shown in the section, look for it on the document's home page.

26. *U.S. government report on a government Web site.*

National Institute of Mental Health's Genetic Workgroup. (1997,

September 19). *Genetics and mental disorders.* Retrieved November

17, 2001, from http://www.nimh.nih.gov/research/genetics.htm

27. *Document on a university Web site.*

Sampson, P. D., Streissguth, A. P., Bookstein, F. L., & Barr, H. M. (2000,

June). On categorizations in analyses of alcohol teratogenesis.

Environmental Health Perspectives, 108(Supp. 3), 421–428. Retrieved

November 17, 2001, from University of Washington School of

Medicine, Fetal Alcohol and Drug Unit Web site: http://depts

.washington.edu/~fadu/sampson.pdf

28. *Stand-alone document.* If no author is given, start the entry with the document title.

Zimbardo, P. G. (1999). *Stanford prison experiment.* Retrieved November

17, 2001, from http://www.prisonexp.org/

29. *Archived newsgroup or mailing list message.* As with newspaper articles located through a home-page search (example 22), use only the first page of the archive because the search string is a temporary URL. If an electronic discussion message is not archived or otherwise retrievable, it should not be cited in the reference list. Such a document can, however, be cited in the text as a personal communication (see example 9 in "APA In-Text Citations").

Strauss, L. (2001, February 2). K12>target: Which is best to use for

plagiarism? [Msg 1]. Message posted to comp.internet.net-

happenings newsgroup, archived at http://groups.google.com/

groups?hl=en&group=comp.internet.net-happenings

30. *E-mail message.* These messages are considered personal communication and so are identified only in the in-text citation (see example 9 in "APA In-Text Citations"), not in an entry in the reference list.

AUDIOVISUAL MEDIA

31. *Motion picture or other nonprint source.* Give the name of the originators and, in parentheses, their function. Identify the medium (for example, "Motion picture," "Videotape," "Audiotape," "Slide," "Chart," or "Art work") in brackets immediately

after the name of the work, before the period. At the end of the entry, give the location and name of the distributor or the location of the work of art.

National Geographic Society (Producer). (1986). *Gorilla* [Videotape].

Washington, DC: National Geographic Society.

Delaunay, S. (Artist). (1958). *Colored rhythm no. 698* [Painting]. Buffalo:

Allbright-Knox Art Gallery.

32. *Television program.* For a single episode in a series, use the basic form of a selection in an edited book (see example 8), with the scriptwriter in the author position and the series producer in the editor position. Identify the program type (for example, "Television broadcast" or "Television series") in brackets immediately after the title. The director's name can be included in parentheses after the title.

Levy, P. R. (1994). The Mission [Television series episode]. In P. L. Stein

(Producer), *Neighborhoods: The hidden cities of San Francisco.* San

Francisco: KQED.

To cite a series or a special, use the basic form for a book (see example 1), with the series producer in the author position and "Producer" in parentheses after the name. Use the same form to cite a particular broadcast of a regularly scheduled news program, but add the date of the broadcast after the year.

Burns, K., & Novick, L. (Producers). (1998). *Frank Lloyd Wright* [Television

special]. New York: Public Broadcasting Service.

APA Manuscript Form

In addition to following the general conventions described under the alphabetical entry **manuscript form**, APA style also covers other aspects of the appearance of the finished manuscript. (See the sample pages illustrated on page 114.) Students who are preparing laboratory reports and technical papers may want to consult the APA manual for additional information about preparation of tables and figures and treatment of statistical and mathematical copy.

MARGINS AND SPACING Use default word-processor settings for margins: at least one inch at the top, bottom, and sides. Double-space all lines.

FONT Use a 12-point serif font, such as Times or Times Roman.

TITLE PAGE AND HEADINGS Center the title on the page. Follow APA's conventions of capitalization for titles: Capitalize all major words (including those following the hyphen in **compound words**) and all words of four letters or more; capitalize **conjunctions, articles,** or **prepositions** only if they have four letters or more; capitalize the first word after a colon or a dash.

Double-space and center your name, the instructor's name, the course name and number, and the date on separate lines underneath the title.

If there is an abstract, put it on the page following the title page, with the heading "Abstract" centered at least an inch from the top of the page.

On the first page of text, type the title again, centered at least an inch from the top of the page. Double-space, and then start the first line of the text.

PAGE NUMBERS Beginning with the title page, number all pages (except artwork and figures) consecutively in the upper right-hand corner, about half an inch from the top of the page and at least an inch from the right-hand edge of the page. Type the short title (the first two or three words of the title) five spaces to the left of the page number, in case the pages get separated. You can automatically set page numbers and headers with the header function of most word-processing programs.

CORRECTIONS AND INSERTIONS Do not strike out errors or ink in corrections. If you are using a word processor, make the corrections and print out fresh pages. If you are using a typewriter, use correction fluid or a ribbon with correction tape. (Your corrections are more likely to line up if you proofread and correct before you take the page out of the typewriter.) Do not put corrections in the margins or write on the manuscript. Retype any page that has more than two corrections.

BLOCK QUOTATIONS A quotation longer than forty words should be set off from the rest of the text. Indent it five to seven spaces from the left margin, and double-space it. Do not indent the first line of the quotation more than the other lines. If the quotation is two or more paragraphs long, indent the first line of the second and subsequent paragraphs an additional five to seven spaces.

Add an in-text citation (usually the page number, which is preceded by "p.") one space after the final punctuation mark of the quotation.

> Breuer and Freud (1895) noted that sometimes the connection between
> a hysterical symptom and its precipitating event is quite clear. They give
> the following example:
>
> > A highly intelligent man was present while his brother had an
> > ankylosing hip-joint extended under an anesthetic. At the instant at
> > which the hip-joint gave way with a crack, he felt a violent pain in
> > his own hip-joint, which persisted for nearly a year. (p. 15)

APA

Sample APA Manuscript Pages

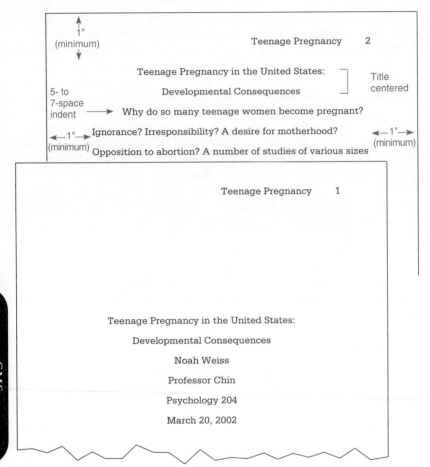

CMS Style

The Chicago Manual of Style, 14th ed. (Chicago: U of Chicago P, 1993), presents two styles of documentation. One uses author-date citations in the text paired with a reference list, much like the MLA and APA styles. The other—the one that is explained here—uses numbered endnotes or footnotes and, with long manuscripts, a bibliography. This style is often used in history, art history, and other humanities disciplines.

CMS style was originally intended for authors and editors of book-length manuscripts. It has been adapted for students as *A Manual for Writers of Term Papers, Theses, and Dissertations,* 6th ed. (Chicago: U of Chicago P, 1996), by Kate Turabian (revised by John Grossman and Alice Bennett).

Occasionally, the recommendations in these two books differ. For example, CMS prefers endnotes to footnotes because they are less expensive to typeset; however, Turabian recommends footnotes for dissertations, theses, and other papers that will be stored on microfilm. For a typical research paper written as a class assignment, endnotes are generally preferable. In the pages that follow, we note other differences between CMS and Turabian; find out which your instructor prefers. For more information, see the FAQs page on the CMS Web site, <http://www.chicagomanualofstyle.org/cmosfaq.html>.

CMS

continued

CMS Documentary Notes

Whether you use footnotes at the bottoms of the text pages or endnotes on a separate page at the end of the paper, you should number them consecutively throughout the paper. As one of the last steps before you finish your paper, check the note numbers to make sure that none has been accidentally omitted or repeated.

For the note numbers in the text, use Arabic numerals typed slightly above the line. Most word processors and many typewriters can raise characters by half a line, and most word processors can reduce the type size (from 12 to 9 or 10 points, for example) to produce a superscript number ([1]). Note numbers should be placed at the end of a sentence or a clause, after the punctuation mark (with the exception of a dash, which should follow the note number).

For the numbers preceding the notes themselves, type the numeral on the same line as the note (and in the same type size), followed by a period and a space. If you are using a computer program that generates footnotes with superscript numbers, most instructors will accept that style.

According to CMS, footnotes in manuscripts submitted for publication must be double-spaced, but in academic papers not intended for publication, single spacing with a double space between notes is acceptable; Turabian recommends single spacing of both footnotes and endnotes, with a double space between notes. The first line of each note should be indented by the same amount that paragraphs are indented. Either italics or underlining can be used for the titles of books and other works.

Footnotes appear on the bottom of the same page of text where the corresponding note numbers appear. A short rule (about twenty characters long) separates the text and the footnotes. If the last footnote on a page runs over to the following page, the continuation is also separated from the text with a short rule.

BOOKS

BASIC FORM FOR CMS NOTE FOR NONPERIODICAL REFERENCES

Book:

    1. Anna A. Author and Barney B. Author, <u>Title of Work</u>

(Location: Publisher, 2002).

Chapter or part of a book:

    2. Anna A. Author, "Title of Chapter," in <u>Title of Book</u>, ed.

Enid E. Editor and Edward E. Editor (Location: Publisher, 2002),

xx–xx.

CMS

1. *Book with one author.* The author's name is not reversed. The name of the book is underlined or italicized, and the important words are capitalized. Publication information—place of publication, name of publisher, and date of publication—is enclosed in parentheses. The page number of the information being cited follows the publication information; page numbers are not necessary if the entire work is being cited. For inclusive page numbers, you need to include only the digits that have changed in the second number; for example, 321–5 (instead of 321–325) or 547–55 (instead of 547–555).

    1. Julie Roy Jeffrey, <u>Frontier Women: The Trans-Mississippi West</u>

<u>1840–1860</u> (New York: Hill and Wang, 1979).

2. *Book with two or three authors.*

> 2. Dennis Tedlock and Barbara Tedlock, <u>Teaching from the American Earth: Indian Religion and Philosophy</u> (New York: Liveright, 1975), 75.

3. *Book with more than three authors.* In a note, the name of the first author can be followed by "et al." or "and others." The bibliography entry, however, customarily lists all the authors (with the name of only the first one inverted).

> 3. Travis Hudson et al., <u>The Eye of the Flute: Chumash Traditional History and Ritual as Told by Fernando Librado Kitsepawit</u> (Santa Barbara, Calif.: Santa Barbara Museum of Natural History, 1977), 20.

4. *Book with a group or corporate author.* If a work published by an organization has no author's name on the title page, show the organization as the author in the reference note.

> 4. University of Chicago Press, <u>The Chicago Manual of Style</u>, 14th ed. (Chicago: University of Chicago Press, 1993).

5. *Book with an editor.* Begin the entry with the name of the editor (or editors), followed by the abbreviation "ed." (or "eds.").

> 5. H. Shelton Smith, Robert T. Handy, and Lefferts A. Loetscher, eds., <u>American Christianity</u> (New York: Scribner's, 1960), 146.

6. *Book with an editor or translator and an author.* Unless the translator or editor is the point of the reference, the author's name comes before the title and the translator's or editor's name or both come after. Use the abbreviation "trans." for "translator." (Note that the two-part publication information in this entry indicates that the source is a reprint of a book published relatively recently; data for both the original and the reprint are given. Example 7 shows the treatment for a reprint of an older, classic work.)

> 6. Carlos Fuentes, <u>Burnt Water</u>, trans. Margaret Sayers Peden (New York: Farrar, Straus and Giroux, 1980; reprint, New York: Noonday Press, 1986).

7. *Foreword or introduction.* Use this kind of note only when the foreword or introduction itself is the source of information. The name of the book author follows the title of the book. (Note that the publication information here shows the original date of publication as well as the date this classic work was reprinted.)

> 7. Tony Tanner, introduction to <u>Pride and Prejudice</u>, by Jane Austen (1813; reprint, ed. Tony Tanner, New York: Penguin, 1980), x–xii.

8. *Book without a listed author or editor.* If no author is shown for a book, begin the note with the name of the book.

8. Dorothea Lange, with an essay by Christopher Cox, vol. 5 of

Aperture Masters of Photography (New York: Aperture, 1987).

9. *Book edition other than the first.*

9. Lacy Baldwin Smith, This Realm of England, 5th ed. (Lexington,

Mass.: D. C. Heath, 1988), 177–8.

10. *Selection in an edited book.* The name of the selection or chapter is enclosed in quotation marks. The name of the book is underlined or italicized. The name of the editor (or editors) is preceded by "ed." (an abbreviation for "edited by").

10. John Garrard, "Parties, Members and Voters after 1867," in

Later Victorian Britain, ed. T. R. Gourvish and Alan O'Day (New York:

St. Martin's Press, 1988), 145.

11. *Letter in a published collection.*

11. Victoria to Vicky, 28 January 1863, Queen Victoria in Her

Letters and Journals, ed. Christopher Hibbert (New York: Viking Penguin,

1985), 170.

12. *Volume in a multivolume series.* The volume title may either precede or follow the series title. If the volume does not have a separate title, include the volume number after the title of the series; if the note refers to specific pages, however, give the volume number with the page numbers at the end of the citation.

12. Paul L. Hughes and James F. Larkin, eds., Tudor Royal

Proclamations, vol. 1 of The Early Tudors (1485–1553) (New Haven: Yale

University Press, 1964), 80.

13. C. Peter Ripley, ed., The Black Abolitionists' Papers, vol. 1

(Chapel Hill: University of North Carolina Press, 1985).

OR

13. C. Peter Ripley, ed., The Black Abolitionists' Papers (Chapel Hill:

University of North Carolina Press, 1985), 1:111.

13. *Reference book.* It is not necessary to provide the facts of publication in notes for well-known reference books. If the encyclopedia or dictionary is organized in

CMS

alphabetical order, a page number is not necessary. Instead, use the abbreviation "s.v." (for *sub verbo*, "under the word") and the name of the entry where the information can be found. Citations for information from reference books are generally not included in the bibliography.

> 14. Dictionary of American Negro Biography, s.v. "Roudanez, Louis
>
> Charles."

PERIODICALS

BASIC FORM FOR CMS NOTE FOR PERIODICAL REFERENCES

Periodical paginated by volume:

> 1. Anna A. Author and Barney B. Author, "Title of Article,"
>
> Title of Periodical xx (2002): xxx–xx.

Periodical paginated by issue:

> 1. Anna A. Author and Barney B. Author, "Title of Article,"
>
> Title of Periodical xx, no. 10 (2002): xx–xx.

---

14. *Article in a journal.* The article title is enclosed in quotation marks. The journal title is underlined or italicized. The volume number follows the name of the journal. If there is an issue number, it may be included after the volume number either in parentheses (in which case the date follows the page number) or preceded by "no." (the abbreviation for "number"). Issue numbers must be included for journals paginated by issue rather than by volume or year. The date of publication is enclosed in parentheses and followed by a colon and the page number (or numbers) of the information being cited.

> 1. Alistair Thomson, "Fifty Years On: An International Perspective
>
> on Oral History," Journal of American History 85 (1998): 581–96.

> 2. James E. Packer, "Trajan's Glorious Forum," Archaeology 51, no. 1
>
> (1998): 32–41.

OR

> 2. James E. Packer, "Trajan's Glorious Forum," Archaeology 51(1):
>
> 32–41 (1998).

15. *Article in a magazine.* A reference to an article in a general-interest magazine does not need to include the volume number; if it does not, the date of the issue is not enclosed in parentheses and the page number is separated from the date by a comma rather than a colon. Whichever style you choose for your paper, use it consistently.

3. Tamala M. Edwards, "Family Reunion," Time, 16 November 1998, 85–6.

OR

3. Tamala M. Edwards, "Family Reunion," Time 152, no. 21 (16 November 1998): 85–6.

16. *Article in a daily newspaper.* If the section of the paper is identified, include its name, number, or letter. When the entry includes section number, page number, and column number, use the abbreviations "sec.," "p.," and "col." to avoid confusion (see example 19, note 8). If the city is not named in the title of the newspaper, add it to the title in parentheses.

4. Mellgren, Doug, "Polar Bears' Realm: Armed Tourists and Adventure Converge in an Arctic Outpost," Travel, St. Louis Post Dispatch, 21 February 1999, T5.

17. *Unsigned article.* Start with the article title if no author is named.

5. "Warning: Hazardous Mulches," Organic Gardening, May/June 1998, 12.

18. *Interview, published or broadcast.*

6. Huston Smith, interview by Bill Moyers, The Wisdom of Faith: A Personal Philosophy, Part 5, Public Broadcasting System, 28 April 1996.

19. *Review.* Start with the name of the reviewer and the title of the review (if any). After the words "review of," identify the work reviewed by title and author (or other relevant information, such as director, performers, producer, type of production, location and date of a live performance). Finally, give the name, date, and page number (or numbers) of the periodical where the review appeared.

7. John J. O'Connor, "An England Where Heart and Purse Are Romantically United," review of Pride and Prejudice (BBC/A&E television production), New York Times, 13 January 1996, 13(L).

CMS

8. Bosley Crowther, review of Pride and Prejudice, dir. Robert Z. Leonard (MGM movie), New York Times, 9 August 1940, p. 19, col. 1.

OTHER SOURCES

20. *Online source.* Because electronic sources are developing so quickly, the style for citing them is still developing. Consequently, the style shown here is that of Kate Turabian's *Manual for Writers of Term Papers, Theses, and Dissertations*, 6th edition (1996), rather than *The Chicago Manual of Style*, 14th edition (1993). The basic principle in both, however, is to provide the author, title, and date information that would be provided for a print source plus enough "publication" information to enable a reader to retrieve the document. The date the document was accessed must also be included, because online documents are often modified or updated.

BASIC FORM FOR CMS NOTE FOR ONLINE SOURCES

1. Anna A. Author, "Title of Web Page," Title of Web Site [type of source] updated 30 November 2002, accessed 15 December 2002; available from URL; Internet.

Web site.

9. National Archives and Records Administration, "Exhibit: Titanic Memorandum," American Originals [database online] updated 15 April 1998, accessed 16 April 1998; available from http://clio.nara.gov/exhall/ originals/titanic.html; Internet.

Article from an online journal.

10. George A. Bray III, "Scalping during the French and Indian War," Early American Review 2, no. 3: 1998 [journal online] updated 12 February 1998, accessed 6 November 1998; available from http://earlyamerica.com/ review/1998/scalping.html; Internet.

Online book.

11. Eugene Field, The Love Affairs of a Bibliomaniac (New York: Scribner's, 1896) [book online] accessed 29 October 1998; available from

http://etext.lib.virginia.edu/cgbin/browse-mixed?id=FieLove&tag;

plpublic&images=images; Internet.

Online posting (Listserv/mailing list or Usenet/discussion list).

Give the author's name, the subject line (in quotation marks), the date the message was created, the name of the list (if there is one), the e-mail address of the mailing list or discussion list, the description "online posting," the date of access, and the Web address if the posting was accessed in an archive on the Web.

12. Sean Cubitt, "Re: Film Literacy/Production" [online posting],

18 August 1998, in Film-Philosophy <film-philosophy@mailbase.ac.uk>

accessed 9 September 1998; available from http://www.mailbase.ac.uk/

lists/film-philosophy/files; Internet.

21. *CD-ROM, diskette, or magnetic tape.* Give the same author, title, and date information as for a print source, including any edition, version, or release number. In addition, describe the medium of the source (such as "CD-ROM"), its publisher or vendor, and its date of publication.

13. Steven Schmitz and Janet C. Christopher, "Trouble in

Smurftown: Young Gangs and Moral Vision on Guam," Child Welfare 76,

no. 3 (1997): 411–28 [abstract on CD-ROM]; available from SilverPlatter,

Social Welfare Abstracts 31247.

22. *Film, video recording, or other visual material.* Because there are so many kinds of visual materials (not only movies on cassette but also films and slides), one rule cannot cover them all. The citation note should provide whatever information is necessary to describe the source, to indicate its relevance to the researcher, and to enable a reader to retrieve it.

14. Pride and Prejudice, directed by Robert Z. Leonard, produced by

Hunt Stromberg, starring Greer Garson and Laurence Olivier, MGM/UA,

1940, videocassette.

23. *Sound recording.* The entry for a record, tape, or compact disc (spelled *disk* by CMS) usually begins with the name of the composer. Collections or anonymous works begin with the title. Underline or italicize the title of a recording; enclose the name of a selection in quotation marks. The name of the performer usually follows the title; if the purpose of the citation is to emphasize the performer, however, the entry may begin with the performer's name. For publication information, use the name of

CMS

the recording company and the number of the recording. Other information—such as copyright date and kind of recording—may be added.

15. Joaquin Rodrigo, "Concierto de Aranjuez," on <u>Rodrigo:</u>

<u>Conciertos</u>, Pepe Romero and Academy of St. Martin-in-the-Fields, Sir

Neville Marriner, Philips compact disk 432 828-2.

24. *Public document.* Citations for printed public documents should generally include the country, state, or other government division issuing the document (unless all the documents being cited are issued by the same government); the legislative body, executive department, court, or agency (including the name of any subsidiary division); the title of the document (underlined or italicized); the name of the author or editor, if given; the report number or other identification needed to locate the document; the publisher if different from the issuing body; the date; and the page number, unless the entire work is being cited. If you are citing a large number of public documents, you may find it helpful to consult the *Chicago Manual* (pp. 602–28) for its many examples.

16. U.S. Department of Commerce, Bureau of the Census, <u>Negro</u>

<u>Population 1790–1915</u> (Washington, D.C., 1918).

25. *Legal reference.* A note for a decision by a federal court begins with the title of the case (CMS says to underline or italicize it; Turabian says to underline or italicize it only in the text). The source is identified by volume number, the abbreviated title of the official court report (in the example below, "U.S." stands for *United States Supreme Court Reports*), and the page number. In the first note citing the decision, include the year in parentheses. Federal court decisions are usually cited only in the text or notes and not in the bibliography. If your paper has many legal citations, consult *The University of Chicago Manual of Legal Citation* (1989) or *The Bluebook: A Uniform System of Citation,* 17th ed. (Harvard Law Review Association, 2000).

17. <u>Brown v. Board of Education</u>, 347 U.S. 483 (1954).

26. *Unpublished dissertation or thesis.* The title is enclosed in quotation marks. The work is identified as a dissertation or thesis in the parentheses enclosing the publication information, which consists of the name of the college or university and the date.

18. James Hugo Johnston, "Race Relations in Virginia and

Miscegenation in the South, 1776–1860" (Ph.D. diss., University of

Chicago, 1937).

27. *Personal communication.* Citations for information gained in personal conversations or by letter, e-mail, or telephone may be included in the text, in informal

notes, or in more formal ones. Because personal communications are not usually available to the public, they do not need to be included in a bibliography.

> 19. Theodore Thomas informed me by telephone in January 1998 that the film had been seven years in the making.

OR

> 19. Theodore Thomas, telephone conversation with author, 10 January 1998.

28. *Secondary source.* Include publication information for both the primary source (if that information is available) and the secondary source. If the purpose of the note is to indicate where you found the primary-source information, list the primary source first. If, however, you are focusing on the secondary source's quotation of the primary source, start the note with the secondary source.

> 20. Burr Cartwright Brundage, Lords of Cuzco: A History and Description of the Inca People in Their Final Days (Norman: University of Oklahoma Press, 1967), 160, quoted in John Felstiner, Translating Neruda: The Way to Macchu Picchu (Stanford, Calif.: Stanford University Press, 1980), 264.

OR

> 21. John Felstiner, Translating Neruda: The Way to Macchu Picchu (Stanford, Calif.: Stanford University Press, 1980), 264, quoting Burr Cartwright Brundage, Lords of Cuzco: A History and Description of the Inca People in Their Final Days (Norman: University of Oklahoma Press, 1967), 160.

CMS Shortened Notes

The first time a source is cited, the note should contain complete publication information, as shown in the preceding examples. Subsequent references to a source, however, may be shortened, using only the last name of the author (or authors) and the page reference. (If two or more authors have the same last name, use their initials or first names in all notes.) The title of the work should be included in long papers, such as theses and dissertations; in shorter papers, include it only if two or more works by the same author are cited. A long title may be shortened to a key phrase.

1. *Shortened reference to a book.*

>   1. Jeffrey, 125.

OR

>   1. Jeffrey, <u>Frontier Women</u>, 125.

2. *Shortened reference to a part of a book.* If a title is necessary, use the title of the chapter or selection and not the title of the book.

>   2. Garrard, "Parties, Members and Voters," 145.

3. *Shortened reference to an article.* If a title is necessary, use the article title and not the name of the periodical.

>   3. Dunbar-Nelson, "People," 78.

If the article is not signed, use the article title, or a shortened version of it.

>   4. "Garrison Predicts Success," 2.

4. *"Ibid." for successive references to the same source.* If there are two or more notes in a row to the same page of the same work, the abbreviation "ibid." (short for the Latin *ibidem,* meaning "in the same place") may be used for the second and subsequent notes.

>   5. Ibid.

If the second note is to a different page in the work, use "ibid." and the page number.

>   6. Ibid., 130.

CMS Bibliography

For short papers with only a page or two of notes, a bibliography may be optional because the reader can easily spot the bibliographical information for the sources consulted. For longer papers, a separate bibliography is an aid to the reader because it can be difficult to locate the first note for a source among pages and pages of notes. Find out whether your instructor wants you to provide a bibliography.

Bibliography entries contain essentially the same information as the first note for a source but differ from notes in format. First, the name of the author (the first author, if there is more than one) is reversed because the bibliography is arranged alphabetically by last name. Second, the elements in a bibliographical entry are separated by periods rather than commas, and parentheses are not used around the publication information. The examples that follow explain additional variations for specific kinds of sources.

The first line of a bibliography entry begins at the left margin, and subsequent lines are indented. Turabian specifies an indention of five spaces and single spacing within entries but double spacing between them. CMS specifies an indention of three to four spaces for the second and subsequent lines and double spacing both within and between entries. Find out which style your instructor prefers.

The bibliography may be titled "Selected Bibliography," "Works Cited," or "Sources Consulted." This last choice is appropriate if you have used interviews or other nonprint sources.

1. *Book with one author.*

Jeffrey, Julie Roy. Frontier Women: The Trans-Mississippi West 1840–1860.

New York: Hill and Wang, 1979.

2. *Book with more than one author.* Semicolons may be used to separate the names of three or more authors.

Hudson, Travis; Thomas Blackburn; Rosario Curletti; and Janice Timbrook.

The Eye of the Flute: Chumash Traditional History and Ritual as

Told by Fernando Librado Kitsepawit. Santa Barbara, Calif.: Santa

Barbara Museum of Natural History, 1977.

Tedlock, Dennis, and Barbara Tedlock. Teaching from the American Earth:

Indian Religion and Philosophy. New York: Liveright, 1975.

3. *Book with a group or corporate author.*

University of Chicago Press. The Chicago Manual of Style. 14th ed.

Chicago: University of Chicago Press, 1993.

4. *Book with an editor.*

Smith, H. Shelton; Robert T. Handy; and Lefferts A. Loetscher, eds.

American Christianity. New York: Scribner's, 1960.

5. *Book with an editor or translator and an author.*

Fuentes, Carlos. Burnt Water. Translated by Margaret Sayers Peden.

New York: Farrar, Straus and Giroux, 1980; New York: Noonday

Press, 1986.

6. *Foreword or introduction.*

Tanner, Tony. Introduction to Pride and Prejudice, by Jane Austen. 1813.

Reprint, edited by Tony Tanner, New York: Penguin, 1980.

7. *Book without a listed author or editor.* List the entry alphabetically by the first main word in the title. If the first word is "A," "An," or "The," you may transpose it to the end of the title, preceded by a comma.

Dorothea Lange. With an essay by Christopher Cox. Vol. 5 of Aperture

Masters of Photography. New York: Aperture, 1987.

8. *Book edition other than the first.*

Smith, Lacy Baldwin. This Realm of England. 5th ed. Lexington, Mass.:

D. C. Heath, 1988.

9. *Selection in an edited book.*

Garrard, John. "Parties, Members and Voters after 1867." In Later

Victorian Britain, edited by T. R. Gourvish and Alan O'Day, 152–89.

New York: St. Martin's Press, 1988.

10. *Letter in a published collection.*

Victoria. Letter to Vicky, 28 January 1863. Queen Victoria in Her Letters

and Journals, edited by Christopher Hibbert. New York: Viking

Penguin, 1985.

11. *Volume in a multivolume series.*

Hughes, Paul L., and James F. Larkin, eds. Tudor Royal Proclamations.

Vol. 1 of The Early Tudors (1485–1553). New Haven: Yale University

Press, 1964.

12. *Article in a journal.*

Packer, James E. "Trajan's Glorious Forum." Archaeology 51, no. 1 (1998):

32–41.

13. *Article in a magazine.*

Edwards, Tamala M. "Family Reunion." Time, 16 November 1998, 85–6.

14. *Article in a daily newspaper.* News items are rarely listed separately in bibliographies; articles from special sections are treated like articles from general-interest magazines.

Mellgren, Doug. "Polar Bears' Realm: Armed Tourists and Adventure

Converge in an Arctic Outpost." Travel, St. Louis Post Dispatch, 21

February 1999, T5.

15. *Interview, published or broadcast.*

Smith, Huston. Interview by Bill Moyers. The Wisdom of Faith:

A Personal Philosophy, Part 5. Public Broadcasting System,

28 April 1996.

16. *Review.*

O'Connor, John J. "An England Where Heart and Purse Are Romantically

United." Review of Pride and Prejudice (BBC/A&E television

production). New York Times, 13 January 1996, 13(L).

17. *Online source.*

Web site.

National Archives and Records Administration. "Exhibit: Titanic

Memorandum." American Originals. Database online. Updated

15 April 1998; accessed 16 April 1998. Available from http://clio.

nara.gov/exhall/originals/titanic.html.

Article from an online journal.

Bray, George A., III. "Scalping during the French and Indian War."

Early American Review 2, no. 3 (1998). Journal online. Updated

12 February 1998; accessed 6 November 1998. Available from

http://earlyamerica.com/review/1998/scalping.html.

Online book.

Field, Eugene. The Love Affairs of a Bibliomaniac. New York: Scribner's,

1896. Book online. Accessed 29 October 1998. Available from

http://etext.lib.virginia.edu/cgbin/browse-mixed?id=

FieLove&tag+public&images=images.

Online posting (listserv/mailing list or Usenet/discussion list).

Cubitt, Sean. "Re: Film Literacy/Production." In Film-Philosophy

<film-philosophy@mailbase.ac.uk>. Online posting. 18 August 1998;

accessed 9 September 1998. Available from http://www.mailbase.

ac.uk/lists/film-philosophy/files.

CD-ROM, diskette, or magnetic tape.

Schmitz, Steven, and Janet C. Christopher. "Trouble in Smurftown: Young

Gangs and Moral Vision on Guam." Child Welfare 76, no. 3 (1997):

411–28. Abstract on CD-ROM. Available from SilverPlatter, Social

Welfare Abstracts 31247.

18. *Film, video recording, or other visual material.*

Pride and Prejudice. Directed by Robert Z. Leonard. Produced by Hunt

Stromberg. Starring Greer Garson and Laurence Olivier. MGM/UA,

1940. Videocassette.

19. *Sound recording.*

Rodrigo, Joaquin. "Concierto de Aranjuez." On Rodrigo: Conciertos.

Pepe Romero and Academy of St. Martin-in-the-Fields. Sir Neville

Marriner. Philips compact disk 432 828-2.

20. *Public document.*

U.S. Department of Commerce. Bureau of the Census. Negro Population

1790–1915. Washington, D.C., 1918.

21. *Unpublished dissertation or thesis.*

Johnston, James Hugo. "Race Relations in Virginia and Miscegenation in

the South, 1776–1860." Ph.D. diss., University of Chicago, 1937.

22. *Secondary source.* The page number comes immediately after the title if the
first-mentioned work is a book. The second-mentioned work is treated in note style,

with commas separating the elements and parentheses around the facts of publication of books.

> Brundage, Burr Cartwright. <u>Lords of Cuzco: A History and Description</u>
>
> <u>of the Inca People in Their Final Days</u>, 160. Norman: University
>
> of Oklahoma Press, 1967. Quoted in John Felstiner, <u>Translating</u>
>
> <u>Neruda: The Way to Macchu Picchu</u> (Stanford, Calif.: Stanford
>
> University Press, 1980), 264.

23. *More than one work by an author.* When the bibliography lists more than one work by the same author, a long dash can be used in place of the name in the second and subsequent entries. CMS represents the long dash with three hyphens (---); Turabian specifies an "eight-space line (made by striking the underscore key eight times" (_____). Find out your instructor's preference. The entries may be arranged alphabetically by title (disregarding the introductory articles "A," "An," and "The") or chronologically; use one method or the other consistently throughout the bibliography.

> Dorsey, George A. <u>Traditions of the Skidi Pawnee</u>. Boston: Houghton
>
> Mifflin, 1904.
>
> ---. <u>The Traditions of the Caddo</u>. Washington, D.C.: Carnegie Institution of
>
> Washington, 1905.
>
> ---. <u>The Pawnee Mythology</u>. Washington, D.C.: Carnegie Institution of
>
> Washington, 1906.

CMS Manuscript Form

Because *The Chicago Manual of Style* is intended primarily for manuscripts that are to be published rather than for manuscripts that are themselves the final product, the format presented here is the one recommended in *A Manual for Writers of Term Papers, Theses, and Dissertations* by Kate Turabian; its guidelines are more appropriate for most student research papers. Some departments and disciplines prefer formats that are not identical to these, however. Be sure to check with your instructor.

MARGINS Leave at least one inch at the top, bottom, and sides. Start the first page of the text, the endnotes, and the bibliography about two inches from the top of the page.

TITLE PAGE For a term paper, center the name of the university or college near the top of the page. Toward the middle of the page, center the full title of the paper, the course name (including department and course number), the date, and your name.

PAGE NUMBERS   The title page counts as page 1, but it is not numbered. The page number on the first page of text should be centered between the last line of type and the bottom edge of the page. Subsequent pages should be numbered in the top right corner, about three-quarters of an inch from the top edge of the paper and an inch from the right edge.

LINE SPACING   The general text should be double-spaced. In papers not intended for publication, footnotes, endnotes, and bibliographies may be single-spaced, with double spaces above and below each entry.

BLOCK QUOTATIONS   Quotations of two or more lines of poetry or eight or more lines of prose should be set off as block quotations, which are single-spaced and separated from the general text with a double space above and below. Block quotations are indented four spaces from the left margin; paragraph indentions are an additional four spaces. Quotations of poetry should be line for line as in the original. Because block quotations are set off from the text, they should not begin and end with quotation marks.

CORRECTIONS AND INSERTIONS   If you are using a typewriter, you can use correction paper, correction fluid, or self-correcting typewriter ribbon to delete or insert a character. If more than one character needs to be corrected, the page should be retyped. If you are using a computer, make corrections on screen, and print out a clean copy of the paper.

Sample CMS Manuscript Pages

Following are a sample title page, text pages, a notes page, and a list of works cited for a paper in CMS format.

LOYOLA UNIVERSITY NEW ORLEANS

CREOLES OF COLOR IN NEW ORLEANS:
SHATTERED DREAMS AND BROKEN PROMISES

AMERICAN HISTORY FROM
RECONSTRUCTION TO THE PRESENT
HISTORY 320

JANUARY 23, 2000

BY
KAREN BATTLE

CMS

Title page.

2″

There is no state in the Union, hardly any spot of like size on the globe, where the man of color has lived so intensely, made so much progress, been of such historical importance and yet about whom so comparatively little is known. His history is like the Mardi Gras of the city of New Orleans, beautiful and mysterious and wonderful, but with a serious thought underlying it all. May it be better known to the world someday.
Alice Dunbar-Nelson, "People of Color in Louisiana"[1]

← 1″ →

As early as 1815, with promises of compensation from General

← 1″ → Andrew Jackson for participation in the Battle of New Orleans, the

free Black people of New Orleans patiently awaited the fulfillment

of their strong desire for equality with Whites. Dubbed "free

persons" or "Creoles" of color, the group remained--for nearly two

centuries--in the difficult "center" position in New Orleans society:

Block ——→ They shared neither the privileges of the master class nor
quotation   the degradation of the slave. They stood between--or rather
indented   apart--sharing the cultivated tastes of the upper caste and
4 spaces   the painful humiliation attached to the race of the enslaved.[2]

With slaveholders and well-established property owners among

the class, many free Blacks identified their interests with those of

the governing White society. The result was the separation of the

educated and propertied free Blacks from the majority of their race,

with whom they shared a common legal status.[3]

Rule →——
above
footnote   1. Alice Dunbar-Nelson, "People of Color in Louisiana," in The
Works of Alice Dunbar-Nelson, ed. Gloria T. Hull (New York: Oxford
University Press, 1994), 322.
      2. Charles E. O'Neill, S.J., foreword to Our People and Our
History, by Rodolphe L. Desdunes (Baton Rouge: Louisiana State
University Press, 1973), ix.
      3. Donald E. Everett, "Demands of the New Orleans Free
Colored Population for Political Equality, 1862-1865," Louisiana
Historical Quarterly, April 1955, 43.

2 ←—— Page number centered
on first text page

First text page for paper with footnotes.

As the years dragged on and the size and wealth of the free Black population of New Orleans continued to grow, strong dissatisfaction with the Creole example of uplift and opportunity to those still enslaved began to emerge in the White community. In an address to the Louisiana legislature in 1857, Governor Robert C. Wicliffe proposed a somewhat unrealistic solution to the free Black "problem":

> Public policy dictates that immediate steps be taken at this time to move all free negroes now in the State when such removal can be effected without violation of the law. Their example and association have a most pernicious affect [sic] upon our slave population.[4]

In January 1860 a group of about one hundred free Blacks from surrounding rural parishes, who felt that conditions could only worsen, left for Haiti from the port of New Orleans. Free Black New Orleanians, however, failed to see any reason for such an action. Possessing a combined estimated value of about $20 million of the city's wealth, the Creoles of color decided to stick it out and prepare themselves for the long and arduous struggle for what they felt was theirs by right of birth.[5]

---

4. Quoted in Brenda Marie Osbey, "Faubourg Tremé: Community in Transition, Part 2," New Orleans Tribune, January 1991, 13.
5. Ibid.

Text page with footnotes.

2″

There is no state in the Union, hardly any spot of like size on the globe, where the man of color has lived so intensely, made so much progress, been of such historical importance and yet about whom so comparatively little is known. His history ←—1″—→ is like the Mardi Gras of the city of New Orleans, beautiful and mysterious and wonderful, but with a serious thought underlying it all. May it be better known to the world someday.
Alice Dunbar-Nelson, "People of Color in Louisiana"[1]

←—1″—→

As early as 1815, with promises of compensation from General Andrew Jackson for participation in the Battle of New Orleans, the free Black people of New Orleans patiently awaited the fulfillment of their strong desire for equality with Whites. Dubbed "free persons" or "Creoles" of color, the group remained--for nearly two centuries--in the difficult "center" position in New Orleans society:

Block —→ They shared neither the privileges of the master class nor
quotation the degradation of the slave. They stood between--or rather
indented apart--sharing the cultivated tastes of the upper caste and
4 spaces the painful humiliation attached to the race of the enslaved.[2]

With slaveholders and well-established property owners among the class, many free Blacks identified their interests with those of the governing White society. The result was the separation of the educated and propertied free Blacks from the majority of their race, with whom they shared a common legal status.[3]

Note—→   As the years dragged on and the size and wealth of the free
number
raised   Black population of New Orleans continued to grow, strong
1/2 line
and   dissatisfaction with the Creole example of uplift and opportunity to
reduced   those still enslaved began to emerge in the White community. In
an address to the Louisiana legislature in 1857, Governor Robert C.
Wicliffe proposed a somewhat unrealistic solution to the free Black

2

CMS

First text page for paper with endnotes.

5

NOTES

1. Alice Dunbar-Nelson, "People of Color in Louisiana," in The Works of Alice Dunbar-Nelson, ed. Gloria T. Hull (New York: Oxford University Press, 1994), 322.

2. Charles E. O'Neill, S.J., foreword to Our People and Our History, by Rodolphe L. Desdunes (Baton Rouge: Louisiana State University Press, 1973), ix.

3. Donald E. Everett, "Demands of the New Orleans Free Colored Population for Political Equality, 1862-1865," Louisiana Historical Quarterly, April 1955, 43.

4. Quoted in Brenda Marie Osbey, "Faubourg Tremé: Community in Transition, Part 2," New Orleans Tribune, January 1991, 13.

5. Ibid.

6. Everett, 44.

7. Ibid., 45.

8. Ibid., 46.

9. Virginia R. Dominguez, White by Definition (Piscataway, N.J.: Rutgers University Press, 1986), 135.

10. John W. Blassingame, Black New Orleans: 1860-1880 (Chicago: University of Chicago Press, 1973), 131.

11. Brenda Marie Osbey, "Faubourg Tremé: Community in Transition, Part 3," New Orleans Tribune, August 1991, 15.

12. Rayford W. Logan and Michael R. Winston, eds., Dictionary of American Negro Biography (New York: W. W. Norton, 1982), 534.

CMS

First page of endnotes.

6

WORKS CITED

Blassingame, John. Black New Orleans: 1860-1880. Chicago:
     University of Chicago Press, 1973.

Desdunes, Rodolphe. Our People and Our History. Baton Rouge:
     Louisiana State University Press, 1973.

Dominguez, Virginia R. White by Definition. Piscataway, N.J.:
     Rutgers University Press, 1986.

Dunbar-Nelson, Alice. "People of Color in Louisiana." In The Works
     of Alice Dunbar-Nelson, edited by Gloria T. Hull. New York:
     Oxford University Press, 1994.

Everett, Donald E. "Demands of the New Orleans Free Colored
     Population for Political Equality, 1862-1865." Louisiana
     Historical Quarterly, April 1955, 43.

Logan, Rayford W., and Michael R. Winston, eds. Dictionary of
     American Negro Biography. New York: W. W. Norton, 1982.

O'Neill, Charles E., S.J. Foreword to Our People and Our History,
     by Rodolphe L. Desdunes. Baton Rouge: Louisiana State
     University Press, 1973.

Osbey, Brenda Marie. "Faubourg Tremé: Community in Transition,
     Part 2." New Orleans Tribune, January 1991, 13.

---. "Faubourg Tremé: Community in Transition, Part 3." New
     Orleans Tribune, August 1991, 15.

---. "Faubourg Tremé: Community in Transition, Part 4." New
     Orleans Tribune, September 1991, 14.

Wall, Bennett H. Louisiana: A History. Wheeling, Ill.: Forum Press,
     1990.

Bibliography.

CSE (Formerly CBE) Style

The style manual published by the Council of Science Editors (CSE; formerly Council of Biology Editors)—*Scientific Style and Format: The CBE Manual for Authors, Editors, and Publishers,* 6th ed. (New York: Cambridge UP, 1994)—is the basic guide for most writing in the life sciences and medicine. A 7th edition is in preparation. In addition to extensive treatment of the conventions for scientific terminology, it presents two systems of documenting references: a name-year system similar to that of APA and a citation-sequence system, which uses superscript numbers in the text that refer to a numbered list of references. (Some scientific journals use some variant of one of these systems, such as citation numbers enclosed in parentheses in the line of text rather than above it; check with your instructor about the preferred citation system for your class.) For style information, see CSE's Web site, <http://www.councilscienceeditors.org>; follow the "publications" link to the "scientific style and format" link.

The major difference between the CSE system of numbered notes and that of CMS is that the references in CSE are assigned a number by order of first mention in the paper and the number is repeated whenever that reference is cited in the paper. In general, the goal of the CSE style for entries in the reference list is to minimize the number of keystrokes made by the typist: there are no periods after initials; names of journals and publishers are abbreviated; and neither italics nor quotation marks are used with titles of books, journals, or articles.

CSE

CSE In-Text Citation Numbers

Superscript numbers in the text refer to numbered references in the reference list at the end of the paper. References are numbered according to the order in which they are first used in the text: the first reference cited is 1, the second is 2, and so on. Each time the reference numbered 1 is cited in the text, the superscript 1 is used. Two or more citation numbers in one place are separated by a comma (for example, "4,5"); a sequence of three or more consecutive citation numbers, however, is treated as an inclusive number separated by a hyphen (such as "2-4") rather than as a series (that is, "2,3,4"). The numbers are placed at the point of citation rather than at the end of a sentence or a clause, differing from the custom for MLA, APA, and CMS styles.

The two prime factors most frequently cited[1,2] are evolutionary history

and mode of transmission.

The superscript numbers in this example correspond to entries 1 and 2 of the paper's reference list.

CSE Numbered List of References

The reference list, which begins on a new page after the end of the text, should be titled "References" or "Cited References." (Sources that you consulted but did not cite in the text may be listed under a separate heading, such as "Additional References" or "Bibliography.") The entries are numbered sequentially according to their first mention in the text.

The basic order of elements in a reference entry is the name of the author or authors, the title of the book or article, publication information, and pages. Each element ends with a period; periods are not used after initials or abbreviations. A comma is used to separate items of equal importance, such as authors' names. A semicolon is used to separate items that are parts of an element but are not directly related, such as the date of publication of a journal and the volume number or the publisher of a book and the year of publication. A colon indicates that what follows is subordinate to the material before it, such as a subtitle or the page numbers following the volume number of a journal. Examples of the most common kinds of references are shown here and explained in more detail in the *CBE Manual*; for more specialized examples, consult the *National Library of Medicine Recommended Formats for Bibliographic Citation* (Bethesda, MD: National Library of Medicine, 1991), which is the primary source of CSE citation style.

BOOKS   The formats described here can apply to booklets, pamphlets, and brochures as well as to books.

BASIC FORM FOR CSE NOTE FOR NONPERIODICAL REFERENCES

Book:

   1. Author AA, Author BB. Title of work. Location: Publisher: 2002.

   512 p.

Chapter or part of a book:

   2. Author, AA. Title of chapter. In: Editor BB, Editor CC, editors.

   Title of book. Location: Publisher; 2002. p xx-xx.

---

   1. *Book with one or more authors.* The names of all authors are reversed. If there are more than ten authors, the first ten are listed, followed by "and others." First initials rather than first names are used in most cases. No periods are used after the initials, and no comma is used between the last name and the initials.

   Only the first word, proper nouns, proper adjectives, and capitalized abbreviations (such as AIDS) are capitalized in the title. In contrast to the APA documentation system, which also uses a lowercase style for titles, the first word of a subtitle is not capitalized in CSE bibliographical entries, nor are titles italicized or underlined.

   The name of the publisher is usually shortened. Drop conventional commercial designations, such as "Company," "Inc.," and "Press," unless doing so would cause ambiguity. In that case, abbreviate the term—"Pr" for "Press," for example. (Appendix 2 in the *CBE Manual* further explains the rules for shortening publishers' names

CSE

and provides a list of examples.) The last element in book entries is the total number of pages in the book (including back matter, such as the index) followed by "p" (for "pages").

1. Mandelbrot BB. The fractal geometry of nature. San Francisco:

   WH Freeman; 1995. 460 p.

2. *Book with one or more editors.* Follow the names with the word "editor" (or "editors").

2. Briggs DEG, Crowther PR, editors. Paleobiology: a synthesis.

   Cambridge (MA): Blackwell Scientific; 1992. 608 p.

3. *Book with an organization as author.* Shorten organization names according to the CSE rules for shortening publishers' names (described in example 1).

3. British Medical Assoc. A code of practice for sterilisation of

   instruments and control of cross infection. London: British Medical

   Assoc; 1989. 58 p.

4. *Book without a named author or editor.* To indicate that no author or editor is listed on the title page or elsewhere, start the entry with "[Anonymous]."

4. [Anonymous]. Social aspects of AIDS prevention and control

   programmes. Geneva: World Health Organ; 1988. 174 p.

5. *Book edition other than the first.* Include the edition number in abbreviated form after the title. Use "rev ed" as the abbreviation for "revised edition."

5. McCurnin DM, editor. Clinical textbook for veterinary technicians.

   2nd ed. Philadelphia: WB Saunders; 1993. 816 p.

6. *Translated book.* Include the name of the translator after the title. If there is an editor in addition to the author, put the editor's name after the translator's, and separate the two with a semicolon. After the number of pages, the title in the original language may be given.

6. Spindler K. The man in the ice: the discovery of a 5,000-year-old body

   reveals the secrets of the Stone Age. Osers E, translator. New York:

   Random House; 1994. 305 p. Translation of: Mann im eis.

7. *Volume in a multivolume series.* The title of the series precedes the volume number and title of the volume being cited. The total number of pages of the volume is not given.

7. Legendre P, Legendre L, editors. NATO ASI series. Volume G14,

Developments in numerical ecology. Berlin: Springer-Verlag; 1989.

8. *Chapter or part of a book by the author of the book.* The title of the book follows the author's name. The title of the part (as well as any other pertinent identification, such as the number or type of the part) follows the publication information. The page numbers of the part are the last element in the entry. In inclusive page numbers, only the changed digits in the second number are shown.

8. Bakker RT. The dinosaur heresies. New York: Zebra; 1986. The twilight

of the dinosaurs; p 442-4.

9. *Chapter or part of a book not by the author or editor of the book.* The entry begins with the name of the author of the part and the title of the part. Then the book is identified. The last element in the entry, following the publication information, is the page numbers of the part.

9. Benton MJ. Red queen hypothesis. In: Briggs DEG, Crowther PR, editors.

Paleobiology: a synthesis. Cambridge (MA): Blackwell Scientific; 1992.

p 119-23.

PERIODICALS

BASIC FORM FOR CSE NOTE FOR PERIODICAL REFERENCES

1. Author AA. Title of article. Title of Periodical 2002;xxx:xx-xx.

---

10. *Article in a journal.* If there are more than ten authors, list the names of the first ten, followed by "and others." Capitalize only the first word, proper nouns, proper adjectives, and capitalized abbreviations (such as AIDS) in article titles. To indicate a type of article—such as editorial, interview, or letter to the editor—enclose the descriptor in square brackets immediately after the article title.

Journal titles longer than one word are abbreviated according to the standard form used in most biological and medical journals: articles, conjunctions, and prepositions are dropped unless they are part of a name or a scientific or technical term; at least the last two letters of all remaining words are dropped (for example, "Microbiology" is abbreviated "Microbiol" and "Journal" is abbreviated "J"). The first letter of each word in a journal title is capitalized. Appendix 1 in the *CBE Manual* provides a table of standard abbreviations of words that are frequently used in journal titles.

The month and issue number may be omitted for journals that are paginated by volume. The year, volume number, and inclusive page numbers are separated by

CSE

punctuation marks that have no space before or after them. In inclusive page numbers, only the digits that change are included in the second number.

> 10. Lenski RE, May RM. The evolution of virulence in parasites and
>
>   pathogens: reconciliation between two competing hypotheses.
>
>   J Theoret Biol 1994;169:253-65.

11. *Article by an organizational author.*

> 11. North Am Assoc for the Study of Obesity. Position paper: guidelines
>
>   for the approval and use of drugs to treat obesity. Obes Res
>
>   1995;3:473-8.

12. *Article on discontinuous pages.* Use a comma and a space between discontinuous page numbers.

> 12. Pugh CB, Waller AE, Marshall SW. Physical activity and public health.
>
>   JAMA 1995;274:533, 535.

13. *Article in a journal paginated by issue.* If each issue of a periodical begins with page 1 (instead of only the first issue each year), include the issue number in parentheses after the volume number.

> 13. Frederich RC. Leptin levels reflect body lipid content in mice:
>
>   evidence for diet-induced resistance to leptin action. Nat Med
>
>   1995;1(12):11-4.

14. *Article in a supplement to an issue.* Include the supplement number and the abbreviation "Suppl" in parentheses after the volume number.

> 14. Piot P, Kapita BM, Were JBO. The first decade and challenge for the
>
>   1990s. AIDS 1991;5(1 Suppl):1S-5S.

15. *Newspaper article.* Names of newspapers and magazines are not abbreviated. If the location of a newspaper is not included in its title, add that information in parentheses after the title. The date of the article is given in year-month-day form, and a three-letter abbreviation is used for the month. Because the pagination can be different in different editions, the section and column as well as the page should be identified.

> 15. Yoon CK. Clues to redwoods' mighty growth emerge in fog. New York
>
>   Times 1998 Nov 24; Sect D:1(col 1).

16. *Magazine article.* If a general-interest magazine uses volume and issue numbers, the entry can be formatted exactly like that of a journal article paginated by

issue (see example 13). If not, use the date of publication in year-month-day form; the month may be written out in full or abbreviated.

16. Menon S. Indus Valley, inc. Discover 1998 Dec:67-71.

OTHER SOURCES

17. *Conference proceedings.* The editor may be a person or an organization. If the report has a title that is different from the conference name, include it after the editor's name. After the date and location of the conference, include the publication and page information that would be included for a book.

17. World Council of Churches [WCC], editor. Report of second WCC

international consultation on AIDS and pastoral care; 1988 Dec 12-20;

Moshi, Tanzania. Geneva: WCC/Christian Commission; 1990. 237 p.

18. *Scientific or technical report.* Begin the entry with the name of the author or issuing agency. The publisher may be the sponsoring organization or government agency rather than a commercial publishing company. If there is a report number (identified with "Report nr") or a contract number (identified with "Contract nr"), include it as a separate element between the date of publication and the number of pages. End the entry with an availability statement, including the publication number, if there is one.

18. National Center for Health Statistics (US). Health, United States, 1998

with socioeconomic status and health chartbook. Hyattsville, MD:

National Center for Health Statistics; 1998. 460 p. Available from:

DHHS, Washington; PHS 98-1232.

19. *Dissertation or thesis.* After the title, specify, in square brackets, the type of document (such as "dissertation" or "MSc thesis"). As publication information, give the location and name of the institution granting the degree and the year the document was completed. Include an availability statement at the end of the entry if the document was found somewhere other than the library of the institution for which the document was written.

19. Seip D. Factors limiting woodland caribou populations and their

interrelationships with wolves and moose in southeastern British

Columbia [dissertation]. Seattle: University of Washington; 1990. 60 p.

Available from: University Microfilms, Ann Arbor, MI; AAD14-94.

20. *Audiovisual material.* The title and identification of the medium come before the name of the author or editor. The entry also includes the name of the producing company, if it is different from the publisher, and a physical description—such as

CSE

the number of cassettes, the running time, or the slide size. An availability statement and a description of accompanying materials (such as an instructor's guide or a script) may be included at the end of the entry.

> 20. Battered [videocassette]. Grant L. New York: HBO Project Knowledge;
>
> 1991. 1 videocassette: 56 min, sound, color, 1/2 in. Accompanied by:
>
> study guide. Available from: Ambrose Video Publishing, New York, NY.

ELECTRONIC SOURCES   In addition to the information that would be given for a printed book or journal article, an entry for an electronic source needs to identify the type of medium and provide enough information to enable retrieval of the document. If the document is one that can be modified or updated at any time, the date of access needs to be included in the entry.

The impending 7th edition of *Scentific Style and Format* will include many more examples of Internet citations, based on the *National Library of Medicine Recommended Formats for Bibliographic Citation*. In the meantime, a supplement dealing with Internet citations is available as a pdf file on the NLM Web site at <http://www.nlm.nih.gov/pubs/formats/internet.pdf>.

21. *Electronic journal article.* Although CSE does not require the online address, it is useful to add it to ensure that the article can be retrieved.

> 21. Pechenik JA, Wendt DE, Jarrett JN. Metamorphosis is not a new
>
> beginning. BioScience Online [serial online] 1998 Nov; 48(11):901-10.
>
> Available from: American Institute of Biological Sciences via the
>
> Internet; http://www.aibs.org/latitude/latpublications.html. Accessed
>
> 1998 Nov 17.

22. *Electronic book or monograph.*

> 22. Casey D. Primer on molecular genetics. Oak Ridge, TN: Human Genome
>
> Management Information System, Oak Ridge National Laboratory,
>
> US Dept of Energy, 1991-92 (updated 1997 June). Available from:
>
> Human Genome Project Information via the Internet; http://www.
>
> ornl.gov/hgmis/publicat/primer/intro.html. Accessed 1997 July 14.

CSE Manuscript Form

Like CMS, CSE is intended for publishers and editors of books and journals rather than for students. Because CSE deals with the content more than the form of various elements of a paper, the manuscript form described here is based on that generally recommended for college papers. Different disciplines have different specifications for research papers, however, so find out whether your instructor has any particular requirements for your papers.

In general, scientific papers have a critical-argument structure and begin with an abstract, which summarizes the contents of the paper, usually in one paragraph. Then they pose a question or hypothesis (in a section usually titled "Introduction"), present and assess evidence for and against the hypothesis, and reach a conclusion (in a section titled "Conclusion" or "Discussion and Conclusion"). Research reports (such as lab reports or reviews of the literature about a particular topic) usually also include a section titled "Methods" or "Methods and Materials." It follows the introduction and describes the way the research was done. The list of references (usually titled "References" or "Cited References") begins on a separate page after the conclusion of the paper.

MARGINS AND SPACING Leave at least one inch at the top, bottom, and sides. Double-space throughout the paper, including block quotations and the reference list.

FIRST PAGE Begin with your name, the name of the course, and the date on separate lines, each starting at the left-hand margin. Then double-space and center the title. The abstract (titled "Abstract") follows the title after two double spaces. If there is room after the abstract, the introduction can begin on the first page as well. (Some instructors prefer a separate title page; be sure to find out.)

TITLE For scientific papers, the title should be as specific as possible—without being excessively long. It should, if possible, start with the word or term representing the most important aspect of the subject paper. A subtitle can be used to describe research design (such as "A Randomized, Controlled Trial").

HEADINGS To indicate the main divisions of the paper—such as the abstract, the introduction, the conclusion, the reference list—use headings. You may also use subheadings within these divisions to indicate subtopics. Typically, the first level of heading is centered on the page, with two double spaces above it, and the second level starts at the left margin, also with two double spaces above it.

PAGE NUMBERS Page numbering starts with the first page. The numbers are typed in the upper right corner, about half an inch from the top of the page.

CSE

BLOCK QUOTATIONS A quotation that is too long to be efficiently inserted in your running text should be indented from the left margin. Do not put quotation marks around such a quotation. If the text leading into the quotation does not clearly identify the source, include a citation after the closing punctuation of the quoted material. Follow the paragraphing of the original. That is, if the original started with an indented paragraph, indent the first line of the quotation; otherwise, do not indent it. Similarly, follow the capitalization in the original. Use **ellipsis points** to indicate any omission.

ITALIC AND BOLD TYPE According to the conventions of scientific and mathematical writing, some terms are written in italics and others in bold type (such as vectors in mathematical expressions). If you are using a word processor, you can easily switch to italic or bold type. If you are using a typewriter, however, you must indicate italics by underlining the word or letter. To indicate boldface, draw a wavy line underneath the word or letter (for example, "matrix $\underset{\sim}{A}$").

Sample CSE Manuscript Pages

Following are a sample title page, text pages, and a references list for a paper in CSE format.

1″

½″

1

Eric Gerard Smith

Biology 310

3 December 1995

Predicting Parasitic Virulence through a Synthesis

of Spatial and Temporal Factors

Title centered

Abstract ◄————————————— Heading centered

Why do some parasites kill the host they depend on while others coexist with their host? Two prime factors determine parasitic virulence: the manner in which the parasite is transmitted and the evolutionary history of the parasite and its host. Parasites that are transmitted horizontally tend to be more virulent than those transmitted vertically. Parasites that colonize a new host species tend to be more virulent than parasites that have coevolved with their hosts. It used to be assumed that parasite-host interactions inevitably evolve toward lower virulence, but this assumption has been contradicted by studies showing conservation of or increase in virulence over time. The modulation of virulence in parasite-host systems can be predicted by using a model that synthesizes spatial (transmission) and temporal (evolutionary) factors.

Introduction

Why do certain parasites exhibit high levels of virulence within their host populations while others exhibit low virulence? The two prime factors most frequently cited[1,2] are evolutionary history and mode of transmission. Incongruently evolved parasite-host associations are characterized by high virulence, while

Two notes for one citation

CSE

First page.

2

Single
note

congruent evolution may result in reduced virulence[2]. Parasites
transmitted vertically (from parent to offspring) tend to be less
virulent than parasites transmitted horizontally (between unrelated
individuals of the same or different species). Studies that show an
increase in virulence during parasite-host interaction, such as
Ebert's experiment[3] with *Daphnia magna*, necessitate a synthesis
of traditionally discrete factors to predict a coevolutionary outcome.
Changes in virulence during parasite-host interaction are better
described as modulation than as increase or decrease, because the
word *modulation* implies the potential for an inclusive, predictive
paradigm for parasite-host interaction.

Scientific
terms
may be
italicized
or
underlined

Methods

Evolutionary history and mode of transmission will first be
considered separately in this paper and then integrated by means
of an equation discussed by Antia, Levin, and May[4] and a model
proposed by Childs, Mills, and Glass[5]. Transmission is defined by
host density and specific qualities of host-parasite interaction. It is
a spatial factor that gives direction to the modulation of virulence.
Evolution is a temporal factor that determines the extent of the
modulation. The selective equilibrium model gives it great potential
for accurate predictability of a broad range of parasite-host
interactions.

Conclusion

Traditional assumptions about the factors determining
parasitic strategy have been largely apocryphal, ignoring
contradictory evidence[1]. Equilibrium models synthesize the

CSE

Second page.

4

temporal (i.e., evolutionary) factors and the spatial (i.e., transmission) factors characteristic of parasite-host systems. Time is required to modulate virulence, and spatial factors, such as host density and transmission strategy, determine the direction of the modulation.

The development of an inclusive, accurate model has significance beyond theoretical biology, given the threat to human populations posed by pathogens such as HIV[10]. Mass extinctions, such as the Cretaceous event, may have resulted from parasite-host interaction[21], and sexual reproduction (i.e., recombination of genes during meiosis) may have evolved to increase resistance to parasites[22]. Parasitism constitutes an immense, if not universal, influence on the evolution of life, with far-reaching paleological and phylogenetic implications. A model that synthesizes the key factors determining parasitic virulence and can predict the entire range of evolutionary outcomes is crucial to our understanding of the history and future of species interaction.

CSE

Last page.

5

Cited References

1. Esch GW, Fernandez JC. A functional biology of parasitism: ecological and evolutionary implications. London: Chapman and Hall; 1993. Evolutionary aspects; p 231-67.

2. Toft CA, Aeschlimann A. Parasite-host associations: coexistence or conflict? Oxford: Oxford Univ Pr; 1991. Introduction, Coexistence or conflict?; p 1-12.

3. Ebert D. Virulence and local adaptation of a horizontally transmitted parasite. Science 1994;265:1084-6.

4. Antia R, Levin BR, May RM. Within-host population dynamics and the evolution and maintenance of microparasite virulence. Am Nat 1993; 144:457-72.

5. Childs JE, Mills JN, Glass GE. Rodent-borne hemorrhagic fever viruses: a special risk for mammalogists? J Mammal 1995;76:664-80.

6. Gage KL, Ostfeld RD, Olson JG. Nonviral vector-borne zoonoses associated with mammals in the United States. J Mammal 1995;76:695-715.

7. Krebs CJ. Ecology: the experimental analysis of distribution and abundance. New York: HarperCollins; 1994. Natural regulation of population size; p 322-48.

8. Hotez PJ, Pritchard DI. Hookworm infection. Sci Am 1995;272:355-6.

9. Krebs JW, Wilson ML, Childs JE. Rabies: epidemiology, prevention, and future research. J Mammal 1995;76:681-94.

CSE

Reference list first page.

Style Manuals

In addition to the styles described in detail in this section, many professional organizations publish manuals that prescribe reference formats for publications in their fields. The following list is a sampling of style manuals used in various disciplines.

CHEMISTRY: Dodd, Janet S., ed. *The ACS Style Guide: A Manual for Authors and Editors.* 2nd ed. Washington, DC: American Chemical Soc., 1997.

GEOLOGY: Bates, Robert L., Rex Buchanan, and Marla Adkins-Heljeson, eds. *Geowriting: A Guide to Writing, Editing, and Printing in Earth Science.* 5th ed. Alexandria, VA: American Geological Inst., 1995.

JOURNALISM: Goldstein, Norm, ed. *The Associated Press Stylebook and Briefing on Media Law.* Cambridge, MA: Perseus, 2000.

LAW: Columbia Law Review. *The Bluebook: A Uniform System of Citation.* 17th ed. Cambridge: Harvard Law Rev., 2000.

MATHEMATICS: American Mathematical Society. *AMS Author Handbook.* Providence: American Mathematical Soc., 1996. (Free upon request from AMS: 800/321–4267 or as a pdf file from <http://www.ams.org/books

MEDICINE: American Medical Association. *American Medical Association Manual of Style.* 9th ed. Baltimore: Williams and Wilkins, 1998.

PHYSICS: American Institute of Physics. *AIP Style Manual.* 4th ed. New York: American Inst. of Physics, 1990.

CSE

THE ALPHABETICAL ENTRIES

Note to the Reader: You will get more benefit from *Writing from A to Z* if you first read **Composing Processes**, on pages 3–21, which provides a framework for using the information in the alphabetically arranged entries. The entries are alphabetized strictly by letter, ignoring the spaces between words. For example, *a lot/a lot* follows **almost/most** and precedes **already/all ready**. Within the entries, bold type identifies terms that have their own entries; you can use these cross-references to move around in the book freely and explore a topic in as much or as little detail as you wish. As in a dictionary, the headings at the tops of the left and right pages identify the first and last entries on each two-page spread. A comprehensive index lists topics not only by the terms used in the entries but also by other terms that users may think of instead (for instance, "dots, spaced" and "periods, spaced" for **ellipsis points**).

a/an

A and *an* are indefinite **articles**; *indefinite* indicates that whatever the article points to belongs to the category named but is not a specific member of it.

> The operator dialed *a* number. [Not a specific number but just some number. Contrast "The operator dialed *the* number"; the definite article, *the*, indicates that a specific number is referred to.]

The *sound* (not the letter) that follows *a* or *an* determines which should be used: Use *an* before vowel sounds (the sounds of *a, e, i, o,* or *u*); use *a* before any consonant sound.

> The film's plot is summarized in *a* one-page review. [Say the word *one* aloud; the first *sound* is that of a consonant, *w* (as in *won*), even though the first letter is a vowel, *o*.]

> He arrived *an* hour early. [Although the *h* in *hour* is a consonant, the *h* is silent, and the word begins with a vowel sound.]

> It was *a* historic event. [The consonant *h* is pronounced, so *a* precedes the consonant sound.]

> *An* unexpected scholarship offered Carlos *a* unique opportunity. [*Unexpected* begins with a vowel sound (*u*); *unique* begins with a consonant sound (*y*).]

> He bought *an* SLR camera. [The letter *S* is here pronounced *ess*, which begins with a vowel sound.]

> *A* sonar operator detected the wreck. [*Sonar* begins with a consonant sound.]

abbreviations

Like symbols, abbreviations—shortened forms of words or phrases—are especially useful in tables, bibliographies, and other places where space is at a premium. In most text, however, keep abbreviations to a minimum, except for those commonly used with dates or figures (for instance, *A.D.* 735, 11:15 *a.m.*) and those for titles conventionally abbreviated when they appear with names (*Mr. Bruce Lee, Jr.; Dr. Anna Cortez* or *Anna Cortez, M.D.; Ms. Adams*). Abbreviate the names of organizations and other terms only if you are sure that all your readers will understand the abbreviations readily. A good rule of thumb: When in doubt, spell it out.

Except for commonly used abbreviations (*U.S., a.m.*), spell out a term the first time you use it, and give its abbreviation in parentheses. Thereafter, you can use the abbreviation alone.

> The National Aeronautics and Space Administration (NASA) has accomplished much in its short history. But is NASA worth what it costs?

Punctuation and Capitalization

Usage of **periods** and of **capital letters** with abbreviations varies; check current practice for specific abbreviations in an up-to-date dictionary. Note also that various professional organizations, such as the Modern Language Association of America (MLA) and the American Psychological Association (APA), have their own preferred forms of abbreviation. For bibliographic information on various association style guides, see **Research Processes,** pages 61, 99, 114–15, 139, and 153.

Do not divide and hyphenate an abbreviation at the end of a line.

Do not add a **period** at the end of a sentence that ends with an abbreviation that uses a final period.

> The official name of the company is Data Base, Inc. [not Inc..]

Acronyms and Initialisms

An acronym is an abbreviation pronounced as a word (usually formed by combining the first, and sometimes other, letters of several words).

AIDS	Acquired Immunodeficiency Syndrome
NATO	North Atlantic Treaty Organization
RAM	random-access memory
ROM	read-only memory

An initialism is formed in the same way as an acronym and, like an acronym, is used as a name for the thing it stands for, but its letters are individually pronounced.

FTP	file transfer protocol
FBI	Federal Bureau of Investigation
CIA	Central Intelligence Agency
CPR	cardiopulmonary resuscitation

Acronyms and initialisms follow most of the same rules. They are written without periods and in capital letters (unless they have been fully integrated into the language as common nouns—for example, *radar, sonar, scuba, laser*—in which case they are no longer thought of as abbreviations and they follow the same rules as any other words). If in doubt, consult a dictionary.

Form the plurals of acronyms or initialisms by adding an *-s*, with or without an **apostrophe** (but be consistent).

CDs or CD's   VCRs or VCR's

Measurements

Here are some common abbreviations for units of measurement. Except for abbreviations such as *in.* (inch), which could be misread as a word (*in*), most abbreviations of measurements do not require periods. If in doubt, consult a dictionary or the style guide for the academic discipline in which you are writing.

In college writing, do not abbreviate measurements except in tables or graphs.

bu	bushel		F	Fahrenheit
C	Centigrade, Celsius		ft	foot, feet
cal	calorie		gal.	gallon
cm	centimeter		hp	horsepower
doz	dozen		hr	hour

in.	inch	qt	quart
KB	kilobyte	rpm	revolutions per minute
km	kilometer	sec	second
lb	pound	T	tablespoon
m	meter	tsp	teaspoon
min	minute	yd	yard
oz	ounce	yr	year
pt	pint		

The plural of abbreviations of units of measurement is usually the same as the singular: 1 *cm* and 3 *cm* (not 3 *cms*).

Personal Names and Titles

Personal names generally should not be abbreviated.

Charles	*Thomas*	*William*	*George*
~~Chas.~~	~~Thos.~~	~~Wm.~~	~~Geo.~~
∧	∧	∧	∧

Spell out an academic, civil, religious, or military title when it does not precede a proper name.

doctor
The ~~Dr.~~ was surprised by the patient's temperature.
∧

When preceding a name, some (but not all) titles are customarily abbreviated. (See also **Ms./Miss/Mrs.**)

Dr. Smith   Mr. Mills   Ms. Katz

An abbreviation of a title may follow the name; however, it should not duplicate a title before the name.

Dr. William Smith~~, Ph.D.~~

OR   ~~Dr.~~ William Smith, Ph.D.

When addressing **letters** and including names in other documents, normally spell out titles that precede a name (exceptions: *Mr., Mrs., Ms., Dr.*):

Professor Charles Matlin

Captain Juan Ramirez

The Honorable Mary J. Holt

The Reverend James MacIntosh

The following list gives common abbreviations for personal and professional titles. Where alternative forms are given with a **slash** between them, the first is the one recommended by the Modern Language Association of America (MLA).

Atty.	Attorney
BA/B.A.	Bachelor of Arts
BS/B.S.	Bachelor of Science
Capt.	Captain
Col.	Colonel
CPA/C.P.A.	Certified Public Accountant
DA/D.A.	Doctor of Arts
DD/D.D.	Doctor of Divinity
DDS/D.D.S.	Doctor of Dental Science (or Surgery)
Dir.	Director
Dr.	Doctor (used with any doctor's degree)
Drs.	Plural of Dr.
EdD/Ed.D.	Doctor of Education
Esq.	Esquire (used after a lawyer's name)
Hon.	Honorable
JD/J.D.	Doctor of Law (Latin *Juris Doctor*)
Jr.	Junior (spelled out only in formal contexts, such as formal invitations)
LLB/LL.B.	Bachelor of Laws
LLD/LL.D.	Doctor of Laws
Lt.	Lieutenant
MA/M.A.	Master of Arts
MBA/M.B.A.	Master of Business Administration
MD/M.D.	Doctor of Medicine (Latin *Medicinae Doctor*)
Messrs.	Plural of Mr. (French *Messieurs*)
Mmes.	Plural of Mrs. (French *Mesdames*)
Mr.	Mister (spelled out only in formal contexts, such as formal invitations)
Mrs.	Married woman (abbreviation for Mistress)
Ms.	Woman of unspecified marital status
MS/M.S.	Master of Science
Msgr.	Monsignor
PhD/Ph.D.	Doctor of Philosophy

Prof.	Professor
Rep.	Representative
Rev.	Reverend
RN/R.N.	Registered Nurse
Sen.	Senator
Sgt.	Sergeant
Sr.	Senior (spelled out only in formal contexts, such as formal invitations)
St.	Saint

Company Names

Many companies include in their names such terms as *Brothers, Incorporated, Corporation*, and *Company*. If these terms appear as abbreviations in the official company names, use the abbreviated forms: *Bros., Inc., Corp.*, and *Co.* If such terms are not abbreviated in the official names, spell them out.

Similarly, use the **ampersand** (&) only if it appears in the official company name. (Note: The ampersand is not used in MLA style.)

Only when space is limited should you abbreviate titles of organizational units such as Department (*Dept.*) and Division (*Div.*).

Other Terms When in Parentheses, Tabular Material, or Documentation

When used within regular text, most words should be spelled out. However, the following abbreviations may be used to conserve space in material in parentheses, tabular material, or documentation.

abbr.	abbreviation
acad.	academy
adapt.	adapted by, adaptation
anon.	anonymous
app.	appendix
assn.	association
assoc.	associate, associated
attrib.	attributed to
aux.	auxiliary
b.	born
bk. or bks.	book or books
c., ca.	around this date (Latin *circa*)

cf.	compare (Latin *confer*)
ch. or chs.	chapter or chapters
col.	column
comp.	compiled by
cond.	conducted by, conductor
contd.	continued
d.	died
dept.	department
div.	division
ed.; eds.	editor, edited by, edition; editors, editions
e.g.	for example (Latin *exempli gratia*)
e-mail or E-mail	electronic mail
esp.	especially
et al.	and others (Latin *et alia*)
etc.	and so forth (Latin *et cetera*)
ex.	example
fig.	figure
fr.	from
fwd.	foreword, foreword by
govt.	government
hist.	history, historian, historical
i.e.	that is (Latin *id est*)
illus.	illustrated by, illustrator, illustration
inc.; Inc.	including; Incorporated
inst.	institution
intl.	international
introd.	introduced (or introduction) by
irreg.	irregular
misc.	miscellaneous
ms. or mss.	manuscript or manuscripts
narr.	narrator, narrated by
natl.	national
NB/N.B.	take note (Latin *nota bene*)
n.d.	no publication date
no.	number
n.p.	no publisher or no place (city)

n. pag.	no pagination
orig.	original, originally
p. or pp.	page or pages
par.	paragraph
PS/P.S.	postscript
pseud.	pseudonym
pub., publ.	published by, publisher, publication
qtd.	quoted
reg.	registered, regular
rept.	reported, reported by
rev.	revised, revised by, revision, review
rpt.	reprint, reprinted by
sec., sect.	section
soc.	society
supp. or supps.	supplement or supplements
trans.	translator, translated by
vol. or vols.	volume or volumes

Courses of Study

Avoid **clipped forms** (such as *poli sci, psych, soc,* and *econ*) for courses of study.

$$\text{composition} \qquad\qquad\qquad \text{economics}_\odot$$

I enjoyed freshman ~~comp~~ but thought I might fail ~~econ.~~

Geographical Locations

Generally, in text, spell out names of cities and countries (except for long multiword names such as *United States of America,* which is abbreviated *U.S.* as an adjective) and other place names. Spelling out such names avoids possible misunderstanding and makes reading easier. The following list includes geographical abbreviations often used in addresses.

Ave.	Avenue	N.E., NE	Northeast
Blvd.	Boulevard	St.	Street
Ct.	Court	S.W., SW	Southwest
Dr.	Drive		

Postal Abbreviations

The U.S. Postal Service specifies the following abbreviations for states and protectorates in postal addresses.

Alabama	AL	Montana	MT
Alaska	AK	Nebraska	NE
Arizona	AZ	Nevada	NV
Arkansas	AR	New Hampshire	NH
California	CA	New Jersey	NJ
Colorado	CO	New Mexico	NM
Connecticut	CT	New York	NY
Delaware	DE	North Carolina	NC
District of Columbia	DC	North Dakota	ND
Florida	FL	Ohio	OH
Georgia	GA	Oklahoma	OK
Guam	GU	Oregon	OR
Hawaii	HI	Pennsylvania	PA
Idaho	ID	Puerto Rico	PR
Illinois	IL	Rhode Island	RI
Indiana	IN	South Carolina	SC
Iowa	IA	South Dakota	SD
Kansas	KS	Tennessee	TN
Kentucky	KY	Texas	TX
Louisiana	LA	Utah	UT
Maine	ME	Vermont	VT
Maryland	MD	Virginia	VA
Massachusetts	MA	Virgin Islands	VI
Michigan	MI	Washington	WA
Minnesota	MN	West Virginia	WV
Mississippi	MS	Wisconsin	WI
Missouri	MO	Wyoming	WY

The names of the Canadian provinces and territories are abbreviated as follows. (The first abbreviation given for each is the one specified by the U.S. Postal Service.)

Alberta	AB or Alta.
British Columbia	BC or B.C.

Manitoba	MB or Man.
New Brunswick	NB or N.B.
Newfoundland	NF or Nfld.
Northwest Territories	NT or NWT
Nova Scotia	NS or N.S.
Ontario	ON or Ont.
Prince Edward Island	PE or PEI
Quebec	PQ or Que.
Saskatchewan	SA or Sask.
Yukon Territory	YT

Dates and Time

The following abbreviations for periods of time are normally used in formal writing. Other words denoting units of time (for instance, *second, minute, week, month, year, century*) should be spelled out.

AD/A.D.	*anno Domini* [after the beginning of calendar time; used before numerals—*A.D. 1790*]
BC/B.C.	before Christ [before the beginning of calendar time; used after numerals—*647 B.C.*]
BCE/B.C.E.	before the common era [used instead of B.C. by writers who consider B.C.E. religiously neutral]
CE/C.E.	common era [used instead of A.D.]
a.m./A.M.	*ante meridiem* (before noon)
p.m./P.M.	*post meridiem* (after noon)
EST/E.S.T.	Eastern Standard Time

Months and Days

Abbreviate months and days only in documentation and in tables and graphs.

MONTHS

January	Jan.	July	[not abbreviated]
February	Feb.	August	Aug.
March	Mar.	September	Sep. or Sept.
April	Apr.	October	Oct.
May	[not abbreviated]	November	Nov.
June	[not abbreviated]	December	Dec.

DAYS

Monday	Mon.	Friday	Fri.
Tuesday	Tues.	Saturday	Sat.
Wednesday	Wed.	Sunday	Sun.
Thursday	Thurs.		

above

Avoid using *above* to refer to a preceding passage unless the reference is clear. The same is true of *aforesaid, aforementioned, the former,* and *the latter,* which not only risk vagueness but also contribute to a heavy, wooden style. To refer to something previously mentioned, either repeat the **noun** or **pronoun** or construct your paragraph so that your reference is obvious. (See also *former/ latter.*)

Please fill out and submit ~~the above~~ *your time card* by March 1.

absolute phrases

An absolute **phrase** modifies a whole sentence rather than a word or part of a sentence. It usually consists of a **noun** or **pronoun** plus a **participle** or **participial phrase**.

The line being all the way around the block, we decided to see the movie tomorrow.

absolute words

Absolute words (such as *perfect, dead, unique,* and *infinite*) are adjectives or adverbs that cannot logically be compared (used with *more, most, less,* or *least*). However, the comparative and superlative forms are sometimes used in **informal writing**.

The new CD players produce a ~~more perfect~~ *better* sound than the best cassette

players.

Her new song was more ~~unique~~ *unusual* than I had expected.

OR   To my surprise, her new song was *unique.*

abstracts

An abstract briefly summarizes the major points of a longer piece of writing, usually in language similar to that of the piece. Its primary purpose is to enable readers to decide whether to read the work in full. Abstracts are written for many formal reports, some journal articles (especially in the natural and social sciences), and most dissertations, as well as for other long works. Because a long abstract defeats its purpose, abstracts are usually no more than 200 words and may be much shorter. For example, abstracts for articles published in American Psychological Association (APA) journals are limited to 120 words.

Besides accompanying the material being summarized, abstracts may also be collected in periodical indexes, which are often retrievable by computer. These indexes may be directed to a general audience (such as *Dissertation Abstracts International*) or a specific audience (such as *Historical Abstracts*). (See also **Research Processes,** pages 35–60.)

ABSTRACT
Do parents have any important long-term effects on the development of their child's personality? This article examines the evidence and concludes that the answer is no. A new theory of development is proposed: that socialization is context-specific and that outside-the-home socialization takes place in the peer groups of childhood and adolescence. Intra- and intergroup processes, not dyadic relationships, are responsible for the transmission of culture and for environmental modification of children's personality characteristics. The universality of children's groups explains why development is not derailed by the wide variations in parental behavior found within and between societies.

> —abstract of JUDITH RICH HARRIS, "Where Is the Child's Environment? A Group Socialization Theory of Development"

abstract words/concrete words

Abstract words refer to concepts, ideas that cannot be discerned by the five senses. Concrete words create sensory images.

ABSTRACT   work, courage, kind, idealistic, love, go
CONCRETE   scissors, golden, icy, shuffle, stumble

Good writing often uses concrete words to illustrate an idea expressed in abstract words.

> Real (as I will call vine-ripened, soft-walled, acid-flavored, summer-grown) tomatoes are an article of faith, a rallying point for the morally serious, a grail.
> —RAYMOND SOKOLOV, "The Dark Side of Tomatoes"

academic writing

Most academic writing (e.g., abstracts, lab reports, annotated bibliographies, and research proposals) uses standard, written English and presents an informed argument for the general purpose of constructing knowledge. It therefore states a thesis, supports it with evidence (usually gathered by research), and documents all sources. (See also **credibility, documentation, plagiarism, Research Processes.**)

accept/except

Accept, a **verb**, means "receive willingly," "recognize as true," or "agree to undertake."

> Jason *accepts* the premise of the article.
>
> Ginga *accepted* her second job offer.

Except can be a **preposition** meaning "with the exclusion of" or a verb meaning "leave out."

> Everyone met the requirements *except* John. [preposition]
>
> We cannot *except* John from the requirements. [verb]

acceptance letters (See **letters**.)

acknowledging sources (See **Research Processes**, pages 29–34, 46–48, 60–152.)

active voice

In most contexts, choose the active **voice** because it is clearer, more emphatic, and less wordy than the **passive voice**. Active constructions clarify who is performing the action.

> PASSIVE   Election results *are* often *determined* by a small number of voters.
>
> ACTIVE   A small number of voters often *determine* election results.

In some contexts, however, the passive voice is preferable precisely because it deflects attention from the actor.

> Smoking *is prohibited.* [Contrast, for instance, "The management *prohibits* smoking" (active voice).]

A **shift** between active and passive voice in a sentence can be awkward.

> *you have written*
> After your paper ~~has been written~~, reread it for errors in spelling and grammar.
> ⋀

(See also **verbs**.)

adapt/adopt/adept

Adapt, a **verb**, means to "make fit by modification." *Adopt,* also a verb, means to "take voluntarily as one's own" or to "take up and practice."

Jasmine had to *adapt* the new generator to her old engine.

The school board *adopted* the principles set forth by the steering committee.

Adept, an **adjective**, means "thoroughly proficient."

Myron is an *adept* public relations official.

addresses (in text)

For the format of addresses in letters and on envelopes, see **letters.** In text, all items in addresses except the zip code are set off by commas. Do not use a comma within street numbers or in zip codes.

Please send all UPS parcels to my office at 1591 Broadway, New York, NY 10019.

Numbered street names through ten are usually written out.

156 *Fifth* Avenue

BUT   1137 *86th* Court, S.W.

In text, do not abbreviate such words as *street, avenue,* and *suite.* U.S. Postal Service abbreviations for state names are listed under **abbreviations.**

ad hominem fallacy   (See **logic.**)

adjective clauses

An adjective **clause** is a grammatically related sequence of words that includes both a **subject** and a **predicate** and functions as an adjective. Adjective clauses modify a noun or pronoun, which they usually follow. Most adjective clauses begin with a **relative pronoun** (*that, which, who, whom, whose*), but they may also begin with *when, where,* or *why.*

Sam's dream was to open a store *that specialized in comic books.* [The italicized adjective clause modifies *store.*]

That's the school *where I went to second and third grades.* [The italicized adjective clause modifies *school.*]

Adjective clauses can modify nouns and pronouns in all common noun positions: subject, subject complement, and object.

The photography exhibit *that caused so much controversy* is now at the Vought Gallery. [The adjective clause modifies the subject, *exhibit.*]

I have not seen the picture *that caused so much controversy.* [The adjective clause modifies the direct object, *picture.*]

I gave my neighbor, *whose daughter studies art,* a copy of the program guide. [The adjective clause modifies the indirect object, *neighbor.*]

There are several excellent reproductions in the program *that I gave you.* [The adjective clause modifies the object, *program,* of a preposition, *in.*]

The best picture is a self-portrait *that the artist did in 1983.* [The adjective clause modifies the subject complement, *self-portrait.*]

The relative pronoun *that* often can be omitted.

The picture [*that*] I liked best was a portrait of the artist's mother.

(See also **dependent-clause errors.**)

adjectives

An adjective modifies a **noun** or **pronoun.** Descriptive adjectives identify a quality of a noun or pronoun. Limiting adjectives impose boundaries on the noun or pronoun.

a *spicy* novel [descriptive]

the *other* cassette [limiting]

these boots [limiting]

Limiting adjectives include the **articles** *a, an,* and *the;* **demonstrative adjectives** (*this* book, *those* crackers); possessive adjectives (*my* book, *our* picnic); interrogative adjectives (*whose* book, *which* day, *what* idea); numerical adjectives (*two* books, *first* date); and indefinite adjectives (*all* books, *some* roads, *any* ideas).

Placement of Adjectives

An adjective may appear before the noun it modifies or after a **linking verb:** a form of *be* or a word such as *appear, seem, look, touch, feel, taste, become, grow,* or *turn.*

The *small* jobs are given low priority.

No job is too *small.*

An adjective after a linking verb is called a *predicate adjective*. It can modify the subject of the verb (in which case, it is a **subject complement**), or it can modify a **direct object** (in which case it is an **object complement**).

> The auditorium is *full*. [subject complement]
>
> I feel *sorry* for him. [subject complement]
>
> The lack of a raise rendered the promotion *meaningless*. [object complement]

Because some verbs can function both as linking verbs (which are followed by predicate adjectives) and as action verbs (which are modified by adverbs), writers are sometimes confused about which type of modifier to use. If the subject of the verb is to be modified, use an adjective; if the action of the verb is to be modified, use an adverb.

> I feel *bad*. [*Bad* is a predicate adjective modifying *I*, the subject of the linking verb *feel*. Compare "I *am* bad."]
>
> I feel *badly*. [*Badly* is an adverb modifying the action verb *feel*; thus, the sentence refers to an impaired sense of touch. Compare "I *swim* badly."]

(For more on problems with placement of modifiers, see **dangling modifiers** and **misplaced modifiers**.)

Comparison of Adjectives

The *comparative* form of short adjectives adds the **suffix** -er and compares two things. The *superlative* form adds the suffix -*est* and compares three or more things.

> Dave's second film was *funnier* than the first. [comparative]
>
> Dave's third film was the *funniest* of the three. [superlative]

However, many two-syllable adjectives and most adjectives of three or more syllables are made comparative by inserting *more* (or *less*) in front of them and made superlative by inserting *most* (or *least*).

> The weather will be *more* favorable for sailing on the weekend than today. [comparative]
>
> The weather will be *most* favorable for sailing on Sunday. [superlative]

ADJECTIVES WITH IRREGULAR FORMS OF COMPARISON		
	COMPARATIVE	SUPERLATIVE
good	better	best
well	better	best

	COMPARATIVE	SUPERLATIVE
bad	worse	worst
ill	worse	worst
many	more	most
much	more	most
some	more	most
little	less	least

Do not use *more* or *most* before an adjective ending in -*er* or -*est*. Such double comparisons are redundant. For the same reason, do not add -*er* to an already comparative form or -*est* to an already superlative form.

Gina is the ~~most~~ *fastest* sprinter on the team.

Her performance gets ~~more~~ *better* all the time.

At the same time, her competition seems to get *worse~~r~~*.

She recorded her *best~~est~~* time last season.

Multiple Adjectives

When two or more descriptive adjectives modifying the same noun can be reversed and still make sense, or when they can be connected by *and* or *or,* they should be separated by commas. These adjectives are known as *coordinate adjectives.*

The coach is building a *young, energetic, creative* team.

Do not separate the final coordinate adjective from its noun with a comma.

Amelia is a *conscientious, honest, reliable~~,~~* supervisor.

When adjectives modifying the same word make sense in only one order, no commas are needed. These adjectives are known as *cumulative adjectives;* they accumulate as modifiers to form a phrase.

Lee was wearing *his old cotton tennis* hat. [*Tennis* modifies *hat; cotton* modifies *tennis hat; old* modifies *cotton tennis hat; his* modifies *old cotton tennis hat.*]

When limiting and descriptive adjectives appear together, the limiting adjectives precede the descriptive adjectives, with the **articles** usually in the first position.

> *The ten gray* cars were parked in a row. [article, limiting adjective, descriptive adjective]

In English, descriptive adjectives usually follow a particular order (although it may vary depending on intended meaning and emphasis): quality (*beautiful, priceless*), size (*huge, little*), shape (*round, flat, short*), age (*old, new*), color (*blue, white*), origin (*Swedish, Baptist*), material (*cotton, concrete*), and noun used as modifier. Strings of more than three or four adjectives are rare.

> a *beautiful old wooden doll* cradle [adjectives of quality, age, and material and a noun used as a modifier]
>
> a *huge red Persian* carpet [adjectives of size, color, and origin]

Compound Adjectives

Use a **hyphen** to connect two or more words that function as a single adjective before a noun unless the first word is an adverb ending in *-ly* or the pair of words is such a familiar term that no misreading could occur.

> Alice Walker is a *well-known* author. [typical compound adjective consisting of an adverb, *well*, plus the adjective *known*]
>
> BUT Alice Walker is a *highly regarded* author. [adverb ending in *-ly* as the first word of the compound]
>
> What color would be best for the *dining room* chairs? [familiar term that could not cause a misreading]

However, unless a compound adjective is always written with a hyphen, it should not be hyphenated when it follows the noun it modifies. (Consult a dictionary for the accepted form of a compound adjective.)

> As an author, Alice Walker is *well known.*
>
> The work is *time-consuming.* [The dictionary shows *time-consuming* written with a hyphen.]

In a series of compound adjectives, the hyphens are suspended.

> Should the package be sent by *first-, second-,* or *third-class* mail?

Three types of changes can turn nouns and verbs and their modifiers into compound adjectives. First, many modified nouns can become compound adjectives with the addition of *-ed.*

	He pitches with his *left hand.*
BECOMES	He is a *left-handed* pitcher.

Second, many modified verbs can become compound adjectives with the addition of -*ing* or -*ed.*

	The grant proposal *looked* extremely *professional.*
BECOMES	It was an extremely *professional-looking* grant proposal.

Third, when modified nouns of measurement are changed into compound adjectives, they are changed from the plural to the singular.

	Kiko's grandmother was seventy-five *years* old.
BECOMES	Kiko's seventy-five-*year*-old grandmother . . .

Nouns as Modifiers

Nouns often function as adjectives and modify other nouns, as in *potato salad, home economics, telephone book,* and *mail carrier.* Such phrases are direct and concise (contrast *mail carrier* with *person who delivers mail*). However, a long string of noun modifiers can be awkward and confusing. In the following example, some of the noun modifiers should be replaced with possessives or prepositional phrases.

CHANGE	A state college system student financial-aid guidelines overhaul is sorely needed.
TO	An overhaul of the state college system's guidelines for student financial aid is sorely needed.

advanced search

Most major search engines have an advanced search option that you can use to make your search more precise. Advanced-search features include the following:

- Word filter. You can use a template with a menu of **Boolean search** terms or phrases, such as "any of these words," "all of these words," "must include," and "must not include."
- Field limiter. You can look for a word in the text, title, **URL,** or the links on a page.
- Domain limiter. You can search for pages only in a particular domain, such as .edu or .gov.
- Language limiter. You can specify the language of the pages to be searched.

Because advanced-search features vary widely among search engines, be sure to read the instructions in the help files.

adverb clauses

Adverb clauses are whole **clauses** that function as an adverb. They usually begin with a subordinating conjunction (such as *although, as, because, before, than, that, unless, when, where,* and *why*).

> Soledad's cat always came *when it was called.* [The adverb clause modifies *came.*]
>
> *Before you answer,* think a minute. [The adverb clause modifies *think.*]

adverbs

An adverb modifies a **verb,** an **adjective,** another adverb, or an entire **clause.**

> The wrecking ball hit the building *hard.* [The adverb *hard,* modifying the verb *hit,* tells how the ball hit the building.]
>
> The graphics department used *extremely* bright colors. [The adverb *extremely* modifies the adjective *bright.*]
>
> The redesigned brake pad lasted *much* longer. [The adverb *much* modifies another adverb, *longer.*]
>
> *Surprisingly,* the machine failed. [The adverb *surprisingly* modifies an entire clause: *the machine failed.*]

Common Adverbs

Most adverbs answer one of the following questions: Where? When? How? How much? How often?

> Move the throttle *forward* slightly. [Where?]
>
> Replace the thermostat *immediately.* [When?]
>
> Add the bleach *cautiously.* [How?]
>
> Talk *less* and listen *more.* [How much?]
>
> I have worked overtime *twice* this week. [How often?]

Conjunctive Adverbs

Conjunctive adverbs function simultaneously as both **conjunctions** and **adverbs.**

> The drive to the mountain takes six hours; *consequently,* we will leave early Friday morning. [The conjunctive adverb *consequently* connects (relates) the clause before the semicolon to the clause after, which it also modifies.]

EXAMPLES OF CONJUNCTIVE ADVERBS

accordingly	furthermore	meanwhile	still
also	hence	moreover	subsequently
anyway	however	nevertheless	then
besides	incidentally	next	therefore
certainly	indeed	nonetheless	thus
consequently	instead	otherwise	
finally	likewise	similarly	

(See **conjunctive adverbs** for more information and sample sentences.)

Interrogative Adverbs

Interrogative adverbs ask questions. The most common interrogative adverbs are *where, when, why,* and *how.*

> *How* many hours did you study last week?
>
> *Where* are we going when finals are over?
>
> *Why* did you take so long to complete your homework?

Comparison of Adverbs

Most one-syllable adverbs are made comparative by adding *-er* and made superlative by adding *-est.*

> Copier A prints *darker* than copier B.
>
> Copier A prints *darkest* of the three copiers tested.

Most adverbs of two or more syllables are made comparative by inserting *more* (or *less*) in front of them and made superlative by inserting *most* (or *least*).

> Copier A runs *more smoothly* than copier B.
>
> Copier A runs *most smoothly* of all the copiers tested.

A few irregular adverbs change form to indicate comparison. Here are some examples:

	COMPARATIVE	SUPERLATIVE
well	better	best
badly	worse	worst
far	farther, further	farthest, furthest

When in doubt, check a dictionary.

Placement of Adverbs

An adverb may appear almost anywhere in a sentence, but its position may affect the meaning of the sentence. Avoid placing an adverb between two elements where it can be read ambiguously as modifying either.

> Drinking frequently causes liver damage. [Ambiguous: Does *frequently* modify the subject, *drinking*, or the verb, *causes*?]
>
> *Frequently*, drinking causes liver damage. [clear]
>
> Frequent drinking causes liver damage. [clear]

To prevent ambiguity, place adverbs of degree, such as *nearly, only, almost, just,* and *hardly,* immediately before the words they limit.

> CHANGE   Drink Alsatian Alps bottled water *only* for a week, and you'll feel better for a month.
>
> TO   Drink Alsatian Alps bottled water for *only* a week, and you'll feel better for a month.

In the first sentence, *only* could be modifying *drink*—that is, calling for a diet of nothing but Alsatian Alps water. In the second sentence, *only* unambiguously modifies *a week*. (See also **misplaced modifiers** and **squinting modifiers**.)

Depending on the emphasis desired, adverbs can often be placed either before or after the element they modify.

> The gauge dipped *suddenly*. [The placement emphasizes *suddenly*.]
>
> The gauge *suddenly* dipped. [The placement emphasizes *dipped*.]

But beware of unintentional changes of meaning when you move modifiers. Consider the following sentences, which all have different meanings simply because of the relocation of one adverb, *just*.

> He *just* bought flowers for me on Sunday. [modifies *bought* (verb)]
>
> He bought flowers *just* for me on Sunday. [modifies *for me* (prepositional phrase functioning as adverb)]

He bought flowers for me *just* on Sunday. [modifies *on Sunday* (prepositional phrase functioning as adverb)]

Although adverbs can be located in many places in a sentence, depending on the desired meaning or emphasis, normally they should not be placed between verb and object.

slowly
Ana opened ~~slowly~~ the door.
∧

OR

Ana opened the door *slowly.*

OR

Slowly, Ana opened the door.

An adverb may be placed between a helping verb and a main verb, especially if the adverb modifies only the main verb.

The alternative proposal has been *effectively* presented.

Be on guard against awkwardness, however, when you insert an adverb phrase between a helping verb and the main verb.

time and time again
This suggestion has ~~time and time again~~ been rejected.
∧

adverse/averse

Adverse, meaning "opposing," modifies inanimate things such as conditions or opinions. *Averse,* meaning "having a strong dislike (an aversion)," refers to an emotion and thus can modify only living things.

The judge's *adverse* ruling was no surprise, considering her well-known aversion to gambling. The reason she is so *averse* to gambling is not widely known, however.

advice/advise

Advice is a **noun** that means "counsel" or "suggestion."

My *advice* is to send the letter immediately.

Advise is a **verb** that means "give advice."

I *advise* you to send the letter immediately.

affect/effect

As a verb, *affect* usually means "influence or have an impact upon," but it can also mean "put on a false show of."

> The president's plan will not *affect* everyone's taxes. [meaning "influence"]
>
> Although he *affects* a French accent, he has never been out of the United States. [meaning "pretends to have"]

Affect is used as a noun only in psychology and related fields, where it refers to "an emotion or feeling" in a special, technical sense.

Effect can function either as a verb that means "bring about" or "cause" or as a noun that means "result."

> How can we best *effect* the changes that we agree are needed? [verb meaning "bring about"]
>
> What will be the *effect* of these changes on the typical wage earner? [noun meaning "consequence or result"]

agreement (grammatical)

Grammatical agreement means that units of a sentence (such as subject and verb) use the same form to show number, person, gender, or case. (See **agreement of pronouns and antecedents** and **agreement of subjects and verbs.**)

agreement of pronouns and antecedents

Gender	181
Number	182
Compound and Collective Antecedents	183

Every **pronoun** must have a clear antecedent, a **noun** (or sometimes another pronoun) to which it unmistakably refers.

> Studs
> Studs and thick treads make snow tires effective. ~~They~~ are implanted with an
>   ∧
> air gun.

> [Unclear: Which are implanted with an air gun, studs or thick treads or snow tires?]

The antiquated heating system has resulted in an equipment failure.

The heating system
~~This~~ is our most serious problem at present.
  ^

[Unclear: Which is the most serious problem, the antiquated heating system or the equipment failure?]

OR The antiquated heating system has resulted in an equipment failure.

failure
This is our most serious problem at present.
    ^

Computer scientists must constantly struggle to keep up with the profes-
                              cybernetics
sional literature because it is a dynamic field.
                          ^

[There is no noun to which the pronoun *it* could logically refer.]

OR Computer scientists must constantly struggle to keep up with the profes-
           in cybernetics
sional literature because *it* is a dynamic field.
                          ^

Using the **relative pronoun** *which* to refer to a whole clause instead of to a specific noun can be awkward and confusing. Try to avoid these constructions.

CHANGE Fred acted independently on the advice of his consultant, *which* the others thought was wrong. [Unclear: Was the fact that Fred acted independently or was the consultant's advice what the others thought was wrong?]

TO Fred acted independently on the advice of his consultant, much to the distress of the others.

Gender

A pronoun must agree with its antecedent in **gender** (masculine, feminine, or neuter).

Tina picked up *her* gym bag, and Martin picked up *his*.

STRATEGIES FOR AVOIDING GENDER BIAS

Traditionally, a masculine, singular pronoun has been used with singular antecedents whose gender is indefinite, such as *anyone, everyone, person,* and *each.* However, today many people prefer to avoid the implied sexist bias in such usage. Unless a sentence is clearly being used in an all-male or all-female context (in which case *he* or *she* may be the accurate choice), revise it in one of the following ways to include both genders. (See also **nonsexist language.**)

1. Rephrase the sentence to eliminate the gender-specific pronoun.

CHANGE	Each may stay or go as *he* chooses.
TO	Each may choose whether to stay or go.
OR	Each is free to stay or go.

2. Use the plural pronoun *they* instead of a gender-specific singular pronoun (*he* or *she*). Caution: The antecedent of *they* must also be changed to the plural; do not use a plural pronoun when the antecedent is singular (see the discussion of **number** that follows).

	They all may stay or go as *they* choose.
OR	They each may stay or go as they choose.
BUT NOT	*Each* may stay or go as *they* choose. [*Each* is singular; *they* is plural.]

Number

A pronoun must agree with its antecedent in **number** (singular or plural).

> *his or her*
> Every employee must sign ~~their~~ time card.

OR

> *All*   *s*   *s*
> ~~Every~~ employee must sign their time card.

Use singular pronouns with the antecedents *everybody, everyone, anyone, each, either, neither, sort,* and *kind* unless to do so would be illogical because the meaning is obviously plural. (See also *everybody/everyone.*)

> *his or her*
> Everyone pulled ~~their~~ share of the load. [if persons of both genders are involved]

Everyone pulled *their* share of the load. [only in an all-male context]

his ∧

Everyone pulled *their* share of the load. [only in an all-female context]

her ∧

Everyone pulled an equal share of the load. [rephrased to eliminate the plural pronoun *their*]

Compound and Collective Antecedents

A compound antecedent with its elements joined by *and* requires a plural pronoun.

Martha and Joan took *their* briefcases with *them*.

If both antecedents refer to the same person, however, use a singular pronoun.

The respected economist and author departed from *her* prepared speech.

A compound antecedent joined by *or* or *nor* is singular if both elements are singular and is plural if both elements are plural.

Neither the *cook* nor the *waiter* could do *his* job until *he* understood the new computer system.

Neither the *coaches* nor the *players* were pleased by the performance of *their* team.

When one of the antecedents connected by *or* or *nor* is singular and the other plural, the pronoun agrees with the nearer antecedent. Often, however, the result is awkward and the sentence should be rewritten.

Either the *supervisor* or the *operators* will have *their* licenses suspended. [grammatically correct but at least slightly awkward]

Either the *operators* or the *supervisor* will have *her* license suspended. [grammatically correct but very awkward]

The licenses of either the *operators* or the *supervisor* will be suspended. [rewritten to reduce awkwardness]

Collective nouns may take singular or plural pronouns, depending on meaning.

The *committee* adjourned only after *it* had deliberated for days.

The *committee* quit for the day and went to *their* homes.

agreement of subjects and verbs

A **verb** must agree in **number** (either singular or plural) with its **subject**.

> The *snow is* early this year. [A singular noun, *snow,* takes a singular verb, *is.*]

> The band's new *uniforms are* blue. [A plural noun, *uniforms,* takes a plural verb, *are.*]

In tenses that use **helping verbs,** the first helping verb is the only part of the verb that indicates singular or plural.

> The snow *has* started early this year.

> The neighbors *have* been painting their house.

Pronouns as subjects must agree with their verbs in both **number** and **person.**

> *I am* certain, although *we are* still arguing about it, that *he is* to blame. [first-person singular: *I am;* first-person plural: *we are;* third-person singular: *he is*]

Do not let intervening **phrases** and **clauses** mislead you. This problem is especially likely to occur when a plural noun falls between a singular subject and its verb.

> *One* in five of the children *has* the disease.

> The *use* of insecticides, fertilizers, and weed killers, although offering unquestionable benefits, often *results* in unfortunate side effects. [The verb, *results,* must agree with the subject of the sentence, *use,* rather than with the intervening plural nouns.]

Compound Subjects with *and*

When two or more elements are connected by *and,* the subject is usually plural and requires a plural verb.

Chemistry and accounting are both prerequisites for this position.

However, if the elements connected by *and* are thought of as a unit or refer to the same thing, the subject is regarded as singular and takes a singular verb.

Bacon and eggs is a high-cholesterol meal.

If *each* or *every* modifies the elements of a compound subject, use the singular verb.

Each man and woman *has* a patriotic duty to vote.

Every man and woman *has* a patriotic duty to vote.

Compound Subjects with *or* or *nor*

A compound subject with two or more singular elements connected by *or* or *nor* requires a singular verb.

English 1A or English 10A fulfills the requirement.

A compound subject with a singular and a plural element joined by *or* or *nor* requires that the verb agree with the element nearer to it.

Neither the office manager nor the *secretaries were* there.

BUT   Neither the secretaries nor the office *manager was* there.

Either they or *I am* going to write the report.

BUT   Either I or *they are* going to write the report.

Inverted Order (Verb before Subject)

Don't let inverted word order fool you into making an agreement error.

have
From this work ~~has~~ *come* several important *improvements.*
   ∧

[The subject of the verb is *improvements,* not *work.* Compare "Several important improvements *have come* from this work."]

Sentences beginning with *there* or *here* can also cause agreement problems because the subject follows the verb.

There *is* a *virus* in this computer. [*Virus* is the subject; therefore, it takes a singular verb, *is.*]

were
On Halloween, there ~~was~~ a *ghost,* an *astronaut,* a *witch,* and a *pirate* on our front
   ∧

steps, along with one very tired parent.

[Even though each element of the compound subject—*ghost, astronaut, witch, pirate*—is singular, the compound subject is plural and so requires a plural verb: *were*. Compare "A ghost, an astronaut, a witch, and a pirate—along with one very tired parent—*were* on our front steps."]

Flitting among the flowers [there] ~~were~~ *was* the most beautiful ruby-throated *hum-*

mingbird I had ever seen.

[In some inverted sentences, *there* is understood rather than expressed.]

Questions also typically invert the usual subject-verb order.

What *are* the three *subjects* that you like most? [Compare "The three *subjects* that you like most *are* what?"]

What *is* the one *subject* that you like most? [Compare "The one *subject* that you like most *is* what?"]

Indefinite Pronouns

Indefinite pronouns include *all, any, few, many, most,* and *some.* They are singular when they refer to a **mass noun** (*flour* in the following examples). They are plural when they refer to a **count noun** (*books* in the following examples).

All of the flour *is* mixed in next.

All of the books *need* labels.

Most of the flour *has been* contaminated.

Most of the books *are* Hank's.

None is singular with mass nouns, but either the singular or the plural is generally acceptable with count nouns.

None of the flour *is* to be used.

None of the books *are* shelved correctly.

OR   *None* of the books *is* shelved correctly.

The indefinite pronouns *each* and *one* are usually singular.

Each of these videos *has* to be catalogued.

One of the raffle tickets *was* lost.

Relative Pronouns (*who, which, that*)

A verb following a **relative pronoun** (such as *who, which,* or *that*) agrees in number with the noun to which the relative pronoun refers (its **antecedent**).

This is one of those poems *that require* careful analysis. [The relative pronoun *that* refers to *poems* (plural).]

BUT   This is a poem *that requires* careful analysis. [*That* refers to *poem* (singular).]

Collective Subjects

Collective subjects take singular verbs when the group is thought of as a unit and take plural verbs when the individuals are thought of separately. (See also **collective nouns**.)

How long *does* a *couple* wait for a marriage license in this state? [singular]

The *couple have* finally agreed on a June wedding. [plural]

The number of bridesmaids *was* six. [When the word *number* refers to a specific number, it is singular.]

A number of people *were* waiting for the announcement. [When *number* means an approximate number, it is plural.]

Subjects expressing measurement, weight, mass, or total often take singular verbs even when the subject word is plural in form. Such subjects are treated as a unit.

Four years is the normal duration of a college education.

Sixty dollars is the cost of one credit hour.

Some collective nouns, such as *trousers* and *scissors*, are always plural.

His *trousers were* torn by the machine.

BUT   A *pair* of trousers *is* on order.

Subjects with Identical Singular and Plural Forms

A few nouns, such as *series*, have the same form in both singular and plural.

A *series* of meetings *was planned*. [singular]

Two *series* of meetings *were planned*. [plural]

Singular Nouns Ending in s

Some nouns are singular in meaning though plural in form; examples are *athletics*, *mathematics*, *news*, *physics*, and *economics*. These nouns normally take a singular verb.

News of the merger *is* on page 4 of the *Chronicle*.

Economics has been called the dismal science.

Some of these nouns, however, may be either singular or plural, depending on the sense in which they are used.

> *Politics is* the refuge of both idealists and scoundrels. [singular]
>
> BUT His *politics were* far from admirable. [plural]

Subjects with a Subject Complement

Whether a **subject complement** is singular or plural does not affect the verb; the verb agrees with the subject, not the complement.

> The *topic* of his report *was* rivers. [The subject of the sentence is *topic*, not *rivers*.]
>
> The various *oceans are* really one body of water. [The subject of the sentence is *oceans*, not *body*.]

Titles

A book or other work with a plural title requires a singular verb.

> *Bartlett's Familiar Quotations was* stolen from the reference room.
>
> *The Best Years of Our Lives is* one of my favorite films.

Idioms

Some **idioms**, such as *many a,* conventionally take a singular verb, although the form may seem plural. If in doubt, consult a dictionary.

> Many a soldier *was wounded* that day.
>
> BUT Many soldiers *were wounded* that day.

agree to/agree with

When you *agree to* something, you are "giving consent."

> I *agreed to* the hours and wages my new boss proposed.

When you *agree with* something (or someone), you are "in accord" with it.

> I *agree with* the recommendations of the advisory board.

ain't

Ain't is generally considered nonstandard usage and should be avoided in writing (unless used for special effect, as in **dialogue**).

allegory

An allegory is a fictional work intended to convey its **theme** by using literary devices, such as **characterization, plot,** or **setting,** as **symbols** to represent abstract ideas.

alliteration

Alliteration is the repetition of consonant sounds, especially at the beginnings of words. Common in poetry, it is also used occasionally in prose but can easily be overdone.

> O *say* can you *see* . . . ?
> *Pearl Prynne* is a *paradox*, both *bane* and *balm* . . .

all right/alright

All right is always written as two words; *alright* is incorrect.

> *all right*○
> The car was a total loss, but the driver was ~~alright~~.

However, *all right* is informal as well as vague; try to find a more specific word or phrase.

> *not injured*○
> The car was a total loss, but the driver was ~~all right~~.

all together/altogether

All together means "collectively" or "gathered in one place."

> *All together,* the various taxes Sean pays amount to fifty percent of his income.

Altogether means "wholly" or "completely."

> Gardening stops *altogether* here in the winter.

allusion

Allusion promotes economical writing because it is a shorthand way of referring to a large body of material in a few words or explaining a new and unfamiliar idea in terms of one that is familiar. Be sure, however, that your audience is familiar with the material to which you allude. In the following example, the writer brings her point to life by alluding to a popular film hero.

I notice what's going on around me in a special way because I'm a writer. It's like radar, the keen listening and looking of Indiana Jones when he walks into the jungle loud with parrots and monkeys.

—Pat Mora, "A Letter to Gabriela, a Young Writer"

(See also **analogy** and **figures of speech**.)

almost/most

The use of *most* to mean *almost* is colloquial and should be avoided in writing (unless used for special effect, as in **dialogue**).

> New shipments arrive ~~m*o*st~~ *almost* every day.

If you can substitute *almost* for *most* in a sentence, *almost* is the word you need.

a lot/alot

The correct form is two words: *a lot*.

already/all ready

Already means "by or before a specified time."

> We had *already* mailed her present when she arrived for a visit.

All ready means "wholly prepared."

> Laurie was *all ready* for the seminar by Tuesday morning.

a.m./p.m. (or A.M./P.M.)

The abbreviation *a.m.* stands for *ante meridiem*, which means "before noon." The abbreviation *p.m.* stands for *post meridiem*, which means "after noon." These abbreviations should be used only with figures and may be written in capital or lowercase letters.

> The party is scheduled for 6:30 to 8:00 p.m.

ambiguity

Ambiguity occurs when the interpretation of a word, phrase, or passage is uncertain. Faults that can lead to ambiguous writing include **dangling modifiers**, **misplaced modifiers**, ambiguous **pronoun reference**, ambiguous coordination or juxtaposition, ambiguous **word choice**, and **incomplete comparisons**.

Sloppy dishwashing procedures caused several cases of food poisoning.

Dishwashing
~~This~~ is the most serious problem the camp has.
∧

[Ambiguous pronoun reference: Does *this* refer to dishwashing procedures or food poisoning?]

OR   Sloppy dishwashing procedures caused several cases of food poisoning. These cases are the most serious problem the camp has.

does
Sandra values privacy more than Joe.
∧

[Incomplete comparison: Without the added *does*, the sentence can mean that Sandra values privacy more than she values Joe.]

CHANGE   His hobby was cooking, and he was especially fond of cocker spaniels. [Ambiguous juxtaposition: Some transitional statement is needed to clarify the relationship between the two statements.]

TO   His hobby was cooking, *but he had many other interests as well, including dogs.* He was especially fond of cocker spaniels.

Not all
~~All~~ navigators are ~~not~~ talented in mathematics.
∧

[Misplaced modifier: The original means that no navigator is talented in mathematics.]

Ambiguity may also be caused by thoughtless word choice.

CHANGE   The management decided that employee layoffs should be reinstated. [implies that more layoffs are about to occur]

TO   The management decided that the laid-off employees should be reinstated.

American Psychological Association (APA) style (See **Research Processes,** pages 99–114.)

among/between (See *between/among.*)

amount/number

Amount is used with things thought of in bulk (**mass nouns**). *Number* is used with things that can be counted as individual items (**count nouns**).

Although the *number* of donors was large, the *amount* of money collected was not enough.

Avoid using *amount* when referring to countable items.

> I was surprised at the ~~amount~~ of errors in the report.
> ^ *number*

ampersand

The ampersand is the character (&) that stands for the word *and*. It is usually used only in the names of companies, agencies, and the like. In writing or in addresses, spell out *and* unless the ampersand is part of the official name of the organization.

> Procter & Gamble
>
> Johnson & Johnson
>
> BUT   Sears, Roebuck *and* Co.

Some styles, such as MLA, prohibit the use of ampersands. However, other styles, such as APA, allow ampersands in contexts in which space is limited, such as footnotes, reference lists, and tables.

analogy

An analogy is a comparison between similar but unrelated objects or concepts to clarify, or emphasize particular qualities of, one of them. Analogies may be brief or extended, depending on the writer's purpose. In the following paragraph, the writer uses a surprising but effective analogy to convey the feeling of trying to land a tarpon.

> The closest thing to a tarpon in the material world is the Steinway piano. The tarpon, of course, is a game fish that runs to extreme sizes, while the Steinway piano is merely an enormous musical instrument, largely wooden and manipulated by a series of keys. However, the tarpon when hooked and running reminds the angler of a piano sliding down a precipitous incline and while jumping makes cavities and explosions in the water not unlike a series of pianos falling from a great height. If the reader, then, can speculate in terms of pianos that herd and pursue mullet and are themselves shaped like exaggerated herrings, he will be a very long way toward seeing what kind of thing a tarpon is.
>
> —THOMAS MCGUANE, "The Longest Silence"

(For a discussion of false analogies, see **logic**.)

analysis as a method of development

Analysis takes a topic apart and examines or evaluates its parts to determine how they contribute to the quality of the whole. The following example analyzes the faint illumination that exists in the sky on even the darkest nights.

Although the night sky appears dark it is in fact subject to a faint illumination. This comprises the *airglow*—originating in the Earth's upper atmosphere; sunlight diffused through interplanetary space—sometimes termed *zodiacal light,* although this name is more frequently used for its more concentrated cones in the Ecliptic; *galactic light*—starlight diffused through interstellar space; and *stellar light*—direct light from faint stars invisible to the naked eye. The biggest contribution is the stellar light, especially that from stars of about the twelfth magnitude, whose numbers more than make up for their faintness.

—GILBERT E. SATTERTHWAITE, *Encyclopedia of Astronomy*

and/or

The meaning of the phrase *and/or* can usually be expressed more clearly by "____ or ____ or both."

CHANGE   An electric automobile will probably be marketed soon by Ford and/or General Motors.

TO   An electric automobile will probably be marketed soon by Ford or General Motors or both.

Often, simply *or* will convey the necessary meaning.

An electric automobile will probably be marketed soon by Ford or General Motors. [*Or both* may be clear enough in the context or may not be important.]

and etc.

Omit *and.* The abbreviation stands for *et cetera,* which means "*and* others of the same kind." One *and* is sufficient.

However, in most writing, *etc.* should be avoided altogether. (See *etc.*)

anecdote

An anecdote is a brief account of an amusing or interesting incident, used most often to illustrate a point.

He was one of the greatest scientists the world has ever known, yet if I had to convey the essence of Albert Einstein in a single word, I would choose *simplicity.* Perhaps an anecdote will help. Once, caught in a downpour, he took off his hat and held it under his coat. Asked why, he explained, with admirable logic, that the rain would damage the hat, but his hair would be none the worse for its wetting. This knack for going instinctively to the heart of a matter was the secret of his major scientific discoveries—this and his extraordinary feeling for beauty.

—BANESH HOFFMAN, "My Friend, Albert Einstein"

(For another example, see **introduction**.)

annotated bibliography

In an annotated bibliography, each entry is followed by a brief description or evaluation of the subject and scope of the work.

> Applebee, Arthur N. *Contexts for Learning to Write.* Norwood, NJ: Ablex, 1984. A description of a research study of writing instruction in U.S. secondary schools.

ante-/anti-

The **prefix** *ante-* means "prior to" or "in front of."

antecedent   antechamber   antedate

Words with *ante-* are usually spelled as one word and are not hyphenated.
    The prefix *anti-* means "opposite in kind," "opposing," or "serving to prevent."

anticlimax   antiaircraft   antiulcer

Words with *anti-* are usually spelled as one word, but they are hyphenated when *anti-* combines with a proper noun or a word beginning with *i-*.

anti-Russian   anti-inflationary

If you are not sure about the hyphen, consult a dictionary. (See also **prefixes.**)

antecedents

An antecedent is the word or group of words referred to by a **pronoun.** (See also **pronoun reference.**)

> The *poppies* look pretty in *their* new pot. [The antecedent for the pronoun *their* is *poppies.*]

A pronoun must agree in **gender** and **number** with its antecedent. (See **agreement of pronouns and antecedents.**)

> *its*
> The bookstore is having a two-day sale on ~~their~~ entire inventory of notebooks.
>
> [The pronoun, *its*, refers to the singular noun *bookstore.*]

antonyms

An antonym is a word whose meaning is opposite (or nearly opposite) that of another word.

complete/incomplete   easy/hard   hot/cold

Some word pairs that look like antonyms are not.

born/inborn   flammable/inflammable   habitation/inhabitation

If you are not sure, check a dictionary or a thesaurus, which sometimes lists antonyms as well as **synonyms.**

anxious/eager

Careful writers distinguish between *anxious*, meaning "uneasy," and *eager,* meaning "enthusiastic, having a keen interest."

> *eager*
> We were ~~anxious~~ to meet and congratulate her.
>   ^

BUT   He was *anxious* about the results of the examination, fearing that he had not done well.

anyone/any one

Anyone refers to "any person at all." *Any one* is more selective: It refers to a single member of a group.

> Is *anyone* going to the concert?
> I wouldn't go out with *any one* of those boys.

anyways/anywheres

These words are considered nonstandard. Replace them with *anyway* and *anywhere.*

APA style (See **Research Processes,** pages 99–114.)

apostrophes

The apostrophe (') is used to show possession, to mark the omission of letters or numbers, and sometimes to indicate the plural of Arabic numbers, letters, acronyms, and words referred to as words.

To Show Possession

To form the **possessive case** of most singular nouns, acronyms and initialisms, and indefinite pronouns, add an apostrophe and -*s*.

> *New York City's* atmosphere [proper noun]
> the *officer's* decision [common noun]
> *NASA's* program [acronym]

the *FBI's* budget [initialism]

someone's money [indefinite pronoun]

Coordinate and Compound Nouns To show joint possession with coordinate nouns, make only the last noun possessive.

Michelson and Morley's famous experiment on the velocity of light was made in 1887.

To show individual possession with coordinate nouns, make each noun possessive.

The difference between *Tom's* and *Mary's* test results was significant.

With compound nouns, only the last word takes the possessive form.

My *sister-in-law's* car is a red Miata.

Proper Nouns Proper nouns ending in -*s* that are not plural may form the possessive either by an apostrophe alone or by -*'s* which is the more common way today. Whichever method you choose, be consistent.

	Dickens's novels	Garth Brooks's songs
OR	Dickens' novels	Garth Brooks' songs

In names of places and institutions, the apostrophe is sometimes omitted.

Harpers Ferry	Writers Book Club	Veterans Administration

Plural Nouns Use only an apostrophe with plural nouns ending in -*s*. Use an apostrophe plus -*s* for plural nouns that do not end in -*s*.

	the *managers'* meeting	the *waitresses'* lounge
BUT	*men's* clothing	the *children's* bedroom

Possessive Pronouns The apostrophe is not used with possessive pronouns.

yours, its, his, hers, ours, whose, theirs

It's is a contraction of *it is*; *its* is the possessive form of the pronoun *it*. Be careful not to confuse the two words. (See ***its/it's.***)

It's important that the sales force meet *its* quota.

To Show Omission

An apostrophe is used to mark the omission of letters in a contraction or the omission of numbers in a year or decade.

can't	cannot
I'm	I am
I'll	I will
he'd	he would
class of '02	class of 2002

Do not confuse a contraction of a noun with the possessive form of the noun.

Steve's the new president of the student government. [contraction for *Steve is*]

Steve's supporters worked very hard to get him elected. [*Steve* plus possessive -'s]

To Form Plurals

Lowercase Letters and Abbreviations Followed by Periods Add an apostrophe and -s to show the plural of a lowercase letter or of an abbreviation ending with a period.

Her *g*'s and *q*'s were hard to tell apart.

There were too many M.D.'s and not enough nurses.

Capital Letters, Abbreviations without Periods, Numbers, Symbols, Words Referred to as Words Unless confusion could result, you may use either an apostrophe plus -s or merely -s to form the plurals of capital letters, abbreviations without periods, numbers, symbols, and words referred to as words (letters and words used as words are underlined or italicized). However, follow one practice consistently.

	two *X*s [or *X*'s]
BUT	seven *I*'s [not seven *I*s, which could cause confusion with the word *is*]
	his collection of CDs [or CD's]
	5s, 30s, two 100s [or 5's, 30's, two 100's]
	Substitute *and*s for &s. [or *and*'s for &'s]
	The sentence included five *and*s. [or *and*'s]

appeals in argumentation

An effective **argument** relies mainly on the fair presentation of evidence and appeals to reason (see **logic**), but it may also include appeals to the writer's credibility (that is, good will and authority) and appeals to the reader's emotions. All these appeals are legitimate as long as they are used responsibly and appropriately.

appendix/appendixes/appendices

An appendix is a section at the end of a paper or book that adds further information or explanation. (Either *appendixes* or *appendices* may be used as the plural form. Check with your instructor for a preference.)

An appendix can be useful for explanations that are too long for explanatory footnotes but that may be helpful to the reader seeking detailed information about points made in the report. Material appropriate for appendixes includes passages from documents and laws that reinforce or illustrate the text, long charts and tables, letters and other supporting documents, detailed supporting calculations, computer printouts of raw data, and case histories. Appendixes should not be used for miscellaneous bits and pieces of information you were unable to work into the text.

If your paper has two or more appendixes, place them in the order of their reference in the body of the paper. That is, Appendix A is the first appendix you refer to, Appendix B is the next, and so forth.

Begin each appendix on a new page, and give each appendix its own identifying label and title.

Appendix A

Data from the Sample

Identify the appendixes by letter, starting with Appendix A. Should your paper have only one appendix, simply use the label *Appendix* with the title.

List appendixes by title and page number in your table of contents.

application letters (See **letters.**)

appositives

An appositive is a **noun** or a word group functioning as a noun (a noun **phrase**) that renames another noun or word group.

> Cindy Pavelka, *a sophomore on the soccer team,* was named the most valuable player. [The appositive renames *Cindy Pavelka.*]

When an appositive provides information essential to the reader's understanding of the sentence, it is restrictive and should not be separated by commas or other punctuation from the noun or word group it refers to. (See **restrictive and nonrestrictive elements.**)

> The sophomore *Cindy Pavelka* was named the most valuable player. [Without the appositive, the reader would not be able to understand which sophomore.]

An appositive is nonrestrictive when it can be removed without undermining the meaning of the sentence.

His son, *Henry,* has inherited his curiosity. [This sentence refers to a man with only one son, so the name *Henry* is additional information but not essential to understanding the writer's meaning: "His son has inherited his curiosity."]

Nonrestrictive appositives are usually set apart from the rest of the sentence by **commas.** For emphasis, however, or for clarity when the appositives contain commas, you may set them off with **dashes.** A nonrestrictive appositive occurring at the end of a sentence may also be set off with a colon.

The police arrested him on two counts, *speeding and driving without a valid license,* and took him off to jail.

The police arrested him on three counts—*speeding, driving without a valid license, and driving under the influence*—and took him off to jail.

The police arrested him on two counts: *speeding and driving without a valid license.*

An appositive has the same grammatical function as the noun it refers to. When in doubt about the **case** of a **pronoun** in an appositive, you can check it by substituting the pronoun for the noun the appositive refers to.

My boss gave the two of us, Jim and *me,* the day off. [You would say, "My boss gave *me* the day off," not "My boss gave *I* the day off."]

argument

Argumentative writing attempts to convince the audience to adopt your point of view—or at least take it seriously. In an argument, the way you present ideas can be as important as the ideas themselves. An effective argument acknowledges and, if possible, counters conflicting points of view, at all times treating the audience's feelings and opinions with respect. Arguments may include appeals to the reader's emotions and appeals to the writer's credibility (that is, the writer's good will and authority). In college and professional writing, however, arguments rely most heavily on fair presentation of the evidence and appeals to reason, or **logic.**

When you write an argument, maintain a positive tone, and be careful not to wander from your main point, or **thesis.** Avoid **ambiguity** and trivial, irrelevant, or extravagant claims. If the audience is likely to be hostile to your thesis, consider deferring your statement of it until you have built up to it carefully with strong, specific points that support it.

arrangement of ideas (See **emphasis, subordination,** and **methods of development.**)

articles (grammatical)

The articles (*a, an,* and *the*) are considered to be **adjectives** because they modify **nouns,** either limiting them or making them more precise.

Indefinite and Definite

There are two kinds of articles, indefinite and definite. The indefinite articles are *a* and *an*. They denote an unspecified item.

> That was the first time I had run *a* program on our new computer. [The sentence does not refer to a specific program. Therefore, the article is indefinite.]

The choice between *a* and *an* depends on the sound, not the letter, following the article. (See ***a/an.***)

The definite article is *the,* which denotes a particular item.

> That was the first time I had run *the* program on our new computer. [The sentence refers to not just any program but *the* specific program. Therefore, the article is definite.]

In some texts where brevity is crucial, as in telegrams, recipes, tables, or prescriptions, articles may be omitted. As a rule, however, use articles in both formal and informal writing.

Capitalize articles only if they appear as the first word of a **sentence** or of a **title** or subtitle. (See also **capital letters.**)

> *The End of the Big Spenders: The Story of the Crash of 1929*

Articles are ignored when you are alphabetizing a list of works cited.

Usage Determined by Noun Sense

For non-native speakers of English, knowing when to use *a, an, the,* or no article before a noun can be difficult. The choice depends not only on whether the **noun** is singular or plural, count or mass, common or proper but also on whether the noun is used in a specific, nonspecific, or generic sense.

Nouns in a Specific Sense   A noun is used in a specific sense when the audience can be expected to know its identity for one of the following reasons:

1. It has been previously mentioned or is identified by a modifier.

A cat lived with us last winter. *The cat* had only three legs.

2. It refers to an experience shared by the writer and the reader.

The winter solstice was approaching.

3. It is unique in a particular context, such as a system, a location or setting, or an ordered series.

> In 1492, people believed that *the earth* was flat. [The earth is unique in the solar system.]

Misha was in *the garden*. [There is only one garden in a particular location or setting.]

Rose was *the third person* to register for the class. [Rose is the third in a series.]

The or no article should precede nouns used in a specific sense. *The* is used before specific common nouns, singular or plural, and before proper nouns that are plural; that name oceans, rivers, mountain ranges, and other geographic features; or that name regions.

The *Wall Street Journal* is widely read in New York, New Jersey, and *the Northeast* but is less popular west of *the Mississippi*.

No article is used before most other proper nouns.

When *Ed Sanchez* moved back to *Mexico*, he canceled his subscription to *Time*.

Nouns in a Nonspecific Sense   A noun is used in a nonspecific sense when the reader cannot be expected to know its identity or when its identity is not important for one of the following reasons:

1. It was not previously mentioned or is not specifically identified by a modifier.

A dog followed my daughter home from school.

2. It does not refer to an experience shared by the writer and the reader.

A winter storm was approaching.

3. It is not unique but is one among many persons, places, or things.

It was *a* dark and stormy *night*.

A, an, or no article should precede nouns that are used in a nonspecific sense. *A* or *an* is used before singular, common count nouns.

Take *a* large ceramic *bowl* and rub it with *a clove* of garlic.

Salvador Dali was *a* controversial *artist*.

No article is used before plural common nouns and mass nouns.

You can vary this recipe by adding *mushrooms*, *parsley*, or *bacon*.

Nouns in a Generic Sense   A noun is used in a generic sense when it makes a general statement that refers to one of the following:

1. An abstract concept.

Life is what you make it.

2. A category or an example of that category.

The camel is a mammal.

A car is a necessity in our fast-paced world.

The, a, an, or no article can precede nouns used in a generic sense; however, each is used slightly differently. *The* precedes a singular count noun used as the name of a class of items (especially plants, animals, or inventions).

The computer is a wonderful invention.

A or *an* is used before a singular count noun naming a member of a class of items.

A computer is a good investment for people who work at home.

No article is used before an abstract noun or before a plural noun used in a generalization.

Death and *destruction* marked the path of the hurricane.

Computers are time-saving devices.

as

Introducing a subordinate clause with *as* may cause **ambiguity.** Instead, use *because* to express a causal relationship and *while* or *when* to express a time relationship.

CHANGE	As we were having lunch together, he decided to reveal his plans. [ambiguous]
TO	*Because* we were having lunch together, he decided to reveal his plans.
OR	*While* we were having lunch together, he decided to reveal his plans.

as/like

Although in speech *like* is often used as a conjunction instead of *as* ("He thinks just *like* I do"), this usage should be avoided in all but the most informal writing. To introduce a **dependent clause** (remember that a clause includes both a subject and a verb), use the subordinating conjunction *as* (or *as if* or *as though*) instead of the preposition *like*. (For more about introducing clauses with *as,* see **as.**)

	He spoke exactly *as* I did. [The dependent clause *I did* is introduced by the subordinating conjunction *as.*]
BUT	His accent was just *like* mine. [The pronoun *mine* is the object of the preposition *like.*]

Like may be used in **elliptical constructions** that omit the verb from a clause.

> She took to architecture *like a bird to nest building.*

If the omitted portions of the elliptical construction are restored, however, *as* should be used.

> She took to architecture *as a bird takes to nest building.*

As and *like* can both function as prepositions; however, *as* expresses equivalency, and *like* expresses similarity.

> He plays chess *as* a professional. [The sentence means that he is a professional chess player.]

> He plays chess *like* a professional. [This sentence means that he plays as well as a professional but he is not one.]

audience

The first rule of effective writing is to help the audience (even if that audience will be just you—as it is for a diary or journal). You are responsible for how well your audience understands and responds to your message. Concentrate on writing for the needs of specific readers rather than merely writing about certain subjects. Remember that your audience cannot benefit from your facial expressions, voice inflections, and gestures, as listeners can when you speak.

When you are writing for a small audience, you will probably know all or many of its members. Select one person from this group and write "to" that person. When you write for a large audience, imagine a reader who is representative of the group. Whether the audience is large or small, don't try to write without writing *to* someone.

(See also **Composing Processes.**)

audiovisuals

This term refers to a wide range of communication elements that rely on our senses of sight and hearing, from photos, graphs, and illustrations to multimedia events and technology (e.g., PowerPoint or e-mail with sound added). Audiovisuals enhance the audience's experience and understanding. Papers, Web-based projects, and oral presentations can all benefit from well-chosen audio and/or visual elements.

auxiliary verbs   (See **helping verbs.**)

averse/adverse (See *adverse/averse.*)

awful/awfully

The adjective *awful*, though often used informally to mean "very bad," is (like *very bad*) too vague to be effective. Use a more concrete or specific term.

> He felt ~~awful~~ *nauseated* the next morning.

The adverb *awfully*, used to mean "very," is similarly overworked and (like *very*) should be either deleted or replaced by a more descriptive expression.

> By the end of the day I was ~~awfully tired~~ *exhausted*.

> I am ~~awfully~~ sorry.

awhile/a while

Awhile is an **adverb** and is not preceded by a **preposition**. *A while* is a **noun** phrase. It may be preceded by a preposition (usually *for* or *after*); its noun, *while*, can be modified by an adjective.

> Wait *awhile* before calling again. [The adverb *awhile* modifies the verb *wait.*]
>
> BUT Wait for *a while* before calling again. [The noun phrase *a while* is the object of the preposition *for.*]
>
> We waited for *a* long *while* before calling again. [The adjective *long* modifies the noun *while.*]

bad/badly

Bad is an **adjective**. It may precede the **noun** it modifies (a *bad* experience), or it may follow **linking verbs** such as *feel* and *look*.

> Randy felt *bad* when he realized he'd forgotten his mother's birthday.
>
> After the surgery, you will look *bad* for about a week.

Badly is an **adverb** and follows action verbs.

> He performed *badly* on the placement exam.

Badly does not follow linking verbs like *feel* and *look*. That is, saying "Jim looks badly" means literally that Jim's vision is imperfect. (See also *good/well*.)

balanced sentences

When two clauses mirror each other with **parallel structures**, the result is a balanced sentence. Two or more sentences can also be balanced against each other. Balanced sentences are a memorable way to contrast or compare two ideas.

> We must conquer war, or war will conquer us.
> —ELY CULBERTSON, *Must We Fight Russia?*

> Ask not what your country can do for you; ask what you can do for your country.
> —JOHN F. KENNEDY, inaugural address

bandwagon fallacy (See **logic**.)

because

Because is a connective that indicates cause clearly and emphatically. Other connectives indicating cause, such as *for, as,* and *since,* can sometimes be ambiguous.

> *Because*
> ~~As~~ he was banging loudly on the door, Stephanie hesitated.
>   ∧
>
> [*As* could mean *while* or *because*.]

> *Because*
> ~~Since~~ the library was closed, he couldn't complete any homework.
>   ∧
>
> [*Since* could mean *ever since* or *because*.]

For and *inasmuch as* are both more formal than *because*.

He couldn't complete his homework, ~~for~~ *because* the library was closed.

[Note that, when *for* is used as a conjunction, it must be preceded by a comma.]

Punctuating *Because* Clauses

A *because* **clause** before the main clause should be followed by a comma; but when the main clause comes first, a comma is not usually needed.

Because it was starting to snow, they decided to stay inside.

They decided to stay inside *because* it was starting to snow.

begging the question   (See **logic**.)

being as/being that

These **phrases** are considered **nonstandard English**. Replace them with *because* or *since*.

beside/besides

Although some dictionaries accept either word as a **preposition** meaning "in addition to" or "other than," most people use *besides* in this sense and *beside* only as a preposition of location meaning "next to," "apart from," or "at the side of."

Besides the two of us from the English department, three people from the chemistry department were standing *beside* the president when he presented the award.

between/among

Between is normally used to relate two items or persons.

The student union is located *between* the music building and the law library.

Among is used to refer to more than two.

Because he was so tall, she easily spotted him *among* the other guests.

between you and me

Between you and I is incorrect. Because the **pronouns** are **objects** of the **preposition** *between,* the objective form of the **personal pronoun** (*me*) must be used. (See also **case**.)

Between you and I̷, John should party less and study more.
<small>me</small>

bias/prejudice

Both words suggest a preconceived opinion about someone or something. However, *prejudice* usually means a negative opinion not based on facts, whereas *bias* may connote either a positive or a negative feeling.

> His *prejudice* against women should have disqualified him from the Supreme Court. [Because *prejudice* usually has a negative meaning, *against* is the appropriate preposition to use.]
>
> I am *biased* toward the Democratic platform; its principles parallel my own. [*Bias* can be used with *against*, *toward*, or *in favor of*, depending on the meaning.]

bibliography

A bibliography is a section at the end of a paper or a book that lists all the works (books, articles, letters, and other sources) that the author consulted. A list of works cited or a reference list includes only the works cited in the paper. These kinds of lists are more common than bibliographies in undergraduate papers. (See also **Research Processes.**)

block quotations

Occasionally, quoting a long passage or several lines of a poem directly is the best way to illustrate or support a point. Use quotations sparingly, however. Before including a quotation, consider whether **paraphrasing** or **summarizing** would work just as well.

When you use a long quotation, set it off from the rest of the text by indenting it (hence the name *block quotation*). Do not add quotation marks at the beginning or end. Reproduce all internal punctuation marks as they appear in the original. (For formats in MLA, APA, and CMS style, see **Research Processes**, pages 88–89, 90, 113, 132, 136, 148. See also **quotations**, **brackets**, and **ellipsis points.**)

Integrate quotations smoothly into the text; their purpose should be clear to the reader. A block quotation is usually introduced by a **colon** unless the context requires different **punctuation** or none at all.

bookmark

On a **Web browser**, a bookmark (called a Favorite in Internet Explorer) is a tool that lets you save electronic addresses (**URLs**) and return to them at any time.

B   Boolean search

Boolean searches of online databases use operators (such as AND, OR, and NOT) to specify the relationship among search terms. To find out which operators a search engine uses, look in its help file.

The operator AND retrieves pages in which all the search terms are present. Use AND to search for pages about the relation between two concepts. For example, to find out how stress affects vulnerability to disease, use **stress AND disease** to search for pages that contain both terms. Some search engines use a plus sign (+) immediately before the search item instead of AND: **stress +disease.** Some search engines, such as Google, use AND as the default operator, so you don't need to add it.

A few search engines also use NEAR, which is a restrictive form of AND. NEAR retrieves only pages in which the terms are within a few words of each other. To search for an exact phrase, you can enclose it in quotation marks (" ") in some search engines: **"science fiction."**

The operator OR retrieves pages in which at least one of the search terms is present. Use OR to search for synonymous or closely related terms, such as **reggae OR ska.**

The operator NOT retrieves pages in which only one of the terms is present. Use NOT (or AND NOT, depending on the search engine) to limit your search. For example, if you want to find only pages about mustang horses, use **mustang NOT ford** to exclude pages about the Ford Mustang. Some search engines use a minus sign (−) immediately before the term to be excluded instead of NOT: **mustang −ford.**

both . . . and

The construction *both . . . and* is a **correlative conjunction** that requires grammatical and logical balance.

All the houses that we looked at were *both* too expensive *and* too large.

Grammatically, *both* and *and* should be followed by the same constructions. Logically, they should be followed by similar ideas.

Children believe both ~~that~~ *in* Santa Claus ~~is real~~ and *in* monsters.

The connective phrase *as well as* should not replace *and*.

The students need *both* time to study ~~as well as~~ *and* time to play.

(See also **parallel structure**.)

brackets

Square brackets [ ] have two primary functions: to enclose explanatory words inserted in quotations and to serve as parentheses inside parentheses. In MLA style, brackets are also used around **ellipsis points** inserted in a **quotation** to mark an omission.

In Quotations

Brackets (not parentheses) are used to enclose brief explanations or additions inserted in quotations.

> Linguist Bill Bryson observes that most English speakers today "looking at a manuscript from the time of, say, the Venerable Bede [English theologian, A.D. 673–735] would be hard pressed to identify it as being in English."

Brackets around the Latin word *sic* (which means "thus" or "so") indicate that the preceding word (or phrase) is reproduced exactly as it appears in the original, even though it is obviously misspelled or misused.

> The journalist wrote that "bridal [sic] paths meander through the hills above Santa Barbara."

Do not overuse *sic*. You can usually paraphrase a quotation or quote only the part that is correct.

Use brackets when you alter the capitalization of a quotation (see **capital letters**).

In Parentheses

Use brackets instead of additional **parentheses** to set off a parenthetical item within another parenthetical item.

> We should be sure to give Emanuel Foose (and his brother Emilio [1812–82] as well) credit for his role in founding the institute.

brainstorming

Brainstorming is a form of free association used to generate ideas. To brainstorm a topic when working alone, write down whatever occurs to you, no matter how strange or irrelevant it might seem. To brainstorm a topic when working with a group, designate one person to write down the words or phrases as the group members suggest them. Brainstorming can stimulate creative thinking about a topic and reveal fresh perspectives and new connections. Other methods of generating ideas are **clustering, freewriting,** and **outlining.** (See also **Composing Processes,** pages 6–9.)

B

bullets

Bullets are large dots placed before each item in a vertical list. They are visual aids intended to catch the reader's attention. Use them to indicate the organization of the text that follows or to add emphasis to a series. (See also **lists**.)

bunch

Bunch as a **noun** means "things of the same kind" (a *bunch* of grapes). In formal writing, use *group* rather than *bunch* in reference to people. (*Bunch* as a verb means "to group together.")

> *group*
> A ~~bunch~~ of parents organized the student exchange program.
> ^

burst/bursted; bust/busted

Of all these verbs, only *burst* is standard English, appropriate in formal writing. *Bursted* is nonstandard usage; *bust* and *busted* are slang terms.

> The bubble floated across the lawn before it *burst.* [*burst* as past tense]
>
> When we returned to the gym, all the balloons we had used for decoration had *burst.* [*burst* as past participle]

business letters (See **letters**.)

buzzwords

Buzzwords are important-sounding words or phrases that, because of overuse, quickly lose their freshness and precision. They may become popular through their association with science, business, technology, or even sports. We include them in our vocabulary because they seem to give force and vitality to our language. They may be appropriate in technical writing, but in writing for a general audience they sound pretentious. Some current examples are *bottom line, counterproductive, cutting edge, dialogue* (as a verb), *feedback, input, interface* (as a verb), *multitask, no-brainer, outsourcing, parameter, state of the art,* and *world-class* (as an adjective). (See also **jargon**.)

> *confer*
> We need to ~~interface~~ with Multimedia Services.
> ^

call numbers (See **Research Processes**, pages 52–53.)

can/may

Can refers to capability, and *may* refers to possibility or permission.

> I *can* be in Boston for the Marathon. [capability]
>
> I *may* be in Boston for the Marathon. [possibility]
>
> *May* I take a week's vacation to train for the Marathon? [permission]

capital/capitol

Capital means "city serving as a seat of government," "accumulated goods," or "net worth." *Capitol* means "building in which a state legislative body meets," and, in this sense, it is written with a lowercase *c*. When *Capitol* refers to the building in which the U.S. Congress meets, it is capitalized.

capital letters

Capital letters (also called *uppercase letters*) begin certain words, such as **proper nouns,** most words in titles, and the first word of a sentence. The following pages explain general principles of capitalization, but if you are in doubt about a particular word or phrase (*French fries* or *french fries*?) consult a dictionary.

Proper Nouns and Their Derivatives

Proper nouns designate a specific person, place, or thing and are capitalized. Common nouns, which name a general class or category, are not capitalized.

PROPER NOUNS	COMMON NOUNS
President George Bush	a president, the presidency
America, American	a country, a citizen
the White House	a house
the *Queen Elizabeth II*	a ship
the University of Missouri	a university
Christmas	a holiday
January	a month
Dockers	pants
Judaism	a religion
God	a god

Adjectives, nouns, and verbs derived from proper nouns are capitalized.

Balkanize	Jacksonian	Palestinian	Reaganomics

When proper nouns and their derivatives become names for a general class, they are no longer capitalized. Some examples are *titanic, thermos, mimeograph*, and *nylon*. Some proper nouns today are in transition to common nouns (*Teflon/teflon, Levi's/levis*), and dictionaries often show both the capital and the lowercase versions.

People and Groups   Capitalize personal names and nicknames.

Spike Lee	Bill Murray	Susan Sarandon	Sammy Sosa	Amy Tan

Capitalize names of ethnic groups and nationalities and their languages.

African American	Chinese	Latino	Russian

Personal, Professional, and Job Titles   Titles preceding proper names are capitalized.

Dr. Schreiner	Mrs. Lindblad	Sister Mary Catherine

Appositives following proper names are not normally capitalized. (The word *President* is sometimes capitalized when it refers to the chief executive of a national government.)

Joan Kelly Horn defeated Jack Buechner, our former *senator.*

The only exception is an appositive that acts as part of the name.

Catherine the Great   Conan the Barbarian

Capitalize words designating family relationships only when they are part of a proper name or substitute for one.

My favorite shopping partner is my *sister* Mary. [Here, *sister* is a common noun, not part of a name.]

One Christmas we wrote poems about *Aunt* Alice, our dead *aunt.*

The twins thought the poems were funny, but *Mother* disapproved.

The twins thought the poems were funny, but my *mother* disapproved.

Places Capitalize the names of places and geographic regions.

Africa	the Azores	Clark County
Manitoba	St. Louis	Utah

Do not capitalize geographic features unless they are part of a proper name.

He was fond of the *northern part* of Indiana, particularly the *Dunes* area. [part of the proper name *Indiana Dunes National Lakeshore*]

The words *north, south, east,* and *west* are capitalized when they refer to sections of the country. They are not capitalized when they refer to directions.

I may travel *south* this winter.

The *South* may decide next year's election.

Institutions and Organizations Capitalize the names of institutions, organizations, and companies.

Apple Computers	Boston Red Sox	Congress
House Judiciary Committee	Red Cross	United Church of Christ
Urban League		

An organization usually capitalizes the formal names of its internal divisions and departments.

Consumer Products Division   Department of Defense   Faculty Senate

Types of institutions, organizations, and divisions are not capitalized unless they are part of an official name.

Although my thesis adviser was in the *Department of History,* I had a double major in *history* and economics.

When I was in college, I joined *Alpha Sigma Alpha,* a social *sorority.*

I attended *high school* in Webster Groves.

C

Trade Names Capitalize the trademark names of specific brands of products. If you are not sure whether a term is a trademark, consult a dictionary.

Apple Macintosh	Bic	Honda
Reebok	Saran Wrap	Scotch tape

Historical Events and Documents Capitalize historical events, periods, and documents.

the Bill of Rights	the French Revolution	the Iron Age
the Mayflower Compact	the Renaissance	World War II

Religious Terms Capitalize the names of religions, their followers, holy books, and holy days.

Buddhism	Christianity	Islam	Judaism
Catholic	Hindu	Jew	Protestant
the Bible	the Book of Mormon	the Koran	the Talmud
Easter	Passover	Ramadan	

The word *Bible* is capitalized when it refers to the book of scriptures; otherwise, it is not capitalized. (Note that it is not italicized, unlike most book titles. Also note that the adjective *biblical* is not capitalized even when it refers to the Bible.)

My mother goes to church and reads the Bible regularly.

My brother stays home; his bible is *Sports Illustrated.*

Our history course covers *biblical* times.

Names of deities are capitalized.

The Muslims' god is *Allah.* [When *god* is a common noun, it is not capitalized.]

Capitalization of pronouns referring to God is optional, but it is common in religious writing and when confusion about antecedents is possible.

The minister spoke of God and all *His* blessings.

Days of the Week, Months, Holidays Capitalize days of the week, months, and holidays.

Thanksgiving	New Year's Day	December	Tuesday

Do not capitalize seasons of the year.

summer	fall	winter	spring

Scientific Terms Capitalize scientific names of orders, classes, families, and genera, but do not capitalize species or English derivatives of scientific names. (Note also that genera and species are italicized.)

> butterfly, Lepidoptera, lepidopterist [common name, order, English derivative]
>
> *Homo sapiens* [genus: *Homo;* species: *sapiens*]

Capitalize the names of stars, constellations, and planets.

> the Big Dipper   Cassiopeia   Mercury   Pluto

Capitalize *earth* only when it is used as an astronomical term.

> Where on *earth* have you been?
>
> The two planets closest to *Earth* are Mars and Venus.

Abbreviations and Acronyms Capitalize **abbreviations** and acronyms if the words they stand for are capitalized. (There are some exceptions. Consult a dictionary.)

> I.U. (Indiana University)   NASA (National Aeronautics and
>
> in. (inch)   Space Administration)
>
>   radar (radio detecting and ranging)

Titles and Subtitles

Capitalize the initial letter of the first and last words of the title and subtitle of books, articles, essays, plays, films, television programs, musical compositions, records, compact discs, and cassettes. Capitalize all other words in the title except **articles** (*a, an, the*), coordinating **conjunctions** (*and, but, or, nor, for, so, yet*), short **prepositions** (*at, in, on, of*), and the *to* in **infinitives**. Style guides in particular disciplines may have slightly different capitalization conventions; for example, MLA style uses lowercase for all prepositions, regardless of length.

> *Connections: A Multicultural Reader for Writers*
>
> *Winning through Intimidation* [MLA style]
>
> *Through the Looking Glass*

In titles of poems and songs that consist of the first line of the work, follow the capitalization of the line.

> "There's a certain Slant of light" is one of Emily Dickinson's most famous poems.

Hyphenated Compounds

In hyphenated compounds, capitalize all words that would be capitalized without the hyphens.

> "Bait-and-Switch Advertising: Consumers Beware!"
>
> *The Four-Gated City*

Sentences

The first word in a sentence is always capitalized.

> *Whenever* I see you, I have a good time.

The first word of a complete sentence in **quotation marks** is capitalized.

> He announced, "*When* I arrive, we will begin."

A complete sentence enclosed in **dashes, brackets,** or **parentheses** is not capitalized when it is part of another sentence.

> I can't wait to see the new summer movies (last year's were bombs).
>
> I can't wait to see the new summer movies. (Last year's were bombs.)

Capitalization of a question embedded in a sentence but not quoted is optional, but be consistent.

> The issue is, *What* [or *what*] is the university's role in environmental protection?

Capitalization of an independent clause after a **colon** is optional, but be consistent.

> We had to keep working for one reason: *The* [or *the*] deadline was upon us.

If a series of sentences follows a colon, the first word of each one is usually capitalized. If the questions are only a word or phrase, capitalization is optional.

> Today's meeting will deal with two questions: *What* is the university's role in environmental protection? *What* is the university's role in the community?
>
> I have only three questions: *when? where?* and *why?*

Quotations

When you are quoting written material, follow the capitalization of the original or enclose the changed letter in **brackets** to indicate that you have altered the source. Often, you can avoid altering the capitalization by quoting only part of a sentence or passage. (See also **quotations.**)

"Writing is a way of finding out how I feel about anything and everything," explains Pat Mora.

Pat Mora explains that "[w]riting is a way of finding out how I feel about anything and everything."

Pat Mora describes writing as "a way of finding out how I feel about anything and everything."

Traditionally, the first word of each line of poetry is capitalized, but some poets do not follow this convention. When you quote poetry, follow the capitalization of the original.

> In her room at the prow of the house
> Where the light breaks, and the windows are tossed with linden,
> My daughter is writing a story.
> —RICHARD WILBUR, "The Writer"

> in Just-
> spring   when the world is mud-
> luscious the little
> lame balloonman
> whistles   far   and wee
> —E. E. CUMMINGS, "in Just-"

I, O, and Letters

Capitalize the pronoun *I* and the interjection *O* (but do not capitalize *oh* unless it is the first word in a sentence).

> When *I* was five, *I* was an angel in the Christmas pageant.
> One of my favorite carols is "*O* Little Town of Bethlehem."
> *Oh,* how we missed the O'Haras, and *oh,* how they missed us.

In general, capitalize letters that serve as names or indicate shapes.

> I-beam   T-square   U-turn   vitamin B

Miscellaneous Capitalizations

Capitalize the first word in the salutation and in the complimentary close of a letter. (See also **letters.**)

> Dear Dr. Cervetti:
> Sincerely yours,
> Yours truly,

When specifically identified by number, certain units, such as figures in books and rooms in buildings, are normally capitalized.

Figure 12   Fig. 12   Room 434   Rm. 434

Divisions within books are not generally capitalized unless they begin a sentence.

chapter 10   page 54   section 3   line 2

card catalog (See **Research Processes**, pages 52–53.)

caret

A caret (∧) is an editor's mark that indicates where a word or words are to be inserted into the text.

marks
Carets are useful when you are editing a paper.
                      ∧

case (grammatical)

The case of a **noun** or **pronoun** indicates its function in a **phrase, clause,** or **sentence.** There are three cases: subjective, objective, and possessive.

Nouns change form only in the possessive case (with the addition of an **apostrophe** or apostrophe plus -*s*). Pronouns may change form in all three cases, as shown in the table on page 219.

Subjective Case

The subjective case (also called *nominative case*) is used to refer to the person or thing acting. **Subjects** of verbs and **subject complements** are in the subjective case.

She called Jonelle. [subject]

It was *she* who wrote the note. [subject complement]

Pronoun Cases

	Subjective Case	Objective Case	Possessive Case
Personal Pronouns	I	me	my, mine
	we	us	our, ours
	you	you	your, yours
	he	him	his, his
	she	her	her, hers
	it	it	its
	they	them	their, theirs
Relative Pronouns	who	whom	whose
	which	which	whose
	that	that	that

Objective Case

The objective case (also called *accusative case*) is used to refer to the person or thing receiving the action. **Objects** of verbs, **verbals**, and prepositions are in the objective case.

> The photography club chose *her* as the new president. [direct object of the verb *chose*]

> Her grandparents wrote *her* a letter every week. [indirect object of the verb *wrote; letter* is the direct object]

> Our new mechanic seems to like *me*. [direct object of the infinitive *to like,* a verbal]

> Handing *him* her paper, she gave a sigh of relief. [indirect object of the present participle *handing,* a verbal]

> Hiring *her* was the best thing we could have done. [direct object of the gerund *hiring,* a verbal]

> Don't tell; this secret is between you and *me*. [object of the preposition *between*]

Possessive Case

The possessive case (also called *genitive case*) is used for modifiers showing possession or ownership.

> *Dr. Peterson's* credentials appear at the end of *her* article. [*Dr. Peterson's* is a possessive noun; *her* is a possessive pronoun.]

Use the possessive case before a **gerund.**

> The boss objected to *Gerry's* arriving late every morning.

> *My* working has not affected my grades.

The possessive pronoun forms *mine, ours, yours, his, hers,* and *theirs* are used in place of a noun. Note that these possessive forms do not use an apostrophe.

How do you know that this T-shirt is *your/s?*

I know because *mine* doesn't have a hole in it.

Forming Possessive Nouns Singular nouns are usually made possessive by adding -'s. Plural nouns ending in -s need only an apostrophe. Both singular and plural nouns may also be made possessive with the insertion of the word *of* before them.

> The commencement *speaker's* address was well received. [singular noun with -'s]
>
> The address *of* the commencement speaker was well received. [singular noun with *of*]
>
> The *singers'* voices filled the auditorium. [plural noun with apostrophe]
>
> The *children's* drawings adorned the walls of their classroom. [plural noun with -'s]

Proper nouns ending in *s* may take either an apostrophe alone or -'s, which is the more common form. Whichever way you choose, be consistent.

	Dickens's novels	Los Lobos's songs
OR	Dickens' novels	Los Lobos' songs

When several words constitute a single term, only the last word is made possessive.

> The *Department of Energy's* annual budget shows increased revenues for uranium enrichment.
>
> My *brother-in-law's* motorcycle is ten years old.

To show individual possession with coordinate nouns, make both nouns possessive. To show joint possession, make only the last noun possessive.

> The difference between *J. D.'s* and *Marla's* test results is insignificant. [The sentence refers to the separate test results of J. D. and of Marla.]
>
> *Tom* and *Ellen's* car broke down. [The sentence refers to a single car owned jointly by Tom and Ellen.]

Indefinite Pronouns One-syllable **indefinite pronouns** (such as *all, each, few, most, none,* and *some*) require *of* to form the possessive case.

> Both refrigerators were stored in the warehouse, but rust had ruined the surface *of each.*

Longer indefinite pronouns use the -'s form.

Anyone's opinion is welcome.

Tips on Determining the Case of Pronouns

Pronouns in compound constructions should be in the same case.

She and *I* enjoy swimming. [both subjective case—not *her* and *I*]

Give it to *him* and *me*. [both objective case—not *him* and *I*]

His and *my* tapes are on the bookshelf. [both possessive case]

To determine the case of compound pronouns, try out case forms with just one pronoun.

In her report, Keiko mentioned *you* and *me*. ["Keiko mentioned *me*" sounds right. "Keiko mentioned *I*" sounds wrong.]

An **appositive** should be in the same case as the word or phrase it complements.

Two students, Kevin Stein and *I*, were asked to read our poetry. [subjective case for appositive renaming the subject, *students*]

The students selected two poets to represent the creative writers—Kevin Stein and *me*. [objective case for appositive renaming the object, *poets*]

To determine whether to use *we* or *us* before a noun, mentally omit the noun.

We students register on Wednesday. ["We register" sounds right. "Us register" sounds wrong.]

To determine the case of a pronoun that follows *as* or *than* in a **comparison**, mentally add the omitted words.

The redhead is not as handsome as *he* [is handsome]. [You would not write "*him* is handsome."]

Her friend was taller than *she* [was tall]. [You would not write "*her* was tall."]

Who/Whom

Who is the **subjective case** form, and *whom* is the **objective case** form. When in doubt about which form to use, try substituting a **personal pronoun** to see which one fits. If *he, she,* or *they* fits, use *who*.

Who is the senator from District 45? [You would write "*She* (not *her*) is the senator."]

If *him, her,* or *them* fits, use *whom.*

> On *whom* can Jody depend? [You would write "Can Jody depend on *them* (not *they*)?"]

Some writers prefer to begin **clauses** and sentences with *who* instead of *whom,* but others consider this construction ungrammatical, especially in formal contexts.

> *Who* did the voters from District 45 elect? [*Whom* is grammatically correct.]

(See also **who/whom.**)

cause and effect as a method of development

When your purpose is to explain *why* something happened or may happen, you are writing about causes and effects (results, consequences). On the surface, cause-and-effect relationships may seem simple: This happened because of that. In fact, however, causal relationships are rarely simple. Usually there are multiple causes for an effect, and several consequences may spring from a single cause. Moreover, causes and effects tend to occur in chain reactions, like dominoes falling: A cause creates effects, which then become causes of still other effects, and so on. Consider the causal relationships in the following short paragraph.

> The suburb could not have developed without the family automobile. In turn, the growth of suburbia made the automobile king, a necessity of life and in some ways a tyrant. Each family needed a car because suburbanites worked at some distance from their homes and public transportation to many of the new communities did not exist. Because it was necessary for a suburban housewife and mother to cover considerable distances each day, the two-car family became a common phenomenon: one suburban family in five owned two vehicles.
>
> —JOSEPH CONLIN, *The American Past*

(For another example, see **paragraphs.**)

Writing about cause-and-effect relationships requires special care about **logic.**

CBE/CSE style   See **Research Processes**, pages 139–52.)

CD-ROM

CD-ROM is the acronym for Compact Disc—Read Only Memory. CD-ROMs are used to store data (such as library reference resources) and software programs. The information on a CD-ROM can be **downloaded** onto another computer disk or onto your hard drive.

censor/censure

A *censor* is one who supervises conduct and morals by *censoring* (removing or suppressing) objectionable material. *Censure* is strong disapproval or condemnation. For example, members of the U.S. Senate occasionally *censure* one of their colleagues for unethical conduct.

central idea (See **thesis** and **main idea**.)

chair/chairperson/chairman/chairwoman

All four terms are suitable to indicate a presiding officer. To avoid gender bias, however, use *chair* or *chairperson*.

> Ann Winters is the *chair* [or *chairperson*] of the student senate.
>
> After Ben Summers resigned as *chairman* of the student senate, Ann Winters was elected *chairwoman*.

(See also **nonsexist language**.)

characterization

Characterization is the method of developing the traits and personalities of individuals in fiction and drama. Authors may develop their characters through the use of dialogue, action, or motivation. Some characters are said to be "flat," or one-dimensional; other characters are described as "rounded," meaning that they are developed well enough to seem like real people. As a rule, the degree of development depends on the character's function within the **plot**.

charts (See **graphics**.)

Chicago Manual of Style (CMS) (See **Research Processes**, pages 114–38.)

choppy writing

Choppy writing is awkward prose that bumps along following a pattern, usually subject-verb-object. You can avoid or revise choppy writing by varying your sentence patterns—combining short, related sentences, subordinating some sentences to others as **dependent clauses**, and eliminating unnecessary words to turn some **clauses** into **phrases**. (See also **conciseness/wordiness**, **sentence types**, and **sentence variety**.) Compare the following choppy paragraph and the revised version (as the author actually wrote it).

C

CHOPPY
Willie stood up. He walked out onto the bridge. Johnny followed. He stood beside him. The two men leaned forward with their elbows on the rail. They gazed along the tiered apartments. Lucy and her husband stepped out of a parked car. They climbed the stairs. They exchanged a few words with Willie. They climbed back down. They drove away.

REVISED
Willie stood up and walked out onto the bridge. Johnny followed and stood beside him, the two men leaning forward, elbows on the rail, gazing along the tiered apartments. Lucy and her husband stepped out of a parked car, climbed the stairs, exchanged a few words with Willie, then climbed back down and drove away.
—CHILTON WILLIAMSON, JR., *Roughnecking It*

chronological method of development

The chronological **method of development** arranges events in a time sequence, usually beginning with the first event and proceeding to the last.

Narrative essays, laboratory reports, and minutes of meetings are among the types of writing in which information is organized chronologically. The following example comes from an essay.

> The next day General Littlefield summoned me to his office. He was swatting flies when I went in. I was silent and he was silent too, for a long time. I don't think he remembered me or why he had sent for me, but he didn't want to admit it. He swatted some more flies, keeping his eyes on them narrowly before he let go with the swatter. "Button up your coat!" he snapped. Looking back on it now I can see that he meant me although he was looking at a fly, but I just stood there. Another fly came to rest on a paper in front of the general and began rubbing its hind legs together. The general lifted the swatter cautiously. I moved restlessly and the fly flew away. "You startled him!" barked General Littlefield, looking at me severely. I said I was sorry. "That won't help the situation!" snapped the General, with cold military logic.
>
> —JAMES THURBER, "University Days"

circular reasoning (See **logic.**)

cite/site/sight

Cite, a **verb,** means "bring forward" or "quote by way of example, authority, or proof." *Site,* a **noun,** is the location of a building or a plot of land. *Sight,* as a verb, means "to look at" or "to find by looking"; *sight,* as a noun, means "a thing worth seeing" or "the function of seeing."

> His professor felt that Steve should *cite* an authority to reinforce his thesis statement.

The *site* for the new gym is right on top of the old one.

Did the searchers *sight* any survivors?

Her *sight* became so impaired as she aged that she no longer enjoyed going abroad to see the *sights*.

claim

A claim is the point to be proved in an **argument**. (See also **thesis**.)

clarity

No characteristic of writing is more essential than clarity. Clear writing is direct, orderly, and precise. A logical **method of development** and effective **transitions** give your writing **coherence**, enabling the audience to connect your thoughts without conscious effort and to concentrate solely on absorbing your ideas. Techniques of **emphasis** and **subordination** distinguish the key ideas from those of less importance. A consistent **point of view** establishes through whose eyes, or from what vantage point, the subject is presented. **Conciseness** contributes to clarity and saves the reader's time. Careful **word choice** helps you avoid vagueness and **ambiguity**.

classification as a method of development

Classification groups items or subjects into categories to help the audience understand them better. For example, a discussion of rock music might classify it in categories such as heavy metal, acid rock, hard rock, speed metal, and grunge.

In the following passage, an astronomer classifies two types of a rare celestial phenomenon, the supernova.

> Supernovae are divided into two classes according to how their brightness rises and falls: Type I reach their peak brightness in about 20 days, then fade slowly over a year or so; Type II reach their peak in about 30 days, then fade away in about 150 days. Spectral analysis shows that Type I supernovae have much more helium in their envelopes than do Type II, but no definite relationship between the two types has been found. There is some indication that Type II explosions occur in more massive stars, which would mean they are related to stars with iron cores.
>
> —BARRY R. PARKER, *Concepts of the Cosmos*

(For other examples, see **paragraphs**.)

clauses

A clause is a group of words that contains a **subject** and a **predicate**. A clause that can stand alone as a **simple sentence** is an **independent clause** (also called *main clause*). A clause that cannot stand alone is a **dependent clause** (also called *subordinate clause*).

> I was an eighth grader when I read my first banned book. [*I was an eighth grader* is an independent clause; *when I read my first banned book* is a dependent clause.]

Every subject-predicate word group in a sentence is a clause. Each sentence must contain at least one independent clause, with the exception of intentional **sentence fragments** such as exclamations.

Clauses may be connected by a **coordinating conjunction**, a **subordinating conjunction**, a **relative pronoun**, or a **conjunctive adverb**.

> Peregrine falcons are about the size of a large crow, *and* they have a wingspread of three to four feet. [coordinating conjunction connecting two independent clauses]
>
> I like to raise falcons *because* they are such an independent breed. [subordinating conjunction connecting a dependent clause to an independent clause]
>
> It was my grandfather *who* first interested me in these pets. [relative pronoun connecting a dependent clause to an independent clause]
>
> It was hard to overcome my instinctive fear of their claws; *nevertheless,* I continued my hobby. [conjunctive adverb connecting two independent clauses]

A dependent clause may function as a **noun**, an **adjective**, or an **adverb** in a larger sentence. An independent clause may be modified by one or more dependent clauses.

Noun Clauses

Noun clauses function as **subjects, subject complements, direct objects**, or objects of **prepositions**.

> A common rumor is *that mosquitoes can carry the AIDS virus.* [noun clause as subject complement]

Adjective Clauses

An **adjective clause** modifies a noun or pronoun, which it usually follows. Adjective clauses ordinarily begin with a relative pronoun but occasionally begin with *when, where,* or *why.*

> Amanda Martinez, *whom we met yesterday,* showed us the house *where she was born.* [The first adjective clause modifies *Amanda Martinez;* the second modifies *house.*]

Adverb Clauses

An **adverb clause** is a dependent clause that modifies a **verb, adjective,** or **adverb** in another clause. Like adverbs, adverb clauses normally express ideas of time, place, condition, cause, manner, or comparison.

The rain stopped *after we went home.* [time]

The student union is located *where the bookstore used to be.* [place]

If we go back outdoors, the rain will start again. [condition]

The rain stopped *because the weekend was over.* [cause]

The rain stopped *as suddenly as it had started.* [manner]

The new computer-aided weather forecasts are no more reliable *than the old ones were.* [comparison]

Adverb clauses are often introduced by **subordinating conjunctions** (*because, when, where, since, though,* and the like). If the adverb clause follows the main clause, a comma should not normally separate the two clauses. An adverb clause preceding the main clause should be set off by a comma.

Because the singer has such a high-pitched scream, the blare of the amplifiers is even more painful.

Placement of an adverb clause can change the **emphasis** of a sentence.

Rock concerts are fun to attend *unless the music is so loud it hurts your ears.*

Unless the music is so loud it hurts your ears, rock concerts are fun to attend.

An adverb clause cannot act as the **subject** of a sentence.

The increase in
~~Because~~ crude oil prices ~~have increased~~ is the reason gasoline is more expensive
than ever.

OR

Gasoline is more expensive than ever because crude oil prices have increased.

cliché

A cliché is an expression that has been used for so long that it is no longer fresh. Examples are *busy as a bee, cool as a cucumber, better late than never, wear and tear, easier said than done,* and *moving experience.* Because they are so familiar, clichés come to mind easily. However, they give your audience the impression that you haven't thought much about what you are writing. As you revise papers, delete clichés when you can, and instead state the ideas in plain language.

T   *read it*
~~Last but not least,~~ the final step in writing a composition is to ~~go through it with~~
word for word,
~~a fine-toothed comb~~ looking for typos.

On rare occasions, a cliché may be the most efficient means of expressing an idea. For example, "If I can help further, please let me know"—a conventional statement in business letters—may better express your idea than any other choice of words. (See also **figures of speech** and **jargon**.)

clipped forms of words

When the beginning or end of a word is cut off to create a shorter word, the result is called a *clipped form.*

dorm   prof   promo   vet

Although they are acceptable in conversation, most clipped forms should not appear in writing unless they are commonly accepted as part of the special vocabulary of an occupational group.

Apostrophes are not normally used with clipped forms of words (not *'phone,* but *phone*). Because they are not strictly **abbreviations**, clipped forms are not followed by **periods** (not *lab.,* but *lab*).

Do not use clipped forms of **spelling** (*thru, nite,* and the like).

clustering

Clustering is a method of generating and organizing ideas during prewriting. It is similar to **freewriting**, during which you put down ideas as they occur; it differs from freewriting, however, in that it is a more visual representation of ideas. Begin clustering by naming the topic in the middle of the page, circling it, and drawing spokes from the circle to other ideas as they occur to you. Then look for relationships between those ideas, and connect them with lines. These connections may in turn spark additional ideas. When you feel you have written down all the possible ideas, examples, and subtopics, begin your draft by selecting and organizing the ideas within the clusters.

(See also **Composing Processes**, pages 7–9.)

CMS style (See **Research Processes**, pages 114–38.)

coherence

Coherence in writing is achieved by a smooth movement from one idea to another and by a clear indication of the relationships among ideas. Sentences and paragraphs should progress so logically and clearly that readers can follow the development of points without confusion or uncertainty. For suggestions on shaping a logical sequence of ideas, see the various

methods of development listed in this book; for additional examples, see **paragraphs.**

Careful use of words and phrases marking **transitions** is also essential to coherence. Notice the difference between the two paragraphs that follow. The transitional words and phrases have been removed from the first version; they are included in the second version.

WITHOUT TRANSITIONS

She was somewhat familiar with such scenes. They had often made her very unhappy. She had been completely deprived of any desire to finish her dinner. She had gone into the kitchen to administer a tardy rebuke to the cook. She went to her room and studied the cookbook during an entire evening, writing out a menu for the week, which left her harassed with a feeling that she had accomplished no good that was worth the name.

WITH TRANSITIONS

She was somewhat familiar with such scenes. They had often made her very unhappy. *On a few previous occasions* she had been completely deprived of any desire to finish her dinner. *Sometimes* she had gone into the kitchen to administer a tardy rebuke to the cook. *Once* she went to her room and studied the cookbook during an entire evening, *finally* writing out a menu for the week, which left her harassed with a feeling that, *after all,* she had accomplished no good that was worth the name.

—KATE CHOPIN, *The Awakening*

The first paragraph proceeds logically but is choppy. The transitions of the second paragraph provide the smooth flow needed to elicit the reader's understanding and interest. (For a list of transitional words and phrases, see **transitions.**) In longer works, transitions from paragraph to paragraph and from section to section are also essential for clear communication with your audience.

Be sure to check your draft for coherence during the revising process. Having someone else read your paper can be helpful. (See also **Composing Processes.**)

collective nouns

Collective nouns are singular in form but name a group or collection of persons, places, or things.

class	cluster	family	flock
group	herd	jury	staff

When a collective noun refers to a group as a whole, it is treated as singular.

The jury *was* deadlocked; *it* had to be disbanded.

When a collective noun refers to individuals within a group, it is treated as plural.

The jury *were* allowed to go to *their* homes for the night.

(See also **nouns**, **agreement of pronouns and antecedents**, and **agreement of subjects and verbs.**)

colloquial usage

The informal language of everyday conversation (words such as *a lot, picky,* and *know-how*) is often referred to as colloquial. Although colloquial usage is standard English, it may be inappropriate in formal writing. If you are in doubt about whether a word or expression is colloquial, consult a dictionary. Terms labeled *colloquial* or *informal* should usually be reserved for situations in which you want your writing to sound informal or conversational. (See also **informal and formal writing style, diction,** and **English, varieties of.**)

colons

Introducing Explanations or Examples	230
Punctuation and Capitalization with Colons	231
Colons in Titles, Numbers, and Citations	231
Unnecessary Colons	232
Colons versus Semicolons	232

Introducing Explanations or Examples

The colon separates two elements, the second of which explains, amplifies, or illustrates the first. A colon may introduce a complete sentence, a list, or a phrase.

Following my grandmother's Asian traditions, we brought incense to burn at the gravesite, and food: a bowl of rice, fruit, a main dish for his spirit to eat. [Following the colon is a list of kinds of food.]

—Grace Ming-Yee Wai, "Chinese Puzzle"

[T]he presence of the *other,* particularly minorities, in institutions and in institutional life resembles what we call in Spanish a *flor de tierra* (a surface phenomenon): we are spare plants whose roots do not go deep, vulnerable to inclemencies of an economic, or political, or social nature. [Following the colon is a complete sentence expanding on the Spanish phrase.]

—Arturo Madrid, "Diversity and Its Discontents"

A colon may precede a quotation that has been formally introduced or that is longer than one sentence. (See also **block quotations.**)

In her autobiography, prolific mystery writer Agatha Christie (1977) describes the excitement she and her friends felt as young girls standing on the edge of adulthood and contemplating the future:

> The real excitement of being a girl—of being, that is, a woman in embryo— was that life was such a wonderful gamble. . . . The whole world was open to you—not open to your *choice,* but open to what Fate *brought* you. You might marry *anyone.* . . .
>
> —Hilary Lips, *Women, Men, and Power*

A colon lends emphasis to an **appositive** phrase or clause at the end of a sentence.

> I learned from my father while in the first grade one valuable lesson that still affects me now: never be afraid to ask questions.
>
> —Grace Ming-Yee Wai, "Chinese Puzzle"

Punctuation and Capitalization with Colons

A colon is always outside **quotation marks.**

> The following are his favorite "sports": eating and sleeping.

Capitalization of the first word of a complete sentence or a formal question following a colon is optional, but if a series of sentences is introduced by a colon, all the sentences should begin with capital letters. If a quotation beginning with a capital letter follows a colon, the capital is always retained.

> We had to keep working for one reason: *The* [or *the*] deadline was upon us. [complete sentence following colon]
>
> The coach issued the following statement: "*It* ain't over 'til it's over, and it ain't over yet." [quotation following colon]

Begin a list, series, phrase, or word following a colon with a lowercase letter.

> I have only three questions: *when? where?* and *why?*

Colons in Titles, Numbers, and Citations

A colon separates the title and subtitle of a book or article.

> *American Voices: Multicultural Literacy and Critical Thinking*

A colon separates numbers in time references and in biblical citations.

> 11:01 a.m. [11 hours, 1 minute]
>
> Genesis 10:16 [chapter 10, verse 16]

In the expression of proportions, the colon indicates the ratio of one amount to another.

> The cement is mixed with water and sand at 5:3:1. [The colon is read as the word *to*.]

Colons are often used in mathematical ratios.

> $7:3 = 14:x$

A colon follows the salutation in business letters.

> Dear Ms. Jeffers:
> Dear Personnel Director:
> Dear George:

A colon is also used in footnote and reference citations. For examples, see **Research Processes**, pages 61–152.

Unnecessary Colons

Do not insert a colon between a **verb** and an **object** or **complement**.

> The three modes of transportation under consideration are⫽ train, plane, and
>
> automobile.

Do not insert a colon between a **preposition** and an object.

> I applied at schools in⫽ Indiana, Missouri, and Arizona.

Do not insert a colon between *including, such as,* or *for example* and a list.

> The doctor told him to stay away from spicy foods such as⫽ barbecue, salsa, hot
>
> sauce, and curry.

Colons versus Semicolons

Do not use a colon where a **semicolon** is appropriate. The elements separated by a colon are usually grammatically unequal, and what follows the colon explains or illustrates what precedes it. A semicolon separates grammatically equal or parallel elements.

> As long as I could remember, I had been told that a female followed three men during her lifetime: as a girl, her father; as a wife, her husband; as an old woman,

her son. [A colon separates the independent clause and the list. Semicolons separate the three parallel items in the list because they contain commas.]

—JADE SNOW WONG, *Fifth Chinese Daughter*

commas

The comma, which is the most common mark of internal **punctuation**, signals a slight interruption between sentence elements. By indicating sentence structure, it helps readers understand the writer's meaning and prevents ambiguity. By showing where the main part of the sentence begins, the comma helps make the meaning clear in the following examples.

To be good, drivers of five-speed cars must learn to shift smoothly. [Without a comma, the sentence might initially seem to be about "good drivers of five-speed cars."]

When you see a red light, shift down to second. [Without a comma, this sentence temporarily throws the reader off by seeming to have red lights shifting.]

Between Independent Clauses

Use a comma before a **coordinating conjunction** (*and, but, or, nor,* and sometimes *so, yet,* and *for*) that links **independent clauses.**

I had planned to come, but I have changed my mind.

When the independent clauses are short and related, the comma is not necessary but is never wrong.

       The power went out and the computer went down.

OR   The power went out, and the computer went down.

Because the conjunctions *for, so,* and *yet* can also be other parts of speech, a comma is usually necessary even with short clauses to prevent misreading.

> He ran, for the train had started moving.

A **semicolon** may be used instead of a comma if the independent clauses are long and contain commas or other internal punctuation.

> Self-defense specialists offer these tips to help women avoid danger: If someone attacks you, don't panic, because that gives the attacker control over the situation; if the attacker has a weapon, such as a gun or knife, don't be combative; but if a potential assailant tries to get you into a car, don't go, because he will probably try to kill you.

After Introductory Clauses and Phrases

A comma usually follows **introductory clauses or phrases,** signaling where the introductory element ends and the main part of the sentence begins.

Clauses   Use a comma after an introductory **adverb clause.**

> *Since the ozone layer gets thinner every year,* wearing a good sunscreen is wise.

When the adverb clause comes at the end of the sentence, the two clauses may be separated by a comma if they are only loosely related; however, a comma is not essential.

> He should graduate in June, *even though he failed some classes.*

Phrases   Normally, use a comma after an introductory **prepositional** or **verbal phrase.**

> *During her first year of residency,* Dr. Harrison decided she would be a family practitioner. [prepositional phrase]
>
> *Looking up from her magazine,* Maura smiled at me across the room. [participial phrase]
>
> *To enter the contest,* you must fill out the registration form. [infinitive phrase]
>
> *Finals being over,* I began to get ready for the holidays. [absolute phrase]

If an introductory phrase is short and closely related to the main clause, the comma may be omitted unless it is necessary to prevent misreading.

> *In this context* the meaning is different.

To Separate Items in Series

Words, Phrases, or Clauses   Three or more words, phrases, or clauses in a series are separated by commas.

The garden was always *sunny, cool, and fragrant.*

You know you're in trouble when you *charge everything, can't pay off your balance every month, and use one credit card to pay off another.*

Although the comma before *and* may be omitted, using it sometimes prevents ambiguity. The following book dedication shows how a missing comma can cause confusion or worse.

To my parents, William Shakespeare and Marilyn Monroe.

When one or more of the phrases in a series contain commas, separate the phrases with semicolons.

Among the winners were Amanda Sue Smith, gymnast; Betsy Sue Smith, swimmer; and Stacy Sue Smith, basketball player.

Coordinate Adjectives When **adjectives** modifying the same noun can be reversed and still make sense or when they can be separated by *and* or *or,* they should be separated by commas.

She designed a *contemporary, two-story, brick-and-glass* house.

Do not use a comma after an adjective that modifies a phrase.

He was investigating his *damaged garage door opener.* [*Damaged* modifies the phrase *garage door opener.*]

Never put a comma between a final adjective and the noun it modifies.

I was face to face with a huge, angry/ moose.

To Set Off Nonrestrictive Elements

Commas set off nonrestrictive elements—clauses, phrases, and words that add information to but do not limit the words they modify. Unlike restrictive elements, nonrestrictive elements can be omitted without changing the essential meaning of a sentence. (See **restrictive and nonrestrictive elements.**)

The new mall, *which opened last month,* should offer twice as many stores as the old one. [The nonrestrictive clause provides information that is not essential to the meaning of the sentence.]

The mall *that is just being built* will hold twice as many stores as the mall across town. [The restrictive clause is necessary because it identifies which mall.]

Commas (or, occasionally, **dashes** or **parentheses**) signal that an element is nonrestrictive. The meaning of a sentence can depend on whether an element is set off by punctuation, as the following examples illustrate.

She studied longer than anyone else in class, *hoping to get an A.* [Preceded by a comma, the participial phrase *hoping to get an A* is nonrestrictive; it simply adds information about why she was studying.]

She studied longer than anyone else in class *hoping to get an A.* [Without a comma, the participial phrase is restrictive and identifies hopeful classmates.]

Appositives **Appositives,** which are nouns or noun substitutes that rename a nearby noun or noun substitute, can be restrictive or nonrestrictive. A restrictive appositive provides necessary identification and is not set off by commas (my friend Joe; Michael Jackson's album *Thriller*). A nonrestrictive appositive simply adds information and should be set off with commas (my father, Bill; his first car, a blue Pontiac).

Parenthetical and Transitional Expressions Introductory **adverbs** and transitional expressions (including **conjunctive adverbs**), contrasting elements, and other sentence modifiers are usually set off by commas.

Unfortunately, winter storms had closed both roads to the ski resort. [adverb]

Likewise, the storms had closed the airport. [transitional expression]

Undeterred, he got to his feet again. [participle]

He vowed, *however,* that he was going to learn to ski no matter how many times he fell. [conjunctive adverb]

The paper was supposed to be twenty pages, *not ten.* [contrasting phrase]

Commas may be omitted when the word or phrase does not interrupt the continuity of thought or require punctuation for clarity.

Perhaps the oversight was intentional.

The consequences are *nonetheless* serious.

A **conjunctive adverb** or transitional expression (*however, nevertheless, consequently, for example, on the other hand*) that joins two independent clauses is preceded by a **semicolon** and followed by a comma.

His punctuation was perfect; however, his spelling was terrible.

Interjections, Direct Address, Tag Questions Commas set off mild **interjections** (such as *well, why, oh*) and *yes* and *no*.

Well, I think you're right.

No, I don't think you should drive.

Commas are used to set off a name used in **direct address.**

Charlie, would you answer the door?

Tag questions (*shouldn't he? do they?*) should be set off by commas.

The project was finished on time, *wasn't it?*

To Prevent Misreading

Sometimes a comma is necessary to ensure clarity even though it is not required by any other rule or practice.

Whatever will be, will be. [Without a comma, the repeated verb could cause confusion.]

I mended the vase he had knocked over, and replaced the flowers. [Without a comma between them, the two verbs, *knocked over* and *replaced,* might be mistakenly read as a compound verb.]

To Show Omissions

A comma sometimes replaces a word or phrase in **elliptical constructions**. (See also **parallel structure.**)

Some people choose their clothes for style; others, for comfort. [The comma in the second clause replaces *choose their clothes.*]

With Dates, Addresses, Numbers, Names, and Titles

Dates In the month-day-year format, separate the day and the year with a comma. In sentences, a comma also follows the year.

Bill Clinton became the forty-second president of the United States on *January 20, 1993,* at 12 noon.

Do not use commas in the day-month-year format or in dates consisting of only the month and the year.

Bill Clinton became the forty-second president of the United States on *20 January 1993* at 12 noon.

Bill Clinton was first elected president in *November 1992* in a three-way race.

Addresses and Place Names In text, use commas between the elements of an address (except the state and zip code).

Please send the refund to *John Andrews, 11704 Myers Road, St. Louis, Missouri 63119.*

Separate the elements of geographical names with commas. A comma should also set off the state name from the remainder of the sentence.

He was born in *Ossian, Indiana,* in 1983.

Numbers Use commas to separate the digits in long **numbers** into groups of three. A comma in a four-digit number is optional (except that a comma is never used in four-digit years, page numbers, or street numbers).

1,528,200   1528 or 1,528   page 1528

Names and Titles Use a comma to separate names that are reversed.

Scissorhands, Edward

U e a comma between a person's name and an abbreviated title.

Herbert Morris, Jr.   Jane Williamson, Ph.D.

In Correspondence and Documentation

A comma follows the salutation in a personal letter and the complimentary close in both business and personal letters. Use a **colon** after the salutation in a business letter.

Dear Nancy, [personal letter]
Dear Nancy: [business letter]
Sincerely yours,

Use commas between certain elements of footnotes and other documentation. (See **Research Processes,** pages 61–152.)

With Quotations

In a sentence, set off a direct quotation from its attribution with commas.

In 1964, Marshall McLuhan announced, "The medium is the message."
"Don't look back," said baseball great Satchel Paige. "Something may be gaining on you."

Commas are always placed inside **quotation marks.**

The operator listed the call as "collect," which doubled its cost.

Do not use a comma if the quotation ends with a **question mark,** an **ex-clamation point,** or a **dash.**

"I am going to quit school!," he said.

"You're going to do what?," I shrieked.

Do not set off indirect quotations with commas.

Andy Warhol predicted, that everyone will experience fifteen minutes of fame.

Unnecessary Commas

Do not place a comma between a **subject** and a verb or between a verb and its **object**.

> The boys in the band,/had a party.

> The punch press severed,/his left index finger in one swift motion.

Do not use a comma between the elements of a **compound subject** or a compound **predicate**.

> The captain of the cheerleaders,/and the leader of the flag team were both juniors,/
>
> and honor roll students.

Do not put a comma between a **coordinating conjunction**, such as *and* or *but*, and the main clause or phrase it is connecting.

> The coach told them to stop squabbling, but,/they continued to berate each other.

Do not place a comma before the first item or after the last item of a series or between **cumulative adjectives**.

> We are considering installing antitheft devices, such as,/window alarms, dead bolts,
>
> and hidden,/trip wires.

Do not unnecessarily set off a **prepositional phrase** or separate a concluding **adverb clause** from the rest of the sentence. Use commas to enclose only nonrestrictive phrases and clauses.

> They agreed to meet,/promptly at 3:00,/in the jewelry department.

(See also **comma splices** and **run-on sentences**.)

comma splices

Do not join two **independent clauses** with a **comma** only; this error in punctuation is called a *comma splice* (or *comma fault*).

> Aspen was too far away for us to drive there, we decided to fly. [comma splice]

A comma splice can be corrected in several ways. Choose the one that best expresses the relation between the clauses and that sounds the best in

C

the paragraph. The first three methods of revision that follow are appropriate when the two clauses are of equal importance, and the fourth method is best when you want to emphasize one of the clauses.

1. Substitute a **semicolon** for the comma, or substitute a semicolon and a **conjunctive adverb** or a transitional word or phrase (for a list, see **transitions**). When a conjunctive adverb connects two independent clauses, it must be preceded by a semicolon and followed by a comma.

Aspen was too far away for us to drive there; we decided to fly.

OR

Aspen was too far away for us to drive there; *instead,* we decided to fly. [conjunctive adverb]

2. Add a **coordinating conjunction** following the comma.

Aspen was too far away for us to drive there, *so* we decided to fly.

3. Create two sentences. Be aware, however, that putting a **period** between two brief statements may produce two choppy sentences. (See **choppy writing.**)

Aspen was too far away for us to drive there. We decided to fly.

4. Subordinate one **clause** to the other. This method of revision is often the most effective because it emphasizes the more important idea.

Because Aspen was too far away for us to drive there, we decided to fly.

committee

Committee, although it is a **collective noun,** always takes a singular **verb.**

The selection *committee is* considering seven candidates.

To point to the individuals in the committee, use a **phrase** such as *the members of the committee* and a plural verb.

The members of the selection committee are ready to cast their votes.

common knowledge

In research papers, you need not cite a source for what is common knowledge for your audience. Common knowledge may be basic facts known to the public at large, such as that John Lennon was the first Beatle to die. It may also be information commonly known by people in a particular field, such as that women were not allowed on stage during Shakespeare's time.

When you are first doing research in a particular field, you may not know what common knowledge in that field is. If you find a piece of information in a number of your sources without citation, assume that it is common knowledge. However, if you are uncertain, be safe and provide a source citation.

Assertions and controversial claims, such as that Christopher Marlowe wrote some of the plays attributed to Shakespeare, are not considered common knowledge and must always be attributed. Commonly held opinions, such as that junk food is not healthful, need not be attributed to a particular source.

(See also **plagiarizing** and **Research Processes**, pages 28–34.)

common nouns

A common noun specifies a general class of persons, things, places, qualities, or ideas. In contrast, a proper noun names a specific member of the class.

COMMON NOUNS	PROPER NOUNS
woman	Amy Tan
state	Iowa
holiday	Independence Day
book	*The Catcher in the Rye*

When common nouns appear in a title or begin a sentence, they are capitalized. Otherwise, they are lowercased. (For information about the **case**, **number**, and function of common nouns, see **nouns.**)

comparative degree

Most **adjectives** and **adverbs** can be compared. The comparative degree compares two persons or things; the superlative degree compares three or more persons or things. (See also **comparisons.**)

Our kitten is *smaller* than our cat. [comparative]

This kitten is the *smallest* one we've ever had. [superlative]

Most one-syllable words and some two-syllable words use the comparative ending *-er* and the superlative ending *-est*. Most adjectives and adverbs with two or more syllables form the comparative degree by using the word *more* and the superlative degree by using the word *most*.

This chair is *more* comfortable than that one.

This is the *most* comfortable chair in the house.

Some adjectives and adverbs may use either means of expressing degree.

Our neighbor is the *most able* handyman in the neighborhood.

He was the *ablest* handyman in the area.

ADJECTIVES AND ADVERBS WITH IRREGULAR FORMS OF COMPARISON

	COMPARATIVE	SUPERLATIVE
Adjectives		
good	better	best
well	better	best
bad	worse	worst
ill	worse	worst
little	less	least
many	more	most
some	more	most
much	more	most
Adverbs		
ill	worse	worst
badly	worse	worst
far	farther, further	farthest, furthest

Absolute words (*unique, perfect, round*) cannot logically be compared. Careful writers often use the phrase *more nearly* with absolute words to express comparison (*more nearly perfect*). Or they use another modifier, such as *unusual* instead of *unique*.

The superlative form is sometimes used in expressions that do not really express comparison (*best* wishes, *deepest* sympathy, *highest* praise, *most* sincerely).

When the adjective or adverb comes between the two things being compared, add *than* as well as the comparative form.

> Nothing is *lovelier than* a day in June. [*Lovelier* comes between *nothing* and *day.*]
>
> The summer months seem to go *faster than* the winter months. [*Faster* comes between *summer months* and *winter months.*]

compare/contrast

To *compare* things, people, places, qualities, or ideas is to identify the ways they are similar or the ways they are both similar and different. To *contrast* things is to show only how they are different. Comparisons and contrasts are both drawn between elements in the same general class, however.

She *compared* prices at three different stores before buying.

Her style of shopping *contrasted* sharply with her husband's.

In writing about similarities, use *compare to*.

James Watson and Francis Crick *compared* the molecular structure of DNA *to* a zipper.

In writing about similarities and differences, use *compare with*.

We *compared* the features of the new computer *with* those of the old one.

comparison and contrast as a method of development

Comparison and contrast is a **method of development** for presenting similarities or differences or both between two or more things. You can use this method to organize entire essays or single **paragraphs**.

First, decide on your basis of comparison. Suppose, for example, that you are going to compare and contrast movies of the 1950s and movies of the 1990s. After reviewing many movies of both decades, you note several elements that might be bases of comparison: types of plots (both content and development), methods of acting, quality of dialogue or screenwriting, amount of violence shown (if any), and quality and function of accompanying music. You further determine that some features are irrelevant and should not be included in the comparisons: models of cars appearing in the movies, styles of houses, celebrity status of the stars at the time, or size of the casts. Finally, you review all the bases of comparison and limit them to an appropriate number, depending on the length of your writing project.

After you have chosen bases of comparison, select a method of presentation. You might wish to discuss all the elements of the 1950s movies and then all the elements of the 1990s movies, a structure called the *whole-by-whole* (or *block*) *method*. Or you might wish to compare or contrast the elements of both decades of movies one by one, a method called the *point-by-point method*. The following discussion by a college undergraduate is organized according to the whole-by-whole method, describing one type of animal and all its relevant characteristics before going on to describe the other type, its prey, in the same manner.

The big cats of Africa have, like all cats, developed a set of adaptations that allow them to chase down their prey. Besides the forward-oriented eyes and sharp tearing and shearing teeth that are universal in mammalian carnivores, felines have exceedingly flexible backbones and strong shoulder musculature. With this kind of physique, a running cat can reach forward with its fore paws, pull itself rapidly over the ground, bend its back to reach forward with the hind paws, and then straighten the back to begin another stride with its fore paws. In this way, the feline is permitted a long stride for fast sprinting. However, such a strategy is a compromise.

What a cat gains in speed it loses in endurance. The animal tires quickly and cannot run long distances because much of the forward force created by the hind limbs against the ground is lost to the flexibility of the vertebral column.

It is here that the ungulates have "found" their advantage. They are provided with stiff backbones that transmit the force of the hind legs against the ground into forward motion. Thus, although the animal cannot run as fast as its feline predator and does not have as long a stride, it can run farther. If it becomes aware that it is being stalked, it can outrun a would-be killer fairly handily. To aid in perceiving prey, ungulates have laterally oriented eyes, large ears, and a tendency to form herds in which some animals are keeping watch at any given time.

—ANNE NISHIJIMA, "Predator and Prey"

The purpose of this comparison, clearly, is to weigh the advantages and disadvantages of each type of animal. If, on the other hand, your purpose is to emphasize particular features, the information may be arranged according to the point-by-point method, as in the following example:

What is *macho*? That depends which side of the border you come from.

Although it's not unusual for words and expressions to lose their subtlety in translation, the negative connotations of *macho* in this country are troublesome to Hispanics.

Take the newspaper descriptions of alleged mass murderer Ramon Salcido. That an insensitive, insanely jealous, hard-drinking, violent Latin male is referred to as *macho* makes Hispanics cringe.

"*Es muy macho,*" the women in my family nod approvingly, describing a man they respect. But in the United States, when women say, "He's so macho," it's with disdain.

The Hispanic *macho* is manly, responsible, hardworking, a man in charge, a patriarch. A man who expresses strength through silence. What the Yiddish language would call a *mensch*.

The American *macho* is a chauvinist, a brute, uncouth, selfish, loud, abrasive, capable of inflicting pain, and sexually promiscuous.

Quintessential *macho* models in this country are Sylvester Stallone, Arnold Schwarzenegger, and Charles Bronson. In their movies, they exude toughness, independence, masculinity. But a close look reveals their machismo is really violence masquerading as courage, sullenness disguised as silence, and irresponsibility camouflaged as independence.

If the Hispanic ideal of *macho* were translated to American screen roles, they might be Jimmy Stewart, Sean Connery, and Laurence Olivier.

—ROSE DEL CASTILLO GUILBAULT, "Americanization Is Tough on 'Macho'"

(For another example of comparison and contrast, see **paragraphs**.)

comparisons

Incomplete comparisons are a common advertising technique ("38% fewer cavities when you brush your teeth with Brand X"), but they are not appropriate in formal writing, where comparisons must be complete, logical, and clear.

To be complete, comparisons must identify the two things being compared.

than store-bought cookies
Homemade cookies are better.
  ∧

[What are homemade cookies being compared to?]

For comparisons to be logical, the things being compared must indeed be comparable. To make sure that a comparison is logical, check the two parts for **parallel structure**.

's hide
The rhinoceros's hide is almost as tough as the alligator.
  ∧

[It is not logical to compare *hide* with *alligator*.]

For comparisons to be clear, they must be complete and unambiguous. As you revise, consider whether your comparisons can have more than one meaning.

is
Russia is farther from St. Louis than England.
  ∧

it is from
OR   Russia is farther from St. Louis than England.
  ∧

When you are comparing two things of the same kind, use *any other* rather than *any*.

other
This book is better than any I have read.
  ∧

[Without *other*, "this book" is not one of the "(books) I have read."]

complement/compliment

As a **noun**, *complement* means "anything that completes or perfects." As a **verb**, *complement* means "to make complete" or "to enhance."

A *complement* of four students would bring our class to its normal size. [noun]

That teal blouse *complements* your jacket nicely. [verb]

As a noun, *compliment* means "something said in admiration, praise, or flattery." As a verb, *compliment* means "to congratulate" or "to praise."

Jeff's mother *complimented* him on the job he had done cleaning his room. [verb]

The *compliment* from his mother boosted Jeff's morale. [noun]

complements (grammatical)

As a grammatical term, a complement is a word, **phrase**, or **clause** that completes the meaning of the **predicate**.

> The geologist drove a *Jeep*. [word]
>
> To ride with him is *to risk your life*. [phrase]
>
> I was surprised *that he was so reckless*. [clause]

There are four kinds of complements: direct object, indirect object, object complement, and subject complement.

A **direct object** is a **noun** or a word group acting as a noun that indicates what or who receives the action of a **transitive verb**.

> She likes *chocolate*. [noun]
>
> She likes *to work*. [verbal]
>
> She also likes *him*. [pronoun]
>
> She likes *what she does*. [noun clause]

An **indirect object** is a noun or a word group acting as a noun that indicates to whom or for whom the action of a verb is directed. It accompanies a direct object following particular transitive verbs, such as *buy, bring, cause, give, sell, take, tell,* and *wish.*

> Tell *Camille* the story. [*Story* is the direct object; *Camille* is the indirect object.]
>
> Fergus gives his *dog* a new bone every Saturday. [*Bone* is the direct object; *dog* is the indirect object.]

An **object complement** is a noun or an **adjective** that renames or describes the direct object.

> Peggy called him a *jerk*. [*Him* is the direct object; *jerk* (noun) is the object complement.]
>
> He was making her *angry*. [*Her* is the direct object; *angry* (adjective) is the object complement.]

A **subject complement** is a word or a word group following a **linking verb** that renames or describes the **subject**. It may be a **predicate nominative** or a **predicate adjective**.

> Her boyfriend is a *computer scientist*. [*Boyfriend* is the subject; *computer scientist* (predicate nominative) is the subject complement.]
>
> Her brother is *poor*. [*Brother* is the subject; *poor* (predicate adjective) is the subject complement.]

complete subjects and predicates

A complete **subject** is the **simple subject** plus its **modifiers.**

> *The impersonal-looking letter from the college* held the verdict on her future. [*Letter* is the simple subject; the phrase is the complete subject.]

A complete **predicate** is the **simple predicate** and any **objects, modifiers, or complements.**

> She *turned it over nervously in her hands.* [*Turned* is the simple predicate; *it* is the direct object; *over* and *nervously* are adverbs modifying *turned;* *in her hands* is a prepositional phrase modifying *turned.*]

complex sentences

A complex sentence consists of one **independent clause** and one or more **dependent clauses.** The independent clause expresses the main idea, and the dependent clauses express subordinate ideas or emphasize one thought over others.

> *We lost touch with the Scheppers* [independent clause] *after they moved* [dependent clause].
>
> The problem, *which wouldn't be so serious if presidents were limited to one six-year term,* is that the chief executive won't do anything that might hinder his reelection. [dependent clause embedded in independent clause]

Use complex sentences combined with **simple sentences** and **compound sentences** to give your writing variety and interest. In fact, you can sometimes make your meaning more exact if you change one of the independent clauses of a compound sentence to a subordinate clause, creating a complex sentence. (See also **subordination.**)

> The Scheppers moved *and* we lost touch with them. [compound sentence with **coordinating conjunction**]
>
> *After* the Scheppers moved, we lost touch with them. [complex sentence with **subordinating conjunction**]

composing processes   (See **Composing Processes**, pages 1–23.)

compound-complex sentences

A compound-complex sentence combines the features of a **compound sentence** (two or more **independent clauses**) and a **complex sentence** (at least one **dependent clause**).

When I got to our house, I rushed into the yard and called out to her, but no answer came.

—Jamaica Kincaid, "The Circling Hand"

This sentence begins with a dependent clause (*When I got to our house*). The first independent clause contains a compound verb (*rushed* and *called*). The two independent clauses are joined by the coordinating conjunction *but*.

You can often group ideas more effectively and coherently with compound-complex sentences than with other sentence types. However, this type of sentence can sometimes become too complicated. As you revise, pay attention to the clarity of compound-complex sentences; if necessary, divide them into shorter, simpler sentences.

compound sentences

A compound sentence has at least two **independent clauses**.

People makes me grouchy, and I have been trying for months to figure out why.

—Nora Ephron, "*People* Magazine"

The independent clauses express ideas of equal importance and may be combined in one of three ways. They may be joined by a **comma** and a **coordinating conjunction**.

Some people start college right after high school, *but* they can't afford to finish in four years.

The two clauses may be separated by a **semicolon**.

Some students pay for college tuition by working; others are able to secure a scholarship.

Finally, the two clauses may be joined by a semicolon, followed by a **conjunctive adverb**, followed by a comma.

Many students go to school and work part-time; *however,* they rarely finish college in four years.

Independent clauses of similar length and construction make the compound sentence a **balanced sentence**.

I spent my summer vacation in Switzerland, and I traveled to Aruba during the winter break.

Change a compound sentence to a **complex sentence** or a **compound-complex sentence** if the ideas in the clauses are not all of equal importance. (See also **subordination**.)

| CHANGE | I saw the northern lights, and I have always been awed by them, so I stood still and gazed at them. [compound sentence] |
| TO | Seeing the northern lights, which have always awed me, I stood still and gazed at them. [complex sentence] |

compound subjects

A compound subject is two or more subjects for a single verb. When the subjects are connected by *and*, the verb is usually plural.

are
Lisa and Darryl ̵i̵s̵ dressing up as a dragon for Halloween.
      ^

If the nouns joined by *and* function as a single unit, use a singular verb.

Spaghetti and meatballs is my favorite dinner.

A compound subject preceded by *each* or *every* takes a singular verb.

Every new book and journal is catalogued before it is shelved.

When compound subjects are joined by *or* or *nor,* the verb agrees with the nearest subject word.

Neither moon nor stars were visible. [The plural noun, *stars,* takes a plural verb, *were.*]

compound words

A compound word is made of two or more words. Some compound words are hyphenated (*high-tech, low-cost*), some are written as one word (*brainstorm, railroad*), and others are written as two words (*high school, post office*). If you are not certain about the form of a particular compound word, check a dictionary. The meaning of a pair of words can depend on whether they are written as one word or two (*green house/greenhouse, blue book/bluebook*).

Plurals of compound nouns are formed by adding *-s* to the most important word.

also-rans	bird-watchers	mothers-in-law
passersby	raincoats	sweethearts

Possessives of compound nouns are formed by adding *-'s* to the last word.

the letter carrier's reaction   her mother-in-law's secret

For capitalization of compound words in titles, see **capital letters.**

conciseness/wordiness

Concise writing has no unnecessary words. It is achieved only by careful revision. (See also **Composing Processes**, pages 13–23.) Compare, for example, the original and the revised versions of the following sentence.

CHANGE   The payment to which the housing office is entitled should be made promptly so that in the event of a large enrollment, you, as an incoming freshman, may not be denied a place to stay by virtue of your nonpayment.

TO   Pay your housing fee. Then, even if enrollment rises, you will be sure of having a place to stay.

The revision has not only divided one extremely long sentence but also eliminated empty words and phrases and changed a **passive voice** verb to the **active voice**. The following guidelines explain these and other techniques for achieving conciseness.

Eliminate Redundant Elements

Words or phrases that repeat the same idea are redundant.

The cosmetics department was offering a *free gift* with every purchase. [*Free gift* is redundant; gifts are always free.]

EXAMPLES OF REDUNDANT PHRASES

Delete the words in italics in your writing.

advance planning	*close* proximity	*fellow* colleagues
and moreover	*completely* finished	few *in number*
appear *to be*	connect *together*	filled *to capacity*
as to whether	cooperate *together*	*final* outcome
attach *together*	descend *down*	*first* priority
basic essentials	eliminate *altogether*	follow *after*
blue *in color*	*end* product	frown/smile *on his face*
but nevertheless	*end* result	gather *together*

graceful *in appearance*	*new* beginning	sink *down*
habitual/usual custom	*original* source	small/large *in size*
hot-water heater	*passing* phase/fad/fancy	square/round *in shape*
inside *of*	*past* history	strangled *to death*
invited guest	penetrate *into*	*surrounding* circumstances
join *together*	*personal* opinion	*total* annihilation/ extinction/ destruction
joint/mutual cooperation	preplan	
last *of all*	protrude *out*	*true* facts
lift *up*	realization of a dream *come true*	*violent* explosion
local resident	return *back*	worthy *of merit*
may/might *possibly*	separate *apart*	3 p.m. *in the afternoon*
never *at any time*	*serious* danger	

(See also **cliché** and **jargon**.)

Eliminate Empty Words and Phrases

Vague verbs and nouns (such as *to be* verbs, *involve, center around, aspect, element, factor, field, kind, nature*) can lead to wordy sentences. (See also **buzzwords** and **vague words**.)

> *We were arguing about*
> ~~The *nature* of our argument involved~~ whether to go to the 7:15 or the 9:45 show.
> ⋀
>
> *worried*
> The frost ~~was worrisome to~~ the citrus growers.
> ⋀

Intensifiers (such as *very, more, most, best, quite*) and other modifiers can also be empty words. As you revise, consider whether every adverb and adjective is necessary.

He bore a ~~very~~ strong resemblance to his father. [unnecessary intensifier]

The sweater was an ~~absolutely~~ perfect fit. [unnecessary adverb]

Her hometown was ~~rather~~ typical of small-town America. [unnecessary adverb]

Many empty phrases (such as *I think, in my opinion, I am going to discuss, as you know,* and *needless to say*) can be eliminated from a sentence without affecting its meaning. Others, including the following examples, can be reduced to a single word.

EXAMPLES OF EMPTY PHRASES

CHANGE	TO
along the lines of	like
as of that date	then
at present	now
at that point (time)	then
at this point (time)	now
by means of	by
by using (utilizing)	with
due to the fact that	because
during that period	then
for the purpose of	for
for the reason that	because
in order to	to
in spite of the fact that	although, though
in the event that	if
in the neighborhood of	about
owing to the fact that	because
so as to	to
the fact that	that
through the use of	with
until such time as	until

Simplify the Structure

Eliminate Unnecessary Repetition   Although repetition can be intentionally used to emphasize a word or phrase, often it is simply careless writing. Unnecessary repetition can be eliminated by using **elliptical constructions,** by rewording, or by combining sentences.

The house we bought next to the Joneses' ~~house~~ is the best ~~house~~ we have had.

[Use elliptical constructions only in sentences, such as this one, where the reader can readily fill in the omitted words.]

Nearly all ~~the pictures~~ Monet painted*'s* are *ings* ~~pictures~~ of scenery.

[Rewording eliminates not only the repetition of *pictures* but also the redundancy of *pictures painted.*]

Monica was typing a letter/ ~~The letter was~~ to her brother/ ~~It was~~ about her plans

for spring break.

[Combining the three sentences eliminates repetition of both the noun *letter* and the pronoun *it* representing *letter.*]

Turn Nouns into Verbs Many nouns have verb forms, and sentences can sometimes be made less wordy and more direct by using the verb form. Compare, for example, *conduct an investigation* and *investigate.* All-purpose verbs such as *conduct, do, make,* and *perform* often precede nouns that can be changed into verbs.

Susan asked Roque to ~~make a translation of~~ *translate* the song.

The dentist had to ~~perform an extraction of~~ *extract* the tooth.

Eliminate Expletive Constructions Sentences beginning with the **expletives** *there is, there are,* and *it is* can be made more concise by eliminating the expletive.

~~There are~~ *M*any students ~~who~~ are planning to attend the workshop on Friday.

~~It was understood that~~ *W*e ~~would each~~ *agreed to* pay for our own dinners.

Change Passive Voice to Active Voice **Passive voice** constructions are wordier and less direct than **active voice** constructions; compare, for example, *the mail was brought in by us* to *we brought in the mail.* When you do not have a reason for using the passive voice, use the active voice.

the instructor reads
Bluebooks are used when the examinations ~~are read by the instructor~~, and scan-
                                          ^
                                    a computer reads them⊙
tron sheets are used when ~~they are read by a computer.~~
                                                          ^

[The passive voice is preferable for the clauses *Bluebooks are used* and *scantron
sheets are used* because the desired emphasis is on the types of tests used rather
than on who uses them.]

Reduce Clauses to Phrases and Phrases to Words   The previous example can
be made even more concise by turning clauses into phrases.

                              for teacher-read
Bluebooks are used ~~when teachers read the~~ examinations, and scantron sheets are
         for computer-read ones⊙
used ~~when the answers are read by a computer.~~
                                              ^

Turn Negative Sentences into Positive Ones   Positive sentences are less
wordy and easier to understand than negative sentences.

                                                       s
We will ~~not~~ take the trip if the weather ~~does not~~ look good.
                                                         ^

conclusion (ending)

The way you conclude a paper depends on both the **purpose** of your writing and the needs of your **audience**. For example, an essay about a memorable experience could end by reflecting on what you learned from the experience. A **persuasive** essay in which you compare and contrast two items
might end by summarizing the ways in which one is superior to the other.
An **argument** could end by reminding the reader of the points you have made
in support of your **thesis** and perhaps by calling for action.

TYPES OF CONCLUSIONS

REFLECTION
Looking back, I'm surprised I made it through that semester. Sometimes I
wonder if it was worth it. I worked hard, I worried constantly, and I even
began to doubt myself. For all of that, I received a C. Longfellow once wrote:
"Oh, fear not in a world like this / And thou shalt know ere long, / Know
how sublime a thing it is / To suffer and be strong." In my case, those final

lines might more aptly read, "Know how sublime a thing it is / To suffer and be *wrong*."

SUMMARY
If you're shopping for a computer, buy a Mac. It's user friendly, it has better graphics than other personal computers do, and it's cheaper. What more could you want?

CALL FOR ACTION
Join ACLU now if you want to retain your Fourth Amendment rights.

QUESTION
Do you want to return to the days of illegal search and seizure? Do you wish to relinquish your rights to personal privacy? Do you really believe the government should tell you how to live?

ADVICE
Son and father, together, had saved the day—he by holding out for something he enjoyed and I by having the sense, finally, to realize that he was right, and to let go of my dream of how things should be.

This time, anyway.

And then I remembered something else. When my own father took me to Yankee Stadium, I was 6 years old, not 4.

Maybe in a couple of years. . . .

—ANDREW MERTON, "When Father Doesn't Know Best"

Narrative or descriptive papers might conclude with a closing story, some dialogue between the main characters, or a wry or witty comment. Most short academic papers conclude in a final paragraph and do not require a separate conclusion section. Longer projects, such as research papers, may need a conclusion section to emphasize and discuss the findings and their implications.

Whatever kind of conclusion you decide on, it should not introduce new topics, apologize for any real or perceived failings in the paper, or merely stop or trail off. Make sure your paper has a clear sense of closure.

CHANGE   I could go on, but I'm running out of time, so I'll just stop here.

TO   Of course, there are numerous reasons why the educational system should be changed. However, as I've shown in this paper, the main reasons are clear: we need to meet the needs of all students, we need to engage them in learning, and we need to make sure that what they learn in the classroom can be applied to the world of work.

concrete words   (See **abstract words/concrete words**.)

conditional sentences

Conditional sentences contain a **dependent clause** beginning with *if, when,* or *unless* and can express generalizations, predictions, or possibilities. The three types of conditional sentences use different verb **tense** sequences.

Factual conditional sentences express related events that are habitual or governed by a law of nature. The verbs in both clauses are in the same tense— past or present—depending on the time of the action.

> If it *is* a sunny day, I always *go* for a walk.
>
> When water *is heated* to 212 degrees, it *boils*.

Factual conditional sentences can also be used to make requests.

> When the sun *comes* up, you *need* to milk the cows.

Predictive conditional sentences express future events that are planned or are likely to happen. The verbs in the two clauses are in different tenses: the present tense in the dependent clause, and the future tense in the independent clause.

> Unless you *study* for that exam, you *will get* a poor grade.

Imaginative conditional sentences speculate about events that are possible but unlikely, that are completely impossible, or that never happened. The verbs in the two clauses are in different tenses. To talk about an event in the present, use the **subjunctive** *were* in the dependent clause, and use *would, could,* or *might* plus the **infinitive** form of the verb in the independent clause.

> If I *were* you [but I'm not], I *would marry* that man.

To talk about an event in the past, use the **past perfect tense** in the dependent clause and use *would* plus the **present perfect tense** in the independent clause.

> If Hitler *had conquered* Europe [but he didn't], the world *would have been* a much different place.

Do not confuse the imaginative conditional with a noun clause in an indirect quotation ("The instructor asked Karl if he was going to drop the class.").

conjunctions

A conjunction connects words, **phrases**, or **clauses** and indicates the relationship between the elements it connects. For example, the conjunction *and* joins elements; *or* selects and separates them.

When two successive sentences are closely related, you may start the second sentence with a coordinating conjunction to provide a **transition**.

Most students are impressed by how computers can speed revision and enhance a paper's appearance. *But* the bubble bursts when they lose a file or accidentally erase a semester's work.

Types of Conjunctions

Coordinating conjunctions join two words or sentence elements that have identical functions (see also **parallel structures**). The coordinating conjunctions are *and, but, for, nor, or, so,* and *yet.*

Bill *and* John are brothers. [joining two proper nouns]

People are always surprised that I'm able to cook meals *and* bake cookies. [joining two phrases]

She likes tennis, *but* he prefers softball. [joining two clauses]

Correlative conjunctions are conjunctions used in pairs to join grammatically equal words, phrases, or clauses. The correlative conjunctions are *both . . . and, either . . . or, neither . . . nor, not only . . . but also,* and *whether . . . or.*

Raoul will arrive *either* at Midway *or* at O'Hare. [joining two phrases]

When a correlative conjunction joins a singular noun to a plural noun, the verb should agree with the nearest noun. (See also **agreement of subjects and verbs.**)

Neither the students nor the *teacher looks* forward to the Saturday morning class. [The singular third-person form of the verb, *looks,* agrees with the singular noun, *teacher.*]

Subordinating conjunctions connect **dependent clauses** to **independent clauses.** The most frequently used subordinating conjunctions are *after, although, as, because, before, if, since, so, than, that, though, unless, when, where,* and *whereas.*

She went to bed *after* she had finished reading her book.

Punctuation with Coordinating Conjunctions

A **comma** should immediately precede a coordinating conjunction separating two independent clauses, especially if they are relatively long.

The *Life* magazine project was her third assignment, *and* it was the one that made her reputation as a photographer.

A **semicolon** may precede the coordinating conjunction joining two independent clauses that have commas within them.

> Even though it's finals week, we must finish our project; *and* all of our group, including first-year students, will have to contribute.

Conjunctions in Titles

Coordinating conjunctions in the titles of books, articles, plays, movies, and other works should not be capitalized unless they are the first or last word in the title or subtitle. (See also **capital letters**.)

> *Crime and Punishment*
>
> *Neither Fish nor Fowl*

conjunctive adverbs

A conjunctive adverb functions both as an **adverb** modifying the **clause** it introduces and as a **conjunction** joining two **independent clauses**.

> The car ran well for the mechanics; *consequently,* they ignored my complaints.

FREQUENTLY USED CONJUNCTIVE ADVERBS

accordingly	furthermore	meanwhile	still
also	hence	moreover	subsequently
anyway	however	nevertheless	then
besides	incidentally	next	therefore
certainly	indeed	nonetheless	thus
consequently	instead	otherwise	
finally	likewise	similarly	

Two independent clauses joined by a conjunctive adverb require a **semicolon** before and a **comma** after the conjunctive adverb.

> My parents' new house is smaller than their old one; *nevertheless,* they find it very comfortable most of the time.

When the conjunctive adverb is in the middle or at the end of a clause, however, it may be set off by commas; a semicolon alone then separates the two clauses.

My parents' new house is smaller than their old one; most of the time, however, they find it very comfortable.

OR   My parents' new house is smaller than their old one; they find it very comfortable most of the time, however.

A conjunctive adverb that begins a sentence can provide an emphatic **transition**. It is often set off with a comma, unless it flows smoothly into the rest of the sentence and calls for no pause in reading.

Our dog has been nothing but trouble. *Therefore*, he has to go.

connotation/denotation

The denotation of a word is its dictionary definition. The connotations of a word are its emotional associations. For example, *cheap* and *frugal* both refer to a reluctance to spend money, but they have different connotations.

Her grandfather was cheap. [negative connotation]

Her grandfather was frugal. [positive connotation]

Clear writing requires words with both the most accurate denotation and the most appropriate connotations. If you have trouble finding the right word, look in a **thesaurus** for synonyms. But be sure to check a **dictionary** for meanings and usage examples of any unfamiliar synonyms.

consensus

Because *consensus* means "general agreement," the **phrases** *consensus of opinion* and *general consensus* are redundant.

context

Within a text, context is the part of the text that surrounds—and affects the meaning or appropriateness of—a particular word or passage. A reader can often determine the meaning of an unfamiliar word by considering its context. The following sentences show how the meaning of the word *paper* can vary in different contexts.

I start each day with coffee and the morning *paper.*

Before we moved in, we had someone *paper* the bathroom walls.

My entire grade rests on this research *paper.*

Our cat is pedigreed; we have her *papers.*

For a writer, context consists of the rhetorical situation, including the occasion, the writer's **purpose,** and the **audience** for whom the text is being written. For more information, see **Composing Processes.**

continual/continuous

Continual is an **adjective** meaning "recurring in steady and usually rapid succession."

> *Continual* arithmetic drills were the norm in schools fifty years ago.

Continuous, also an adjective, means "marked by uninterrupted flow."

> The *continuous* moan of the wind was so monotonous after three days that Sandy felt like screaming.

contractions

A contraction is a condensed spelling of an expression; an **apostrophe** replaces the missing letters. Use contractions sparingly, if at all, in formal writing.

| cannot | can't | has not | hasn't |
| it is | it's | we will | we'll |

Do not confuse the spelling and punctuation of the contractions *it's, you're, who's, they're,* and *there's* with those of the possessive pronouns *its, your, whose, their,* and *theirs.*

> *You're* the first one in this family to get *your* diploma.

> *There's* never been another Wallen who graduated from college. *They're* especially proud of you, and *theirs* is a proud family.

coordinate adjectives

Coordinate adjectives are two or more **adjectives** that independently modify a **noun**. In contrast to **cumulative adjectives**, coordinate adjectives can be put in a different order and still make sense, and they are separated by a comma.

> *long, dull* movie [coordinate adjectives]

> *quiet piano* music [cumulative adjectives]

coordinating conjunctions

Coordinating conjunctions join two grammatically equal words, phrases, or clauses. The seven coordinating conjunctions are *and, but, for, nor, or, so* and *yet.* (See also **conjunctions**.)

correlative conjunctions

Correlative conjunctions (also called *correlatives*) are pairs of **conjunctions** that join grammatically equal words, phrases, or clauses. The five correlative conjunctions are *both . . . and, either . . . or, neither . . . nor, not only . . . but also,* and *whether . . . or.*

correspondence (See **letters.**)

could have/could of

Could of is nonstandard for *could have.*

> *have*
> I *could of* been a contender.
>   ∧

Council of Science Editors (formerly Council of Biology Editors) (CSE/CBE) style (See **Research Processes**, pages 139–52.)

count nouns

A count noun is a type of **noun** that identifies things that can be separated into countable units. (See also **mass nouns** and **noncount nouns.**)

desks	chisels	envelopes	pencils

There were four *calculators* in the office.

credibility

Credibility—the writer's claim to believability—is important in every rhetorical situation but particularly in persuasive writing; the writer's credibility determines the effectiveness of the argument. In research-based writing, use of credible sources helps establish credibility. Credible sources are usually experts in their fields or others with appropriate credentials. Determining the credibility of Web sources requires extra effort (See **Composing Processes** and **Research Processes**, pages 29–33, 44–46, and 55–56.)

criterion/criteria

Criterion is singular, meaning "an established standard for judging or testing." *Criteria* is the plural form of *criterion* and should not be used as a singular noun.

> *criterion*
> In evaluating this job, we must use three *criteria*. The most important ~~criteria~~ is
>   ∧
>
> publication.

critique

A critique (**noun**) is a written or oral evaluation, especially of a work of art or literature. Do not use *critique* as a **verb** meaning "to review or discuss critically."

prepare a   of
Please ˄critique ˄your rough draft.

CSE/CBE style (See **Research Processes**, pages 139–52.)

cumulative adjectives

Cumulative adjectives are two or more adjectives not separated by **commas**. In contrast to **coordinate adjectives**, they do not make sense in any other order and cannot be connected by *and*.

> *an enormous old redwood* tree [*redwood* modifies *tree; old* modifies the phrase *redwood tree; enormous* modifies the phrase *old redwood tree; an* modifies *enormous old redwood tree*]

cumulative sentences

Cumulative sentences (also known as *loose sentences*) begin with a **subject** and a **predicate** and then add a series of **phrases** or **clauses** that amplify or explain the idea in the independent clause. (See also **periodic sentences** and **sentence types.**)

> A single knoll rises out of the plain in Oklahoma, north and west of the Wichita range. [The subject, *knoll,* and predicate, *rises,* are followed by two prepositional phrases, a pair of adverbs, and another prepositional phrase.]
>
> —N. SCOTT MOMADAY, "The Way to Rainy Mountain"

dangling modifiers

Phrases that do not clearly and logically refer to a **noun** or **pronoun** are called dangling modifiers. Dangling modifiers usually appear at the beginning of a sentence.

> *the operator was*
> While eating lunch in the cafeteria, the computer malfunctioned.
>   ∧

[The sentence does not say who was eating and suggests that the computer was.]

Sometimes, however, they appear at the end of a sentence.

> *the skier is*
> Downhill skiing can be dangerous when inexperienced.
>   ∧

[The sentence does not say who was inexperienced.]

To test whether a phrase is a dangling modifier, check whether the subject of the independent clause is the noun or noun phrase acting in the modifier. If not, the modifier is dangling.

> After finishing the research, the paper was easy to write.

The subject of the independent clause is *paper*. But *paper* did not finish the research, so the modifier is dangling, and the sentence should be recast.

To revise a dangling modifier, you may change the subject of the independent clause.

> *I found that*
> After finishing the research, the paper was easy to write.
>   ∧

Or you may change the phrase into a clause with an explicit subject.

> *Because she hated*
> ~~Hating~~ the very idea of tofu, the recipe was unacceptable to her.
>   ∧

(See also **misplaced modifiers** and **verbals**.)

dashes

The dash can link, separate, and enclose. It is more informal and more emphatic than a **comma** or **parentheses**, so use it sparingly. Compare the effects of the punctuation in the following sentences.

> Only one person—the president—can authorize such activity. [emphasis on *the president*]

263

Only one person, the president, can authorize such activity. [equal emphasis on *one person* and *the president*]

Only one person (the president) can authorize such activity. [emphasis on *one person*]

A dash can indicate a sharp turn in thought, an emphatic pause, or an **interjection** that interrupts a sentence.

The school year will end June 15—unless we have to make up snow days.

You can go shopping—after you mow the lawn.

The sudden snowfall—in early October!—upset our plans.

A dash can be used before a summarizing statement or a repetition that has the effect of an afterthought.

It was hot near the ovens—steaming hot.

Dashes can set off an explanatory or **appositive** series in the middle of a sentence or at the beginning.

Three of the applicants—John Evans, Mary Fontana, and Thomas Lopez—seem well qualified for the job.

Baking, cooking, cleaning—all must be done before the guests arrive for Thanksgiving.

In typing, use two consecutive **hyphens** (--) to indicate a dash, with no spaces before or after the hyphens. A number of computer word-processing programs will make dashes if you hold down the shift and the alt (or option) keys while you press the hyphen key. Others will automatically convert two hyphens into a dash as soon as they are typed.

data

Although many people use *data* as a singular noun (instead of *datum*), it is advisable to treat *data* as a plural noun in formal writing.

The *data are* in, and *they* show improvement in test scores.

database

A database is a collection of data or information that is organized in such a way that it can easily be accessed, managed, and updated. Today, most databases are computerized. (See **Research Processes**, pages 34–60.)

dates

Use **commas** in month-day-year dates between the day, the year, and the rest of the sentence.

October 26, 1956, is the date my mother was born.

Day-month-year dates do not require commas. (This way of writing dates is more common in Europe than in the United States.)

My mother was born on 26 October 1956 in Utah.

Do not use the numerical form for dates (10/26/02) in formal writing or business letters. When the numerical form is used, the order in American usage is month/day/year. For example, 5/7/02 is May 7, 2002. (See also **numbers and symbols.**)

decimals (See **numbers and symbols.**)

declarative sentence (See **sentence types.**)

deductive reasoning (See **logic.**)

defining terms

Terms can be defined either formally or informally, depending on your purpose and on your audience. A formal definition states the term to be defined, places it in a category, and then identifies the features that distinguish it from other members of the same category.

An annual [term] is a plant [category] that completes its life cycle, from seed to natural death, in one growing season [distinguishing features].

An informal definition explains a term by giving a familiar word or **phrase** as a **synonym.**

An invoice is a *bill.* [synonym as subject complement]

Many states have set up wildlife habitats (or *living spaces*). [synonym as appositive in parentheses]

Plants have a symbiotic, or *mutually beneficial,* relationship with certain kinds of bacteria. [synonym as appositive enclosed by commas]

(See also **abstract words/concrete words.**)

Definition Faults

Avoid circular definitions, which merely restate the term to be defined and therefore fail to clarify it.

CIRCULAR   *Spontaneous combustion* is fire that begins spontaneously.

REVISED   *Spontaneous combustion* is the self-ignition of a flammable material through a chemical reaction such as oxidation and temperature buildup.

Avoid faulty "is when" and "is where" definitions, which illogically equate the subject with a *when* or *where* clause.

D

a binding agreement between
A contract is ~~when~~ two or more people ~~agree to something.~~
　　　　　　　　　　^

a facility
A daycare center is *where* working parents can leave their preschool children
　　　　　　　　　　　　^

during the day.

Form for Defined Terms

The word being defined may be in **italics** (or underlined), or it may be set off with **quotation marks**. Whichever form you choose, be consistent.

In this paper, the term "literacy" refers to an individual's capacity to communicate either orally or in writing with other individuals.

definition as a method of development

Depending on the purpose of your paper and on your audience's knowledge of the topic, you may want to give an extended definition of a key term or concept. In the following paragraph, the author defines EQ by first defining the original concept of "emotional intelligence" and then describing the popularization of the concept as EQ.

> The phrase "emotional intelligence" was coined by Yale psychologist Peter Salovey and the University of New Hampshire's John Mayer five years ago to describe qualities like understanding one's own feelings, empathy for the feelings of others and "the regulation of emotion in a way that enhances living." Their notion is about to bound into the national conversation, handily shortened to EQ, thanks to a new book, *Emotional Intelligence,* by Daniel Goleman. Goleman, a Harvard psychology Ph.D. and a *New York Times* science writer with a gift for making even the chewiest scientific theories digestible to lay readers, has brought together a decade's worth of behavioral research into how the mind processes feelings. His goal, he announces on the cover, is to redefine what it means to be smart. His thesis: when it comes to predicting people's success, brainpower as measured by IQ and standardized achievement tests may actually matter less than the qualities of mind once thought of as "character" before the word began to sound quaint.
> —Nancy Gibbs, "The EQ Factor"

(For other examples, see **introductions** and **paragraphs**.)

demonstrative adjectives

A demonstrative **adjective** shows where the thing it modifies is in space or time. The four demonstratives are paired in relation to distance: *this* and *these* suggest here or a close position or time; *that* and *those* suggest there or a remote position or time. They are also paired in relation to **number**: *this* and *that* are singular forms; *these* and *those* are plural forms.

D

This car is the one we bought.

That car would have been impractical.

These car salespeople were helpful and informative.

Those dealers are not to be trusted.

When you use a demonstrative adjective to modify a grouping **noun** such as *class, kind, sort, type,* and *variety,* match the number of the adjective and the noun. Use a singular adjective with a singular noun and a plural adjective with a plural noun.

this class	these classes
this kind	these kinds
this variety	these varieties

The object of the preposition *of* ("this kind," "these kinds *of* ") should also agree in number with the demonstrative adjective and its noun.

This kind of *pears* is best.

These kinds of *pear* are best.

demonstrative pronouns

Demonstrative pronouns (*this, these, that,* and *those*) substitute for nouns. *This* and *that* are used for singular nouns and *these* and *those* for plural nouns. The **antecedent** of a demonstrative pronoun must either be the last noun of the preceding sentence—not the idea of the sentence—or be clearly identified within the same sentence, as in the following examples.

This is the *itinerary* for my vacation.

These are the *places* where we will stay.

That was a *picture* of the Grand Canyon.

Those were the *mules* we rode to the bottom.

Do not use the pronouns *this* and *that* to refer to a whole sentence or to an abstract thought. (See also **pronoun reference**.) One way to avoid this problem is to insert a noun immediately after the demonstrative pronoun, thus turning it into a **demonstrative adjective**.

brownout
The inadequate electrical system has resulted in a brownout. *This* is our most se-
⌃

rious problem at present.

denotation   (See **connotation/denotation**.)

dependent-clause errors

To minimize errors with **adjective clauses**, remember that the **relative pronoun** (*who, whom, whose, that, which*) has two roles: It connects the dependent clause to the independent clause, and it is part of the dependent clause (usually its subject or object).

The hand *that* rocks the cradle rules the world. [*That* refers to *hand* and is also the subject of the dependent clause *that rocks the cradle*.]

The man *whom* I met was going to St. Ives. [*Whom* refers to *man* and is also the object of the dependent clause *whom I met*.]

Do not add a second pronoun to an adjective clause.

We received the sweater that you sent ~~it~~ yesterday.

A stone that ~~it~~ rolls gathers no moss.

Do not use an adjective clause as a subject or object.

The person who
~~Who~~ was working at the site of the blast was killed instantly.
⌃

the person
The mail carrier delivered it to *who* was sitting at the front desk.
⌃

A **noun clause** should begin with a relative pronoun or a **subordinating conjunction** (such as *that, if,* or *whether*), not a preposition.

that
I regret telling my supervisor ~~about~~ my co-worker was lazy.
⌃

In a sentence with an **adverb clause**, do not use a **coordinating conjunction** (such as *and, but,* or *or*) in addition to a subordinating conjunction.

Although I love my new car, ~~but~~ I hate the monthly payments.

dependent clauses

A dependent (or subordinate) **clause** is a word group with a **subject** and a **predicate** that cannot stand alone as a **sentence.** The dependent clause begins with a **subordinating conjunction** (*although, because,* or *since,* for example) or a **relative pronoun** (such as *who, which,* or *that*), and it needs an **independent clause** to complete its meaning. In a sentence, a dependent clause may serve as a **noun,** an **adjective,** or an **adverb.** (See also **subordination.**)

Noun Clauses

A **noun clause** can be a **subject,** an **object,** or a **complement.**

That we had all passed pleased us. [subject]

I learned *that drugs ordered by brand name can cost several times as much as drugs ordered by generic name.* [direct object of verb]

The trouble is *that not all pharmacies carry generic drugs.* [subject complement]

Generic drugs should be available to *whoever wants them.* [object of preposition—use *whoever* rather than *whomever* because the word is the subject of the dependent clause]

He got there first by asking *which way was shorter.* [object of a verbal]

Give *whoever wants one* a copy. [indirect object of verb]

She left home and made herself *what she wanted to be.* [object complement]

Adjective Clauses

An **adjective clause** functions as an adjective by modifying a noun or pronoun in another clause.

The student *whom we met yesterday* showed us her collection of albums, *which includes all of Paul McCartney's work.* [modifying the nouns *student* and *albums*]

The man *who called earlier* is here. [modifying *man*]

The fourth quarter is the period *when defense will be critical.* [modifying *period*]

Adjective clauses may be restrictive or nonrestrictive. If the clause is essential to limiting the meaning of the noun, it is restrictive and not set off by commas. (See also **restrictive and nonrestrictive elements.**)

The quotations *that adorn the book jacket* were compiled from a series of favorable reviews.

If the clause is not intended to limit the meaning of the noun but merely provides further information about it, the clause is nonrestrictive and set off by commas.

Other quotations, *which we chose not to include,* expressed more negative opinions.

If adjective clauses are not placed carefully, they may appear to modify the wrong noun or pronoun.

in the suburbs

The house ~~in the suburbs~~ *that we bought* has increased in value.

[The original sentence implies that we bought the suburbs rather than the house.]

Adverb Clauses

Adverb clauses may express relationships of time, cause, result, or degree. They usually modify verbs but may also modify adjectives, adverbs, or whole clauses.

You are making an investment *when you buy a house.* [time]

A title search was necessary *because the bank would not issue a loan without one.* [cause]

The cost of financing a home will be higher *if discount points are charged.* [result]

Monthly mortgage payments should not be much more *than a person earns in one week.* [degree]

description as a method of development

Effective description uses words to transfer a mental image from the writer's mind to the reader's. The keys to effective description are concrete words; figurative language, such as **metaphor, simile,** or **analogy;** and an orderly sequence. (See also **image/imagery.**)

In the following paragraph, Mark Twain uses most of these strategies to describe the Mississippi when he was a cub pilot.

I still keep in mind a certain wonderful sunset which I witnessed when steamboating was new to me. A broad expanse of the river was turned to blood; in the middle distance the red hue brightened into gold, through which a solitary log came floating, black and conspicuous; in one place a long, slanting mark lay sparkling upon the water; in another the surface was broken by boiling, tumbling rings, that were as many-tinted as an opal; where the ruddy flush was faintest, was a smooth spot that was covered with graceful circles and radiating lines, ever so delicately traced; the shore on our left was densely wooded, and the sombre shadow that fell from this forest was broken in places by a long ruffled trail that shone like silver; and high above the forest wall a clean-stemmed dead tree waved a single leafy bough that glowed like a flame in the unobstructed splendor that was flowing from the sun.

—*Old Times on the Mississippi*

details as a method of development

One of the best ways to engage your reader is to include relevant and specific details. The following paragraph provides details to add strength to the author's assertion that all people, regardless of the color of their skin, share many of the same life experiences.

> But in the main, I feel like a brown bag of miscellany propped against a wall. Against a wall in company with other bags, white, red and yellow. Pour out the contents, and there is discovered a jumble of small things priceless and worthless. A first-water diamond, an empty spool, bits of broken glass, lengths of string, a key to a door long since crumbled away, a rusty knife-blade, old shoes saved for a road that never was and never will be, a nail bent under the weight of things too heavy for any nail, a dried flower or two still a little fragrant. In your hand is the brown bag. On the ground before you is the jumble it held—so much like the jumble in the bags, could they be emptied, that all might be dumped in a single heap and the bags refilled without altering the content of any greatly. A bit of colored glass more or less would not matter. Perhaps that is how the Great Stuffer of Bags filled them in the first place—who knows?
>
> —ZORA NEALE HURSTON, "How It Feels to Be Colored Me"

(For another example, see **paragraphs.**)

determiners

Determiners are words that precede nouns and classify them, identify them, or indicate their quantity. Determiners fall into five categories: **articles, demonstrative adjectives,** possessive adjectives, **numbers** (written as words), and **indefinite pronouns.**

developmental strategies (See **methods of development.**)

Dewey decimal system (See **Research Processes,** pages 52–53.)

diagrams (See **graphics.**)

dialect (See **English, varieties of.**)

dialogue

Dialogue—conversation between two or more people—is distinguished from regular text through the use of **quotation marks.** If a single speaker is quoted for more than one paragraph, place quotation marks at the beginning of every paragraph, but do not close the quotes until the end of the speaker's final paragraph. A change in speakers is signaled by beginning a new paragraph.

> "Did you say something, Sammy?"
> "I said I quit."
> "I thought you did."
> "You didn't have to embarrass them."
> "It was they who were embarrassing us."
> I started to say something that came out "Fiddle-de-doo." It's a saying of my grandmother's, and I know she would have been pleased.
> "I don't think you know what you're saying," Lengel said.
> "I know you don't," I said. "But I do."
>
> —JOHN UPDIKE, "A & P"

diction

Diction means both "choice of words" and "vocal expression or enunciation." The meaning associated with **word choice,** however, is the one pertaining to writing.

dictionaries

A dictionary is a reference book that lists words arranged in alphabetical order. In addition, it gives information about the words' meanings, etymologies (origin and history), forms, pronunciation, **spellings,** uses as **idioms,** and functions as a part of speech. (See Figure D-1.) For certain words, it lists **synonyms** and shows how their meanings are similar but different. It may also provide illustrations, if appropriate, such as a table, a map, a photograph, or a drawing. There are two types of dictionaries: desk dictionaries and unabridged dictionaries.

Elements of a Dictionary Entry

Meaning and Etymology For most words, the enumeration of meanings dominates the length of the dictionary entry. Each meaning is listed in order by number, but the significance of this ordering varies among dictionaries. Some dictionaries give the most widely accepted current meaning first; others list the meanings in historical order, with the oldest meaning first and the current meaning last. A dictionary's preface indicates whether current or historical meanings are listed first. In some dictionaries, a meaning specific

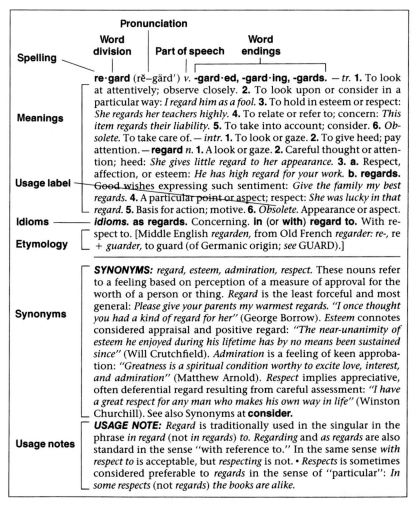

Figure D-1. Dictionary sample entry.

to a certain field of knowledge is so labeled (function, *mathematics*; parallel, *music*).

Information about the origin and history of a word (its etymology) is given in brackets.

Spelling, Word Division, and Pronunciation The entry gives the preferred spelling of the word followed by variant spellings (*catalog/catalogue*), if any. The entry also shows how the word is divided into syllables by inserting a dot between syllables (*re·gard*).

The pronunciation of the word is given in parentheses following the boldfaced entry word. The phonetic symbols (called *diacritical marks*) are explained in a key in the front pages of the dictionary; and an abbreviated symbol key, showing how the symbols should be pronounced, is found at the bottom of each page. Words sometimes have two pronunciations; though both are accurate, the one given first is the preferred pronunciation.

Part of Speech and Word Endings The entry gives the word's **part of speech** (*n*, noun; *v*, verb; *adj*, adjective; and so on). Any irregular forms, such as plurals and verb tense changes, are shown in boldface.

Synonyms Many entries include a listing of **synonyms**, words similar in meaning to the entry word. The listing usually includes a brief discussion of how the meaning of each synonym is distinct from the others.

Usage Usage labels indicate the appropriate (or, in some cases, inappropriate) use of a particular meaning of a word. The most common labels include *nonstandard, colloquial, informal, slang, dialect, archaic, vulgar, British,* and *obsolete*. (See **English, varieties of.**)

Some dictionaries include usage notes as well as labels. These notes, which discuss interesting or problematic aspects of the correct use of a word, are based on the advice of a panel of experts assembled by the dictionary's editors and on actual usage in books, newspapers, and periodicals.

Illustrations and Graphics Some dictionaries include illustrations (usually photographs or line drawings, sometimes charts) to help clarify the meaning of certain words or to put them in context.

Types of Dictionaries

Desk Dictionaries Desk dictionaries are often abridged versions of larger dictionaries. There is no single "best" dictionary, but there are several guidelines for selecting a good one. Choose the most recent edition. The older the dictionary, the less likely it is to have the up-to-date information you need. Select a dictionary with upward of 125,000 entries. Pocket dictionaries are convenient for checking spelling, but for detailed information you'll need the larger range of a desk dictionary. The following are considered good desk dictionaries.

The American Heritage Dictionary of the English Language. 4th ed. 2000. (A searchable online version is available at <http://bartleby.com/61/>.)

Merriam-Webster's Collegiate Dictionary. 10th ed. (A searchable online version is available at <http://www.m-w.com/dictionary>.)

Webster's New World College Dictionary. 4th ed. 1999.

Unabridged Dictionaries Unabridged dictionaries provide complete and authoritative linguistic information. They are impractical for desk use because of their size and expense, but they are available in libraries (perhaps online) and are important reference sources.

Oxford English Dictionary. 2nd ed. The standard historical dictionary of the English language. Its twenty volumes contain over 600,000 words and give the chronological developments of over 240,000 words, providing numerous examples of uses and sources. (Available in print, online, and on CD-ROM.)

Random House Webster's Unabridged Dictionary and CD-ROM. 2nd ed. 1999. Contains about 315,000 entries and uses copious examples. It gives a word's most widely current meaning first and includes biographical and geographical names.

Webster's Third New International Dictionary, unabridged. 1993. Contains over 450,000 entries. Word meanings are listed in historical order, with the current meaning given last. This dictionary does not list biographical and geographical names, nor does it include usage information.

ESL Dictionaries ESL dictionaries are more helpful to the non-native speaker than are regular English dictionaries or bilingual dictionaries. The pronunciation symbols in ESL dictionaries are based on the international phonetic alphabet rather than on English phonetic systems, and useful grammatical information is included both in the entries and in special grammar sections. In addition, the definitions are usually easier to understand than those in regular English dictionaries; for example, a regular English dictionary defines *opaque* as "impervious to the passage of light," and an ESL dictionary defines the word as "not allowing light to pass through." The definitions in ESL dictionaries are usually more thorough than those in bilingual dictionaries. For example, a bilingual dictionary might indicate that *obstacle* and *blockade* are synonymous but not indicate that, although both can refer to physical objects ("The soldiers went around the *blockade* [or *obstacle*] in the road"), only *obstacle* can be used for abstract meanings ("Lack of money can be an *obstacle* [not *blockade*] to a college education").

The following dictionaries and reference books provide helpful information for non-native speakers of English.

Longman Dictionary of American English: A Dictionary for Learners of English. 2nd ed. 1997.

Longman American Idioms Dictionary. 1999.

American Heritage English as a Second Language Dictionary. 1998.

different from/different than

In formal writing, the **preposition** *from* is used with *different*.

The new generation of computers is *different from* earlier generations.

Different than is widely used when it is followed by a **clause**.

The new generation of computers was *different than* we had expected it to be.

differ from/differ with

Differ from means "to be unlike or distinct from."

My opinion of the novel *differs from* Reggie's opinion.

Differ with means "to disagree"; it refers to disagreements between people.

Red and Andy *differ with* each other over almost everything.

direct address

Direct address is a proper or common noun (or phrase) naming the person (or persons) being spoken or written to. Words of direct address are set off by **commas**.

Mary Lu, talk to me!

Don't forget, *all you baseball fans*, that season tickets go on sale today.

direct discourse

In direct discourse, the writer is the speaker, whereas in **indirect discourse**, the writer is recording or repeating the words or thoughts of someone else. When writing, be careful not to shift between the two. (See also **shifts**.)

| DIRECT | Why don't you clean your room? |
| INDIRECT | His mother wondered why he didn't clean his room. |

direct objects

A direct object answers the question *what* or *whom* and follows a **transitive verb**.

I love the *films* of Alfred Hitchcock. [*Films* tells what the speaker loves.]

I love *you*. [*You* is whom the speaker loves.]

(See also **objects**.)

direct quotations

A direct quotation is the exact words someone spoke or wrote. (See also **quotation marks, quotations,** and **indirect discourse.**)

disinterested/uninterested

Disinterested means "impartial, objective, unbiased"; *uninterested* means "without interest" or "indifferent."

> Like good judges, scientists should be passionately interested in the problems they are working on but completely *disinterested* as they evaluate possible solutions.
>
> Despite Jane's enthusiasm, her husband remained *uninterested* in her work.

dividing a word (See **hyphens.**)

division as a method of development (See **analysis as a method of development.**)

documentation

Documentation gives appropriate credit to others whose words or ideas you have used. In American and many other cultures, a failure to give such credit, even if the failure is unintentional, is considered **plagiarism** and is a serious violation of the rules of scholarship. Plagiarism can result in penalties ranging from a failing grade on the paper to a failing grade in the course or even expulsion from school. See also **Research Processes,** especially the discussions of taking notes, paraphrases, and summaries.

document design

Document design involves decisions about what a paper will look like. It encompasses the options for **format** and **manuscript form.** (See also **graphics** and **Research Processes.**)

double (redundant) comparisons

A double comparison is nonstandard, needlessly wordy usage; it should be avoided. (See also **adjectives** and **adverbs.**)

> Our house is the ~~most~~ newest on the block. [double superlative—*most* and *-est*]

> Our flowers are ~~more~~ prettier than our neighbor's. [double comparative—*more* and *-er*]

double negatives

A double negative consists of two negative words used in the same expression. Most double negatives are **nonstandard English** and should not be used in writing.

> *any*
> I *haven't* got ~~none~~.
>   ^

OR

> I have *none*.

Barely, hardly, and *scarcely* are already negative and do not need to be reinforced.

> I ~~don't~~ *hardly* ever have time to read these days.

Two negatives are acceptable only if they are used to suggest the gray area of meaning between negative and positive.

> Joshua is *not unfriendly*. [meaning that he is neither hostile nor friendly]
> It is *not without* regret that I offer my resignation. [implying mixed feelings rather than only regret]

double subjects

A double subject is nonstandard and needlessly wordy.

> My son ~~he~~ likes heavy metal.

OR

> He likes heavy metal.

download

To download is to copy a text or document from another computer source onto a floppy disk or a computer's hard drive.

drafting   (See **Composing Processes**, pages 11–12.)

drawings   (See **graphics**.)

due to/because of

Due to means "a result of" and follows a **linking verb** (such as *be* and *seem*).

Moonlight, regardless of what the poets say, is *due to* the reflection of the sun's rays.

Due to meaning "because of" should not be used as a **preposition** following a nonlinking verb. Replace it with *because of*.

D

We found our way back home ~~due to~~ ^{because of} the moonlight shining on the path.

each

When the **indefinite pronoun** *each* is the subject, it takes a singular **verb**.

Each of the research papers *is* to be written in ten weeks.

When preceded by *each*, singular subjects joined by *and* take a singular verb. When followed by *each,* plural subjects joined by *and* take a plural verb. (See also **agreement of subjects and verbs.**)

Each cat and dog has been groomed. [singular subjects]
The *cats and dogs each have* been groomed. [plural subjects]

When *each* is the antecedent for a pronoun, the pronoun is singular. (See also **agreement of pronouns and antecedents.**)

Each of the girls will have to live with *her* conscience. [not *their*]

editing

Editing is usually one of the last steps in creating a final draft. To edit, read your manuscript carefully for style and sense, and correct problems in grammar, spelling, and punctuation. Consider whether you have used the techniques of **emphasis** and **subordination, conciseness, parallel structure**, and **sentence variety** to make your meaning clear and your writing interesting. Also review your **word choices.**

Although you will undoubtedly edit some sentences as you develop your composition, don't become distracted by editing concerns before you complete your first draft. Ideally, editing and **revising** should be done in separate readings of the manuscript, because revising focuses on the larger elements of content and organization and editing focuses on sentences and words. (See also **Composing Processes**, pages 17–20.)

You can edit on hard copy (paper) or on the monitor screen. If your computer has programs for checking spelling, grammar, or style, use them. However, these programs do not catch all errors or necessarily improve the text. Ultimately, you are responsible for what you write. If particular types of problems—such as consistently misspelled words, omitted commas or apostrophes, or sentence fragments—recur in your writing, draw up a checklist of these problems, and consult it before editing and turning in the final drafts of your papers.

effect/affect (See *affect/effect.*)

e.g.

The **abbreviation** *e.g.* stands for the Latin *exempli gratia,* meaning "for example." Because a perfectly good English equivalent exists (*for example*), there is no need to use a Latin expression or abbreviation except in notes and illustrations where you need to save space. Use punctuation with *e.g.* exactly as you would with *for example.*

either

Like most **indefinite pronouns**, *either* is singular in meaning. As a subject, it takes a singular verb. (See also **agreement of subjects and verbs.**)

> *Either is* fine with me.

When *either* is the antecedent for a pronoun, the pronoun is singular. (See also **agreement of pronouns and antecedents.**)

> *Either* of the choices has *its* merits.

either . . . or

Sentence elements joined by the **correlative conjunction** *either . . . or* should be parallel. (See also **parallel structure.**)

> Pick *either* the green one *or* the blue one.

either/or reasoning   (See **logic.**)

elicit/illicit

Elicit is a **verb** meaning "to draw forth or bring out"; *illicit* is an **adjective** describing an illegal activity. (See also *illegal/illicit.*)

> The lure of easy money *elicited* his desire to engage in *illicit* activities.

ellipsis points

When you omit words in quoted material, use a series of three spaced periods (. . .)—called *ellipsis points, an ellipsis mark,* or *points of suspension*—to indicate the omission. MLA style requires **brackets** [ ] around ellipsis points indicating omissions in a quotation. Compare the following quotation and the shortened version that follows it. (For more about the mechanics of quotations, see **quotations, brackets,** and **Research Processes.**)

ORIGINAL TEXT

As part of its mission to provide care for animals, the M.S.P.C.A. maintains three hospitals in the state, of which Angell is by far the largest. The society also runs eight animal shelters, publishes a bi-monthly magazine called *Animals,* operates a pet cemetery, runs a law-enforcement division, and lobbies the government for the animal protection cause. Even though Angell's interests run counter in some ways to the society's formal goal of *prevention* of cruelty (since the animals are treated after the injury or illness has occurred), the hospital is by far the most illustrious of the M.S.P.C.A.'s operations, and the most expensive.

—JOHN SEDGWICK, "The Doberman Case"

If the omitted part of the quotation is preceded by a period, retain the period and add the three ellipsis points after it. If a punctuation mark other than a period precedes or follows the omitted passage, retain the mark only if it will make the quotation read more smoothly.

As part of its mission to provide care for animals, the M.S.P.C.A. maintains three hospitals [. . .], of which Angell is by far the largest. [. . .] Even though Angell's interests run counter in some ways to the society's formal goal of *prevention* of cruelty [. . .], the hospital is by far the most illustrious of the M.S.P.C.A.'s operations, and the most expensive.

—JOHN SEDGWICK, "The Doberman Case"

Unless there is a particular reason for explicitly noting the omission, ellipsis points are not necessary to indicate the omission of words at the beginning of a quoted passage or the omission of sentences following the passage.

To indicate the omission of one or more lines of poetry, insert a full line of ellipsis points.

Far out of sight forever stands the sea,
Bounding the land with pale tranquility.
[. . . . .]
That is illusion. The artificer
Of quiet, distance holds me in a vise
And holds the ocean steady to my eyes. (1–14)
    —YVOR WINTERS, "The Slow Pacific Swell"

Ellipsis points may occasionally be used for effect to indicate a pause or hesitation.

Don't swim in this water . . . unless you're fond of sharks.

elliptical constructions

In an elliptical construction, a writer omits some words from a sentence to heighten the effect or tighten the style.

The garden was overgrown, the weeds [were] thick and matted.

In my yard, the flowers come first, the garden [comes] second, and the crabgrass [comes] last.

When using an elliptical construction, do not omit words or phrases essential to the meaning. (See also **comparisons**.)

Russia is farther from St. Louis than England. *is* ∧

Elliptical constructions can sometimes make it hard to choose the correct pronoun. When in doubt, mentally insert the omitted words to decide on the correct case.

Consuelo's husband is eight years younger than ~~her~~ [is]. *she* ∧

e-mail

E-mail is electronic mail sent via a local network of computers or the **Internet**. An e-mail address contains a user name, the @ symbol, and the domain name. For example, in the e-mail address <jdoe@mcgraw-hill.com>, the user name is <jdoe> and the domain name is <mcgraw-hill.com>.

E-MAIL NETIQUETTE

1. Proofread an e-mail message before you send it; you may also want to use the spell checker. Make sure that your message is clear and that you have not said anything you will later regret.
2. Keep e-mail messages brief, preferably one screen and no more than two. If what you need to say is longer than that, send a letter or pick up the phone.
3. Keep the subject line short and specific. For example, "May 5 assignment" is a more informative subject line than "Class" if you are e-mailing an instructor.
4. Do not write in ALL CAPITAL LETTERS. They are the e-mail equivalent of shouting and make the message hard to read.
5. Use a salutation, and sign off with your name and e-mail address (also give your phone number if you have asked your correspondent to call you).
6. Fit the **tone** of an e-mail to your **audience** and **purpose**. In general, an e-mail is a more informal communication than a business letter.

(continued)

> 7. Do not write anything in an e-mail that you would be embarrassed to have a third party read; because e-mail is transmitted through system computers, other people, such as the system manager or your employer, can access it.
> 8. If you are responding to a message, quote only as much of it as necessary; do not automatically include a complete copy.

emigrate/immigrate

When people *emigrate,* they go *out of* their country to live or establish residence somewhere else. When they *immigrate,* they come *into* the new country.

> My parents *emigrated* from Poland.
>
> They *immigrated* to the United States.

eminent/imminent/immanent

Eminent is an **adjective** meaning "standing out" or "standing above others in some quality."

> My father was an *eminent* musicologist in his day.

Imminent, also an adjective, means "about to happen" or "hanging threateningly over one's head."

> Examination day was *imminent,* and Tracy was still not prepared.

Immanent, another adjective, means "inherent" and is most often used in religious contexts, such as "belief in a god that is immanent in humans."

emotional appeal (See **appeals to emotion.**)

emphasis

Emphasis is the stress given to ideas according to their importance. Writers achieve emphasis in several ways: by position (for instance, of a word within a sentence or of a sentence within a paragraph); by **repetition;** by selection of **sentence type;** by variation of sentence length; by **punctuation;** by the use of **intensifiers;** by the use of typographical devices, such as **italics** (or underlining); and by direct statement (for instance, by using the terms *most important* and *foremost*).

In Paragraphs

The first and last sentences in a paragraph and the first and last paragraphs in a report or paper tend to be the most emphatic to the reader. The following paragraph builds up to the conclusion of the last sentence.

Energy does far more than simply make our daily lives more comfortable and convenient. Suppose you wanted to stop—and reverse—the economic progress of this nation. What would be the surest and quickest way to do it? Find a way to cut off the nation's oil resources! Industrial plants would shut down, public utilities would stand idle, all forms of transportation would halt. The country would be paralyzed, and our economy would plummet into the abyss of national economic ruin. Our economy, in short, is energy-based.

—*The Baker World*

Another way to achieve emphasis is to follow a very long sentence, or a series of long sentences, with a very short one.

We have already reviewed the problem the department has experienced during the past year. We could continue to examine the causes of our problems and point an accusing finger at all the culprits beyond our control, but in the end it all leads to one simple conclusion. We must cut costs.

Emphasis can also be achieved by the repetition of key words and phrases.

Similarly, atoms *come and go* in a molecule, but the molecule *remains;* molecules *come and go* in a cell, but the cell *remains;* cells *come and go* in a body, but the body *remains;* persons *come and go* in an organization, but the organization *remains.*

—KENNETH BOULDING, *Beyond Economics*

In Sentences

Because the first and last words of a sentence stand out in the reader's mind, the important words should come at the beginning or the end of a sentence. Put your main point in a main clause; put less important details in subordinate clauses.

The earth's history can be understood by examining features, such as moon craters, that reflect geological history. [The sentence emphasizes the earth's history.]

OR

Moon craters are important to understanding the earth's history because they reflect geological history. [The sentence emphasizes moon craters.]

Different emphases can be achieved by the selection of different **sentence types**: a **compound sentence**, a **complex sentence**, or a **simple sentence.**

The report turned in by the police detective was carefully illustrated, and it covered five pages of single-spaced copy. [This compound sentence carries no special emphasis because it contains two coordinate independent clauses.]

The police detective's report, which was carefully illustrated, covered five pages of single-spaced copy. [This complex sentence emphasizes the size of the report.]

The carefully illustrated report turned in by the police detective covered five pages of single-spaced copy. [This simple sentence emphasizes that the report was carefully illustrated.]

In a paragraph of typical **cumulative**, or loose, **sentences** (main idea first), a **periodic sentence**, in which the main idea comes just before the period, will stand out. In the next paragraph, the first sentence, which is the topic sentence, is periodic. The following sentences, which are loose sentences, are examples supporting the topic sentence.

> Finally, completing this whirlwind survey of parasitic insects, there are, I was surprised to learn, certain parasitic moths. One moth caterpillar occurs regularly in the *horns* of African ungulates. One adult, winged moth lives on the skin secretions between the hairs of the fur of the three-fingered sloth. Another adult moth sucks mammal blood in southeast Asia. Last of all, there are the many eye-moths, which feed as winged adults about the open eyes of domestic cattle, sucking blood, pus, and tears.
>
> —ANNIE DILLARD, "The Horns of the Altar"

Balancing sentence parts or making clauses parallel is a technique of emphasis often used in speeches and formal writing. (See also **balanced sentences** and **parallel structure.**)

> If a free society cannot help the many who are poor, it cannot save the few who are rich.
>
> —JOHN F. KENNEDY

An intentional **sentence fragment** is a more informal means of providing emphasis.

> Everyone on our floor has observed the no-smoking policy. Everyone, that is, but Barbara.

The same effect can be achieved within a sentence if a clause is set off with a **dash**. This statement can be made even more emphatic with an **exclamation point**, although exclamation points should be used sparingly to preserve their effect.

> Everyone on our floor has observed the no-smoking policy—everyone, that is, but Barbara!

With Words

Word choice and word order are important means of achieving emphasis. You can make any statement more emphatic by using strong precise **verbs** and by writing in the **active voice** rather than the passive. (See also **sentence variety.**)

stomped
June ~~walked~~ down the aisle.

We considered her
~~Her~~ attitude ~~was considered~~ rude.

Intensifiers (*most, very, really*) can provide emphasis, but they should not be overused.

The final proposal is *much* more persuasive than the first.

Italics (represented by underlining when you type) are another means of emphasis that should be used with caution.

When we consider that many of these people have smoked for their entire adult lives, the fact that they all quit *simultaneously* was even more significant.

Do not use all-capital letters to show emphasis. Doing so is distracting and occasionally confusing because all-capital letters often signify acronyms or **abbreviations.**

Finally, if you really want to get your audience's attention, you may occasionally resort to **hyperbole.**

He sounded like a herd of elephants!

endnotes (See **Research Processes**, pages 116–17.)

end punctuation (See **periods, exclamation points, question marks.**)

English, varieties of

Written English includes two broad categories: standard and nonstandard. Standard English is used in education, government, business and industry, and all professions. It has rigorous and precise criteria for capitalization, **diction, punctuation, spelling,** and **usage.**

Nonstandard English does not conform to such criteria; it is often regional in origin or reflects the special usages of a particular ethnic or social group. As a result, although it may be vigorous and colorful, its usefulness as a means of communication is limited to certain contexts and to people already familiar and comfortable with it in those contexts. It rarely appears in printed material except when it is used for special effect. Nonstandard English is characterized by inexact or inconsistent punctuation, capitalization, spelling, diction, and usage choices. It includes the following forms.

Colloquialisms: A colloquialism is a word or expression characteristic of casual conversation ("That test was a real *bummer.*"). Colloquialisms are appropriate to some kinds of writing (personal letters, notes, and the like) but not to most formal or academic writing. (See also **colloquial usage.**)

Dialect: Dialectal English is a social or regional variety of the language that may be incomprehensible to outsiders. Dialect involves distinct word choices, grammatical forms, and pronunciations. Formal or academic writing, because it aims at a broad audience, should be free of dialect.

E

Localisms: A localism is a regional wording or phrasing. For example, a large sandwich on a long split roll is variously known in different parts of the United States as a *hero, hoagie, grinder, poor boy, submarine,* or *torpedo.* Because not all readers will be familiar with localisms, they should not be used in formal writing.

Slang: Slang is an informal vocabulary composed of facetious **figures of speech** and colorful words used in humorous or extravagant ways. There is no objective test for slang, and many standard words are given slang applications. For instance, slang may use a familiar word in a new way ("She told him to *chill out*"—meaning "relax"), or it may coin new words ("He's a *wonk*"—meaning "a person who works or studies excessively"). Most slang is short-lived and has meaning for only a narrow audience. Thus, although slang may be valid in personal writing or fiction, it should be avoided in formal writing. (See also **slang and neologisms.**)

enthuse, enthused

Formed from the noun *enthusiasm,* these two words are generally considered nonstandard and should be avoided.

equivocation   (See **logic.**)

essay   (See **Composing Processes.**)

essay tests

Some essay examinations must be completed in class; others can be done out of class. Obviously, the advantage of an out-of-class exam is that you can refer to your textbook and lecture notes and take as much time as necessary (before the due date) to plan, organize, write, revise, and proofread. (For more explanation, see **Composing Processes.**) In fact, the only disadvantage of take-home exams is that instructors hold the final product to a higher standard of evaluation. But whether you are writing in or out of class, you need to clarify the instructor's expectations, study and review the material, manage your time, and then analyze the questions, organize your information, and write the answers to the questions.

Clarifying Expectations

When the essay test is announced, try to determine what will be covered—for example, lectures, discussions, textbook chapters, recommended readings, movies or videotapes viewed in class, guest lectures, or peers' reports.

Next find out what sources your instructor considers of primary importance and how the exam will be evaluated. Once you have clarified these expectations, you will know what to study and how much time you will need.

Studying and Reviewing Material

Allot sufficient time to read and review the material that will be covered in the test. As you look through your textbooks and lecture notes, highlight or underline key terms (if you haven't done so already), note points in the text that were emphasized in lecture or discussion, make lists of important ideas or elements covered under specific topics, organize the information in a logical order, and consider using mnemonic devices to help you remember them. (An example of a mnemonic device is remembering the keys on the lines of the treble staff of music—EGBDF—by the phrase Every Good Boy Does Fine.) As you read, imagine the types of questions that might be posed to elicit the information you are studying. Most questions will use one or more of the following modes: **description, defining terms, summarizing, comparison and contrast, analysis,** or **argument.**

When you feel that you have reviewed the material adequately, make up sample questions to describe, define, summarize, compare and contrast, analyze, or argue a point. Practice answering these questions. Practice will tend to lessen your anxiety during the actual test not only because it helps you to study but also because you can check what you missed in your practice answers and further review those weak points. Following are examples of the types of questions you or your instructor might design:

> Describe the political situation in Vietnam that led to the Vietnamese war. [List the key elements and then develop them with facts and illustrations.]

> Define what is meant by the term "social Darwinism." [Tell what it is, what it does, how it works, why it is done, and why it is an issue.]

> Summarize the plot of *To Kill a Mockingbird*. [State the gist of the events in chronological order.]

> Compare and contrast the protagonists in Chekhov's two stories "The Duel" and "The Darling." [Decide whether you will use a point-by-point or whole-by-whole comparison pattern, depending on which is clearer and more concise.]

> Analyze the reasons for the disappearance of the rainforest in South America. [Break down the components of the problem.]

> Which concept is based on a sounder economic rationale—communism or socialism? Present a clear argument supporting your stance. [Draw on various strategies depending on what is appropriate: define terms, compare and contrast, summarize, and analyze information. Clearly state the position you are taking, and support it with ample evidence: facts, authoritative opinions, economic studies, and the like.]

Managing Your Time and Analyzing the Questions

When you receive the essay examination, read all the questions before you begin writing. As you read, underline key terms, and notice how much weight or how many points are assigned to each. Then decide where to begin and how much time to allow for each question, building in enough time to reread and revise. Whenever possible, start with the question you know the most about; that will build your confidence and enhance your fluency.

Organizing Information and Composing a Response

Before you begin to write, make a rough list or outline, or jot down the key elements you know must be addressed. The organization of this information depends to some degree on how the question is phrased, but you may have leeway to decide whether to begin with the most important information (in case you run out of time) or to end with the strongest ideas (because most readers tend to remember the last thing they read). In either case, begin with a clear thesis statement that specifically answers the question, and then list the points you are going to make. Following that introduction, plan to spend one paragraph per point developing your ideas and supporting them with specific facts and information from the text or other sources. When you have covered all the points, restate the thesis and summarize the points you made. Then move on to the next question.

If you have managed your time well, you should have five to ten minutes left to read over your answer. As you read, compare the points in your answer to those on your outline; make sure you have included everything. When you are sure the content is as well developed as possible, read again quickly to make sure your answer is clear and correct.

et al.

Et al. is the **abbreviation** for the Latin *et alia*, meaning "and others." It is generally used only for a work with more than three authors in lists of references or works cited or in parenthetical documentation. Do not italicize or underline the abbreviation. (See also **Research Processes**, pages 64, 68, 101, 104–05, 118, 141.)

Norton, Mary Beth, et al. <u>A People and a Nation</u>. New York: Random, 1983.

etc.

The **abbreviation** *etc.* comes from the Latin *et cetera*, meaning "and the like" or "and so forth." Abbreviations are generally not used in formal writing. When you cannot list all items in a class, use *and so on* or *and the like* rather than *etc.*, or begin the list with *for example, including,* or *such as,* phrases that suggest there are more things in the class than the ones in the list.

> The electronics store has everything you need, *including* coaxial cable, adapters,
> *and*
> connector jacks, wire clips, speaker wire/ ~~etc.~~
>   ∧   ○

In informal writing, if you use *etc.,* do not use *and,* because *and* is part of the meaning of *etc.*

> For the needlepoint class, bring tapestry needles, Dublin linen, scissors, ~~and~~ *etc.*

ethos

In argumentative writing, ethos is an appeal based on the writer's authority and good will.

euphemisms

A euphemism replaces an objectionable, disagreeable, or coarse word or phrase with an agreeable or unobjectionable one.

EUPHEMISM	TRANSLATION
chemical dependency	drug addiction
economically challenged	poor
passed away	died
sanitation engineer	garbage collector

Euphemisms allow writers to distort meaning or hide facts, unwittingly or not (people are *eliminated* instead of *killed* or *downsized* instead of *fired*). However, they also allow writers to be inoffensive and polite. (See also **word choice.**)

everybody/everyone

The pronouns *everybody* and *everyone* are synonyms and may be used interchangeably. They are usually considered singular and so take singular **verbs** and **pronoun** referents.

> *Everybody is* going to Joe's place after the game.
> *Everyone* in my neighborhood *works* during the day.
> *Everybody* wanted to buy a knitting machine of *her* own after the demonstration.
> *Everyone* at this golf course brings *his* lunch on Monday.

Occasionally *everybody* and *everyone* have a meaning so obviously plural that no revision to achieve agreement in number seems a real improvement. This situation is especially likely to occur when the plural pronoun *they* or *their* refers to an antecedent *everyone* or *everybody* in a previous independent clause or sentence.

> *Everyone* laughed at my bad haircut, and I really couldn't blame *them*. [Here, *them* cannot logically be changed to *him or her.*]

Many readers would not object to this sentence, but some would. Depending on the context, possibly *everyone* could be changed to a plural form.

> *All the guests*
> ~~Everyone~~ laughed at my bad haircut, and I really couldn't blame *them*.
>   ∧

Another solution is to change the second clause to eliminate the plural pronoun entirely.

>   *had to agree*⊙
> *Everyone* laughed at my bad haircut, and I really ~~couldn't blame them.~~
>   ∧

The discussions of **agreement of pronouns and antecedents, agreement of subjects and verbs,** and **nonsexist language** provide additional examples of solutions to such problems.

Perhaps the best advice is to know your **audience** and, if in doubt, revise. This policy may be especially sensible in a writing course; usually even the most liberal instructors want to be sure that students understand grammatical principles before they bend the rules.

To emphasize each individual in a group, use *every one*.

> *Every one* of the team members contributed to the victory. [strong emphasis on individuals]

> *Everyone* on the team contributed to the victory. [weak emphasis on individuals]

everyday/every day

Everyday is an **adjective** meaning "common"; *every day* is an adverbial **phrase** meaning "daily."

> During the summer Lola wore her *everyday* clothes *every day,* including Sunday.

evidence

The details that support an **argument** are called *evidence*. They may include statistics, testimony, **examples**, facts, and descriptions. (See also **logic**.)

examples

Examples are the illustrations that support a **thesis** or develop a **paragraph**, a definition, or an idea. Examples may include facts, testimony, descriptions, and **anecdotes**. They not only make your writing clearer and more interesting but also help to persuade the audience that what you say is true. In the following paragraph, the incident in the movie *Shane* is presented as an example of the thesis stated in the first sentence.

> Working on Westerns has made me aware of the extent to which the genre exists in order to provide a justification for violence. Violence needs justification because our society puts it under interdict—morally and legally, at any rate. In *Shane,* for example, when Shane first appears at Grafton's store, he goes into the saloon section and buys a bottle of soda pop. One of the Riker gang (the villains in the movie) starts insulting him, first saying he smells pigs (Shane is working for a farmer), then ridiculing him for drinking soda pop, then splashing a shot of whiskey on his brand new shirt with the words "smell like a man," and finally ordering him out of the saloon. Shane goes quietly. But the next time, when he returns the empty soda bottle and the insults start again, he's had enough. When Shane is told he can't "drink with the men," he splashes whiskey in the other guy's face, hauls off and socks him one, and the fight is on.
>
> —JANE TOMPKINS, *West of Everything*

(See also **defining terms.**)

exclamation points

An exclamation point (!) signals strong feeling: surprise, fear, indignation, or excitement. It cannot, however, make an argument more convincing, lend force to a weak statement, or call attention to an intended irony. Use exclamation points sparingly. (**Emphasis** is better provided through sentence structure and **word choice.**)

An exclamation point is most commonly used after an **interjection, phrase, clause,** or sentence to indicate strong emotion or urgency.

Ouch!   Go away!   Stop that right now!

The exclamation point goes outside quotation marks, unless what is quoted is an exclamation. Do not use a comma or a period after an exclamation point.

I can't believe he answered "four"!
Mikey looked at her and said, "I can't believe I ate the whole thing!"

exclamatory sentences

An exclamatory sentence makes a statement so emphatically that it ends in an **exclamation point**. (See also **sentence types**.)

> These prices are outrageous!
>
> How dare you! Stop shouting this instant!

expletives

An expletive is an expression that occupies the position of some other word, phrase, or clause without adding to the sense. The two common expletives are **it** and **there**.

> *It* is true that Luigi missed the party. [*It* occupies the position of subject, but the real subject is the clause *that Luigi missed the party.*]
>
> *There* are twenty-six letters in the English alphabet. [*There* occupies the position of subject, but the real subject is *letters.*]

Although expletives can be useful in achieving **emphasis** or avoiding awkwardness, they often are unnecessary and create wordy sentences. (See also **conciseness/wordiness**.)

> *We lost*
> ~~There were~~ many orders ~~lost~~ for unexplained reasons.
> ^
>
> *He certainly*
> ~~It is certain that he~~ will go.
> ^

The expletive *it* is idiomatic in expressing certain ideas about time, distance, and weather.

> It's raining, it's pouring.
>
> It's a long, long way from Clare to here.
>
> It's too late for tears.

The expletive *there* is idiomatic in simple statements about the existence of something, especially in narrative or descriptive passages.

> Once upon a time *there* were twelve dancing princesses.

As this example demonstrates, an expletive inverts the usual order of subject and verb (here the subject, *princesses,* comes at the end of the sentence). (See also **inverted sentence order, emphasis,** and **subordination**.)

> Do not begin a declarative sentence with a form of *be;* start the sentence with an expletive instead.

It is
~~Is~~ a beautiful day.
 ^

There are
~~Are~~ many flowers in bloom.
 ^

Do not confuse *it* and *there.*

There
~~It~~ is hardly a cloud in the sky.
 ^

Make sure that the subject (which follows the verb) agrees in **number** with the verb.

 are
There ~~is~~ two birds building a nest in the tree near my house.
   ^

To test whether the verb should be singular or plural, drop the expletive and reverse the order of the subject and verb.

Two birds *are* building a nest in the tree near my house.

explication

Explication is the line-by-line **literary analysis** of a poem or other literary text. This term should not be confused with **paraphrase**, which is a restatement of a passage in your own words. Rather, explications analyze how (or how often) the author uses certain words, why particular words are used (for example, for rhythm or sound or as **figures of speech**, such as **symbols** and **metaphors**), and what effect particular groups of words (such as lines, **stanzas**, or contrasting words) have on the meaning of a work.

explicit/implicit

Explicit is an **adjective** meaning "fully revealed or expressed" or "leaving no question about meaning." To say something explicitly is to state it directly and clearly.

The *explicit* instructions left no doubt about how we were to proceed.

Implicit, also an adjective, means "understood though unexpressed." If something is implicit, it is suggested but not stated directly.

The *implicit* assumption is that the axes represent real numbers.

expository writing

Expository writing, or exposition, informs or explains to the reader by presenting facts and ideas in direct and concise language. Expository writing attempts to explain what its subject is, how it works, or perhaps how it is related to something else. Because exposition is aimed chiefly at the audience's understanding rather than the imagination or emotions, it usually relies less on colorful or figurative language than does writing meant to be mainly either **expressive** or **persuasive**.

> Zoo-related sciences like animal ecology and veterinary medicine for exotic animals barely existed fifty years ago and tremendous advances have been made in the last fifteen years. Zoo veterinarians now inoculate animals against diseases they once died of. Until recently, keeping the animals alive required most of a zoo's resources. A cage modeled after a scientific laboratory or an operating room—tile-lined and antiseptic, with a drain in the floor—was the best guarantee of continued physical health. In the 1960s and early 1970s zoo veterinarians and comparative psychologists began to realize that stress was as great a danger as disease to captive wild animals. Directors thus sought less stressful forms of confinement than the frequently-hosed-down sterile cell.
>
> —MELISSA GREENE, "No Rms, Jungle Vu"

expressive writing

Whatever may be the apparent topic, the real subject of expressive writing is the writer. Whereas **expository writing** deals with facts and ideas, expressive writing aims to convey or simply record the writer's feelings and opinions. This type of writing is usually found in narrative essays, journal entries, and personal letters. It often employs figurative language and descriptive words and phrases that appeal to the audience's imagination. It always tells as much about the writer as about the ostensible topic—in the following passage, the writer's eighth-grade graduation day.

> I hoped the memory of that morning would never leave me. Sunlight was itself young, and the day had none of the insistence maturity would bring it in a few hours. In my robe and barefoot in the backyard, under cover of going to see about my new beans, I gave myself up to the gentle warmth and thanked God that no matter what evil I had done in my life He had allowed me to live to see this day. Somewhere in my fatalism I had expected to die, accidentally, and never have the chance to walk up the stairs in the auditorium and gracefully receive my hard-earned diploma. Out of God's merciful bosom I had won reprieve.
>
> —MAYA ANGELOU, *I Know Why the Caged Bird Sings*

facts (See **logic** and **Research Processes**, pages 28–34.)

fallacies in reasoning (See **logic**.)

false analogy (See **logic**.)

false premise (See **logic**.)

farther/further

Farther refers to distance; *further* refers to a greater degree or extent.

> The high school is *farther* from our house than the junior high is.
>
> Mary Jo argued *further* that, because of the distance, we should drive her to school.

faulty predication

Faulty predication occurs when a subject and predicate do not logically go together.

> ~~The title of~~ Amy Tan's 1995 book is called *The Hundred Secret Senses*.
>
> **OR**
>
> The title of Amy Tan's 1995 book is *The Hundred Secret Senses*.

In this example, the subject and predicate should be either *book* and *is called* or *title* and *is*. A title cannot be called something. (For another example of faulty predication, see *is when/is where*.)

female

The term *female* is usually restricted to scientific, legal, or medical contexts (a *female* patient or suspect). In other contexts, this term sounds cold and impersonal; *girl* or *woman* should usually be used instead. However, be aware of these words' **connotations** about age, dignity, and social position. (See also *male* and **nonsexist language**.)

few/a few

Both *few* and *a few* are used before **count nouns** to indicate a small quantity. However, *few* means "hardly any," whereas *a few* means "some, but not many."

> Teresa is lonely because she has *few* friends.
>
> Jan has *a few* friends who are very dear to him.

297

fewer/less

Fewer refers to items that can be counted (**count nouns**). *Less* refers to mass quantities or amounts (**mass nouns**).

> *Less* vitamin C in your diet may mean more, not *fewer*, colds.

figures (See **graphics**.)

F figures of speech

Figures of speech (or figurative language) usually either state or imply a comparison between two things that are basically unlike but have at least one thing in common. If a device is cone shaped with an opening at the top, for example, you might say that it looks like a volcano; or you might refer to a person given to unpredictable fits of temper as an emotional volcano.

Figures of speech can clarify the unfamiliar by relating a new and difficult concept to a familiar one or by translating the abstract into the concrete. In the process, figures of speech make writing more colorful and graphic.

Use figurative language with care. A figure of speech should not attract more attention to itself than to the point you are making.

> The whine of the engine sounded like ten thousand cats having their tails pulled by ten thousand mischievous children.

Figures of speech should be fresh, original, and vivid. Trite figures of speech, called **clichés**, defeat that purpose. A surprise that comes "like a bolt out of the blue" is not much of a surprise. It is better to use no figure of speech than to use a stale one. (See also **mixed metaphors**.)

Types of Figures of Speech

The most common figures of speech are analogy, hyperbole, simile, and metaphor.

Analogy is a comparison between two objects or concepts in order to show ways in which they are similar. In effect, analogies say "A is to B as C is to D." The resemblance between these concepts is partial but close enough to provide a striking way of illuminating the relationship the writer wishes to establish.

> Pollution affects the environment the way cancer affects the body.

Hyperbole is extreme exaggeration used to achieve an effect or emphasis. It is rarely appropriate in formal writing.

> He *murdered* me on the tennis court.

Simile is a direct comparison of two essentially unlike things, linking them with the word *like* or *as*.

Like a small birdcage, her hat rested precariously on her head, and I expected to see the feathers take flight at any moment.

Metaphor is a figure of speech that points out similarities between two things by treating them as though they were the same thing. Metaphor states that the thing being described *is* the thing to which it is being compared.

He is the sales department's *utility infielder.*

F

FTP

FTP, the abbreviation for File Transfer Protocol, is an electronic format used to exchange Internet files between computers. The transferred files are downloaded into the memory of the receiving computer. In contrast, **HTTP** files are transported from a Web server to a Web browser for viewing rather than downloading. FTP is commonly used to download software programs. The **URL** of FTP sites begins with "ftp://" instead of the more common "http://."

Some FTP sites need to be accessed with DOS commands or a special software program. Others can be accessed with a Web browser. FTP sites usually need to be logged on to with an account and a password. However, some publicly available sites can be accessed with "anonymous FTP," for which "anonymous" is the user ID.

finite verbs

A finite verb is a verb that can function as the sole **verb** of a sentence. (See also **nonfinite verbs.**)

first/firstly

Firstly—like *secondly, thirdly, . . . , lastly*—is an unnecessary attempt to create an **adverb** by adding *-ly. First* is an adverb and sounds less stiff than *firstly.*

Firstly, we should ask for an estimate.

first draft

A first draft is a written piece in which you explore ideas and ways of expressing and organizing them. As you write, you may discover new thoughts and connections, and you may decide to change the focus or direction of your paper. The first draft is the place to make those discoveries.

Some people compose their first draft from an outline; others freewrite their thoughts on the subject and organize them after they see what they have to say. Choose whatever method is most comfortable for you. Do not concentrate on making a first draft grammatically or mechanically perfect. Those changes can come later, when you are **editing.**

When you have finished a first draft, put it aside for a while. Then read it with a fresh eye (or have a peer or colleague read and respond to it), and revise. (See also **Composing Processes,** pages 11–12.)

first-person point of view

The first-person point of view is most often used in personal narratives or accounts of personal experience; it is indicated by the use of the first-person pronoun *I.*

> I confess, without shame, that I expected to find masses of silver lying all about the ground. I expected to see it glittering in the sun on the mountain summits. I said nothing about this, for some instinct told me that I might possibly have an exaggerated idea about it, and so if I betrayed my thought I might bring derision upon myself.
>
> —MARK TWAIN, *Roughing It*

In some academic disciplines, use of the first person is discouraged. However, do not go to awkward lengths to avoid its use.

As a result of this research, ~~this researcher~~ concluded that male students are more
reluctant than females to participate in collaborative learning.

OR

This research suggests that male students are more reluctant than females to participate in collaborative learning.

(See also *I,* **mixed constructions,** and **shifts.**)

flammable/inflammable/nonflammable

Although the *in-* **prefix** usually means "not" (*incapable, incompetent*), both *flammable* and *inflammable* mean "capable of being set on fire." *Nonflammable* is the word to use when you mean "fireproof." To avoid confusion, use *flammable* instead of *inflammable.*

> The cargo of gasoline is *flammable.*
>
> The asbestos suit was *nonflammable.*

focusing the subject (See **Composing Processes**, pages 5–11, and **thesis**.)

follow-up letters (See **letters**.)

fonts (See **typefaces**.)

footnotes/endnotes (See **Research Processes**, pages 116–17.)

F

foreign words

Foreign words in an English sentence are set in **italics** (underlined in typed manuscript).

> The sign in the window said *"Se habla español."*

Many foreign words have been assimilated into English, and some retain accent marks. When in doubt about the treatment of a word, consult a current dictionary. If the word is found in an English dictionary, it does not need to be italicized.

> cliché   de facto   etiquette   résumé   vis-à-vis

foreword/forward

Foreword is a **noun** meaning "introductory statement at the beginning of a book or other work."

> The department chairman was asked to write a *foreword* for the professor's book.

Forward is an **adjective** or **adverb** meaning "at or toward the front."

> Move the lever to the *forward* position on the panel. [adjective]
> Turn the dial until the needle begins to move *forward.* [adverb]

formal writing (See **informal and formal writing style** and **English, varieties of**.)

format

The format of a paper involves the general plan of its organization and the arrangement of its features. (See also **graphics, manuscript form**, and **Research Processes**, pages 60–153.)

former/latter

Former and *latter* should refer to only two items in a sentence or paragraph.

> The president and his trusted aide emerged from the conference, the *former* looking nervous and the *latter* looking downright glum.

Because these terms make the reader look back to previous material to identify the reference, they impede reading and are best avoided.

> *this year's model,*
> Model 19099, had the necessary technical modifications, whereas model 19098,
> *last year's model,* ^
> lacked them, ~~the *former* being this year's model and the *latter* last year's.~~
> ^

fractions (See **numbers and symbols**.)

fragments (See **sentence fragments**.)

freewriting

Freewriting is a method of getting ideas onto paper or the monitor screen without having to worry about structure or mechanical correctness. To freewrite, simply write (nonstop, if possible) everything that comes into your mind for ten or fifteen minutes. Do not worry about continuity or coherence; just keep going. If you get stuck, write the same word over and over until a new thought or direction strikes you. At the end of a freewriting session, you should have a page or two of prose, in which you may find at least one or two ideas interesting enough to develop for a writing assignment.

As well as helping to generate ideas, freewriting is often used in writing journal entries and **first drafts** of papers. (See also **Composing Processes**, pages 6–9.)

further/farther (See *farther/further*.)

fused sentences (See **run-on sentences**.)

future perfect tense

The future perfect tense of a **verb** indicates an action or an event that will be completed at the time of or before another future action or event. It combines *will have* and the **past participle** of the main verb.

> I *will have* barely *started* this project by the time the library closes.

The simple **future tense** is often used instead of the future perfect.

> Joy *will finish* the painting by next weekend. [simple future]
>
> OR
>
> Joy *will have finished* the painting by next weekend. [future perfect]

future tense

The simple future tense of a **verb** indicates an action or an event that will occur after the present. It uses the **helping verb** *will* (or *shall*) plus the main verb. (See also **tenses.**)

> I *will start* the job tomorrow.

gender

Gender, grammatically, refers to the classification of words by sex into masculine, feminine, and neuter (for objects with no specific sex characteristics). The English language assigns gender only to **pronouns** (*he, she, it*) and certain **nouns** (*woman, man*).

Specific individual adults should be referred to with masculine or feminine pronouns (*he, she, him, her*). Avoid using singular masculine or feminine pronouns, however, when gender is not known. Use a plural noun and pronoun or an article instead.

CHANGE	Each student should bring *his* textbook to class every week.
TO	Students should bring *their* textbooks to class every week.
OR	Students should bring *the* textbook to class every week.

When gender is irrelevant in references to animals, babies, or young children, use the neuter pronoun *it*.

> A baby responds with a characteristic whole-body reflex when *it* is startled.

(See also **agreement of pronouns and antecedents** and **nonsexist language**.)

generalizations

Generalizations are conclusions based on a sampling of information. If the sample is broad enough, the generalization may be sound; if the sample is narrow, however, the conclusion may be dismissed as a hasty (or sweeping) generalization. When you are writing, be sure that any generalization you make is supported with sufficient evidence or **examples**. (See also **logic**.)

general-to-specific method of development

A general-to-specific method of development begins with a general statement and then provides facts or **examples** to detail and support that statement. This method can be used in paragraphs or whole papers.

> Beatniks rebelled against what they considered to be the intellectually and socially stultifying aspects of 1950s America. They shunned regular employment. They took no interest in politics and public life. They mocked the American enchantment with consumer goods by dressing in T-shirts and rumpled khaki trousers, the women innocent of cosmetics and the intricate hairstyles of suburbia. They made a great deal of the lack of furniture in their cheap walk-up apartments, calling their homes "pads" after the mattress on the floor.
>
> —JOSEPH CONLIN, *The American Past*

general words/specific words

Writing is more interesting if you use specific words rather than general words. General words can describe or apply to anything; they do not paint an accurate or convincing picture. (See also **abstract words/concrete words**, **vague words**, and **word choice**.)

The movie was ~~really neat~~. *frightening but fun*₀

OR

The movie had *realistic special effects*.

We ~~had a lot of good food~~. *ate spicy tacos, seafood enchiladas, and Spanish rice*₀

gerund phrases

A gerund phrase includes the **gerund** plus its **objects, modifiers,** or **complements**. Like a gerund, it is used as a noun—as **subject, subject complement, direct object, indirect object**, object of a **preposition**, or **appositive**.

Editing my roommate's paper was a difficult task. [gerund phrase as subject]

My least favorite chore is *editing papers*. [gerund phrase as subject complement]

I prefer *typing and proofreading papers*. [gerund phrase as direct object]

The committee awarded *her writing* first prize. [gerund phrase as indirect object]

In addition to *my editing her paper,* she wanted me to revise it. [gerund phrase as object of preposition]

That particular job, *editing her paper,* was more stressful than I had anticipated. [gerund phrase as appositive]

gerunds

A gerund is a **verbal** that ends in *-ing* and is used as a **noun**. It may be a **subject**, a **direct object**, an **indirect object**, an object of a **preposition**, a **subject complement**, or an **appositive**.

Editing is an important writing skill. [subject]

I find *editing* difficult. [direct object]

She gave *skating* the credit for renewing her interest in winter sports. [indirect object]

We were unprepared for their *coming*. [object of a preposition]

Seeing is *believing*. [subject complement]

Melvin's favorite hobby, *skateboarding*, is now illegal downtown. [appositive]

Only the possessive form of a noun or **pronoun** should precede a gerund.

John's working has not affected his grades.

His working has not affected his grades.

Gerunds are commonly used as the names of activities (*swimming, bowling, walking*), as part of idiomatic expressions with *go* (*go hiking, go hanggliding*), and as **direct objects** or **complements** of certain verbs.

The following common verbs use gerunds as complements.

admit	discuss	mind	recommend
anticipate	dislike	miss	require
appreciate	enjoy	object to	resent
avoid	feel like	postpone	resist
can/cannot help	finish	practice	risk
consider	imagine	prefer	suggest
delay	keep (on)	quit	tolerate
deny	mention	recall	understand

Be sure to use gerunds—not infinitives, noun clauses, or **finite verb** constructions—with these verbs.

> *taking*
> I considered ~~to take~~ a walk. [gerund, not infinitive]
> ^

> *taking*
> I considered ~~that I take~~ a walk. [gerund, not noun clause]
> ^

> *walking*   *jogging*○
> I feel like ~~I walk~~ instead of ~~I jog.~~ [gerunds, not finite verbs]
> ^   ^

A few verbs, however, can be used with either an infinitive or a gerund.

attempt	continue	prefer
begin	hate	start
can/cannot bear	like	
can/cannot stand	love	

Four verbs (*stop, remember, forget, regret*) can be followed by either an infinitive or a gerund, but the meaning changes. After *stop*, an infinitive indicates a purpose and a gerund indicates an activity that ceases.

On my way home, I stopped *to talk* to my friend.

I stopped *talking* to my friend after she insulted me.

After *remember, forget,* or *regret,* an infinitive refers to action after the time of the main verb and a gerund refers to action before the time of the main verb.

> I regret to tell you.
>
> I regret telling you.

(For a list of verbs used only with infinitives, see **infinitives**.)

good/well

Good is an **adjective**; *well* is usually an **adverb**.

> Baking bread smells *good.* [adjective]
>
> A perfume tester needs to smell *well.* [adverb]

However, *well* can also be used as an adjective to describe someone's health.

> She is not a *well* woman.
>
> Jane is looking *well.*

(See also *bad/badly*.)

Google

This Internet search engine (URL: <http://www.google.com>) leads the list of search engines recommended by the Librarians' Index to the Internet (<http://www.lii.org>) because it is comprehensive, fast, and easy to use, and it consistently delivers relevant results. See also **Internet, Research Processes** (pages 54–60), and **World Wide Web.**

Gopher

During the early 1990s, Gopher was an Internet application used to access hierarchically organized text files. It was replaced by **HTTP.** Most Gopher files have now been converted to Web sites that are more easily accessed by Web search engines. The **URL** of Gopher sites begins with "gopher://" instead of the more common "http://."

grammar

Grammar is commonly thought of as the set of rules and examples showing how a language should be used in writing and in speech. Considered in this way, grammar describes the **usage** of a language.

Grammar, more formally, is the characteristic system of the classes of words, their inflections, and their functions and relations in a **sentence.** That is, grammar is the study and description of the **syntax** and word formation of a language.

graphics

Especially in our visually oriented society, no discussion of effective writing is complete without a discussion of graphics. In addition to the kinds of illustrations discussed in this section, **headings, lists, typefaces, tables,** and all the other elements of **manuscript form** can be considered graphic features.

Graphics have always been important, but computer technology has made it easy for writers to vary typefaces, to use boldface and italic type, and to create **tables** and **graphs.** Graphic options, however, should always serve the **audience** and **purpose** of the paper. Most authorities agree that the greatest danger in the new ease with which graphic effects can be created is the temptation to overdo—to use too many typefaces, for example. A graphic element without purpose or meaning just makes the writer look foolish.

Although writers use many kinds of visuals, we will concentrate in this section on five: the pie chart, line graph, multiple bar graph, segmented bar graph, and combined line/bar graph.

All graphs, charts, diagrams, and photographs should be numbered and labeled with a brief descriptive title (for example, "Figure 1. Age distribution of U.S. population, 1996"). The source of the graphic should also be given (as shown in the examples on the following pages); if the source is from the Internet, include the date published (or, if that is not available, the date accessed) and the electronic address, or **URL.** Each graphic should be referred to in the text (for example, "As Figure 1 shows, the largest age group in the United States in 1996 was . . ."). Unless it is very complex, the graphic should be no larger than half a page. It should ideally be placed on the same page as the text reference; if the text reference comes at the bottom of the page, the graphic should be placed on the following page.

(See also **Research Processes.**)

Pie Charts

Suppose you are doing a paper on aging in American society and want to show visually that the percentage of older Americans is increasing. If you are comparing the size of different age brackets in a given year, a pie chart is a good choice of graphic. In the pie chart, you present percentages as if they were slices of a pie. The entire pie equals one hundred percent of the data (in this case, of the U.S. population). The slices indicate the percentages of the population falling within the Census Bureau age brackets. You might use a different pie chart for each year you are analyzing.

As you can see from the pie chart in Figure G-1, it's difficult to distinguish the variance between some age brackets. If it is important for your audience to see these distinctions, you can add the percentage labels to the chart (as shown in Figure G-1). If you have more than seven variables, a pie chart can become confusing. But if you are comparing fewer than eight things

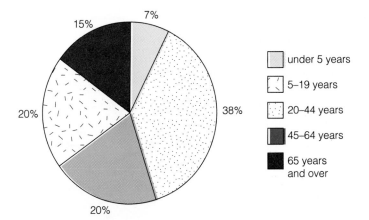

Figure 1. Age distribution of U.S. population, 1996. From U.S. Bureau of the Census, *Current Population Reports,* Series P-25, Nos. 917 and 1095, and *Population Paper Listing* 57; accessed 24 Nov. 2001 <http://www.census.gov/population/www/estimates/popest.html>.

Figure G-1. Pie chart and caption.

and if the disparity between the sizes is relatively large, a pie chart can enhance your paper.

Line Graphs

To show trends in your subject, you might use a line graph. Line graphs allow readers to see increases and decreases over time. The line graph in Figure G-2 compares the population distribution at four points over a 120-year period. Because of their use in scientific documents, line graphs look more formal than pie charts; they have the advantage of allowing the audience to distinguish numerical values more easily.

Multiple Bar Graphs

Multiple bar graphs can be effective if used wisely. Don't use them to compare too many variables; if you do, the bars become an indecipherable mountain range, and the audience becomes lost in the valleys and peaks. The multiple bar graph is effective if the variables on the horizontal axis are being examined individually (distribution in a single year) as well as collectively (comparison of changes from year to year), as shown in Figure G-3. Because of its inherent visual appeal and the ease with which readers can distinguish among items, the multiple bar graph combines some of the best features of the pie chart and the line graph.

G

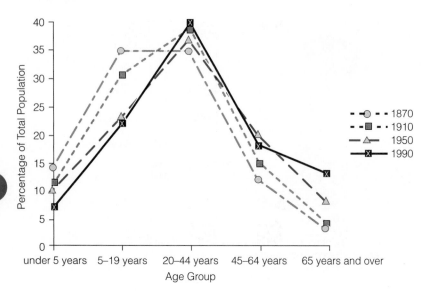

Figure 2. U.S. population distribution by age, 1870, 1910, 1950, 1990. From U.S. Bureau of the Census, *Current Population Reports,* Series P-25, Nos. 311, 917, 1095, and *Population Paper Listing* PPL-91; published 2 Apr. 2001 <http://www.census.gov/population/estimates/nation/popclockest.txt>.

Figure G-2. Line graph and caption.

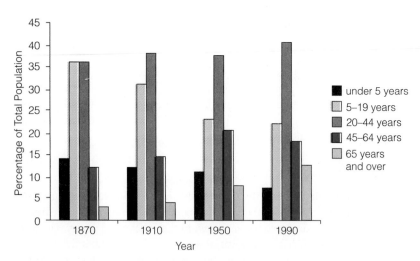

Figure 3. U.S. population by age, 1870, 1910, 1950, 1990. From U.S. Bureau of the Census, *Current Population Reports,* Series P-25, Nos. 311, 917, 1095, and *Population Paper Listing* PPL-91; published 2 Apr. 2001 <http://www.census.gov/population/estimates/nation/popclockest.txt>.

Figure G-3. Multiple bar graph and caption.

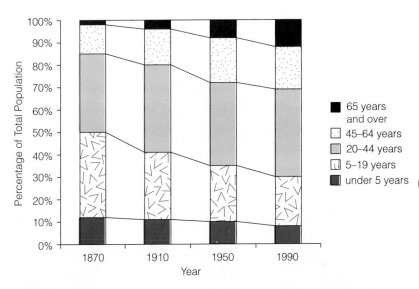

Figure 4. U.S. population distribution by age, 1870, 1910, 1950, 1990. From U.S. Bureau of the Census, *Current Population Reports,* Series P-25, Nos. 311, 917, 1095, and *Population Paper Listing* PPL-91; published 2 Apr. 2001 <http://www.census.gov/population/estimates/nation/popclockest.txt>.

Figure G-4. Combined line and segmented bar graph and caption.

Other Kinds of Graphs

If you have a graphing program on your computer, you may be able to make other kinds of graphs and charts as well, such as segmented bar graphs or combined bar and line graphs. Figure G-4, a combined line and segmented bar graph, is another way to display the information shown in Figures G-2 and G-3. Whereas Figures G-2 and, to a lesser extent, G-3 emphasize the highs and lows in population distribution, Figure G-4 makes it easier to perceive the changes in the population brackets. Figure G-4 would be the most useful if your main purpose was, for example, to show the growth in the over-sixty-five age bracket. If your software graphing program allows it, experiment with different types of graphs to see which one will help you make your point most effectively.

Other Visual Material

You may wish to consider visual materials other than graphs as you explore the best ways to present your content. Photographs are useful if you are discussing the way something looks, and diagrams or flowcharts can help your audience understand a complicated process or the relationships among a group (such as a family).

G

Figure 5. Diego Rivera, *Día de las Flores,* Los Angeles County Museum of Art; rpt. in *Diego Rivera Web Museum;* accessed 24 Nov. 2001 <http://www.diegorivera.com/ diaflores.html>.

Figure G-5. Scanned-in art and caption.

If you use a scanned image (such as a painting or a map) from a Web site, be sure to identify it and credit the source, as shown in Figure G-5. For student papers, it is generally not necessary to obtain reprint permission from the work's owner (who may not be the person who put the image on the Web site), but it would be necessary if you were using the image in a paper that was to be published.

If you use a diagram or drawing traced or photocopied from another source, be sure to give proper credit. Label only the parts that are necessary to your discussion, and simplify the drawing or diagram if it is more complex than you need.

graphs   (See **graphics**.)

G

had/had of

Had of is nonstandard usage for *had*.

If only I had ~~of~~ called her, she might not have been so angry.

had ought/hadn't ought

These phrases are nonstandard. Drop the *had*.

You ~~had~~ ought to call your mother today.

You ~~hadn't~~ ought to do that.
not (inserted above, with caret)

half

Either *half a* (or *an*) or *a half* is appropriate usage.

Felix ate *half a* loaf of bread for breakfast.
Sarah told me she'd work *a half* day in my place.

Avoid using *a half a* (or *an*) in formal writing.

Let it boil for *a half* ~~an~~ hour.

OR

Let it boil for ~~a~~ *half an* hour.

hanged/hung

Hanged is the past-tense verb to use when referring to death by hanging; *hung* is the correct past tense for all other meanings of *hang*.

hasty generalization (See **logic**.)

headings

Headings tell the reader where the major sections and subsections of a document begin and end. They also identify the content that follows them. Headings at the same level should be in the same style and size of type and should be grammatically consistent (see **parallel structure**). Formats for headings may depend on the requirements of an instructor, on formal specifications from a customer or employer, or on the field in which the document is being written. (See also **graphics**.)

healthful/healthy

Something that is *healthful* promotes good health. Something that is *healthy* has good health. Carrots are *healthful*; people can be *healthy*.

helping verbs

A helping verb (also called *auxiliary verb*) is added to a main **verb** to indicate **tense** and sometimes **mood** and **voice**. A helping verb and a main verb constitute a **verb phrase**. The principal helping verbs are the various forms of the verbs *be (am, is, are, was, were, been, being)*, *have (has, had, having)*, and *do (does, did)*. Other helping verbs are *shall, will, may, can, must, ought, might, should, would,* and *could*. (See also **modal auxiliaries**.)

> I *am* going.
>
> I *did* go.
>
> I *should have* gone.
>
> I *would have been* gone if I hadn't waited for Pat.
>
> The order *was* given.

To express the past tense with the helping verb *do* in questions and negative statements, put only *do* in the past tense. Do not change the main verb.

What *did* you ~~learned~~ in that class?
           ^learn

When a form of or *have* is used as a helping verb in the present tense, it is the only part of the verb that indicates person and number.

> The dispatcher *is* waiting for a reply.
>
> *Does* it look like what you wanted?
>
> The package you sent *has* just arrived.

he/she, his/her

Because English has no singular **personal pronoun** that refers to both sexes, the word *he* has traditionally been used when the sex of the **antecedent** is unknown.

> Whoever is appointed [either a man or a woman] will find *his* task difficult.

Because the use of a masculine **pronoun** to refer to an unspecified person is offensive to many readers or simply illogical, it is better to rewrite the sentence in the plural or avoid the use of a pronoun altogether.

P   *s*   *they*
A̶ p̶hotographer cannot take good pictures unless h̶e̶ understand̶s̶ the concept of
   ∧   ∧
framing.

                              the
Whoever is appointed will find h̶i̶s̶ task difficult.
                              ∧

The **phrases** *he or she* and *his or her* are an alternative solution, but they are clumsy when used too often.

Whoever is appointed will find *his or her* task difficult.

(See also **agreement of pronouns and antecedents** and **nonsexist language**.)

himself/hisself

Hisself is nonstandard; instead, use *himself*.

Lucas *himself* greeted me at the door.

Cesar hurt *himself* playing soccer.

homonyms (See **spelling**.)

hopefully

Hopefully means "in a hopeful manner." Careful writers do not use it to mean "I hope" or "it is hoped."

We hope
H̶o̶p̶e̶f̶u̶l̶l̶y̶ the sun will come out tomorrow.
    ∧

however

However may be either a **conjunctive adverb** (signaling a contrast between ideas) or a simple **adverb**. When it is a conjunctive adverb placed between two independent clauses, it is preceded by a semicolon and followed by a comma. When it appears later in a clause, it is preceded and followed by commas.

I'd like to go with you; *however,* my schedule is just too full. [placed between independent clauses]

I'd like to go with you; my schedule, *however,* is just too full. [appears later in the second clause]

When *however* is a simple adverb, it is not set off with punctuation.

However much I'd like to go, I simply do not have the time. [simple adverb modifying *much*]

hyperbole

Hyperbole is exaggeration to achieve emphasis or a humorous effect. It is a **figure of speech** often employed in advertising and comedy, but it should seldom be used in formal writing.

That mechanic charges a *gazillion dollars* for a tune-up.

There is *nothing on earth* like Ambia perfume.

H

HTML

HTML, the abbreviation for Hypertext Markup Language, is the set of codes used to create **World Wide Web** documents. These codes, or tags, tell a Web browser how to display a Web page's words and images. For example, the tag <P> is used to format a block of text as a paragraph.

HTTP

HTTP, the abbreviation for Hypertext Transfer Protocol, is the set of rules computers use to transmit and receive text, graphic, and multimedia files on the **World Wide Web.** When you type in a **URL** or click on a hypertext link, your browser sends an HTTP request to the Internet address indicated by the URL. The server at that address processes your request and sends the file you requested. The URL of HTTP files begins with "http://."

hyphens

The hyphen's primary functions are to link words and sometimes numbers and to divide words at the ends of lines.

With Compound Words

The hyphen joins **compound words** and compound **numbers** from twenty-one to ninety-nine and fractions when they are used as modifiers. When in doubt about whether or where to hyphenate a word, check a dictionary.

able-bodied   brother-in-law   one-sixteenth
self-contained   twenty-one

With Modifiers

Two-word and three-word unit **modifiers** that express a single thought are hyphenated when they precede a **noun** (an *out-of-date* car, a *clear-cut* decision). Do not hyphenate **cumulative adjectives** (a *new digital* computer) or unit modifiers formed with an **adverb** ending in -*ly* (a *rarely used* computer, a *badly needed* vacation).

The presence or absence of a hyphen can alter the meaning of a sentence. Use a hyphen when it is needed for clarity.

	She was a dynamic systems analyst.
COULD MEAN	She was a dynamic-systems analyst.
OR	She was a dynamic systems-analyst.

When the modifying **phrase** follows the noun it modifies, it is not hyphenated.

Our office equipment is *out of date*.

A hyphen is always used in a unit modifier or a noun that begins with a letter or numeral.

UNIT MODIFIERS	NOUNS
A-frame house	H-bomb
five-cent candy	9-iron
nine-inch gap	T-square

If a series of unit modifiers all end with the same term, it does not need to be repeated; for smoothness and brevity you may "suspend" the hyphens and use the modified term only at the end of the series.

CHANGE	The third-floor, fourth-floor, and fifth-floor rooms have recently been painted.
TO	The third-, fourth-, and fifth-floor rooms have recently been painted.

With Prefixes and Suffixes

A hyphen is used after a **prefix** when the root word is a **proper noun**.

anti-Stalinist   post-Newtonian   pre-Sputnik

If there is a possibility of misreading, a hyphen can be used to separate the prefix and the root word, especially if the root begins with the letter that ends the prefix. When in doubt, consult a dictionary.

anti-inflationary   co-worker   non-native   re-draw

In some cases, a hyphen is inserted after the prefix to change the meaning. *Re-cover* means "to cover anew," but *recover* means "to recuperate." Other words whose meaning can be changed with a hyphen include *re-sent* and *resent, re-form* and *reform,* and *re-sign* and *resign.*

A hyphen is used when *ex-* means "former."

ex-partners   ex-wife

The **suffix** *-elect* is hyphenated.

president-elect   commissioner-elect

To Divide Words

Hyphens are used to divide words at the end of a line. Avoid dividing words whenever possible; if you must divide them, use the following guidelines for hyphenation (or consult a dictionary).

DIVIDE

- Between syllables (but leave at least three letters on each line): let-ter
- Between the compound parts of compound words: time-table
- After a single-letter syllable in the middle of a word: sepa-rate
- After a prefix: pre-view
- Before a suffix: cap-tion
- Between two consecutive vowels with separate sounds: gladi-ator

DO NOT DIVIDE

- A word that is pronounced as one syllable: shipped
- A **contraction**: you're
- An **abbreviation** or acronym: NCAA

Divide a word spelled with a hyphen only after the hyphen. If the hyphen is essential to the word's meaning, do not divide the word.

Other Uses of the Hyphen

Hyphens should be used between letters showing how a word is spelled.

In his letter, Dean misspelled *believed* b-e-l-e-i-v-e-d.

Hyphens identify prefixes, suffixes, or written syllables.

Re-, *-ism*, and *ex-* are word parts that cause spelling problems.

A hyphen can stand for *to* or *through* between letters and numbers. (However, when a number, letter, or date is preceded by the word *from,* the word *to* must be used instead of a hyphen.)

pages 44-46 the Detroit-Toledo Expressway

A-L and M-Z from A to Z

H

I

Always capitalize the personal pronoun *I*.

When writers wish to emphasize objectivity, as in formal academic and scientific writing, they avoid *I* and other first-person pronouns (such as *my, we, our*), often using **passive voice** constructions instead.

CHANGE	I conducted the experiment . . .
TO	The experiment was conducted . . .

In much writing, however, and especially in **expressive writing** and some **persuasive writing**, *I* and other first-person pronouns are both natural and appropriate.

> I went to the woods because I wished to live deliberately, to front only the essential facts of life, and see if I could not learn what it had to teach, and not, when I came to die, discover that I had not lived. I did not wish to live what was not life, living is so dear, nor did I wish to practice resignation, unless it was quite necessary. I wanted to live deep and suck out all the marrow of life, to live so sturdily and Spartan-like as to put to rout all that was not life, to cut a broad swath and shave close, to drive life into a corner, and reduce it to its lowest terms, and, if it proved to be mean, why then to get the whole and genuine meanness of it, and publish its meanness to the world; or if it were sublime, to know it by experience, and be able to give a true account of it in my next excursion.
>
> —HENRY DAVID THOREAU, *Walden*

idioms

Idioms are groups of words that, when used together, have a special meaning apart from their literal meaning. People who "run for office," for example, need not be track stars; this idiom means they are seeking public office.

Although idioms are most troublesome to people who are not native speakers of a language, even native speakers of English sometimes have trouble remembering which **preposition** idiomatically follows certain **verbs** and **adjectives**. The following box gives some of those combinations. Consult a dictionary for idioms that do not appear here. (See also **phrasal verbs**.)

PREPOSITIONS IN IDIOMS

abide *by* (a decision)	accused *by* (a person)
abide *in* (a place)	accused *of* (a deed)
according *to*	acquaint *with*
accountable *for* (actions)	
accountable *to* (a person)	*(continued)*

321

adapt *for* (a purpose)
adapt *from* (a source)
adapt *to* (a situation)

agree *on* (terms)
agree *to* (a plan)
agree *with* (a person)

analogy *between* (two things)
analogous *to*
analogy *with* (something)

angry *at, about* (an action or
   a thing)
angry *with* (a person)

apply *for* (a position)
apply (one thing) *to* (another thing)
apply *to* (someone)

argue *for, against* (a policy)
argue *with* (a person)

arrive *at* (a decision, conclusion)
arrive *in* (a place)

blame (an action) *on* (someone)
blame (someone) *for* (an action)

capable *of*

charge *for* (a service)
charge *with* (a crime)

compare *to* (an unlike thing)

compare *with* (a thing of the same
   kind)

comply *with*

consist *in* (a characteristic, cause)
consist *of* (ingredients)

convenient *for* (a purpose)
convenient *to* (a place)

correspond *to, with* (something
   being compared)
correspond *with* (the recipient of
   a letter)

deal *in* (a product)
deal *with* (people or things)

depend *on*

deprive *of*

different *from* (not *than*)

differ *from* (something being
   compared)

differ *on, about, over* (an issue)
differ *with* (a person)

excerpt *from* (not *of*)

forbid *to* (not *from*)

identical *with, to*

impose *on, upon*

in accordance *with*

inferior *to*

inseparable *from*

liable *for* (actions)
liable *to* (an authority)

opposition *to*

possibility *of*

prefer (one thing) *to* (a second
   thing)

prevent *from*

prior *to*

rely *on, upon*

reward *by* (an action)
reward *for* (an accomplishment)
reward *with* (a gift)

sensitive *about* (a slight, an
   offense)
sensitive *to* (an external condition)

similar *to*

substitute *for*

superior *to*

thoughtful *of*

unequal *in* (qualities)
unequal *to* (a challenge)

wait *at* (a place)
wait *for* (a person, event)
wait *on* (a customer)

i.e.

The **abbreviation** *i.e.* stands for the Latin *id est,* meaning "that is." Because a perfectly good English expression exists (*that is*), use the Latin expression or abbreviation only in notes and illustrations where you need to save space.

When you use *i.e.,* punctuate it as follows: If *i.e.* connects two **independent clauses**, precede the abbreviation with a **semicolon** and follow it with a **comma.** If *i.e.* connects a **noun** and **appositives,** precede and follow it with commas. Do not underline or italicize *i.e.*

> Initial critical disdain, i.e., a scathing review in the *Times,* influenced some viewers.

ie/ei spelling   (See **spelling.**)

if

In formal writing, when you use *if* to express a condition contrary to fact, use the **subjunctive** form of the verb.

> *If* I *were* president, I would step down after one term.

illegal/illicit

Illegal is an **adjective** meaning "unlawful" or "not authorized by law."

> Embezzling the company's retirement funds is illegal.

Illicit, also an adjective, means "not permitted," which is taken to mean "not permitted by law, society, or custom." Thus, illicit acts may or may not be illegal, but illegal acts are always illicit.

> Incest is *illicit* everywhere in the world.

illustrations   (See **graphics.**)

image/imagery

An image is a vivid description that appeals to the senses. Images are most often found in poetry, although writers can also use images to make their prose more striking or memorable. (See also **figures of speech.**) For example, in "The Angry Winter," Loren Eiseley brings to life scientific information about the ice age by including sensory images of winter, such as this cold and silent scene.

> As I snapped off the light the white glow from the window seemed to augment itself and shine with a deep, glacial blue. As far as I could see, nothing moved in the long aisles of my neighbor's woods. There was no visible track, and certainly

no sound from the living. The snow continued to fall steadily but the wind, and the shadows it had brought, had vanished.

immigrate/emigrate (See *emigrate/immigrate*.)

imminent/eminent/immanent (See *eminent/imminent/immanent*.)

imperative mood

The imperative mood of a verb expresses commands and direct requests. It is always used in the present tense. Quite often in imperative sentences, the subject (*you*) is understood.

> [You] *Watch* out for the broken step! [Use an **exclamation point** instead of a period after an urgent command.]
>
> [You] *Take* the A-train to 57th Street.

The other moods of verbs are **indicative** and **subjunctive**. (See also **sentence types**.)

implicit/explicit (See *explicit/implicit*.)

imply/infer

Imply means "express indirectly" or "suggest." *Infer* means "derive as a conclusion." Both are **verbs**.

> Her tone *implied* doubt.
>
> The teacher *inferred* from the quality of the work that the assignment had been done at the last minute.

in/into/in to

In means "inside of"; *into* implies movement from the outside to the inside. *Into* is a **preposition**; *in to* is an **adverb** followed by a preposition.

> The textbooks were *in* the storeroom, so she sent her assistant *into* the room to get them.
>
> The pumpkin turned *into* Cinderella's coach. [*Turn* is used here to mean "convert or transform" and requires *into*.]
>
> Turn the form *in to* the Admissions Office. [*Turn* here means "deliver" and requires *in*.]

incidentally/incidently

Incidently is a common misspelling. The correct spelling is *incidentally*.

incomplete comparisons

Comparisons are incomplete when they do not identify both things being compared or when a needed word or phrase has been omitted.

than store-bought ones
Homemade cookies are better.
                                    ∧

[The comparison did not identify what homemade cookies were being compared to.]

does
I enjoy field hockey more than Aletha.
                                      ∧

[The comparison might have been read to mean "more than I enjoy Aletha."]

incomplete sentences (See **sentence fragments** and **sentence types**.)

increasing order of importance as a method of development

Increasing order of importance (also called *climactic order*) presents the point of least importance first and builds, point by point, to the most important idea at the end. The method is effective when the **conclusion** is not the anticipated one or is not an agreeable or popular one. Another advantage is that the **audience** finishes the piece with the main point fresh in mind.

The disadvantage of the method of increasing order of importance is that it begins weakly, with the least important information. However, the method can be used to great effect when the writer skillfully leads readers to the final important detail and leaves them at that high point.

One of the many ill effects of alcohol, perhaps the least important—though this might sound odd at first—is its effect on the body. To be sure, alcohol rots the liver and destroys the brain. But that's the business of the individual. This is a free country, and the choice to destroy oneself is an individual matter. Or it would be if there were not other considerations, the family being one. More important than what alcohol does to the individual is what it does to the family of the alcoholic. In the majority of cases, it leads to the dissolution of the alcoholic's family, with all of the misery that divorce entails, especially for children. And even if alcoholism doesn't lead finally to divorce, it still inevitably causes misery to the other family members, who are guilty only of tolerating the behavior of the drunken mother or father. But most important by far—at least from society's point of view— is the collective effect of alcoholism on the nation at large. Statistics show that, taken together, the nation's alcoholics significantly reduce American productivity on the one hand (because of days absent and work done shoddily) and significantly increase the cost of medical insurance and care on the other. For all of these reasons, but especially the last, it seems to me that we should not tolerate excessive drinking one day more.

—Barry J. Gillin

incredible/incredulous

Incredible means "hard to believe"; *incredulous* means "disbelieving" or "skeptical."

The hikers told a story of *incredible* adventures.

We were *incredulous* about some of their claims.

indefinite adjectives

Indefinite **adjectives** designate an unspecified quantity.

any day   *other* students   *some* classes

indefinite pronouns

The most common indefinite pronouns are *all, another, any, anybody, anyone, anything, both, each, either, everybody, everyone, everything, few, many, most, much, neither, nobody, none, no one, one, other, several, some, somebody, someone, something,* and *such.* Most indefinite pronouns take singular verbs and pronouns, unless the meaning is obviously plural.

Each of the writers *has* a unique style.

Everyone in our class *has* completed the test.

Everyone laughed at my haircut, and I couldn't really blame *them.*

A few indefinite pronouns always take plural verbs and pronouns, however.

Many are called, but *few are* chosen.

Several were aware of the problem, and *they* vowed to address it.

Because only the indefinite pronouns that are singular can form the possessive, an **apostrophe** and *-s* are used to form it.

Everyone's test has been completed.

(See also **agreement of subjects and verbs** and **agreement of pronouns and antecedents**.)

independent clauses

An independent clause (or main clause) is a group of words containing a **subject** and a **predicate** that can stand alone as a separate sentence.

My grades were not as good as I had expected, although I did pass every class.

The second, unitalicized clause in the example is a **dependent clause**; although it contains a subject and predicate, it cannot stand alone as a sentence. (For combinations of dependent and independent clauses, see **sentence types**.)

indexes

The research tools called indexes are lists of articles published in periodicals and are of two basic types, general or specialized. Their purpose is to simplify the process of locating current information about most topics. They are published in print form, on CD-ROMs, and online. Reference librarians can help you use indexes efficiently and effectively. (See **Research Processes**, pages 48–52.)

indicative mood

The indicative mood is the **verb** form used for declarative statements and questions.

> The high temperature on Sunday *broke* a record for December.
>
> This *has been* a lovely fall.
>
> When *will* the semester *be* over?

The other moods of verbs are **imperative** and **subjunctive**. (See also **sentence types**.)

indirect discourse

In contrast to **direct discourse**, indirect discourse (or an indirect quotation) paraphrases someone's words. **Quotation marks** are not used.

> Will Rogers said, "I never met a man I didn't like." [direct discourse]
>
> Will Rogers said he never met a man he didn't like. [indirect discourse]

An indirect question reports a question instead of asking it directly; in this form no question mark is necessary.

> She wanted to know what time the bus arrived.

(See also **commas, paraphrasing, quotations**.)

indirect objects

The indirect object of a **transitive verb** is a **noun** or a **pronoun** that indicates who or what receives the action of the verb. Pronouns that function as indirect objects are in the **objective case**. (See also **objects**.)

> She will give *me* an answer tomorrow. [*Me* is the indirect object; *answer* is the direct object.]

With certain verbs, including those listed here, the indirect object must be expressed as a **prepositional phrase**, which comes after the direct object.

the book to

Li Peng dedicated his father ~~the book~~.

admit	introduce	recommend
announce	mention	repeat
dedicate	open	report
describe	outline	return
explain	prescribe	speak
indicate	propose	suggest

The indirect object may also be expressed in a prepositional phrase with other verbs. Use the preposition *to* after verbs such as *give, tell,* and *send,* which imply an action or transaction between two individuals. Use the preposition *for* after verbs such as *make, sing,* and *buy,* which suggest an action on behalf of someone or something else.

When the direct object is a pronoun or when the indirect object is accompanied by a lengthy modifier, the indirect object must come after the direct object.

to my sister

I loaned ~~my sister~~ it the following day. [The pronoun *it* is the direct object.]

The instructor gave a study guide to the students who attended the last class. [The *who* clause modifies *students,* the indirect object.]

indirect quotations   (See **indirect discourse.**)

inductive reasoning

Inductive reasoning leads from particular instances to a conclusion. (See also **logic.**)

infer/imply   (See **imply/infer.**)

infinitive phrases

An infinitive phrase includes an **infinitive** (often accompanied by *to*) and its **object,** plus any **modifiers.**

This team should be able *to resist the temptations of fame and fortune.*

An infinitive phrase can serve as **noun, adjective,** or **adverb** in a **sentence.**

Claudia is bone weary and wants *to go home.* [noun]

Her desire *to collapse on a sofa and put up her feet* is almost overpowering. [adjective]

But she must carry on *to meet the deadline.* [adverb]

An infinitive phrase serving as a noun may be an **appositive**, a **complement**, an object, or a **subject** in the sentence.

Brandon's goal, *to finish the project on time,* may be unrealistic. [appositive]

The intent of most advertising is *to encourage people to buy a product.* [subject complement]

They propose *to build their home this fall.* [direct object]

To catch the perfect wave is every surfer's dream. [subject]

An introductory infinitive phrase becomes a **dangling modifier** when its implied subject is not the same as the subject of the **independent clause**. The implied subject of the infinitive in the following sentence is *you* or *one,* not *communication.*

To have a good relationship with someone, ^(you should focus on) communication ~~is vital.~~

OR

To have a good relationship with someone, ^(one should focus on) communication ~~is vital.~~

infinitives

An infinitive is the plain, or uninflected, form of a **verb** (*go, run, fall, talk, dress, shout*) and is generally preceded by the word *to,* which in this case is not a preposition but rather the sign of an infinitive.

It is time *to go* to school.

Let me *show* you the campus. [*To* is not used with the infinitive after certain verbs, including *let, make, help, see,* and *hear.*]

An infinitive is a **verbal** and may function as a **noun**, an **adjective**, or an **adverb**.

To pass is not the only objective. [noun]

These are the classes *to take.* [adjective]

He was too tired *to study.* [adverb]

The infinitive may reflect two **tenses**: the present and (with a **helping verb**) the present perfect.

to go [present tense]

to have gone [present perfect tense]

Do not use the present perfect tense when the present tense is sufficient.

> I should not have tried *to* ~~have~~ *go* ~~gone~~ so early.

Infinitives of **transitive verbs** can express both **active** and (with a helping verb) **passive voice.**

> to hit [present tense, active voice]
>
> to have hit [present perfect tense, active voice]
>
> to be hit [present tense, passive voice]
>
> to have been hit [present perfect tense, passive voice]

Splitting Infinitives

A split infinitive occurs when an adverb or an adverb phrase is placed between the sign of the infinitive, *to,* and the infinitive itself. A modifier, especially a long one, between the two words can often be awkward; in most cases, it is preferable not to split an infinitive.

> He planned *to* *complete the forms* as soon as possible ~~complete the forms~~.

Sometimes, however, splitting an infinitive is necessary to prevent awkwardness or ambiguity. Compare the following sentences.

> He opened the envelope unexpectedly *to find* the missing papers. [*Unexpectedly* seems to modify *opened* rather than *find.*]
>
> He opened the envelope *to find* unexpectedly the missing papers. [This sentence is awkward.]
>
> He opened the envelope *to* unexpectedly *find* the missing papers. [Splitting the infinitive is the least awkward way to modify *find.*]

Special Problems with Infinitives

Infinitives do not show past tense, number, or person. Do not add *-ed* or *-s* to them.

> Toan asked me to work~~ed~~ with him at the radio station.

> Jenny likes to ~~studies~~ *study* in the third-floor lounge.

The **particle** *to* is usually omitted after the **helping verbs** *can, could, will, would, shall, should,* and *must* (but not after *need, have,* and *ought*); after sensory verbs (such as *see, hear, watch,* and *listen*); and after a few other verbs such as *help, make,* and *let.*

Frequently, I watch the children ~~to~~ play in the neighborhood park. The sound of

their voices makes me ~~to~~ remember my childhood in Vietnam.

To indicate purpose, use an infinitive (rather than a gerund) as a **complement** ("I enrolled in this class *to meet people*"). Also use an infinitive as a complement with the following common verbs.

afford	demand	mean	request
agree	deserve	need	require
allow	expect	offer	seem
appear	fail	order	swear
arrange	force	permit	teach
ask	hesitate	persuade	tell
beg	hope	plan	threaten
cause	instruct	prepare	wait
command	intend	pretend	want
compel	invite	promise	warn
consent	learn	propose	wish
dare	make	refuse	
decide	manage	remind	

The following verbs can be used with either an infinitive or a gerund as a complement.

attempt	continue	prefer
begin	hate	start
can/cannot bear	like	
can/cannot stand	love	

With four verbs (*forget, regret, remember, stop*) that can be followed by either an infinitive or a gerund as a complement, the meaning changes according to which is used. After *stop,* an infinitive indicates a purpose and a gerund indicates an activity that ceases.

On my way home, I stopped *to talk* to my friend.

I stopped *talking* to my friend after she insulted me.

After *remember, forget,* or *regret,* an infinitive refers to action after the time of the main verb and a gerund refers to action before the time of the main verb.

I cannot forget *to hand* in that paper.

I cannot forget *handing* in that paper.

(For a list of verbs that are used only with gerunds as complements, see **gerunds**.)

informal and formal writing styles

Style is the way language functions to reflect the writer's personality and attitudes in particular situations. For example, a letter to a friend would be relaxed, even chatty, in **tone**, whereas a job application **letter** would be restrained and deliberate. The style appropriate for one situation may not be appropriate for another.

Standard English can be divided into two broad categories of style—formal and informal. Understanding the distinction can help you use the appropriate style. However, no clear-cut line divides the two categories; in fact, some writing may call for a combination of the two.

Formal writing is most evident in scholarly and academic articles, lectures, and legal documents. Material written in a formal style is usually impersonal and objective because the subject matter is more important than the writer's personality. Unlike informal style, formal style does not use **contractions, slang**, or dialect. (See also **English, varieties of.**) The paragraph you are reading now is written in formal style.

An informal writing style is relaxed and conversational. It is the style found in most personal (as opposed to business) letters and popular magazines. There is little distance between writer and audience because the tone is personal. Contractions and **elliptical constructions** are common. Consider the following passage, which illustrates how an informal writing style may use **slang** for special effects and have something like the cadence and structure of spoken English while conforming to the grammatical conventions of written English.

> Imagine "The Wizard of Oz" with an oversexed witch, gun-toting Munchkins and love ballads from Elvis Presley, and you'll get some idea of this erotic hellzapoppin from writer-director David Lynch. Lynch's kinky fairy tale is a triumph of startling images and comic invention. In adapting Barry Gifford's book *Wild at Heart* for the screen, Lynch does more than tinker. Starting with the outrageous and building from there, he ignites a slight love-on-the-run novel, creating a bonfire of a movie that confirms his reputation as the most exciting and innovative filmmaker of his generation.
>
> —PETER TRAVERS, *Rolling Stone*

Requests can be made with various levels of formality by varying the helping verb. The level of politeness you use depends on your relationship with the person to whom you are making the request.

Please fax me a copy of that report. [polite request]

Could you *please* fax me a copy of that report? [more polite]

Would you *please* fax me a copy of that report? [even more polite]

informative writing (See **expository writing**.)

ingenious/ingenuous

Ingenious means "marked by cleverness and originality"; *ingenuous* means "straightforward" or "characterized by innocence and simplicity."

FDR's *ingenious* plans for the New Deal were intended to move the United States out of the Great Depression.

Maria's solution seemed *ingenuous*, but it reflected a sophistication and cunning few of us knew she possessed.

in order to

Often the phrase *in order to* is a meaningless filler dropped without thought into a sentence.

~~In order to~~ start the engine, open the choke and throttle, and then press the starter.
To

input

Input is correctly used as a noun or verb in the context of computers. In formal writing on other topics, it should be avoided because it is a **buzzword**.

Johnson gave us some useful ~~input.~~
suggestions.

inquiry letters (See **letters**.)

in regards to

Use *in regard to, with regard to, as regards,* or *regarding.* The plural noun *regards* means "good wishes" or "affection."

In regards to your letter of May 14 . . .

OR   *Regarding* your letter of May 14 . . .

inside/inside of

Inside can function by itself as a preposition; *of* is unnecessary.

The switch is just *inside* ~~of~~ the door.

Inside of meaning "in less time than" is colloquial and should be avoided in formal writing.

> They were finished *inside ~~of~~* an hour.

OR   They were finished *within* an hour.

insure/ensure/assure

Assure means "to promise," "to reassure," or "to convince." *Ensure* and *insure* both mean "to make sure or certain," but only *insure* is widely used in the sense of guaranteeing the value of life or property.

> I *assure* you that the paper will be done on time.

> We need a bibliography to *ensure* that the information is complete.

> This paper is so good it ought to be *insured* against theft.

intensifiers

Intensifiers are **adverbs** that add emphasis. Examples are *very, quite, really,* and *indeed.* However, unnecessary intensifiers can weaken your writing. When revising your draft, either eliminate intensifiers that do not make a definite contribution or replace them with specific details.

> The team was ~~quite~~ happy to receive the ~~very~~ good news that it had been awarded
> $1,000
> a ~~rather substantial monetary~~ prize for its participation in the tournament.
>   ∧

As an intensifier, *too* means "more than enough, excessive." It is not interchangeable with *very,* which means "extremely, in a high degree."

>   very
> My cousin was ~~too~~ happy when he won the scholarship.
>   ∧

intensive pronouns

Intensive pronouns are **pronouns** formed with *-self* or *-selves* that emphasize another pronoun or a noun. (See also **reflexive pronouns.**)

> He opened the door *himself.*

interjections

An interjection is a word or **phrase** standing alone or inserted into a **sentence** to exclaim or to command attention. Grammatically, it has no connection to the sentence. An interjection can be strong (*Ouch! Ugh!*) or mild (*My, Oh*).

A strong interjection is followed by an **exclamation point.**

> *Ouch!* That bee sting really hurts!

A weak interjection is followed by a **comma.**

> *Well,* if you don't like it, leave.

An interjection inserted into a sentence may need a comma before and after it or no commas at all.

> The time, *indeed,* has come.
> What *in the world* did you mean by that?

Internet

The Internet is a global network of computers. It includes many protocols, or information formats—not only the "http" (hypertext transfer protocol) of the **World Wide Web** but also FTP (**file transfer protocol**), **Gopher** (a text-oriented search protocol), and telnet (a protocol that lets you **log on** to another computer, such as the one housing the library's central catalog, from your computer). You can access the Internet through your university's computer system or an Internet service provider, such as America Online.

interrogative sentences

An interrogative sentence asks a question and ends with a **question mark.** (See also **sentence types.**)

> Which coat is yours?
> How many subjects were interviewed?

interviews

Sometimes interviewing an expert is the best way to get information you need for a research paper or other project. To ensure a successful interview, you need to prepare for it.

When you call or write to request the interview, (1) explain who you are, (2) briefly describe the purpose and proposed length of the interview (request no more of your interviewee's time than absolutely necessary), (3) ask when would be a convenient time for the interview (keep your own deadline in mind), and (4) ask for permission to tape the interview.

In preparation for the interview, learn as much as possible about the interviewee and the topic, and prepare a list of specific questions. Design the questions to elicit more than yes or no as an answer. Never try to improvise an interview, and never use it to gather information that is readily available elsewhere. When you arrive for the interview, be prepared to guide it pleasantly but purposefully.

GUIDELINES FOR INTERVIEWS

1. Use the list of questions you have prepared, but if some answers prompt additional questions, ask them.
2. Let the interviewee do the talking. Don't try to impress him or her with your knowledge of the subject or your opinions about it.
3. If the interview drifts off track, be ready to steer it back with a specific question.
4. Take only memory-jogging notes during the interview. Do not ask the interviewee to slow down so that you can take detailed notes. If you want to tape-record the interview, obtain permission beforehand. Recording allows you to concentrate on asking questions and listening to answers rather than on taking notes. There are three possible disadvantages to tape-recording, however: It may make the interviewee nervous, it may lure you into simply recording whatever the interviewee says rather than directing the interview with specific questions, and the tape may be faulty or the recorder may fail to capture everything because it was not set loudly enough.
5. Immediately after leaving the interview, make detailed notes from your interview notes. Do not postpone this step. No matter how good your memory is, you will forget some important points.

If you include information from the interview in a paper, use the proper style to document your source both within your text and in the list of works cited. (See **Research Processes,** pages 84, 108, 121, 141.)

intransitive verbs

Intransitive verbs are **verbs** that do not take a **direct object.**

The audience *laughed.*

The hummingbird *flitted* from flower to flower. [An intransitive verb may be followed by a prepositional phrase or other adverbial modifier.]

introduction (opening)

The introduction of a piece of writing has two purposes: to indicate your subject and to catch the audience's interest. It should be natural, not forced; an awkward introduction will only puzzle readers, who will be unable to establish a meaningful connection between the introduction and the body of the paper. If you find writing an introduction difficult, try composing it late, even last, in the writing process. Many writers find that an effective introduction occurs to them as their perspective develops in the course of writing.

Don't assume that your audience will instinctively know your attitude toward the subject or will be predisposed to read what you have written. To engage the audience's interest, try one of the following strategies.

Definition

Opening with a definition is effective if it gives the audience new information or new understanding. It loses its effectiveness if the audience is familiar with the definition or if the opening is contrived ("Webster defines *literature* as . . .").

> What is the new loyalty? It is, above all, conformity. It is the uncritical and unquestioning acceptance of America as it is—the political institutions, the social relationships, the economic practices. It rejects inquiry into the race question or socialized medicine, or public housing, or into the wisdom or validity of our foreign policy. It regards as particularly heinous any challenge to what is called "the system of private enterprise," identifying that system with Americanism. It abandons evolution, repudiates the once popular concept of progress, and regards America as a finished product, perfect and complete.
>
> —HENRY STEELE COMMAGER, "Who Is Loyal to America?"

Interesting Characteristics

If your subject has some unusual characteristics, you can use one or more of them to open your piece and capture the audience's attention and interest. The following introduction, for example, uses the notion of eccentricity to make readers curious about Norton I.

> During the Gold Rush of 1849 and the years that followed, San Francisco attracted more than any city's fair share of eccentrics. But among all the deluded and affected that spilled through the Golden Gate in those early years, one man rose to become perhaps the most successful eccentric in American history: Norton I, Emperor of the United States and Protector of Mexico.
>
> —JOAN PARKER, "Emperor Norton I"

Surprising Statistic or Fact

Sometimes you can open with an interesting or startling statistic or fact.

> During a six-month period in 1973, the *New York Times* reported the following scientific findings:
>   A major research institute spent more than $50,000 to discover that the best bait for mice is cheese. . . .
>
> —JERRY MANDER, "The Walling of Awareness"

Anecdote

A brief narrative of an amusing, peculiar, or interesting incident—an **anecdote**—can provide a striking introduction.

> At just about the hour when my father died, soon after dawn one February morning when ice coated the windows like cataracts, I banged my thumb with a hammer. Naturally I swore at the hammer, the reckless thing, and in the moment of swearing I thought of what my father would say: "If you'd try hitting the nail it would go in a whole lot faster. Don't you know your thumb's not as hard as that hammer?" We were both doing carpentry that day, but far apart. He was building cupboards at my brother's place in Oklahoma; I was at my home in Indiana, putting up a wall in the basement to make a bedroom for my daughter. By the time my mother called with the news of his death—the long distance wires whittling her voice until it seemed too thin to bear the weight of what she had to say—my thumb was swollen.
>
> —Scott Russell Sanders, "The Inheritance of Tools"

Background

Providing some background or historical material about your subject may arouse the audience's concern and interest.

> The problem lay buried, unspoken for many years in the minds of American women. It was a strange stirring, a sense of dissatisfaction, a yearning that women suffered in the middle of the twentieth century in the United States. Each suburban wife struggled with it alone. As she made the beds, shopped for groceries, matched slipcover material, ate peanut butter sandwiches with her children, chauffeured Cub Scouts and Brownies, lay beside her husband at night—she was afraid to ask even of herself the silent question—"Is this all?"
>
> —Betty Friedan, "The Problem That Has No Name"

introductory clauses or phrases

Use a **comma** to set off an introductory adverbial **clause** or **phrase** unless the word group is very short and there is no likelihood of misreading.

> *As we pulled onto the highway,* the snow started coming down.
> *Almost immediately* we decided to turn back.

Use a comma after an introductory **participial phrase**, **infinitive phrase**, or **absolute phrase**.

> *Blowing into five-foot drifts,* the snow soon blocked our way. [participial phrase]
> *To tell you the truth,* we were lost. [infinitive phrase]
> *The blizzard finally behind us,* we breathed a sigh of relief. [absolute phrase]

inverted sentence order

In inverted sentence order, the **subject** follows the **verb**. Inverted order is especially common in sentences that begin with *there is* or *there are*. (See also **expletives**.)

> There *is* a right *way* to do things—and a wrong way. [The subject of the sentence, *way*, is preceded by the verb, *is*.]

Writers also sometimes invert sentence order to add **emphasis**.

> Blessed *are* the *meek*. [The subject of the sentence, *meek*, follows the verb, *are*.]

(See also **agreement of subjects and verbs** and **sentence variety**.)

irony

Irony is achieved by language suggesting a meaning that contrasts with its literal meaning. For example, humorist Art Buchwald employs irony when he says, "The most important argument for collecting taxes from the elderly is that it would lower the tax burden on helpless corporations and conglomerates who are struggling to make ends meet."

When writing a **literary analysis**, you might focus on one of the types of irony. When authors use *verbal irony*, they give a character's words more than one meaning. When authors use *structural irony*, it pervades the literary work. The **persona** in Jonathan Swift's essay "A Modest Proposal," for example, appears to be proposing that we eat the children of the Irish poor, when actually he is pointing out the foibles of government policy toward the Irish. In drama, playwrights sometimes use *dramatic irony* by developing scenes in which the audience is aware of an outcome different from the one a character anticipates. Irony may also be *tragic, cosmic, romantic,* or *situational*. In each case, the author shares with the reader or audience knowledge of which the characters are unaware.

irregardless/regardless

Irregardless is nonstandard. Use *regardless* or *irrespective* instead.

> ~~Irregardless~~ *Regardless*
> of the difficulties, we must find a way to get Mr. Eliot out of the bank.

irregular verbs

Irregular verbs are **verbs** that do not form the **past tense** and the **past participle** by adding -*d* or -*ed*.

COMMON IRREGULAR VERBS

PRESENT	PAST	PAST PARTICIPLE
arise	arose	arisen
awake	awoke or awaked	awaked or awoke
be (is, am, are)	was, were	been
beat	beat	beaten
become	became	become
begin	began	begun
bend	bent	bent
bite	bit	bitten or bit
blow	blew	blown
break	broke	broken
bring	brought	brought
build	built	built
burst	burst	burst
buy	bought	bought
catch	caught	caught
choose	chose	chosen
cling	clung	clung
come	came	come
cost	cost	cost
creep	crept	crept
dig	dug	dug
dive	dived or dove	dived
do	did	done
draw	drew	drawn
dream	dreamed or dreamt	dreamed or dreamt
drink	drank	drunk
drive	drove	driven
eat	ate	eaten
fall	fell	fallen
fight	fought	fought
find	found	found
fly	flew	flown

PRESENT	PAST	PAST PARTICIPLE
freeze	froze	frozen
get	got	gotten or got
give	gave	given
go	went	gone
grow	grew	grown
have	had	had
hear	heard	heard
hide	hid	hidden
hurt	hurt	hurt
keep	kept	kept
know	knew	known
lay (put)	laid	laid
lead	led	led
lend	lent	lent
lie (recline)	lay	lain
lose	lost	lost
make	made	made
prove	proved	proved or proven
read	read	read
ride	rode	ridden
ring	rang	rung
rise	rose	risen
run	ran	run
say	said	said
see	saw	seen
send	sent	sent
shake	shook	shaken
shrink	shrank or shrunk	shrunk or shrunken
sing	sang or sung	sung
sink	sank or sunk	sunk
sit	sat	sat
sleep	slept	slept
speak	spoke	spoken

(continued)

PRESENT	PAST	PAST PARTICIPLE
spin	spun	spun
spring	sprang or sprung	sprung
stand	stood	stood
steal	stole	stolen
sting	stung	stung
stink	stank or stunk	stunk
strike	struck	struck or stricken
swear	swore	sworn
swim	swam	swum
swing	swung	swung
take	took	taken
teach	taught	taught
tear	tore	torn
throw	threw	thrown
wake	woke or waked	waked or woken
wear	wore	worn
write	wrote	written

is when/is where

When you are **defining terms**, do not use *is where* or *is when* clauses. A definition tells *what* a thing is, not "where" or "when" it is.

> *a binding agreement between*
> A contract is ~~when~~ two or more people ~~agree to something.~~
>   ∧   ○

> *a place*
> A day care center is *where* working parents can leave their preschool children during the day.   ∧

it

The **pronoun** *it* has a number of uses. First, *it* can refer to an object or idea or to a baby or animal whose sex is unknown or unimportant. *It* should have a clear **antecedent**.

> Darwinism strongly influenced nineteenth-century American thought. *It* even affected economics.

> The Moodys' baby is generally healthy, but *it* has a cold at the moment.

It can also serve as an **expletive.**

> *It* is necessary to sand wood before painting it.

However, your writing can often be more direct if you do not use *it* as an expletive.

> *We*
> ~~It is~~ seldom ~~that we~~ go.
>   ∧

(See also *its/it's.*)

italics

Italics (indicated on the typewriter by underlining) are a style of type. *This sentence is printed in italics.*

For Emphasis

Words that are defined or that require special **emphasis** in a sentence are sometimes italicized. To create emphasis in formal writing, **word choice** and sentence structure are preferable to italics.

> By *texts* we mean not only books but also newspaper and magazine articles, government documents, advertisements, and letters. [Italics are used for a term being defined.]

> What are the arguments *against* the idea, and what are the arguments *in favor of* it? [Italics are used for emphasis; the meaning would be just as clear without italics, however.]

Titles of Works

In text, titles of works that are published or produced as separate entities are italicized (or underlined). Shorter works—such as book chapters, magazine articles, and songs—are enclosed in **quotation marks.** (The treatment of titles is somewhat different in various styles of documentation. See **Research Processes,** pages 61–153.)

Books and Literary Works

> *A Tale of Two Cities*   *The University of Chicago Spanish Dictionary*

Titles of holy books and legislative documents are not italicized.

> the Bible   the Koran   the Magna Carta

Titles of chapters in books, essays, and short stories are enclosed in quotation marks.

"A Modest Proposal"   "Rip Van Winkle"

"Male and Female in Hopi Thought and Action"

Titles of poetry collections and long poems are italicized; titles of short poems are enclosed in quotation marks.

The Iliad   *The Waste Land*   "The Road Not Taken"

Titles of plays are italicized.

King Lear   *Raisin in the Sun*

Magazines and Newspapers

Titles of magazines and newspapers are italicized; titles of articles are enclosed in quotation marks.

the *Los Angeles Times*   *National Geographic*

"Sex, Race, and Box Office" in *Image,* the Sunday magazine of the *San Francisco Examiner*

Titles of comic strips are italicized.

Doonesbury   *The Far Side*

Films and Television and Radio Programs

Aladdin   *Jeopardy*   *Malcolm X*

A Prairie Home Companion   *Sense and Sensibility*   *The X-Files*

Titles of individual episodes are enclosed in quotation marks.

Albums and Long Musical Works

Bizet's *Carmen*   *The Joshua Tree*   *Thriller*

Titles of songs and other short musical compositions are enclosed in quotation marks.

"Amazing Grace"   "The Minute Waltz"   "Peel Me a Grape"

Painting and Sculpture

Leonardo da Vinci's *Mona Lisa*   Michelangelo's *David*

Software

Excel   WordPerfect

Names of Vehicles and Vessels

The names of ships, trains, spacecraft, and aircraft (but not the companies that own them) are italicized.

They sailed to Africa on the Onassis *Clipper.*

Model and serial designations are not italicized.

Boeing 747   DC-7

Words, Letters, and Figures

Words, letters, and figures mentioned as such are italicized.

The word *inflammable* is often misinterpreted.

I need to replace the *s* and *6* keys on my old typewriter.

Foreign Words

Foreign words and phrases that have not been assimilated into the English language are italicized; foreign words that have been fully assimilated need not be italicized. Refer to an up-to-date dictionary if you are in doubt about a particular word.

Flavio ordered *chilaquiles* and I ordered breakfast tacos.
—SANDRA CISNEROS, "*Bien* Pretty"

Genus and species names, which are in Latin, are italicized.

Three types of orchids are easy and reliable to grow: *Cattleya, Paphiopedilum,* and *Phalaenopsis.*
—"Elegant and Easy," *Sunset*

its/it's

Its is a possessive **pronoun**; *it's* is a **contraction** of *it is* or *it has.*

It's important that the university live up to *its* public relations image.

It's been three months since I heard from him.

I

jargon

Jargon is the specialized vocabulary of a particular field or group. If all your readers are members of a particular group, jargon may be an efficient means of communicating with them. But if you are writing for a general audience, eliminate jargon. If some technical terms are necessary, define them the first time you use them. (See also **buzzwords.**)

For example, when author and doctor Oliver Sacks describes neurological disorders for general readers, he sometimes uses medical terminology, but he describes the maladies in plain English first. In "The Lost Mariner," Sacks's first description of the amnesia of one of his patients is in nonmedical vocabulary: "I found an extreme and extraordinary loss of recent memory—so that whatever was said or shown to him was apt to be forgotten in a few seconds' time." Sacks later quotes a psychiatrist's assessment of this patient in medical jargon: "His memory deficits are organic and permanent and incorrigible."

journals

Journals are often used in writing classes to encourage students to experiment with language, explore ideas, or respond to assignments. Because of their exploratory, reflective nature, journals are rarely judged on the basis of grammar or mechanics but rather on the length or depth of an entry. Students are often encouraged to **freewrite** in their journals to allow their creativity to emerge.

keyword

Keywords are the search terms used in Internet searches. (See **Boolean search** for advice about combining keywords and searching for phrases; see also **Research Processes**, pages 41–42 and 56–57.)

kind of/sort of

Kind of and *sort of* mean "category of" or "type of." The **article** *a* should not follow either term.

What *kind of a̶* movie is it?

In formal writing or speech, neither term should be used to mean "somewhat," "more or less," or "rather."

rather
The movie told a s̶o̶r̶t̶ ̶o̶f̶ sad story.
　　　　　　 ∧

later/latter

Later refers to time; *latter* means the second of two groups or things referred to or the last item referred to in a series. (See also *former/latter.*)

> Nancy arrived first; Peggy got there *later.*
>
> Between sailing and swimming, I prefer the *latter.*

lay/lie, set/sit

The confusion writers sometimes have between *lay* and *lie* is similar to the confusion between *set* and *sit*. *Lay* (like *set*) is a **transitive verb** that means "place or put." *Lie* (like *sit*) is an **intransitive verb** meaning "rest on a surface."

> Now I always *lay* [*set*] my glasses next to my computer. [present tense]
>
> My glasses always *lie* [*sit*] next to my computer. [present tense]
>
> Twice last week I *laid* [*set*] my glasses on the kitchen counter. [past tense]
>
> Twice last week my glasses *lay* [*sat*] on the kitchen counter all day. [past tense]
>
> I forgot where I *had laid* [*had set*] my glasses. [past participle]
>
> I found that my glasses *had lain* [*had sat*] on the kitchen counter all day. [past participle]

lead/led

The **past tense** of the verb *lead* is *led*.

> We asked Frank to *lead* us; he *led* us to the Schwarzenegger film festival.

learn/teach

Learn means "to gain knowledge." *Teach* means "to impart knowledge."

>   *taught*
> Ms. Hoover ~~learned~~ me well.
>   ^
>
> OR
>
> I *learned* a lot from Ms. Hoover.

leave/let

Leave, as a **verb**, should not be used as a synonym for *let*, meaning "allow," in formal writing.

> *Let*
> ~~Leave~~ him get that door for you.
> ^

347

lend/loan

Lend and *loan* both have a long history as **verbs,** but some writers prefer *lend.* *Loan* (which can also be a **noun**) can be used as a verb only in a literal sense, whereas *lend* can be used in either a literal or a figurative sense.

You can *lend* [or *loan*] them the money if you wish.

"Friends, Romans, countrymen, *lend* me your ears. . . ."

—WILLIAM SHAKESPEARE, *Julius Caesar*

less/fewer (See *fewer/less.*)

letters

Basic Considerations

Because a business letter determines your reader's impression of you, thoughtfulness, correctness, and neatness are all essential. Whatever the occasion and purpose may be, remember that your letter will be read by a busy human being who has feelings just as you do. Therefore, get to the point, be clear and objective, and always be polite (especially if you are writing about something that has made you anxious or angry). Keep both your own purpose and your reader's situation and interests clearly in mind as you write. Then reread your first draft and revise it until you are satisfied that it is as effective as you can make it; type the letter in a traditional business format so that your reader will focus on what you are saying rather than on how your letter looks; and proofread the letter carefully—several times, if necessary—before you mail it. Keep a copy for future reference.

Although the types of business letters are numerous, the following discussion focuses on a few that are of special interest to college students—letters associated with getting a job—as well as letters of inquiry, which everyone needs to write from time to time. (See also **memorandums** and **résumés**.)

Business Letter Format

Type single-spaced on only one side of letterhead stationery or 8½-by-11-inch, unruled, white bond paper, and use a matching standard-size envelope. Center the letter on the page inside a "picture frame" of white space. The right, left, and top margins should be about 1 to 1½ inches.

The two most common formats for business letters are the *full block style* (see Figure L-1, a typical business letter that illustrates each of the elements discussed in the following paragraphs) and the *modified block style* (see Figures L-2, L-3, and L-4). In the full block style, every line begins at the left margin; this style is usually used with letterhead stationery. In the modified block style, the return address, the date, and the closing are indented to the center of the page.

L

Heading If you are not using letterhead stationery, type your full address (street, city, state, and zip code) 1 to 1½ inches from the top of the page. Spell out address designations, such as *Street, Avenue,* and *West.* The state name may be abbreviated; use the two-letter U.S. Postal Service **abbreviation.**

Date If you are using plain stationery, type the date on the line below the address. If you are using letterhead stationery, type the date two lines below the letterhead. Spell out the name of the month.

Inside Address Two to four lines below the date, type the recipient's full name and job title, the name of the company or institution (if appropriate), and the address. The inside address is always aligned on the left margin.

Salutation Place the salutation, or greeting, two lines below the inside address, also aligned on the left margin. In business letters, the salutation ends with a **colon.**

Use the recipient's title (such as *Mr., Ms., Dr.*) unless you are on a first-name basis. Address women without a professional title as *Ms.,* whether they are married or unmarried, unless they have expressed a preference for *Miss* or *Mrs.* If the recipient's first name could be either a man's or a woman's, use both the first and the last names in the salutation (*Dear K. H. Jones:*).

If you do not know the name of the recipient, use a title appropriate to the context of the letter (*Dear Personnel Director, Dear Customer Service*

<table>
<tr><td>Letterhead</td><td>

Mahwah News & Sun
618 Main Street
Mahwah, NJ 07430

(201) 788-1234
FAX: (201) 788-4900
</td></tr>
<tr><td>Date</td><td>May 3, 2002</td></tr>
<tr><td>Inside address</td><td>

Mr. Stanley Clayton
Billing Department
Philadelphia Photo Research Services
26142 Market Street
Philadelphia, PA 19103
</td></tr>
<tr><td>Salutation</td><td>Dear Mr. Clayton:</td></tr>
<tr><td>Body</td><td>

Enclosed is your invoice dated April 29, 1999, showing a balance due of $6,240.00. However, we paid this bill in full on March 26, 1999, as shown by the enclosed copy of our canceled check (check number 51643) made out to your firm in the amount of $6,240.00.

Please credit our account for this amount and send us a new invoice showing this transaction.

If you have any questions, please call Mahwah News & Sun during regular business hours and ask to speak to me.
</td></tr>
<tr><td>Complimentary closing</td><td>Sincerely,</td></tr>
<tr><td>Signature</td><td>*Marjorie Bedard*</td></tr>
<tr><td>Typed name
Title</td><td>

Marjorie Bedard
Accounting Manager
</td></tr>
<tr><td>Notations</td><td>

MB/pf
Enclosure: Invoice No. 87300; copy of check 51643
cc: A. L. Evans, Treasurer
</td></tr>
</table>

Figure L-1. Business letter (full block style).

1824 Franklin Place
Blue Hill, Maine 04614
May 15, 2002

University of Maine
Music Department
125 Liberty Street
Orono, Maine 04469

Dear Personnel Director:

An announcement was recently posted on the Student Union bulletin board of Husson College that you are seeking a part-time music research assistant. I would like to apply for that position.

I am a senior at Husson College, with a major in music history, and will graduate in June. In the previous two years (as described in the enclosed résumé), I held a similar position at Husson College, working as research assistant to Dr. Pamela Hetu. During two summers, I worked at the Brattleboro Music Camp as librarian and general research assistant. I think that these employment experiences and my educational background qualify me for the position you are seeking to fill.

I am available for an interview at your convenience and will be happy to give you any additional information you may need. My telephone number is (207) 374-6606.

Sincerely,

Estelle Sanford

Estelle Sanford

Enclosure: Résumé

Figure L-2. Sample application letter (modified block style).

9347 Pardu Drive
Oakland, CA 94621
August 5, 2002

Ms. Beverly Mendoza
Personnel Manager
West Coast Express Courier Services
6452 Airline Road
San Francisco, CA 94104

Dear Ms. Mendoza:

I am seeking a position in marketing so that I may use my education and experience to help market services and products. At a recent business meeting, I spoke to Mr. Pavel Deucher on your staff, and he told me that an entry-level marketing position was open at West Coast Express. I would like to apply for that position.

I graduated from Stanford University in June with a Bachelor of Business Administration degree in marketing. During my sophomore and junior years at Stanford, I was enrolled in the Business Majors' Work-Study Program. Through this program, I received valuable marketing and business training from several area firms (see the enclosed résumé for details). In my senior year, I worked part-time as a marketing assistant for Robinson Business Products, a firm I trained with in the work-study program.

I would like to meet with you for an interview whenever it is convenient for you. I can be reached at my home, telephone (510) 555-2830.

Sincerely yours,

Christian Noyes

Enclosure: Résumé

Figure L-3. Sample application letter.

23 Park Place
New York, NY 10016
November 5, 2002

Ms. Courtney Plunksett
Personnel Department
Computers, Inc.
1675 21st Avenue
Brooklyn, NY 11232

Dear Ms. Plunksett:

Thank you for granting me the interview on Monday. In particular, thank you for giving me a tour of the offices and manufacturing facilities so that I could learn more about Computers, Inc. I am impressed with the company's organization, efficiency, and management.

The position you described to me is very attractive. I believe that my education and experience qualify me to do the job successfully.

I look forward to hearing from you in the near future.

Yours truly,

Henry King

Henry King

Figure L-4. Follow-up letter to job interview.

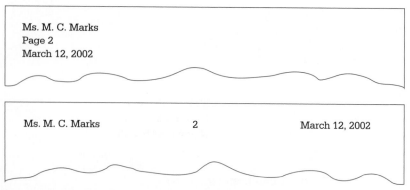

Figure L-5. Headings for the second page of a letter.

Representative), or replace the salutation with an "attention line" to the appropriate department (*Attention: Membership Committee*) or a "subject line" (*Subject: 2001–02 Membership Fees*).

Body Begin the body of the letter two lines below the salutation. Single-space within paragraphs, and double-space between paragraphs. (Indenting the first line of each paragraph five to ten spaces is acceptable but is considered more informal than the unindented block style.)

Be concise, direct, and considerate. In the opening paragraph, state the letter's purpose. Include supplementary information in a middle paragraph or two, and conclude your letter with a brief paragraph that both establishes good will (with a phrase such as "I look forward to meeting with you" or "I appreciate your prompt attention") and expresses what needs to be done next ("I am available for an interview at your convenience" or "I hope to receive the refund from you within a few days").

Second Page If a letter requires a second page, always carry over at least two lines of the body text; do not use a second page for only the letter's closing. The second page (and all subsequent pages) should have a heading with the recipient's name, the page number, and the date. The heading may go in the upper left-hand corner or across the page, as shown in Figure L-5.

Closing The complimentary closing begins two lines below the body of the letter. *Sincerely, Sincerely yours,* or *Yours truly* are common endings for business letters. As shown by the examples, the initial letter of the first word is capitalized. Punctuate the ending with a **comma.**

Four lines below the closing, type your full name. If you are writing in an official capacity, type your title on the next line. Your signature goes above

```
Leslie Warden
3814 Oak Lane
Lexington, KY 40514



                              Marjorie Bedard
                              Accounting Manager
                              Mahwah News & Sun
                              618 Main Street
                              Mahwah, NJ 07430
```

Figure L-6. Business envelope.

your typed name. Unless you are on a first-name basis with the recipient, sign your full name.

Notations At the bottom of the last page of a business letter, brief notations may show who typed the letter, whether any materials are enclosed with the letter, and who is receiving a copy of the letter. The *typist's initials* (in lowercase letters) are separated from the letter writer's initials (in capital letters) by a colon or a slash (*SBR:nlg* or *SBR/nlg*). If the writer is also the typist, no initials are needed.

An *enclosure notation* alerts the recipient that the envelope contains material (such as a résumé or an article) in addition to the letter. You can either name the enclosures or indicate how many there are. In either case, you must also mention the enclosed materials in the body of the letter.

Enclosure: Résumé and Letter of Recommendation

OR

Enc. (2)

A *copy notation* tells the reader who is receiving a copy of the letter.

cc: Dr. Charles Larson

Envelope

The recipient's address on the envelope should be identical to the inside address of the letter. Start the first line in the approximate center of the envelope. The return address (your name and address) goes in the upper left-hand corner. See Figure L-6.

Application Letter

The desired outcome of a job application letter is an interview. But the letter first must catch the attention of the person responsible for selecting new hires from among many candidates. Thus, the application letter should present your education, talents, and experience in as favorable a light as possible.

When you draft a job application letter, be sure to consider its three objectives: to get the reader's notice, to present your qualifications clearly and confidently, and to request an interview. Be concise, but provide sufficient detail to give the reader the following information:

1. *The type of work you are seeking or the specific job title.* Personnel managers review many letters each week. To save them time, state your job objective directly at the beginning of the letter.

I am seeking a position in an engineering department where I can use my computer science training to solve engineering problems.

2. *Your source of information about the job.* If you have been referred to a prospective employer by one of its employees, a placement counselor, a professor, or someone else, say so either before or right after you state your job objective.

During the recent NOMAD convention in Washington, DC, a member of your sales staff, Mr. Dale Jarrett, told me of a new opening for a sales assistant in your Dealer Sales Division. My college course work in selling and my experience in various part-time sales jobs qualify me, I believe, to be a candidate for this position.

3. *A summary of your qualifications for the job,* specifically education, work experience, and activities showing initiative or leadership skills. If you are applying for a specific job, be sure to mention any pertinent information not included on the more general **résumé** you will enclose with your letter.

4. *A reference to your résumé* for additional information.

5. *A request for an interview,* including information about where you can be reached and when you will be available for the interview.

Type your letter, proofread it carefully for errors, and keep a copy for future reference. (See also **Composing Processes.**)

The two sample letters of application (Figures L-2 and L-3) illustrate the use of these guidelines. The first is written by a college senior, the second by a recent college graduate. (Both letters use the modified block form.)

Follow-up Letter

If you are successful in obtaining a job interview, jot down pertinent information you learned during the interview as soon as possible after you leave, while the information is still fresh in your mind. (This information can be especially helpful in comparing job offers.) A day or two later, send the interviewer a brief note of thanks, saying that you find the job attractive (if true) and feel you can fill it well. The sample in Figure L-4 is typical.

Acceptance Letter

Respond within a week to an acceptable job offer. To begin the letter, say how pleased you are to accept the offer. Then, to avoid any confusion, specify the job you are referring to and the salary that has been offered.

In the second paragraph, refer to any pertinent details that were discussed during the job interview, such as a date for beginning the job. Conclude the letter by noting that you are looking forward to beginning your new job.

Inquiry Letter

A letter of inquiry requests answers to particular questions. You will not always get a response, but you can improve your chances of success by following these suggestions.

1. Be concise, specific, and clear in wording your questions.
2. Write your questions as a numbered list if at all possible.
3. Keep the list of questions as short as possible.
4. Thank your reader for taking the time and effort to reply.
5. Include the address to which the answers should be sent.

To further encourage a response, enclose a stamped, self-addressed envelope.

liable/likely

The term *liable* means "legally subject to" or "responsible for."

Employers are held *liable* for their employees' decisions.

In writing, *liable* should retain its legal meaning. Where a condition of probability is intended, use *likely*.

likely
Rita is ~~liable~~ to be promoted.
    ^

library classification systems (See **Research Processes**, pages 52–53.)

library research (See **Research Processes**, pages 35–60.)

lie/lay (See **lay/lie, set/sit.**)

like/as (See *as/like*.)

limiting the subject (See **Composing Processes.**)

linking verbs

A linking verb links the **subject** to the **subject complement** (a **noun** or **modifier** that renames or describes the subject). The most common linking verb is *be* in its various forms. Other verbs that may function as linking verbs include *become, remain, seem,* and verbs that convey the senses (*look, feel, sound, taste, smell*).

> Careful editing *is* essential to a well-written paper.
>
> She *became* an industrial engineer.
>
> The repair crew *looked* tired.

A few verbs may function either as linking verbs or as **transitive** or **intransitive verbs.** If a form of *be* may be substituted, the verb is probably a linking verb.

> He *grew* angry. [linking verb, equivalent in meaning to *became*]
>
> He *grew* African violets in his office. [transitive verb]
>
> The African violets *grew* profusely. [intransitive verb]

If your native language does not require a verb between a subject and a subject complement, pay special attention when you revise and edit to make sure that every sentence has a **verb** (not just a **participle,** such as *being.*)

> *is*
>
> Ivan very handsome.
> ^

listing

Listing is a prewriting technique that helps you generate, organize, and focus your thoughts. Listing can be a form of **brainstorming** or **clustering.** Once you have a possible subject in mind (or one is assigned to you), start writing down every idea that pops into your head. When you have generated a list, rearrange ideas, organize topics into logical groups, and omit items that are irrelevant or lead in unproductive directions. (See also **Composing Processes.**)

lists

To emphasize a series of points—perhaps the characteristics of a thing or the steps in a process—use a vertical, or displayed, list. Lists can be bulleted, numbered, or lettered alphabetically. Use **bullets** if the order of the items in the list is not important; use numbers or letters if the items need to be presented in a certain order, as in the steps in a process.

The items in a list should be parallel. They should be all single words or all phrases or all sentences. If they are phrases, they should be constructed alike; for example, they might all begin with an infinitive.

To format and introduce vertical lists, follow these guidelines (many word-processing programs use the same formatting guidelines):

- Indent the bullets, numbers, or letters at least half an inch from the left margin.
- Use a hanging indent for each item in the list; that is, start the second and subsequent lines of the item under the first word of the first line, not under the bullet, letter, or number. (This list uses a hanging indent.) On most of today's word-processing programs, margins can easily be set for a hanging indent.
- Follow numbers or letters with a period. (For a list run into the text, enclose numbers or letters in **parentheses**.)
- If you introduce the list with an **independent clause** (such as the introduction to this list), follow the clause with a **colon**.
- If you introduce the list (usually a list of words or phrases) with an incomplete clause that ends with a verb, do not follow the clause with any punctuation (just as you would not put a punctuation mark between a verb and a direct object).

literary analysis

When instructors ask students to write about literature, they generally expect them to write a literary analysis. Perhaps the easiest approach is to write a paper describing what you liked and disliked about a play, poem, or work of fiction. Once you have determined your likes and dislikes, back up these assertions with quotations and examples from the literary work.

Depending on the literary genre, the level of the course, and the length of the assigned paper, a literary analysis might focus on one or several literary elements and techniques. For example, when writing about literature or drama, you might focus on the **characterization**, the **setting**, or the **plot** of the work. If you were writing about Toni Morrison's novel *Beloved,* you might discuss the development of the character of Sethe and how Morrison portrays her as a mother. If you were writing about Henrik Ibsen's play *A Doll's House,* you could examine how the setting (in Norway) contributes to the atmosphere of the play and reflects the cold personality of the husband, Torvald. If you were writing about Peter Ackroyd's novel *The Trial of Elizabeth Cree,* you could focus on how the structure of the plot contributes to the suspense of the story and allows for the surprising ending. Exploring any one of these elements (characterization, setting, plot) could result in a well-developed short paper; an examination of all three elements in a single work would yield an interesting longer essay. You could also use the **comparison and contrast** method of development to examine two similar works.

In addition to these basic elements of literature, a literary analysis could focus on **point of view, theme, tone, metaphor** and **simile,** or **symbolism** and **allegory.** If you were looking at Henry James's well-known short novel *The Turn of the Screw,* for example, you might want to discuss the innovative use of point of view. The story is told through the eyes of a character who is obviously deranged, so the audience gets a skewed version of the events. If you wanted to discuss the point of view of a poem, you would consider the poet's **persona** in the poem, or the voice assumed by the poet. In Edgar Arlington Robinson's poem "How Annandale Went Out," the poet assumes the persona of a doctor. In Langston Hughes's poem "A Theme for English B," the poet assumes the persona of a college student. By exploring the point of view in a poem—that is, by asking who the speaker is—you gain insight into the poet's purpose and intentions.

Writing about a theme is a common approach to literary analysis. If you were writing about J. D. Salinger's novel *Catcher in the Rye,* you might focus on the theme of hypocrisy, and if you were analyzing Margaret Atwood's novel *The Handmaid's Tale,* you might want to explore how the author uses the backlash against feminism as a theme. If you are struck by how an author creates an effect through the use of language, you might want to build your literary analysis around tone. In Edgar Allen Poe's story "The Fall of the House of Usher," the author uses various means to establish a feeling of dread, and in Denise Levertov's "The Mutes," the poet uses verbal irony to convey her feelings about sexual harassment.

Exploring figurative language is another basis for a literary analysis, but it is often more appropriate for poetry than for prose works. An **explication** of a poem focuses on how the poet uses such figurative language as metaphor and simile to add meaning to a poem. If you were writing about Hamlet's famous soliloquy, "To be or not to be," you might discuss the meanings and emotions that Shakespeare evokes with such figurative phrases as "the slings and arrows of outrageous fortune," "the whips and scorns of time," and "shuffled off this mortal coil." Another approach to literary analysis is to focus on a work's use of symbolism or allegory. For example, Shakespeare uses the rose as a symbol of love in many of his poems, and Hawthorne uses the snake as a symbol of evil. Other works contain a central allegory, such as Robert Frost's poem "The Road Not Taken," in which a choice about a fork in the road is an allegory for a choice about a life path. Similarly, George Orwell's novel *Animal Farm* is an allegory about totalitarianism.

Whatever the focus of your literary analysis, you need to take certain steps to generate a clear, convincing, organized, and well-developed essay. Plan on reading the play, poem, or work of fiction more than once. While you are reading the work, use your **journal** to explore possible ideas and directions for your essay. After you have determined a focus,

- Read closely and repeatedly, marking all relevant examples.
- Determine the function of each example.
- Decide which one (or ones) to use.
- Study the structure of the examples you have chosen.
- Trace how and where they are used.
- Look for relationships between your focus and other elements.
- Examine how these relationships contribute to the meaning and accessibility of the work.

Next, prepare to present your analysis in essay form. When beginning to write, follow the steps described in **Composing Processes**, for they apply to the writing of any paper. In the introduction to your essay, present your **thesis** about the role of your focus (which might be characterization, setting, theme, tone, metaphor, or the like) in the literary work. In the body of your essay, expand and develop the thesis by citing and explaining all relevant examples and discussing the relationship of your focus to the work in general, to its message, or to your knowledge of the author's beliefs.

In addition to the steps of the composing processes, you need to follow certain conventions used in writing about literature. In the introduction, include the title of the work, the author, and a brief summary of the plot. When describing the action of the work, use the **literary present** tense. To avoid **plagiarism**, carefully follow the guidelines for quotations, paraphrasing, summarizing, and documentation that are explained in **Research Processes**.

literary present

When you write about literature or other works of art, verbs normally should be in the literary present. This convention is based on the idea that the work continues to exist in the present even if the author or artist is long dead.

In his poetry, Melville *writes* scornfully about the waste of war.

In Homer's *Odyssey*, Ulysses and his men *are* temporarily turned into pigs.

little/a little

Little and *a little* are used to modify **mass nouns**, but *little* has a more negative connotation than does *a little*. (See also *few/a few*.)

I have *little* money in the bank. I can't afford to eat out.

I have *a little* money in the bank. Let's treat ourselves to a night out.

logic

Logic is the study of reasoning. In almost all of your writing, and especially in writing intended to persuade someone to accept or at least respect your point of view, attention to logic is essential. Philosophers ranging from Aristotle twenty-five centuries ago to Stephen Toulmin in our own day have defined various systems of logic. Despite important differences, all these systems have a common aim: to move from true premises by valid reasoning—called *inference*—to a conclusion that is also true, or at least highly probable.

Deductive Reasoning

Deductive reasoning, which is essentially mathematical, can be illustrated by the structure known as the *syllogism* (from a Greek word meaning "propositions considered together").

> All human beings are mortal.
>
> Socrates is a human being.
> _____
>
> Therefore, Socrates is mortal.

The first two statements of the syllogism are called the *premises*. The third statement is the *conclusion*. The distinctive feature of deductive logic is that if the reasoning is valid, the conclusion is guaranteed by the premises. That is, if the premises are true and the reasoning is valid, the conclusion must be true—as in the example.

Validity is not the same as truth; *validity* merely refers to the form of the reasoning. A valid deductive argument can be built on false premises, with the result that the conclusion, too, will be false.

> All human beings are purple.
>
> Socrates is a human being.
> _____
>
> Therefore, Socrates is purple.

And invalid reasoning will lead to a false conclusion even though the premises are true.

All human beings are mortal.

Socrates is mortal.

Therefore, all human beings are Socrates.

A deductive argument in which the premises are true and the reasoning is valid is said to be sound. Soundness—valid reasoning from true premises— is what the writer of a deductive argument must strive for.

Inductive Reasoning

Inductive reasoning arrives at a conclusion by examining a sampling of information that suggests (but can never guarantee) that the conclusion is true. In other words, whereas deductive reasoning deals with certainty, inductive reasoning deals with probability. To take a simple example, if you flick the light switch a hundred times and the light comes on every time, you conclude that the light will come on the next time you flick the switch. But, of course, it may not come on; the bulb may have burned out or been removed, or the power may have been shut off.

Because the world is an uncertain place, most arguments deal with probabilities rather than certainty. The methods of science, too, are based primarily on inductive reasoning: Until an experiment has been repeated several times with the same results, the findings are regarded as tentative. Even when the conclusion appears almost certain, the scientist keeps an open mind. In an inductive argument, the more evidence, the better the evidence, and the better the writer's reasoning from the evidence, the more convincing the writer's conclusion will be.

The Toulmin Model

The Toulmin model of argument, devised by British philosopher Stephen Toulmin, cuts through the distinction between inductive and deductive to establish the elements of any argument. Always there is a *claim*, essentially the matter to be proved. The claim is based upon information, or data (what Toulmin calls *grounds*). In Toulmin's words, "the claim . . . can be no stronger than the grounds that provide its foundation." But how do we know that the alleged grounds really do provide support for the claim being considered—that they "are not just irrelevant information having nothing to do with the claim in question"? The answer, Toulmin says, is *warrants*—rules or formulas from law, science, personal experience, or other sources appropriate to the topic—that do establish the connection between the grounds and the claim. Finally, in order to be trustworthy, the warrants must themselves be subject to *backing*. For instance, "legal statutes [offered as warrants] must have been validly legislated; scientific laws . . . thoroughly checked out; and so on."

Fallacies

Fallacies are types of faulty reasoning. Usually, they are due to careless thinking; but they may also be used deliberately, as they are in much propaganda and advertising, to mislead. Following are some of the most common fallacies.

Ad hominem is Latin for "to the man." It is a form of argument that attacks the person rather than the issues.

> Our new professor looks like Homer Simpson. How can we take him seriously?

An *appeal to pity* tries to distract the audience from the legitimate issues by focusing attention on the arguer's irrelevant miseries.

> I deserve a raise. My car is in the shop, I'm behind in my mortgage payments, and my wife left me with three children to raise alone. [The listed misfortunes may be reasons for needing a raise, but they are not reasons for deserving a raise.]

The *bandwagon fallacy*—a favorite of advertisers and politicians—is a tactic children often resort to, asserting that something is good or right because "everyone else is doing it."

> Four out of five doctors surveyed recommend Brand X painkiller for their patients.

Begging the question is circular reasoning. It merely restates in the conclusion (usually in other words) what has been asserted in the premise.

> Because women are not well suited for fighting, they do not do well in combat duty in the armed forces.

The *either/or fallacy* erroneously assumes that only two alternatives are possible when, in fact, others exist.

> A new car may be expensive, but do you want me to drive around in this junk pile for the rest of my life?

Equivocation misleads by using a term in two different senses.

> We should not raise taxes. Life is taxing enough as it is.

A *false analogy* makes the erroneous assumption that because two objects or ideas seem similar in some ways, they must be similar in other ways. For instance, a political dictator defended the execution of sexual offenders by drawing false analogies between immoral behavior and physical disease and between the population as a whole (or the state) and a diseased body.

> If your finger suffers from gangrene, what do you do? Let the whole hand and then the body become filled with gangrene, or cut the finger off?

False cause (sometimes called *post hoc, ergo propter hoc,* meaning "after this, therefore because of this") wrongly assumes that because one event happened after another event, the first somehow caused the second.

> Our new police uniforms have worked wonders. They were issued on September 2, and in the six months since then, arrests have increased forty percent.

Hasty generalizations (also called *sweeping generalizations*) are conclusions based on too little, faulty, or misunderstood evidence. No matter how certain you are of the general applicability of an opinion, use with caution such all-inclusive terms as *anyone, everyone, no one, always,* and *never.*

> Management is never concerned about employees.
>
> Computer instructions are always confusing.
>
> Anyone can see that taxes should not be raised.

A *non sequitur* is a statement that does not logically follow from a previous statement. Non sequiturs may reflect faulty reasoning, but they often occur when a writer simply neglects to express some logical link in a chain of thought.

> He enjoyed cooking and was especially fond of cocker spaniels. [The missing link in this alarming sentence is that cooking was one of his interests but he had others, including cocker spaniels.]

A *red herring* is an irrelevancy thrown into an argument to divert the attention from the real issue at hand.

> Before you start worrying about the budget deficit, you'd better take care of those laid-off defense workers.

The *slippery slope fallacy* falsely assumes that if one event is allowed to occur, it will inevitably lead to a whole chain of consequences.

> If we continue to allow legal abortions, the next steps will be the elimination of the physically and mentally undesirable and finally the killing of anyone we don't like for any reason at all.

Biased or Suppressed Evidence

A conclusion reached from self-serving data, questionable sources, or purposely incomplete facts is illogical and dishonest. If you were asked to prepare a report on the acceptance of a new policy and you distributed questionnaires to only those in favor of the policy, the resulting evidence would be biased. If you *purposely* ignored people who believed the policy was ineffective, you would also be suppressing evidence. Any writer must be concerned about the fair presentation of evidence, especially in reports that recommend or justify actions.

Fact versus Opinion

Distinguish between fact and opinion. Facts include verifiable data or statements, whereas opinions are personal conclusions that may or may not be based on facts. For example, it is a fact that distilled water boils at 100°C; it is an opinion that distilled water tastes better than tap water. To prove a point, some writers mingle facts with opinions, obscuring the differences between them. This tactic is, of course, unfair to the audience. Be sure to distinguish facts from opinions in your writing so that your audience can clearly understand and judge your conclusions.

> The new milling machines produce parts that are within two percent of specification. [This sentence is stated as a fact that can be verified by measurement.]
>
> The milling machine operators believe that the new models are safer than the old ones. [The word *believe* identifies the statement as an opinion—later statistics on the accident rates may or may not verify the opinion as a fact.]

The opinions of experts are often accepted as evidence in court. In writing, too, experts' testimony can help you convince the audience that your views are sound. Be on guard, however, against flawed testimonials. For example, a chemist may well make a statement about the safety of a product for use on humans, but the chemist's opinion is not as trustworthy as that of a medical researcher who has actually studied the effects of that product on humans. When you quote the opinion of an authority, be sure that his or her expertise is appropriate to your point, that the opinion is a current one, and that the expert is indeed highly respected.

log on/log off

To log on is to go through the necessary steps on your computer to get **online.** Depending on the age and complexity of your computer system, logging on may require simply entering your password, or it may entail additional steps. Logging off is the process of getting offline, either by entering certain words or letters (such as *quit* or *q* in Telnet) or by clicking particular icons on the computer screen.

logos

Logos is the appeal to reason in an **argument**. It is based on **logic** and the fair presentation of reliable evidence.

loose/lose

Loose, an **adjective**, means "free from restraint" or "not fitting tightly."

He wore a *loose* shirt for his workout.

Lose, a **verb**, means "miss from one's possession," "fail to win," or "go astray."

They are going to *lose* the game if they keep dropping the ball.

lots

Lots is an informal way of expressing quantity. In formal writing, *many,* *much,* or a specific amount is more appropriate.

> *several hours*
> We had l̶o̶t̶s̶ ̶o̶f̶ ̶t̶i̶m̶e̶ to spare.
>   ∧

L

main clauses (See **independent clauses**.)

main idea

In a paper, the main idea (also called the *central idea*) is the **thesis**. In a paragraph, the main idea is the focus of the **topic sentence**. Usually, the main idea is directly stated, but sometimes it is implied. In either case, making sure that everything in a paper (or a paragraph) is related to the main idea is the key to achieving **unity**. For ways to develop a main idea, see **methods of development**.

main verb (See **helping verbs** and **verb phrases**.)

male

Use *male* in legal, medical, or scientific writing (*the male subjects, in a study of ten males*). Its objective, impersonal **connotation** suits these fields. In other writing, use *boy* or *man*. However, be sensitive to these words' connotations about age, dignity, race, and social standing within the context of your writing. (See also *female* and **nonsexist language**.)

man/mankind

The terms *man* and *mankind* have traditionally been used to represent all human beings. However, many people now feel that this terminology ignores and, by implication, denigrates the other half of the human race—women. Whenever possible, use a gender-neutral alternative, such as *humanity* or *people*. (See also **nonsexist language**.)

manuscript form

Some details of manuscript form vary according to the requirements of the instructor or of the academic field in which you are writing. The most common formats are those prescribed by the Modern Language Association of America for the humanities; by the American Psychological Association for the social sciences; by *The Chicago Manual of Style* for history, art history, and other humanities; and by the Council of Biology Editors for the life sciences and medicine. These styles are described in **Research Processes**. Certain conventions of manuscript form, however, are common to nearly all papers. Unless you are instructed otherwise, follow the conventions presented here.

Print out or type final drafts on one side of 8½-by-11-inch bond typing paper, not erasable or onionskin paper. If you are using a continuous-feed printer, remove the perforated feeder strips from the sides of the paper and separate the pages. If you do not have access to a computer or typewriter, your paper should be legibly handwritten in blue or black ink on 8½-by-11-inch notebook paper that has widely spaced lines (to leave room for corrections).

Whatever method you use, the print or writing should be legible. If you use a computer or typewriter, choose a conventional font or **typeface** rather than a script or other unusual style. Courier is a legible typeface that looks like traditional typewriting; Times and Times Roman are also considered very readable. With a typewriter or dot-matrix printer, use a ribbon that has sufficient ink. With a laser or ink-jet printer, make sure you have an adequate supply of ink in your cartridge.

Double-space throughout your paper: title, block quotations, tables and captions, **appendixes,** reference lists and notes—*everything.* Use one-inch margins (except for page numbers) unless you are given other instructions.

Indent the first word of each paragraph half an inch (five spaces if you are using a typewriter).

If you are using a computer, do not justify the lines (justified type can be difficult to read); leave the right margin uneven. Avoid dividing words at the end of lines unless absolutely necessary. (For conventions on breaking words between lines, see **hyphens.**)

Begin each part of the paper—such as the abstract, the reference list, and the appendixes—on a new page. Center the heading at the top of the page. The heading should not be underlined, enclosed in **quotation marks** (unless, of course, it is a **quotation**), or written in all-capital letters.

The upper right-hand corner is a good place for page numbers. To help the reader if the pages become separated, type your last name before the page number on each page, unless instructed otherwise.

(See also **graphics.**)

mapping (See **clustering** and **outlining.**)

mass nouns

Mass nouns name concrete things that are not countable, such as *water, silver,* and *bread.* In contrast, **count nouns** name things that are countable, such as *raindrops, knives, questions,* and *houses.* Mass nouns usually take singular verbs.

> Much *water has* poured into the reservoir.
>
> The *money is* all his.

(See also **agreement of subjects and verbs, indefinite pronouns,** and **noncount nouns.**)

may/can   (See *can/may.*)

maybe/may be

Maybe spelled as one word is an **adverb** meaning "possibly."

We'll go to Spain someday, *maybe.*

May be spelled as two words is a **verb phrase** meaning "is perhaps."

She *may be* the only musician in the room.

media/medium

The singular **noun** is *medium;* it takes a singular verb. The plural form is *media;* it takes a plural verb.

The *medium* you choose for a landscape painting *is* important in setting the tone.

Many *media are* accepted in Norden's art class.

Newer dictionaries (such as *The American Heritage Dictionary of the English Language,* published in 1992, and the online Merriam-Webster dictionary at <http://www.m-w.com/cgi-bin/dictionary>) indicate that *media* is starting to be accepted in some contexts as a singular mass noun when it refers to the agencies of mass communication, as in "the *news media has* given the American public more than it wants to know about Washington scandals."

memorandums

Called *memos* for short, business memorandums (or memoranda) are routinely used within organizations for internal communications of all kinds— to announce policies, confirm conversations, exchange information, delegate responsibilities, request information, transmit documents, instruct employees, and report results. Memos should be brief and to the point, and they should ordinarily deal with only one subject.

Memo Format

Although memo format varies somewhat among companies and institutions, all memos begin with four lines that give the date, the name of the author, the name of the recipient, and the subject of the memo. (See Figure M-1.) Instead of signing the memo, the author usually initials his or her name. Recipients of copies are listed at the end of the memo.

Simpson & Row Publishing Company
MEMORANDUM

DATE: September 6, 2002
TO: Art Jones, Heidi Moder
FROM: Sylvia Santuzi ℒℴ
SUBJECT: Cover for Michelle Burns: The Politics of
            the Environment

Here is the artwork for the cover of the Burns book. I think
the art studio did a particularly good job conveying the
essence of the environment in this montage. I need to
have your feedback on it in a day or two so that I can
discuss it with Burns when she comes in for the meeting
on Friday. In particular, consider these five areas.

1.   Does the cover work with the book's content?
2.   Are the colors acceptable? (Think taste, style,
     appeal.)
3.   Is there anything jarring or offensive in the
     montage? (Think about students and professors.)
4.   Has anything important not been depicted here?
     What?
5.   Does the artwork meld with the image of Simpson &
     Row we've been trying to promote?

If changes need to be made, please be specific in your
comments and criticisms. Why does the change need to
be made? What particular things need to be changed?
How would you change it?

Please respond with your comments and answers to the
questions by Wednesday, September 8, at the latest. I
know you're both busy, but we do have to get moving on
this cover. And I want Burns to be satisfied with the job
we're all doing.

I appreciate your help.

mab
Copies: Gerard Marin, Vice President
          Lisa Carl, Marketing Manager

M

Figure M-1 Typical memo format.

Structure and Tone

The first paragraph should concisely describe the topic and purpose of the memo and include necessary background information ("As we agreed at yesterday's meeting," for example). The last paragraph should describe any action that is required.

To make the contents readily apparent to a reader skimming the memo, use highlighting techniques such as numbered lists and subheads.

The level of formality depends on the audience and the purpose. A project report to a superior should be more formal, for example, than the sharing of information with a peer.

(See also **letters**.)

metaphor

A metaphor is a **figure of speech** that implies a comparison between two unlike things. (A **simile** is an explicit comparison using *like* or *as*.)

> *The building site was a beehive,* with iron workers on the tenth floor, plumbers installing fixtures on the floors just beneath them, electricians busy on the middle floors, and carpenters putting the finishing touches on the first floor.

Metaphors can help clarify, describe, and explain. For example, naming the tube that carries oxygen from a spacecraft to spacewalking astronauts an *umbilical cord* emphasizes its life-sustaining nature.

A word of caution: A **mixed metaphor** can result in an incongruous and perhaps laughable statement.

> Hawkins offered a proposal to *iron out* the *bottlenecks*.

metasearch engine

Metasearch engines search a number of search engines simultaneously and retrieve about 10% of the search results from each one. Because no two search engines search exactly the same database or index keywords in the same way, metasearch engines can help you check that you have not missed any important Web sites. (For a list of metasearch engines, see **Research Processes**, page 55.)

methods of development

Finding the most appropriate method (or methods) of developing the topic of your paper will make both the writing and the reading easier as the paper moves smoothly and logically from **introduction** to **conclusion**. There are several common methods of development, each best suited to particular purposes.

If you are writing a set of instructions, for example, you know that your audience needs a **chronological method of development**—this step first, this next, and so forth.

In writing about a new topic that is in many ways similar to another, more familiar topic, you may wish to compare the new topic to the familiar one. In doing so, you are using either **analogy** or **comparison as a method of development**.

If you are explaining an airplane crash, you might begin with the crash and trace backward to its cause, or you might begin with the cause of the crash (for example, a structural defect) and show the sequence of events that led to the crash. Either way, you are using **cause and effect as a method of development**. You can also use this approach to develop a solution to a problem, beginning with the problem and moving on to the solution, or vice versa. (See also **problem-solution as a method of development**.)

If you are writing about the software for a new computer system, you might begin with a general statement of the function of the total software package, then explain the functions of the larger routines within the software package, and finally deal with the functions of the various subroutines. This approach is the **general-to-specific method of development**.

Still another approach to a topic is to begin with the least important facts or ideas and build to a climax—**increasing order of importance as a method of development**.

Methods of development often overlap, and it is a rare paper that relies on only one. The important thing is to select a primary method of development for the paper as a whole and then use others as appropriate.

misplaced modifiers

A **modifier** is misplaced when it appears to modify the wrong word or phrase. To ensure clarity, place modifiers as close as possible to the word, phrase, or clause they are intended to modify.

Misplaced Words

Adverbs are especially likely to be misplaced because they can appear in several positions within a sentence.

> We *almost* lost all the parts.
> We lost *almost* all the parts.

The first sentence means that all the parts were *almost* lost (but they were not), and the second sentence means that a majority of the parts (*almost*

all) were in fact lost. To avoid confusion, place the adverb immediately before the word it is intended to modify.

> *Not all*
> ~~All~~ navigators are ~~not~~ talented in mathematics.
> ∧
>
> [When *not* precedes *talented*, the implication is that *no* navigator is talented in
> mathematics.]

Misplaced Phrases and Clauses

To ensure clarity, place phrases and clauses near the words they modify.
Note the two meanings possible when the italicized phrase is shifted in the
following sentences.

> The sedan *without the accessories* sold the best. [Different types of sedans were
> available, some with and some without accessories.]
>
> The sedan sold the best *without the accessories*. [One type of sedan was available,
> and the accessories were optional.]

Awkward placement of long phrases and clauses can interrupt the grammatical flow of a sentence. An adverb phrase or clause between the subject
and the verb or between the verb and the object or complement can make
reading difficult.

> *B*   *traffic*
> ~~Traffic,~~ *because of the accident,* had to be rerouted.
>   ∧
>
> [Placement between subject and verb is awkward.]

> *the parcel*   *it.*
> I securely wrapped / *before I mailed* / ~~the parcel~~ /
>   ∧   ∧   ∧
>
> [Placement between verb and direct object is awkward.]

A phrase or clause between a helping verb and a main verb or between
to and an **infinitive** can also be awkward.

> *B*   *I will*
> ~~I will,~~ *before I wear the jacket again,* sew on the button.
>   ∧
>
> [Placement between main and helping verb is awkward.]

> *because of the long line*
> We had to / ~~*because of the long line*~~ / buy tickets for the later show.
>   ∧
>
> [Placement between *to* and infinitive is awkward.]

Squinting Modifiers

A modifier squints when it can be interpreted as modifying either the sentence element before it or the one after it. Correct a squinting modifier by changing its position or by rephrasing the sentence.

too often
Working late ~~too often~~ leads to inefficiency.
                              ∧

OR

Habitually working
~~Working~~ late ~~too often~~ leads to inefficiency.
          ∧

(See also **dangling modifiers**.)

misspelled words (See **spelling**.)

mixed constructions

Mixed constructions usually occur in first drafts and are due to hasty writing. The writer starts a sentence with one kind of structure in mind (such as a prepositional phrase followed by a subject and a verb) but, in the course of trying to put the idea into words, unintentionally switches to another structure halfway through the sentence. Untangle mixed constructions during revision of your paper.

M

R
~~By~~ ╱equiring all cars to use unleaded gasoline is intended to reduce air pollution.

[The sentence structure switches between *gasoline* and *is,* and the sentence lacks a subject.]

OR

By requiring all cars to use unleaded gasoline, the federal government intends to reduce air pollution.

The blizzard had closed the roads, but ~~which~~ the snowplows were trying to re-
                                                them
open before morning.
     ∧

[This sentence gets sidetracked at *but which. But* is a word that links two independent clauses; *which* is a word that links a subordinate clause to an independent clause.]

OR

The blizzard had closed the roads, which the snowplows were trying to reopen before morning.

mixed metaphors

A mixed metaphor is the illogical combination of two **metaphors**, or implied comparisons.

Let us resolve that the British lion shall never pull in its horns.

MLA style (See **Research Processes**, pages 61–98.)

modal auxiliaries

Modal auxiliaries are **helping verbs** that express ability, probability, advice, wishes, or requests. The following are the most common modal auxiliaries:

| can | may | must | shall | will |
| could | might | ought | should | would |

Modal auxiliaries precede the **infinitive**, or plain, form of a verb, and they do not change to agree with the number or the person of the subject.

If I *can* afford the cost, I *may* buy a computer.

You *ought* to check the newspaper ads regularly. [*To* is used with the infinitive after *ought* but not after the other modal auxiliaries.]

Entering students *should have taken* the assessment tests. [When a modal auxiliary precedes another helping verb, such as *have* or *be,* the helping verb is in the infinitive form.]

modem

Modems (the word comes from *mo*dulator and *dem*odulator) connect computers via telephone lines, cable, or DSL and enable users to transfer **e-mail,** Web documents, and other information. A modem may be internal (inside your computer) or external.

Modern Language Association (MLA) style (See **Research Processes**, pages 61–98.)

modes, rhetorical (See **Composing Processes, expository writing, expressive writing,** and **persuasive writing.**)

modified block style (See **letters**.)

modifiers

Modifiers limit, describe, or qualify the meaning of a word or word group. They are words, **phrases**, or **clauses** that add details, interest, and precision to writing.

> The rain fell. [This sentence is without modifiers.]
>
> The *light spring* rain fell *softly*. [Details are provided by modifiers.]

Modifiers act as **adjectives** or **adverbs**. Adjectives modify **nouns** or **pronouns**.

> *seventeen* elephants   *that* dog
>
> *lucky* you   *bright* lights

Adverbs modify **verbs**, adjectives, and other adverbs. They may also modify phrases, clauses, or entire sentences.

> The graphics department used *extremely* bright colors. [The adverb *extremely* modifies the adjective *bright*.]
>
> The redesigned brake pad lasted *much* longer. [The adverb *much* modifies another adverb, *longer.*]
>
> The wrecking ball hit the building *hard*. [The adverb *hard*, modifying the verb *hit*, tells how the ball hit the building.]
>
> *Surprisingly*, the machine failed. [The adverb *surprisingly* modifies an entire clause, *the machine failed.*]

(See also **dangling modifiers** and **misplaced modifiers**.)

mood (grammatical)

Mood in grammar identifies the **verb** form used to express whether an action or state is considered a fact, command, possibility, or wish. The **indicative mood** states a fact or opinion or asks a question. The **imperative mood** gives a command or direction. The **subjunctive mood** expresses a wish or suggestion or states a circumstance contrary to fact.

Indicative Mood

The indicative mood can be conjugated in all **tenses**.

> The dial setting *is* correct.   The setting *was* correct.
>
> *Will* the setting *be* correct?   The setting *had been* correct the day before.

M

Imperative Mood

The imperative mood is expressed only in the second-person form of the present tense, and the implied subject, *you,* is not expressed.

Install the wiring today.

Please *let* me know if I can help.

Subjunctive Mood

Except for *be,* verbs have a distinctive subjunctive form only in the third-person singular of the present tense; the -*s* is dropped.

	Jason insisted that he *take* charge of the project. [subjunctive]
BUT	He always *takes* charge. [indicative]
	If I *were* going, I would leave on Wednesday. [subjunctive; form of *be*]
BUT	I *am* going, and I will leave on Wednesday. [indicative; form of *be*]

Mood Shift

Be careful not to shift needlessly from one mood to another within a sentence.

Re-cap the tubes of paint, and ~~you should~~ clean the brushes.

[The shift from imperative to indicative is awkward and unnecessary.]

Ms./Miss/Mrs.

Ms. is a convenient form of addressing a woman, regardless of her marital status, and it is now almost universally accepted. *Miss* is used to refer to an unmarried woman, and *Mrs.* is used to refer to a married woman. Some women indicate a preference for *Miss* or *Mrs.,* and such a preference should be honored. An academic or professional title (*Doctor, Professor, Captain*) should take precedence over *Ms., Miss,* or *Mrs.* (See also **letters.**)

must have/must of

Must of is a nonstandard expression. The correct usage is *must have.*

have
I *must ~~of~~* forgotten to turn off the heat.

narration

Narration is storytelling, the presentation of a series of real or fictional events in a chronological sequence. That sequence may not always be straightforward, however. Like many movies (movies are always narrative in form), a written narrative may use flashbacks, beginning in the middle or even at the end of the story and then going back to examine the events that led up to that point. Much narrative writing explains how something happened. Thus, it is closely related to **cause and effect as a method of development**.

Narrative writing depicts events in a chronological, exact sequence. It tells a story by ordering events in time, by using verb **tenses** to show past and present, and by using transitional words relating to time (*after, before, first, now, then*). Narrative writing also presents a consistent **point of view** in relation to the writer through the use of **person**.

Writers can narrate a story from either the first-person or the third-person point of view. If authors write as participants in experiences, they use first-person narration. In the following excerpt from a chapter in Maxine Hong Kingston's novel *The Woman Warrior*, the author writes as a woman talking to her daughter.

> "I remember looking at your aunt one day when she and I were dressing; I had not noticed before that she had such a protruding melon of a stomach. But I did not think, 'She's pregnant,' until she began to look like other pregnant women, her skirt pulling and the white tops of her black pants showing. She could not have been pregnant, you see, because her husband had been gone for years. No one said anything. We did not discuss it. In early summer she was ready to have the child, long after the time when it could have been possible."
>
> —"No Name Woman"

If authors write as observers about someone else's experiences or about an object or event, they use third-person narration.

> Mr. Pontellier . . . fixed his gaze upon a white sunshade that was advancing at a snail's pace from the beach. He could see it plainly between the gaunt trunks of the water oaks and across the stretch of yellow camomile. The gulf looked far away, melting hazily into the blue of the horizon. The sunshade continued to approach slowly. Beneath its pink-lined shelter were his wife, Mrs. Pontellier, and young Robert Lebrun. When they reached the cottage, the two seated themselves with some appearance of fatigue upon the upper step of the porch, facing each other, each leaning against a supporting post.
>
> "What folly! to bathe at such an hour in such heat!" exclaimed Mr. Pontellier. He himself had taken a plunge at daylight. That was why the morning seemed long to him.
>
> "You are burnt beyond recognition," he added, looking at his wife as one looks at a valuable piece of property which has suffered some damage.
>
> —KATE CHOPIN, *The Awakening*

N

Once a narrative is under way, it should not be interrupted by lengthy explanations or analysis. Explain only what is necessary for readers to follow the action.

For further information about sequencing narratives, see **chronological method of development**.

neither . . . nor

Neither . . . nor is a **correlative conjunction**—the pair of words connects parallel parts of sentences, such as antecedents or subjects. When both antecedents are singular, *nor* should be followed with a singular verb or pronoun; if one antecedent is singular and the other plural, the verb or pronoun should agree with the closest antecedent. (See **agreement of subjects and verbs** and **agreement of pronouns and antecedents**.)

> Neither fame nor wealth *is* enough to lure her from retirement. [singular antecedents]

> Neither the dog nor the two cats *show* any loyalty to *their* master. [The closer antecedent is plural; therefore, both the verb and the pronoun must be plural.]

The elements following *neither* and *nor* should be parallel.

> *plentiful jobs*
> Neither the high salaries nor the ~~fact that jobs are plentiful~~ can attract me to a city
> where I feel unsafe.

noncount nouns

In contrast to **count nouns**, which may be made plural, noncount nouns are always singular. Noncount nouns include **mass nouns** (such as *water, silver,* and *bread*), abstract nouns (such as *beauty, intelligence,* and *evidence*), categorical nouns (such as *furniture, luggage,* and *machinery*), and most **gerunds** (such as *swimming, bowling,* and *jogging*).

Because noncount nouns are always singular, the pronouns and verbs that follow them must also be singular.

> The lab *equipment is* in need of repair, but we can't afford to get *it* fixed.

Different **adjectives** expressing quantity precede count and noncount nouns.

COUNT NOUNS	NONCOUNT NOUNS
few, a few	little, a little
many, several	much

In addition, only count nouns can be preceded by the adjectives *each* and *every* and by the **articles** *a* and *an*.

Some nouns can be used as either count or noncount nouns.

Death is the only certainty in *life*. [*Death* and *life* are abstract nouns in this sentence.]

The drunken driver was responsible for six *deaths*. [*Death* is a count noun in this sentence.]

The baby's bib was covered with *egg*. [In this sentence, *egg* is a mass noun.]

The recipe calls for three *eggs*. [In this sentence, *eggs* is a count noun.]

none

With **mass nouns,** *none* takes a singular verb. With **count nouns,** *none* can take either a singular or a plural verb, although some writers prefer to use a singular verb.

None of the material *has* been ordered. [Always use a singular verb with a mass noun—in this case, *material*.]

None of the clients *has* [*have*] been called yet. [A singular or plural verb can be used with a plural count noun (*clients*).]

(See also **agreement of subjects and verbs.**)

N

nonfinite verbs

A nonfinite verb, or **verbal,** is a verb form used as an adjective, adverb, or noun. It cannot function as the verb of a sentence, as can a **finite verb.**

non sequitur fallacy (See **logic.**)

nonsexist language

Use inclusive language rather than language that stereotypes or excludes individuals on the basis of gender. Avoid stereotyped assumptions about gender roles.

spouses

All medical school graduates and their ~~wives~~ are invited to the centennial
                                          ∧

celebration.

[The word *wives* implies that all the graduates are men.]

Candidates for the university presidency are Daniel Scott, president of EXL In-

dustries, and ~~Mrs.~~ Arlene Hoffman, dean of students ~~and mother of two.~~

[Only the woman's marital and parental status is noted. If such information is relevant, it should be given for men as well as women; if it is not, it should be deleted.]

Do not use pronouns that exclude either sex. (See also **agreement of pronouns and antecedents.**)

Doctors   *their*
~~A doctor~~ must constantly update ~~his~~ medical knowledge.

[Make the antecedent and the pronoun plural.]

OR

A doctor must keep informed about new medical developments. [Revise the sentence to eliminate the pronoun.]

OR

A doctor must constantly update his or her medical knowledge. [This alternative, using both masculine and feminine pronouns, becomes awkward if it is repeated too often.]

Avoid *man* compounds or gender-specific occupational titles when referring to both men and women or when the gender is not known or is irrelevant.

humans
About one-fifth of ~~mankind~~ speak Chinese.

sales representative
The ~~salesman~~ will call at 3 p.m.

sculptor
Louise Nevelson was a world-famous ~~sculptress.~~

GENDER-NEUTRAL ALTERNATIVES

INSTEAD OF	USE
actor, actress	actor
alumnae, alumni	graduates
anchorman	anchor
busboy, busgirl	server's helper, server's (*or* serving) assistant

INSTEAD OF	USE
businessman, businesswoman	businessperson, business executive
cavemen	cave dwellers, cave people
chairman, chairwoman	chair, presiding officer, convener, leader, moderator, coordinator
cleaning lady, maid	housekeeper, office cleaner
clergyman	member of the clergy, minister, pastor
coed	student
comedienne	comedian
congressman	representative, senator, member of Congress, legislator
craftsman	craftsperson, artisan, craftworker
deliveryman	delivery clerk, courier
fireman	firefighter
fisherman	fisher, angler
forefathers	ancestors, forebears
foreman	supervisor, leader; head juror
freshman	first-year student
garbageman	garbage collector
handyman	repair person, repairer
heiress	heir, inheritor
heroine	hero, protagonist
housewife	homemaker
laymen	laypeople, laity
mailman	mail carrier, letter carrier, postal worker
male nurse	nurse
man (noun)	person, human being, one, individual, you, I
man (verb)	operate, staff, work, serve on (in, at)
man-hours	worker-hours, employee-hours, staff-hours
mankind	humans, humanity, humankind, human beings, human societies, people, we, us
man-made	handmade, hand-built, synthetic, manufactured, fabricated, machine-made, constructed

(continued)

N

INSTEAD OF	USE
manpower	personnel, staff, labor, workers
meter maid	meter reader, meter attendant
middleman	contact, go-between, intermediary, agent
newsman	reporter, journalist
old wives' tale	superstition
poetess	poet
policeman, policewoman	police officer
repairman	repairer, technician
right-hand man	right hand, chief assistant, lieutenant
salesman, saleswoman, saleslady, salesgirl	salesclerk, salesperson, sales representative
spaceman	astronaut, space traveler
spokesman, spokeswoman	spokesperson, representative
sportsmanship	fair play, fairness
statesmanlike	diplomatic
stewardess	flight attendant
suffragette	suffragist
waiter, waitress	server
watchman	guard
weatherman	weather forecaster, meteorologist
workman	worker
workmanlike	efficient, skillful

nonstandard English

Nonstandard English consists of forms and usages that are not used by educated speakers and writers, such as *anyways, could of,* and *ain't.* Some dictionaries identify nonstandard words. (See **English, varieties of.**)

note taking (See **Research Processes,** pages 46–48.)

not only . . . but also

Not only . . . but also is a **correlative conjunction.** The pair should connect **parallel structures.**

Marisol not   maintains
~~Not~~ only ~~maintaining~~ a 4.0 average,/but ~~Marisol~~ also works part-time and is cap-

tain of the swim team.

Also may be omitted, especially with short constructions.

> He speaks *not only* Spanish *but* French, Italian, and German.

Do not use a comma when *not only . . . but also* connects two words or phrases; use a comma only with clauses.

> Mexico City is not only smoggy,/but also crowded.

noun clauses

A noun clause is a **dependent clause** that functions as a **subject,** an **object,** a **subject complement,** or an object of a **preposition.**

> *Whichever one you choose* will be fine. [noun clause as subject]
>
> Choose *whichever one you like.* [noun clause as object]
>
> The problem is *that you cannot make up your mind.* [noun clause as subject complement]
>
> I will pay for *whichever one you choose.* [noun clause as object of preposition]

noun phrases (See **phrases.**)

nouns

A noun names a person, thing, quality, idea, place, or action. Nouns can be **proper nouns** or **common nouns.**

Proper Nouns

A proper noun names a particular person, thing, idea, place, or action. Proper nouns are capitalized.

April	Chevrolet	Christianity	East Coast	Kansas City
Mark Twain	Passover	Pulitzer Prize	Sturm und Drang	Vietnam War

Common Nouns

A common noun names a general class of persons, things, qualities, ideas, places, or actions. All nouns except proper nouns are common nouns. A few nouns (*Democrat/democrat*) are both proper and common.

book	chisel	city	country	honesty
love	revolution	squirrel	student	

An abstract noun names a quality or idea not detectable by the five senses. (See also **abstract words/concrete words.**)

courage	cowardice	decency
discord	friendship	harmony

A concrete noun names things that can be detected by the senses.

apple	chord	door	pin
sky	tree	water	

A **count noun** names discrete objects or concepts that can be counted.

birds	cars	footballs	inches
magazines	questions	videos	

A **mass noun** names substances without subdivisions, things that do not have individual units and cannot be counted. (See also **noncount nouns.**)

dirt	foam	hay
hydrogen	milk	sunshine

A **collective noun** names a group of persons, things, qualities, ideas, places, or actions. Its form is singular, but its meaning is plural.

committee	crowd	family
group	team	

Noun Functions

Nouns may serve as subjects of **verbs,** as objects of verbs and **prepositions,** as **complements,** and as **appositives.**

The *boat* sank. [subject of *sank*]

Chris parked the *car.* [direct object of *parked*]

The police officer gave *Lisa* a ticket. [indirect object of *gave*]

The event occurred within a *year.* [object of the preposition *within*]

An equestrian is a *person* who rides horses. [subject complement]

We elected Ellis *group leader.* [object complement]

Ginnie Tobias, the *treasurer,* gave her report last. [appositive]

Some nouns are used as **adjectives** and **adverbs**.

The *office* buildings are tall in New York City. [adjective]

Gloria came *home.* [adverb]

Making Nouns Possessive

Singular Nouns To form the **possessive case** of most singular nouns, add an **apostrophe** and *-s.*

New York City's atmosphere   the table's finish

Singular nouns that end in multiple -s sounds may take either an apostrophe and -s or only an apostrophe to show the possessive case, but be consistent in whatever practice you choose.

	conscience's sake	appearance's sake
OR	conscience' sakes	appearance' sakes

Proper Nouns Proper nouns that end in -s may form the possessive with either an apostrophe alone or an apostrophe and -s, which is the more common way today. Whichever method you choose, however, be consistent.

	Dickens's novels	Los Lobos's songs
OR	Dickens' novels	Los Lobos' songs

In names of places and institutions, the apostrophe is sometimes omitted.

Harpers Ferry   Writers Book Club   Veterans Administration

Coordinate and Compound Nouns To show joint possession with coordinate nouns, make only the last noun possessive.

The *Hawks and Blue Jays'* rematch was an exciting game.

To show individual possession with coordinate nouns, make both nouns possessive.

The difference between *Keisha's* and *Marianne's* grade point averages was less than a tenth of a point.

With compound nouns, only the last word takes the possessive form.

> My *sister-in-law's* car is a red Miata.

Plural Nouns   Plural nouns that end in -s need only an apostrophe to show the possessive case.

> the *architects'* design   the *waitresses'* lounge

Plural nouns that do not end in -s need an apostrophe and -s to show the possessive case.

> *men's* clothing   the *children's* bedroom

Both singular and plural nouns may be made possessive with the insertion of the word *of* before them.

> the president's statement   the statement of the president
> the books' covers   the covers of the books

Making Nouns Plural

Most nouns form the plural by adding -s.

> *Dolphins* are capable of communicating with people.

Those ending in -s, -z, -x, -ch, and -sh form the plural by adding -es.

> How many size *sixes* did we produce last month?
> The letter was sent to all the *churches.*
> Technology should not inhibit our individuality; it should fulfill our *wishes.*

Those ending in a consonant plus -y form the plural by changing -y to -ies.

> The fruit salad contained fresh *cherries.*

Some nouns ending in -o add -es to form the plural, but others add only -s.

> One tomato plant produced twelve *tomatoes.*
> Sheila made *tacos* for dinner.

Some nouns ending in -f or -fe add -s to form the plural; others change the -f or -fe to -ves.

> cliff/cliffs   fife/fifes   knife/knives

Some nouns require an internal or other change to form the plural.

> woman/women   child/children   mouse/mice   goose/geese

Some nouns do not change in the plural form.

Fish swam lazily in the clear brook while a few wild *deer* mingled with the *sheep* in a nearby meadow.

Compound nouns written as hyphenated or separate words form the plural in the main word.

sons-in-law   high schools

Compound nouns written as one word add *-s* to the end.

Use seven *tablespoonfuls* of freshly ground coffee to make seven cups of coffee.

If in doubt about the plural form of a word, look it up in a dictionary. Most dictionaries give the plural form if it is made in any way other than by adding *-s* or *-es*.

nowhere/nowheres

Nowheres is nonstandard usage; use *nowhere*.

They were *nowheres* to be seen.

number (grammatical)

Number in grammar refers to the categories of singular (one thing) and plural (more than one). Number is a property of **nouns, pronouns,** and **verbs.**

N

Nouns

Form the plural of most nouns by adding *-s* or *-es* to the singular forms.

Homes in the two new *subdivisions* come equipped with microwave *ovens* and satellite *dishes.*

The chess *students* played five *matches.*

Some nouns, though, require a change in spelling to show the plural.

foot/feet   tooth/teeth   man/men   person/people

Pronouns

The singular and plural forms of pronouns differ, with the exception of *you.*

SINGULAR	PLURAL
I	we
you	you
he, she, it	they

Verbs

Form the singular of most regular verbs in the third **person**, present **tense**, and indicative **mood** by adding -s or -es.

he persuades   she teaches   it swims

The third-person plural is the plain, uninflected form.

they persuade   they teach   they swim

The verb *be* changes form to indicate the plural, except with *you*.

SINGULAR	PLURAL
I *am*	we *are*
you *are*	you *are*
he, she, it *is*	they *are*

(See also **agreement of subjects and verbs** and **irregular verbs**.)

numbers and symbols

The guidelines for using words or figures to represent numbers and words or symbols vary among disciplines. In MLA style (commonly used in English and foreign language courses), the basic rule is to spell out numbers that can be written in a word or two and to use figures for the others. In APA style (commonly used in the social sciences), words are generally used to express numbers from one to nine and figures to express 10 and above. In CMS style (used in the humanities and history), words are generally used for whole numbers from one through ninety-nine. In CSE style (formerly CBE style; used in science and mathematics), figures are used for quantities of any kind (not only 5 *mg* but also 3 *hypotheses*).

No matter what the rules of a particular discipline are, however, a number at the beginning of a sentence is always written out (or the sentence is recast so that the number does not come first), and related numbers in the same sentence are expressed alike.

Seventy
~~70~~ people attended the meeting.
∧

OR

The meeting drew 70 [or *seventy*] people.

                  4   *16*   *64*
The cells in the petri dish multiplied from ~~four~~ to ~~sixteen~~ to ~~sixty-four~~ to 256 in
           ∧   ∧   ∧

five days.

The following guidelines for the use of figures are suitable for papers in English and humanities courses. For guidelines for other disciplines, see the list of style manuals in **Research Processes,** page 153.

When to Use Figures

Dates

March 20, 1999 [**comma** between date and year]

March 1999 [no comma between month and year]

March 6, March 6th, *or* March sixth [any of the forms is acceptable, but be consistent]

6 B.C., A.D. 723 [*B.C.* follows the year, *A.D.* precedes it]

the twentieth century [write out centuries]

twentieth-century art [hyphenate the adjective form of centuries]

the sixties, the 1960s, *or* the '60s [any of these forms is acceptable, but be consistent]

Times

3:15 p.m. [use figures with *a.m.* and *p.m.*]

three o'clock [use words with *o'clock*]

Addresses

34829 Lincoln Way, St. Louis, MO 33345

449 West 68th Street

N

Decimals, Fractions, and Percentages

12.75 gallons, 4.8 inches [do not use symbols or abbreviate measurements, except in tables and graphs]

12½ feet [use figures for fractions with whole numbers]

half a cup, three-quarters of an hour [write out simple fractions]

ninety-nine percent, 2.45 percent [use the symbol % only in tables and graphs]

Scores and Statistics

a 33–7 score   an average class size of 27   a ratio of 5 to 1

Amounts of Money

$12.95 [use the symbol $ with specific amounts]

$243 billion [use the symbol $ with a combination of figures and words for round amounts of $1 million and over]

twenty dollars [round amounts may be written out]

thirty-five cents [use the symbol ¢ only in tables and graphs]

Divisions of Books and Plays

volume 3   chapter 21   page 401

act I, scene ii [some instructors may prefer Arabic numbers: act 1, scene 2]

Cardinal and Ordinal Numbers

A cardinal number expresses a specific quantity.

one pencil   *two* typewriters   *three* airplanes

An ordinal number expresses degree or sequence.

first quarter   *second* edition   *third* degree

In most writing, an ordinal number should be spelled out only if it is a single word (*tenth,* but *27th*) or modifies *century* (*twenty-first* century).

Symbols

Use symbols, such as %, ¢, @, ", +, and =, only in graphs and tables, not in the body of a paper. The one exception is the dollar sign ($), which may be used with specific dollar amounts (*$4.75, $120 million*) in the text. (See also **ampersand.**)

object complements

An object complement is a **noun** or **adjective** that either describes or re-names the **direct object**.

> They call her a *genius*. [noun]
>
> We painted the house *white*. [adjective]

The most common verbs permitting object complements are *appoint, call, consider, designate, keep, leave, make, name,* and *render.*

objective case

Pronouns that function as **objects** of **verbs** or **prepositions** are in the objective case: *me, you, him, her, it, us, them, whom, whomever.* (See also **case**.)

objects (grammatical)

An object in grammar is a **noun** or a word or a word group acting as a noun that is influenced by a **verb**, a **verbal**, or a **preposition**. An object can be a **direct object**, an **indirect object**, or an object of a preposition. Any expression serving as a noun—**pronoun**, **gerund**, **infinitive**, noun **phrase**, or **noun clause**—may be an object.

Direct Object

A direct object receives the action of a **transitive verb** and answers the question *what* or *whom*.

> Miguel bought *a snowmobile*. [noun phrase]
>
> Shannon loves *skiing*. [gerund]
>
> The hungry athletes wanted *to eat*. [infinitive]
>
> I found *her*! [pronoun]
>
> Snowman's Mart has *just what I want*. [noun clause]

Indirect Object

An indirect object follows certain transitive verbs (such as *bring, give, send,* and *tell*). It answers the question *to whom, to what, for whom,* or *for what.* Indirect objects accompany direct objects and usually precede them.

> Dee brought *her mother* the chair.
>
> The charitable foundation gives *the poor* of our city new hope.

Objects of Prepositions

An object of a preposition is a noun or noun equivalent preceded by a **preposition**. The preposition and the object constitute a **prepositional phrase**.

> We ate lunch *in the park*.

> Garbage *with a high paper content* has been turned into protein-rich animal food.

occasion

Occasion is the context for an act of writing. It is an element of the **rhetorical situation**. It determines the appropriate length; the amount of time needed to plan, organize, draft, and revise; and the formality of the **tone**. (See **Composing Processes**, pages 3–4, 6.)

off/off of

Off of is nonstandard usage: *of* is unnecessary.

> I fell *off ~~of~~* the ladder.

OK/O.K./okay

The expression *okay* (also spelled *OK* or *O.K.*) should be avoided in formal writing.

>   *approved*
> Mr. Sturgess ~~gave his okay to~~ the project.
>   ^

>   *acceptable to*
> The solution is ~~okay with~~ me.
>   ^

on account of/because of

The **phrase** *on account of* is a wordy substitute for *because of*.

>   *because*
> She felt that she had lost her job ~~on account~~ *of* the shrinking defense budget.
>   ^

online

When your computer is online, it is connected to another computer by a modem or other device, allowing you to do such things as access the **Internet**. A computer is not online when it is not actively connected to another computer or network; it can still be used for functions such as word processing while offline.

only

Only should be placed immediately before the word or **phrase** it modifies. The placement of *only* can change the meaning of a sentence.

> *Only* he said that he was tired. [He alone said he was tired.]
>
> He *only* said that he was tired. [He actually was not tired, although he said he was.]
>
> He said *only* that he was tired. [He said nothing except that he was tired.]
>
> He said that he was *only* tired. [He was nothing except tired.]

openings   (See **introductions**.)

oral presentations/reports

Many classes, especially those in business administration, require oral presentations or reports. Following are some basic guidelines for preparing an informal classroom presentation.

If the oral report is to present information you have not yet written about or researched, follow the steps described in **Composing Processes** to create a manuscript. Then you need to decide how to present it to your **audience**.

As a rule, the audience will consist of your instructor and classmates; since you know them, consider what they know about your topic and what information they will find interesting. If the instructor has not indicated that the report should fulfill a special **purpose**, decide whether your purpose is to inform, entertain, or persuade. This decision will determine how you select and organize your material.

When you have decided on a purpose, consider how to get your audience's attention immediately. A good **introduction** will engage your listeners. Examine the introduction strategies, and choose the one best suited for your purpose. Next, select the main points you will present, and decide how to illustrate and call the audience's attention to them. Plan to use examples, illustrations, statistics, or stories to back up each point; to further engage the audience, highlight each point with a visual aid (no more than one per point), such as **graphics** on posters, flipcharts, overhead transparencies, slides, or handouts. Whatever visual aids you choose, be sure they are clear, concise, and easily visible from the back of the room. Pay special attention to making clear **transitions** between points in an oral report so that the audience can follow you. Finally, be sure your presentation has a conclusion; don't trail off. Plan to summarize, thank your audience, and ask if there are any questions.

With these basics in place, confirm the amount of time allotted for your presentation, and decide whether you will speak from a complete manuscript or rely on notes. If you use a manuscript, print it triple-spaced in a large font. Be sure to number the pages. There are few situations more disconcerting than standing in front of a room full of people trying to figure out which page comes next. Next, practice reading the report aloud. Make the sentences short, highlight key words, and mark places where you will pause. Practice enough so that during the presentation you will be able to look up and make eye contact with audience members. When the manuscript is marked, read it aloud again to time yourself. One triple-spaced page of text usually takes two minutes to read.

If you prefer a more spontaneous approach, outline your presentation on notecards. Be sure to insert clear transitions, highlight key words, and write in specific references to visual aids so that you won't forget to use them.

Whether you speak from a manuscript or notes, it is absolutely essential that you practice the presentation. If possible, tape-record yourself or present the report to someone else to get feedback on whether you are speaking clearly and at a moderate pace, whether your voice is engaging (as opposed to monotonous), and whether you rely on fillers such as *uh, really, you know,* or *like.* Practice in front of a mirror to become aware of your facial expressions and to ensure that you maintain an appropriate degree of eye contact with your audience. Make the practice as realistic as possible, referring to the visual aids or speaking in the room where the presentation is scheduled to take place. The more you practice, the better you will feel when you are standing in front of the class.

organization

A piece of writing must be well organized to communicate the writer's thoughts clearly and efficiently to an audience. Most successful writing—whether an essay, article, letter, or memorandum—has at least three major divisions: (1) an **introduction**, which engages the audience's attention, states the **topic**, and indicates at least the general direction of what will follow; (2) a middle (also called *body*), which develops the topic or **thesis**; and (3) a **conclusion**, which leaves the audience with a sense of completion. (See also **Composing Processes.**)

Good organization also involves the writer's use of clear and appropriate **methods of development**—comparison, definition, cause-and-effect, classification, and so forth—for the piece as a whole and for its various parts or sections, including individual **paragraphs**. The **coherence** of a piece of writing—that is, the ease with which the audience can follow the progression of ideas or images and relate them to one another—depends heavily on organization. (See also **logic.**)

Outlining is a useful way for writers to check their organization as they are revising.

outlining

In the planning and revision stages, an outline can help make writing logical and coherent. An informal outline—a **thesis** statement and a list of ideas—is helpful in planning a composition. A formal outline, which shows the sequence and relative importance of ideas, can be used both during planning and during revision to judge the paper's organization.

A formal outline has a conventional system of indented letters and numbers.

```
Thesis
    I. Major idea
        A. Supporting idea for I
            1. Example or illustration of A
            2. Example or illustration of A
                a. Detail for 2
                b. Detail for 2
                    (1) Detail for b
                    (2) Detail for b
        B. Supporting idea for I
    II. Major idea
```

The headings can be either phrases or sentences (used as **topic sentences** in the composition). To help ensure parallel treatment of the points at each level, make the headings for each level grammatically parallel. (See also **parallel structure.**)

If you make an outline of your draft during revision, this overview can help you spot weaknesses in logic and organization. An outline can show where you strayed from the topic. It can show repetition of an idea under two or more major heads, which may mean that you need to rethink the structure, the **method of development,** or even the **thesis.** If almost all the heads are the same level, you may need to combine some of them or work on **subordination** and **emphasis.** If you have only one subdivision under a head, you should either incorporate it into the main idea or provide at least one additional supporting point.

overstatement (See **hyperbole.**)

page format (See **manuscript form** and **Research Processes**, pages 86–98, 112–14, 131–38, 146–52.)

paragraphs

A paragraph is a group of sentences that support and develop a single idea. A good paragraph has **unity**, **coherence**, and a pattern of **organization**.

Unity

When every sentence in the paragraph contributes to developing the core idea, which is usually stated in a **topic sentence**, the paragraph has unity.

Although the topic sentence may appear anywhere in a paragraph, typically it is the first sentence.

> *The stance reporters have taken toward media advisers has changed dramatically over the past twenty years.* In *The Selling of the President* (1969), Joe McGinnis exposed the growing role of media advisers with a sense of disillusion and even outrage. By 1988 television reporters covered image-makers with deference, even admiration. In place of independent fact correction, reporters sought out media advisers as authorities in their own right to analyze the effectiveness and even defend the truthfulness of campaign commercials. They became "media gurus" not only for the candidates but for the networks as well.
>
> —Kiko Adatto, "The Incredible Shrinking Sound Bite"

Sometimes, however, the topic sentence falls logically in the middle of a paragraph.

> It is perhaps natural that psychologists should awaken only slowly to the possibility that behavioral processes may be directly observed, or that they should only gradually put the older statistical and theoretical techniques in their proper perspective. But it is time to insist that science does not progress by carefully designed steps called "experiments" each of which has a well-defined beginning and end. *Science is a continuous and often a disorderly and accidental process.* We shall

not do the young psychologist any favor if we agree to reconstruct our practices to fit the pattern demanded by current scientific methodology. What the statistician means by the design of experiments is design which yields the kind of data to which *his* techniques are applicable. He does not mean the behavior of the scientist in his laboratory devising research for his own immediate and possibly inscrutable purposes.

—B. F. SKINNER, "A Case History in Scientific Method"

Occasionally, a paragraph can lead to a concluding topic sentence.

> In those years, a revolution in computerized library technology took place; as recently as a year and a half before completion the power capacity of the building had to be restudied and upgraded. The flexibility that was supposed to be built into the plan has proved to be more theoretical than practical in spite of modular design; the movable partitions weigh two hundred pounds. Twenty years ago libraries and museums avoided destructive natural light like the plague. But even at that time, the new filtering and reflective glass that has created a radical and agreeable change in their architecture was being developed. Today the idea of the windowless behemoth is dead. Two of the architects who started with the project are also dead, and most of the others are retired. *The Madison Library, in fact, could be called dead on arrival.*
>
> —ADA LOUISE HUXTABLE, "Washington's Stillborn Behemoth"

Coherence

Coherence enables readers to follow a writer's train of thought effortlessly because the relation of each idea to those before and after is clear. Many things contribute to coherence, especially these: holding to one **point of view**, one attitude, one **tense**; using appropriate transitional words and phrases (see **transitions** and **conjunctions**); using **parallel structures**; providing **pronouns** with clear antecedents; and incorporating **repetition** of key words and phrases.

In the following paragraph by Rachel Carson, note how the italicized transitional phrases develop the idea in the topic sentence by moving the reader smoothly from one example to the next.

Topic Sentence	*Many of the natural wonders of the earth owe their existence to the fact that once the sea crept over the land, laid down its deposits of sediments, and then withdrew.* There is Mammoth Cave
Transition	in Kentucky, *for example,* where one may wander through miles of underground passages and enter rooms with ceilings 250 feet overhead. Caves and passageways have been dissolved by ground water out of an immense thickness of limestone, deposited by
Transition	a Paleozoic sea. *In the same way,* the story of Niagara Falls goes back to Silurian time, when a vast embayment of the Arctic Sea crept southward over the continent. Its waters were clear,

Transition

Transition

for the borderlands were low and little sediment or silt was carried into the inland sea. It deposited large beds of hard rock called dolomite, and in time they formed a long escarpment near the present border between Canada and the United States. *Millions of years later,* floods of water released from melting glaciers poured over this cliff, cutting away the soft shales that underlay the dolomite, and causing mass after mass of the undercut rock to break away. *In this fashion* Niagara Falls and its gorge were created.

—Rachel Carson, *The Sea around Us*

In the first paragraph of the next example, coherence is achieved largely by repetition of the phrase *we fear* in a series of **parallel structures**. The phrase appears again at the beginning of the next paragraph as a transition to a list of the ways we superstitiously try to protect ourselves against what we fear.

We fear the awesome powers we have lifted out of nature and cannot return to her. *We fear* the weapons we have made, the hatreds we have engendered. *We fear* the crush of fanatic people to whom we readily sell these weapons. *We fear* for the value of the money in our pockets that stands symbolically for food and shelter. *We fear* the growing power of the state to take all these things from us. *We fear* to walk our streets at evening. *We* have come to *fear* even our scientists and their gifts.

We fear, in short, as that self-sufficient Eskimo of the long night had never *feared.* Our minds, if not our clothes, are hung with invisible amulets: nostrums changed each year for our bodies whether it be chlorophyll toothpaste, the signs of astrology, or cold cures that do not cure: witchcraft nostrums for our society as it fractures into contending multitudes all crying for liberation without responsibility.

—Loren Eiseley, "The Winter of Man"

Development

Paragraphs may be organized in a variety of ways, depending on your purpose. Shown here are examples of six of the most common methods: **details, process, comparison and contrast, classification** and division, **cause and effect**, and **definition**. Elsewhere in this book, you will find examples of other **methods of development: analysis, chronological method, description, examples, general-to-specific, increasing order of importance, problem-solution,** and **spatial**.

Details A comparison of two paragraphs will show the value of details in developing a paragraph.

After she suffered a stroke, her body became shrunken and distorted. She couldn't work, so she lay in bed all day. She also couldn't cook or prepare a meal.

Now notice how details help to give a better idea of the problems caused by a stroke and to intensify the audience's response.

> After she suffered a stroke, her serenely imposing figure had shrunk into an unevenly balanced, starved shell of chronic disorder. In the last two years, her physical condition had forced her retirement from nursing, and she spent most of her days on a makeshift cot pushed against the wall of the dining room next to the kitchen. She could do very few things for herself, besides snack on crackers, or pour ready-made juice into a cup and then drink it.
>
> —JUNE JORDAN, "Many Rivers to Cross"

Process A process is usually best described by presenting its steps in chronological order. Sometimes a description of the physical setting and the materials used is also helpful. In the following paragraph, for example, the description of the calf roper's equipment is necessary to the explanation of the process of calf roping.

> Calf ropers are the whiz kids of rodeo: they're expert on the horse and the ground, and their horses are as quick witted. The cowboy emerges from the box with a loop in his hand, a piggin' string in his mouth, coil and reins in the other, and a network of slack line strewn so thickly over horse and rider, they look as if they'd run through a tangle of kudzu before arriving in the arena. After roping the calf and jerking the slack in the rope, he jumps off the horse, sprints down the length of nylon, which the horse keeps taut, throws the calf down, and ties three legs together with the piggin' string. It's said of Ray Cooper, the defending calf-roping champion, that "even with pins and metal plates in his arm, he's known for the fastest ground work in the business; when he springs down his rope to flank the calf, the result is pure rodeo poetry." The six or seven movements he makes are so fluid they look like one continual unfolding.
>
> —GRETEL EHRLICH, "Rules of the Game: Rodeo"

Comparison and Contrast Two things can be compared point by point or whole by whole (block). The following paragraph is a point-by-point comparison of wealth and poverty in New York City. For an example of a whole-by-whole comparison, see the first example in **comparison and contrast as a method of development.**

> No novelist would dare put into a book the most extreme of the dizzying contrasts of wealth and poverty that make up the ordinary texture of life in today's cities. The details are too outlandish to seem credible. Directly under the windows of the $6 million apartments that loom over Fifth Avenue, for instance, where grandees like Jacqueline Onassis or Laurence Rockefeller sleep, sleep the homeless, one and sometimes two on each park bench, huddled among bundles turned gray by dirt and wear. Across town last Christmas the line of fur-coated holiday makers waiting outside a fashionable delicatessen to buy caviar at only $259.95 a pound literally adjoined the ragged line of paupers waiting for the soup kitchen to open at the

church around the corner. In the shiny atriums of the urban skyscrapers where 40-year-old investment bankers make seven figures restructuring the industrial landscape, derelicts with no place to go kill time. And every train or bus commuter knows that his way home to suburban comfort lies through a dreary gauntlet of homelessness and beggary.

—MYRON MAGNET, "The Rich and the Poor"

Classification and Division Classification and division (or *partition*, as it is sometimes called) are closely related. Classification groups numerous items into categories. Division breaks a single item into its parts. Both are powerful strategies for explaining complex topics. The first example that follows illustrates classification. The second example divides the writer's subject into parts.

Supernovae are divided into two classes according to how their brightness rises and falls: Type I reach their peak brightness in about 20 days, then fade slowly over a year or so; Type II reach their peak in about 30 days, then fade away in about 150 days. Spectral analysis shows that Type I supernovae have much more helium in their envelopes than do Type II, but no definite relationship between the two types has been found. There is some indication that Type II explosions occur in more massive stars, which would mean they are related to stars with iron cores.

—BARRY R. PARKER, *Concepts of the Cosmos*

We all listen to music according to our separate capacities. But, for the sake of analysis, the whole listening process may become clearer if we break it up into its component parts, so to speak. In a certain sense we all listen to music on three separate planes. For lack of a better terminology, one might name these (1) the sensuous plane, (2) the expressive plane, (3) the sheerly musical plane. The only advantage to be gained from mechanically splitting up the listening process into these hypothetical planes is the clear view to be had of the way in which we listen.

The simplest way of listening to music is to listen for the sheer pleasure of the musical sound itself. That is the sensuous plane. . . .

The second plane on which music exists is what I have called the expressive one. Here, immediately, we tread on controversial ground. . . .

The third plane on which music exists is the sheerly musical plane. Besides the pleasurable sound of music and the expressive feeling that it gives off, music does exist in terms of the notes themselves and of their manipulation. Most listeners are not sufficiently conscious of this third plane.

—AARON COPLAND, "How We Listen to Music"

Cause and Effect The first sentence in the following paragraph introduces the idea that the invention of photography (the cause) changed how people saw the world (the effect). The subsequent sentences present consequences of that invention.

When photography was being introduced, it was life-enriching and vista-opening; but once it was achieved, once everybody had a camera, the people were looking in their cameras instead of looking at the sight they had gone to see. It had an attenuating effect. A picture came to mean less and less, simply because people saw pictures everywhere. And the experience of being there also somehow meant less because the main thing people saw everywhere was the inside of their view-finders, and their concern over their lens cap and finding the proper exposure made it hard for them to notice what was going on around them at the moment.
—DANIEL BOORSTIN, "Technology and Democracy"

Definition The author of the following paragraph repeats the word *home* as he enlarges its conventional definition.

The flesh is home. African nomads without houses decorate their faces and bodies instead. The skull is home. We fly in and out of it on mental errands. The highly developed spirit becomes a citizen of its own mobility, for home has been inter-nalized and travels with the homeowner. Home, thus transformed, is freedom. Everywhere you hang your hat is home. Home is the bright cave under the hat.
—LANCE MORROW, "The Bright Cave Under the Hat"

Length

Although there are no simple formulas for paragraph length, a good rule of thumb is that each typewritten page should have at least one paragraph break. A paragraph longer than a page should be divided or reorganized. If you are confused about when to break a paragraph, use the following questions for guidelines:

- Can the reader tell that I'm moving from my introduction to the body of the essay?
- Am I shifting from one idea to another?
- Am I moving from one time or place to another?
- Should I break here to emphasize this point?
- Would a break help to illustrate the difference between these two points?
- Can the reader tell that I'm now moving into my conclusion?

The following set of paragraphs helps to illustrate where and when to break. Paragraph one introduces the husky, paragraph two introduces Dr. Rentko, and paragraph three emphasizes the seriousness of the situation.

Down that row of runs, the husky has started to croon again. A handsome, bush-coated dog with the mismatched irises—one brown, one pale blue—that are char-acteristic of his breed, he lies unhappily on the floor, his head sheathed in an Elizabethan collar, a plastic cone that keeps him from gnawing at the bandages swathed tightly around his middle. Three nights back he came in barely able to breathe.

Dr. Virginia Rentko, a cheerful second-year resident with a thick mane of dark hair, was on duty when the husky arrived. She couldn't get a stethoscope on him, the dog was in such a state of anxiety. . . . X-rays, however, showed a clear case of pneumothorax: air was leaking out of his lungs, through balloonlike pockets called blebs and bullae, and getting trapped inside his chest cavity, keeping his lungs from fully expanding.

Dr. Rentko plunged a syringe into the husky's chest to drain off the trapped air. But she filled up one syringe, then another and another; air was seeping into the animal's chest faster than the syringes could tap it off.

—JOHN SEDGWICK, "The Doberman Case"

Sometimes a paragraph of only one sentence or two is useful. In **dialogue**, for instance, a new paragraph signals each change of speaker, making possible a series of one-word paragraphs such as the following:

"No!"
"Yes."
"Why?"

A short paragraph often makes a good bridge, or **transition**, between paragraphs or parts of a paper. And short paragraphs next to longer ones can also provide emphasis. In the following example, two paragraphs—the first of average length, the second just a single sentence seven words long— conclude the essay from which they are taken. Notice the powerful emphasis achieved by the short final paragraph.

If the Civil Rights Movement is "dead," and if it gave us nothing else, it gave us each other forever. It gave some of us bread, some of us shelter, some of us knowledge and pride, all of us comfort. It gave us our children, our husbands, our brothers, our fathers, as men reborn and with a purpose for living. It broke the pattern of black servitude in this country. It shattered the phony "promise" of white soap operas that sucked away so many pitiful lives. It gave us history and men far greater than Presidents. It gave us heroes, selfless men of courage and strength, for our little boys and girls to follow. It gave us hope for tomorrow. It called us to life.

Because we live, it can never die.

—ALICE WALKER, "The Civil Rights Movement: What Good Was It?"

Knowing when to combine paragraphs is just as important as knowing when to break them. As the following paragraphs illustrate, choppiness can be equally confusing.

A dog who cowers in fear when a human reaches out a hand might also have been abused.

Just the opposite with this husky. Far from retreating before Dr. Rentko, the dog was coming on too strong with her. He would try to bite her every time she came in.

"He was trying to dominate me," she says. So she had to bully him right back. She put him on a short leash, took him outside the hospital, and told him to sit. To her surprise, he sat. And he heeled on the way back.

There have been no further problems. Now she is concerned that perhaps she went a little far. "I think I'll go in there and love him up a little bit," Dr. Rentko says.

The husky perks up—his mismatched eyes brighten—as the doctor comes near. She drives her hands into his thick fur. The husky croons.

—JOHN SEDGWICK, "The Doberman Case"

Although there are quotations from Dr. Rentko, these passages contain no actual dialogue, so they need not be broken after her statements. Moreover, every passage is related to the topic sentence, which intends to show "Just the opposite with this husky." Maintain clarity and coherence by combining short paragraphs that relate to the topic sentence.

parallel structure

In a parallel structure, sentence elements (words, **phrases,** or **clauses**) that are alike in function are also alike in construction. Parallel structure— whether within a sentence or throughout a paragraph—clarifies meaning and adds a pleasing symmetry.

That red sunflower is gaudy, gargantuan, and gross. [parallel words]

Andy was dying to go to the fair, to eat cotton candy, and to ride the loop-the-loop. [parallel phrases]

Parallel structure can draw together related ideas, as in the preceding sentences, or it can contrast dissimilar ones, as in the next example. (See also **balanced sentences.**)

Marcella believed in God and country, but George believed in nothing.

The symmetry and rhythm of parallel structure contribute to the power of many famous speeches, as illustrated in the following excerpt from the Gettysburg address. (For another example, see **paragraphs.**)

But in a larger sense, *we cannot dedicate—we cannot consecrate—we cannot hallow*—this ground. The brave men, *living* and *dead,* who struggled here, have consecrated it far above our poor power to *add* or *detract. The world will little note nor long remember what we say here,* but *it can never forget what they did here.*

—ABRAHAM LINCOLN

Faulty Parallelism

Faulty parallelism can occur when elements in a series do not have the same grammatical form.

> When you evaluate college brochures, consider the variety and number of courses
>
> offered in your field, the quality and mix of extracurricular activities, and ~~if~~ the
>   *age*   *suitability of the*
> ~~college has modern~~ and ~~suitable~~ computer facilities.
>   ^   ^
>
> [Because the first two items in the series are phrases beginning with a pair of nouns, express the third item as a phrase in the same form rather than as a clause.]

Faulty parallelism can also be caused by the attempt to group together in a series things that are not logically comparable.

> The university offers special training to help displaced workers move into pro-
>
> fessional and technical careers such as data processing, bookkeeping, customer
>   *service*
> ~~engineers~~, and sales ~~trainees.~~
>   ^
>
> [Occupations—data processing and bookkeeping—cannot logically be compared to people—customer engineers and sales trainees.]

Elements joined by a **conjunction** should also be parallel.

>   *by*
> You may travel to the new museum either *by train* or ~~there is a~~ bus.
>   ^
>
> [The coordinate conjunction, *either . . . or,* joins different grammatical forms: a prepositional phrase, *by train;* and a clause, *there is a bus.*]

OR

> You may travel to the new museum by either *train* or *bus.*
> [The coordinate conjunction joins parallel grammatical forms: nouns.]

> Gustavo went shopping for groceries and ~~to get~~ a dishpan.
>
> [The conjunction, *and,* joins different grammatical forms: a prepositional phrase, *for groceries;* and an infinitive phrase, *to get a dishpan.*]

paraphrasing

Paraphrasing is one of the three ways you can incorporate information from other people into your own writing (the other two ways are **summarizing** and **quotation**). Summarizing condenses, or boils down, the source material to the briefest form consistent with your purpose, and quoting reproduces the source material exactly. In contrast, paraphrasing restates the source material in detail but *in your own words*. Therefore, you do not need to use **quotation marks** (except for any distinctive expressions retained word for word from the original—that is, quoted—in your paraphrase or summary). Use a paraphrase to simplify a complex concept or to highlight details that are especially relevant. (See also **Research Processes**, beginning on page 25.)

Whether you quote, paraphrase, or summarize, remember that you must give proper credit to your source in order to avoid **plagiarism**. The only exception is information that is **common knowledge**. For instance, it is common knowledge that Independence Day in the United States is celebrated on July 4. If you used that information from a source, you would not have to give credit. However, if you were presenting someone's opinion about the appropriateness of celebrating the Fourth of July, or summarizing someone's description of the different ways the day is celebrated in different regions, you would need to give credit to your source. The line between common knowledge and specialized knowledge or opinion is not always clear. The best advice is to give credit if you are in doubt.

Following is a quoted passage, together with a plagiarized version of it, a paraphrase of it, and a summary of it.

ORIGINAL TEXT

One of the major visual cues used by pilots in maintaining precision ground reference during low-level flight is that of object blur. We are acquainted with the object-blur phenomenon experienced when driving an automobile. Objects in the foreground appear to be rushing toward us while objects in the background appear to recede slightly. There is a point in the observer's line of sight, however, at which objects appear to stand still for a moment, before once again rushing toward him with increasing angular velocity. The distance from the observer to this point is sometimes referred to as the "blur threshold" range.

—WESLEY E. WOODSON and DONALD W. CONOVER,
Human Engineering Guide for Equipment Designers

PLAGIARIZED VERSION

An important visual cue that pilots use to maintain ground reference during low-level flight is object blur, a phenomenon that is familiar to those who drive a car. Close objects appear to be rushing toward us, and distant objects appear to recede slightly. At a middle point, however, objects appear to stand still before rushing toward us with increasing speed. The distance from us to this point is the "blur threshold" range.

PARAPHRASE

In *Human Engineering Guide for Equipment Designers,* Wesley E. Woodson and Donald W. Conover explain how pilots apply the notions of "object blur" and "blur threshold" range to preserve their orientation while flying low, much as drivers do when traveling along a highway. Object blur is the visual effect in which near objects seem to speed toward the driver while distant objects seem to move away. At some point in between, though, objects seem to momentarily be stationary; the distance from this point to the driver is the blur threshold range (210).

SUMMARY

In *Human Engineering Guide for Equipment Designers,* Wesley E. Woodson and Donald W. Conover explain that low-flying pilots use object blur and especially the "blur threshold" range as important visual cues (210).

Note that the plagiarized version does not acknowledge the source and changes little, whereas the paraphrase is in different, somewhat less technical, language, although it is approximately as long as the original because it restates the material completely. The summary, which merely captures the main point, is much briefer.

parentheses

Parentheses enclose expressions that may help the reader's understanding but are not essential for meaning. Parenthetical expressions include **abbreviations, clauses, phrases, sentences,** words, and in-text citations of sources (see **Research Processes,** beginning on page 63).

A basic English unit of measure for distance is the foot (ft).

The late 1990s did not generally usher in another fin de siècle (a French phrase meaning "end of the century") of fashionable despair and decadence, as occurred in the late 1890s.

Parentheses also enclose letters or numbers that label items in a list in a sentence.

The course will cover (1) the writing process, (2) the paragraph, (3) the sentence, (4) the mechanics of writing, and (5) the essay.

Punctuation with Parentheses

When a comma follows a parenthetical expression, it is put outside the closing parenthesis. When a parenthetical expression is at the close of a sentence, the ending punctuation is put outside the closing parenthesis.

In the *Star Wars* trilogy, the human characters, Han Solo (Harrison Ford) and Princess Leia (Carrie Fisher), are often overshadowed by the antics of the robots R2D2 and C3PO and the wisecracks of the Wookie (a very tall, hairy alien).

When a complete sentence within parentheses stands independently, the first word of the sentence is capitalized and the ending punctuation goes inside the final parenthesis.

For example, if the death of one's spouse is rated as one hundred points, then moving to a new house is rated by most people as worth only twenty points, a vacation thirteen. (The death of a spouse, incidentally, is almost universally regarded as the single most impactful change that can befall a person in the normal course of his life.)

—ALVIN TOFFLER, *Future Shock*

Some writers prefer to use **brackets** instead of additional parentheses to set off a parenthetical item that is already within parentheses.

We should be sure to give Emanuel Foose (and his brother Emilio [1812–82] as well) credit for his part in founding the institute.

parenthetical elements (See **restrictive and nonrestrictive elements.**)

participial phrases

A participial phrase consists of a **participle** plus its **object** or **complement**, if any, and modifiers. Like the participle, a participial phrase functions as an **adjective** modifying a **noun** or **pronoun.**

The team *winning the most games* wins the trophy.

Discovering his team was ahead, he decided to stay.

The ground, *blanketed by snow,* sparkled in the sun.

Dangling Participial Phrases

A dangling participial phrase occurs when the noun or pronoun that the participial phrase is meant to modify is not stated in the sentence. (See also **dangling modifiers.**)

he became less efficient.
Being unhappy with the job, ~~his efficiency suffered.~~
                              ^

[His *efficiency* was not unhappy with the job; what the participial phrase really modifies—*he*—is not stated but merely implied.]

Misplaced Participial Phrases

A participial phrase is misplaced when it is too far from the noun or pronoun it is meant to modify and so appears to modify something else. (See also **modifiers.**)

rolling around in the bottom of the drawer.
~~Rolling around in the bottom of the drawer,~~ I found the missing earring/
                                                                          ^

P

participles

A participle is a **verbal** that can function as part of a verb phrase (was *parking, had *painted*), as an **adjective** before a noun (a *parking* ticket, a *painted* fence), or as part of a **participial phrase** modifying a noun (the fence *painted* by Huck).

The **present participle** is formed by adding *-ing* to the plain, or **infinitive,** form of the verb (*looking, waiting*). Used with a *be* verb (*am, are, is, was, were*), it expresses an action in progress.

> Kristina is *revising* her essay.
>
> The taxi driver was *waiting.*
>
> Jimmy may be *going* to summer school. [Use *be* after a **modal auxiliary,** such as *may.*]

The **past participle** of regular verbs is formed by adding *-d* or *-ed* to the plain, or infinitive, form (*shared, waited*). The past participles of most **irregular verbs** end in *-en, -n,* or *-t,* and the vowel may be different from that of the infinitive form (for example, *blow* becomes *blown, choose* becomes *chosen, send* becomes *sent*). To check the past participle of a particular irregular verb, consult a dictionary.

The past participle is used with *have* verbs to form the **perfect tenses** (have *lived,* had *sung,* will have *read*). It is used with *be* verbs to form the **passive voice** (is *played,* were *driven*).

A participle cannot be used as the verb of a sentence; the result is a **sentence fragment.**

> The committee chair was responsible. Her vote *being* the decisive one. [with handwritten edit: `, h` inserted, making "responsible, her"]
>
> OR
>
> The committee chair was responsible. Her vote *was* the decisive one.

The present and past participles of emotive verbs such as *bore, excite, interest, amuse, annoy, please,* and *tire* have very different meanings. The present participle describes an experience or a person causing an experience. The past participle describes a person's response to an experience.

> The lecture was very ~~bored~~ *boring* because I am not ~~interesting~~ *interested* in growing orchids. [handwritten corrections: *boring* above *bored*, *interested* above *interesting*]

particles

Particles are words with unique functions that are not included in the conventional **parts of speech.** Examples are *not,* the negative particle, and the sign of the infinitive. Other particles combine with verbs to form **phrasal verbs** (such as *out* in *look out* and *up* in *touch up*).

parts of speech

A part of speech is a class of words grouped according to their function in a sentence.

If a word *names* something, it is a **noun** or **pronoun**. If it makes an *assertion* about something, it is a **verb**. If it *describes* or *modifies* something, it is an **adjective** or an **adverb**. If it *joins* or *links* two elements of a sentence, it is a **conjunction** or a **preposition**. If it expresses an exclamation, it is an **interjection**.

If you are in doubt about what part of speech a word is, look it up in the dictionary. Each of its functions is identified by an abbreviation (*n, prn, vb, adj, adv, conj, prep, int*).

Use **context** and word-part clues (especially **suffixes**) to determine a word's part of speech and its meaning. The word *desert,* for instance, can be a noun meaning "a dry, barren, often sandy region with little vegetation," a noun meaning "something deserved," or a verb meaning "to forsake or leave." If you note that in the following sentence *desert* is preceded by the infinitive marker *to,* you will identify it as a verb.

Helmut chose to *desert* because the noise at the front lines frightened him.

passive voice

The passive voice includes a *be* verb and the **past participle** of a **transitive verb** (a verb that can take a direct object). The doer of the action either is not named or is named at the end of the sentence in a **prepositional phrase** beginning with *by.*

The Blue Jays *were defeated.* [Who or what defeated them is not named.]

The Blue Jays were defeated *by the Hornets.*

With an **active voice** verb, the doer of the action is the **subject** of the sentence.

The Hornets defeated the Blue Jays.

In general, the active voice makes writing more concise and vigorous. However, the passive voice is preferable in some circumstances. Use it when the doer of the action is irrelevant, when the doer is less important than the receiver of the action, or when naming the doer would be impractical or undiplomatic.

The house *was painted* just last summer.

Ann Bryant *was presented* with a Phi Beta Kappa key by President Howe.

Taking photographs *is not permitted* during the performance.

You can use the passive voice in all tenses and forms.

The team *is defeated.* [present tense]

The team *was defeated.* [past tense]

The team *will be defeated.* [future tense]

The team *is being defeated.* [present progressive]

The team *had been defeated.* [past perfect]

The team expects *to be defeated.* [infinitive]

The team hates *being defeated.* [gerund]

Change-of-state verbs, such as *open, close, change, show, increase, decrease, break,* and *burst,* take the active voice more frequently in English than in other languages.

The door *opened* slowly. [rather than *The door was opened slowly.*]

A few idiomatic constructions are expressed only in the passive voice.

The library *is located* on the corner of Twelfth and Vine.

Kai *was born* in 1960.

past participle

The past participle of regular **verbs** adds -*d* or -*ed* to the infinitive (*shared, waited*). The past participle of most **irregular verbs** ends in -*en,* -*n,* or -*t,* and the vowel may be different from that of the infinitive form (for example, *blow* becomes *blown, choose* becomes *chosen, send* becomes *sent*). To check the past participle of a particular irregular verb, consult a dictionary.

With *have* verbs, the past participle forms the **perfect tenses** (have *lived,* had *sung,* will have *read*). With *be* verbs, it forms the **passive voice** (is *played,* were *driven*).

The past participle can also be used as a **modifier** before a noun or as part of a **participial phrase.**

Raisins are *dried* grapes.

The documentary, *introduced* at the Sundance Festival, won several awards.

past perfect tense

The past perfect tense of a **verb** combines *had* and the **past participle.** It refers to an event or action that took place before another past event or action. (See also **tenses** and **perfect tenses.**)

I *had studied* Spanish for six years before I felt confident speaking it.

past tense

The past tense (also called the *simple past tense*) of a **verb** refers to an action, event, or state in the past. (See also **irregular verbs** and **tenses**.)

> Lorna *called* yesterday.
>
> A face *appeared* in the window.

pathos

Pathos is the appeal to the audience's emotions and opinions in an **argument**.

peer response

One of the best forms of feedback on a paper is peer response. Peer response sessions may be formally arranged by the instructor or informally set up with a friend or classmate, but in either case, having a peer read your draft and respond to it lets you know the effect of your writing on an audience. Such feedback can be invaluable when you revise. (See also **Composing Processes**, pages 15–17.)

per

Per is acceptable in expressions of ratio (*per annum, per capita, per diem*), but it should not be used in the sense of "according to" (*per your request, per her order*).

percent/per cent/percentage

The spelling *percent* is the preferred form. Except in tables, use the word *percent*, which always follows a number, rather than the symbol %.

> The basic tax rate for the state is six *percent*.

The word *percentage*, which usually follows an adjective, refers to a general result or portion.

> A high *percentage* of the voters favor the bottle bill.

perfect tenses

Perfect **tenses** of **verbs** combine a form of *have* and a **past participle**. They all refer to an event or action begun in the past. The **present perfect** (*has* or *have* plus the past participle) refers to an action or event begun in the past and lasting until the present.

> I *have waited* for forty-five minutes.

The **past perfect** (*had* plus the past participle) refers to an action or event begun in the past and completed in the past before another action or event.

I *had waited* forty-five minutes before I decided to leave.

The **future perfect** (*will have* plus the past participle) refers to an action or event that began in the past and will be completed in the future.

By seven o'clock, I *will have waited* for fifty minutes.

periodical index   (See **Research Processes**, pages 48–51.)

periodic sentences

A periodic sentence (also called a *climactic sentence*) presents subordinate ideas and modifiers before the main idea. Use a periodic sentence occasionally for **emphasis**, as shown by the second sentence of the following example. (See also **sentence types**.)

I didn't even pay much attention to my parents' accented and ungrammatical speech—at least not at home. *Only when I was with them in public would I become alert to their accents.*

—RICHARD RODRIGUEZ, "Aria: A Memoir of a Bilingual Childhood"

periods

A period usually indicates the end of a declarative or imperative sentence. (See also **exclamation points**.)

I need more information. [declarative]

Send me any information you may have on the subject. [imperative]

A period may also end a polite request or a question to which an affirmative response is assumed (a **question mark** would also be correct).

Will you please send me the free coupons you advertised.

(See **run-on sentences** and **sentence fragments** for discussions of difficulties with use of the period after sentences.)

Periods can also indicate omissions when used as **ellipsis points** or in **abbreviations** (*Ms., Dr., Inc.*). Use periods after initials in names.

W. T. Grant   J. P. Morgan

If an abbreviation that ends with a period comes at the end of a sentence, do not add another period.

Please meet me at 3:30 p.m.

Use periods as decimal points with **numbers**.

109.2 $540.26   6.9%

Use periods following the numbers in numbered **lists** and in **outlines**.

1.

2.

3.

Periods with Other Punctuation

A period is conventionally placed inside **quotation marks**.

> The word *prissy* means "prim and precise."
>
> Farah said, "Let's go to the park on Friday."

A period goes after the **parenthesis** at the end of a sentence, unless the parentheses enclose a complete new sentence.

> One of Anne Tyler's popular novels from the 1980s was later made into a movie (*The Accidental Tourist*).
>
> The basic steps in the dyeing procedure are given below. (Also see the section on matching colors.)

person (grammatical)

Person is the form of a **personal pronoun** indicating the speaker, the person spoken to, or the person (or thing) spoken about. A **pronoun** representing the speaker is in the *first person*.

> *I* could not find the answer in the text.

If the pronoun represents the person or persons spoken to, it is in the *second person*.

> *You* are handling the situation well.

If the pronoun represents the person or persons spoken about, it is in the *third person*.

> *They* received the news quietly.

	SINGULAR	PLURAL
First person	I, me, my	we, ours, us
Second person	you, your	you, your
Third person	he, him, his she, her, hers it, its	they, them, their

Identifying pronouns by person helps writers avoid illogical shifts from one person to another. A common error is to shift from the third person to the second person.

> Writers should spend the morning hours on work requiring mental effort, for
> *their minds are*
> ~~your mind is~~ freshest in the morning.
>   ^

OR

> *You* should spend the morning hours on work requiring mental effort, for *your* mind is freshest in the morning.

(See also **case** and **number.**)

persona

The persona is the speaker in a poem or the voice an author takes on to make a statement or create an effect.

personal pronouns

Personal pronouns refer to specific individuals or things. These **pronouns** have different forms in different **cases.** Used as **subjects,** they are in the subjective case: *I, you, he, she, it, we,* and *they.* Used as **objects,** they are in the objective case: *me, you, him, her, it, us,* and *them.* And they have two forms in the **possessive case:** as adjectives (*my, your, his, her, its, our,* and *their*) and as noun equivalents (*mine, yours, his, hers, its, ours,* and *theirs*). (See also **agreement of pronouns and antecedents** and *I.*)

personification

Personification is a **figure of speech** that attributes personal or human qualities to an inanimate object or abstraction.

> The seeds on my carpet were not going to lie stiffly where they had dropped like their antiquated cousins, the naked seeds on the pine-cone scales. They were travelers.
>
> —LOREN EISELEY, "How Flowers Changed the World"

persons/people

Persons is acceptable with a specific number (4,986 *persons*) or in a legal or official context ("Carpool lanes are restricted to vehicles carrying more than two *persons*"). In all other contexts, use *people.*

$\overset{people}{\text{Many } \cancel{persons} \text{ have never heard of our school.}}$

persuasive writing

Unlike **expressive writing**, which emphasizes the writer's experience, focusing on the writer's feelings and opinions, and **expository writing**, which emphasizes the **topic**, focusing on facts and ideas, persuasive writing emphasizes the **audience**—that is, it aims to change the audience's mind or move the audience to action. Thus, it often employs appeals to the emotions as well as to **logic**. (See also **argument**.)

phenomena/phenomenon

Phenomena is the plural of *phenomenon*, which means "a rare or significant occurrence, event, or person."

> A total eclipse of the sun is an impressive *phenomenon*.

> Of all the celestial *phenomena*, a total eclipse of the sun is the most impressive.

phrasal verbs

English verbs can combine with **particles** to form two- or three-word units called *phrasal verbs*. The words that make up phrasal verbs usually have different meanings together than they have separately. (See also **idioms**.) For instance, the definition of *put up with*, "to tolerate or endure," is unrelated to the meaning of either *put* or *up*. Most ESL dictionaries provide phrasal-verb definitions after the main-verb entry.

Some phrasal verbs can be separated by a direct object, but others cannot.

> Please *hand in* your homework.

OR   Please *hand* your homework *in*.

BUT   Let's *go over* some examples.

NOT   Let's *go* some examples *over*.

If the phrasal verb can be separated and the direct object is a **pronoun**, however, it must go between the verb and the particle.

> Please hand *it* in.

NOT   Please hand in *it*.

COMMON PHRASAL VERBS

The parentheses ( ) indicate that a direct object may be placed between the verb and the particle.

break up (with)	grow up	show up
bring ( ) up	hand ( ) in	shut ( ) off
call ( ) back	hand ( ) out	shut ( ) up
call ( ) off	hang out ( )	speak out
call ( ) up	hang ( ) up	speak up
catch on	have ( ) on	stand up for
catch up (with)	help ( ) out	stay up
check in	keep on	take after
check ( ) out	keep ( ) out	take care of
check up on	keep up (with)	take ( ) in
cheer ( ) up	leave ( ) out	take ( ) off
come out	look after	take ( ) out
cross ( ) out	look on	take ( ) over
cut ( ) out	look out (for)	tear ( ) down
drop in	look ( ) over	tear ( ) up
drop ( ) off	look ( ) up	think ( ) over
drop out (of)	make ( ) up	throw ( ) out
figure ( ) out	pick ( ) out	try ( ) on
fill ( ) in	pick ( ) up	try ( ) out
fill ( ) up	put ( ) away	try out (for)
find ( ) out	put ( ) back	tune ( ) in (to)
get along (with)	put ( ) off	turn ( ) down
get away (from)	put ( ) on	turn ( ) off
get ( ) back	put up with	turn ( ) on
give ( ) back	quiet ( ) down	wake ( ) up
give in (to)	run across	watch out (for)
give ( ) up	run into	wear ( ) out
go out (with)	run out of	wrap ( ) up
go over	show ( ) off	use ( ) up

(Other phrasal verbs appear under *idioms.*)

phrases

A phrase is a word group that acts as a single **part of speech** but does not have both a **subject** and a **verb**. Thus, unlike a **clause**, a phrase cannot make a complete statement. Instead, a phrase may function as an **adjective, adverb, noun,** or verb. Phrases are generally classified according to the part of speech of their main word: prepositional phrase, verbal phrase, noun phrase, and verb phrase. Two types of phrases, however, are known by their function: appositive phrase and absolute phrase.

Prepositional Phrases

A **prepositional phrase** consists of a **preposition** plus its object (a noun, pronoun, or word group functioning as a noun) and any **modifiers.** Prepositional phrases usually function as adjectives or adverbs.

> *After the hurricane* [functions as an adverb], the residents *of the coastal towns* [functions as an adjective] returned *to their homes* [functions as an adverb].

Verbal Phrases

The three types of verbal phrases are participial phrases, infinitive phrases, and gerund phrases.

A **participial phrase** consists of a **present** or **past participle** and any objects or modifiers. Participial phrases always function as adjectives.

> *Looking pleased with herself,* the child curtsied after her recital.

An **infinitive phrase** consists of an **infinitive** and any objects or modifiers. Infinitive phrases can function as adjectives, adverbs, or nouns.

> They want *to know his secret.* [functions as a noun]
>
> The need *to begin immediately* should be obvious. [functions as an adjective]
>
> We must work *to increase our outreach.* [functions as an adverb]

A **gerund phrase,** which consists of a **gerund** and any objects or modifiers, always functions as a noun.

> *Preparing a term paper* is a difficult task. [functions as a subject noun]
>
> She liked *writing with the computer.* [functions as a direct object noun]

Verb Phrases

A **verb phrase** consists of a main verb and any **helping verbs.**

> The cable company *was collecting* higher fees than it *had been authorized* to charge.

Noun Phrases

A noun phrase consists of a noun and any modifiers.

Many large universities use computers.

Appositive Phrases

Appositive phrases describe or rename a noun. They consist of a noun and any modifiers and may begin with *such as, for example, that is,* or *in other words.* Appositive phrases are usually enclosed by commas.

Chow-chow, *a marinated vegetable relish,* is a familiar dish in Pennsylvania Dutch communities.

Absolute Phrases

An **absolute phrase** consists of a noun and a participle plus any modifiers. Whereas other kinds of phrases modify a word, absolute phrases modify the rest of the sentence in which they appear.

Her heart pounding wildly, she reached for the light switch.

plagiarism

Plagiarism is passing off another person's words or ideas as your own. It is unethical and unprofessional, and it is illegal once a work has been published. To avoid plagiarism, you must give credit to the person who had the idea or wrote the words and must refer to your source. Use quotation marks around every direct quotation, and document it properly. Also document paraphrases and summaries of other people's ideas. You do not, however, need to document **common knowledge.** For tips on avoiding plagiarism and detailed guidance on using and documenting sources, see **Research Processes.** (See also **paraphrasing, summarizing, quotations,** and **signal phrases.**)

Because rules about plagiarism vary from one country to another, ESL learners should carefully study **Research Processes,** pages 29–33. Consult an instructor or writing-lab tutor if you have any questions about the use of source material in a research paper.

plot

Plot is the sequence of events in a drama or a piece of fiction. Plots can convey tragedy, comedy, mystery, romance, or satire—or a combination of these genres. A unified plot has a clear-cut beginning, middle, and end. The beginning often includes exposition—an explanation of what occurred before the action began. The middle usually involves a complication that leads to a climax. This turning point or crisis leads to the dénouement (outcome), in which questions are answered, fates are determined, and mysteries are solved.

plurals   (See **nouns** and **spelling**.)

plus

Plus should not be used to join two **independent clauses**.

> *and*
> The house has not been painted in fifteen years, ~~plus~~ the roof is leaking.
>   ∧

p.m./a.m.   (See *a.m./p.m.*)

point of view

A writer's interpretation of and connection to the written work is called the point of view. To indicate point of view, a writer uses **personal pronouns** in the first, second, or third person. The first person is used to show that the writer is involved, either as spectator or as doer.

> *I* saw the storm approaching.
> *We* drove to Disneyland.

The second person is used to give directions, instructions, or advice.

> Enter the data after pressing the enter key once. [The second-person pronoun, *you*, is implied.]

The third person indicates that the narrator is writing about other people or is describing a phenomenon.

> *They* bought tickets to Des Moines.
> The hibiscus is a tropical flower, but *it* also grows in California.

Do not unnecessarily shift the point of view in a sentence, a paragraph, or a composition. (See also **narration** and **shifts**.)

In a **literary analysis**, point of view takes on added dimensions. A first-person narrator uses first-person pronouns and is a participant in the story. In contemporary novels, different narrators often take turns telling their parts of the story. For example, in Amy Tan's novel *The Kitchen God's Wife*, the chapters alternate between the mother's and the daughter's point of view, both told in the first person. This strategy lets the audience decide with whom to agree or empathize. The first-person narrator may be a main character, a minor character, or an observer.

P

When authors write in the third person, they often take an omniscient point of view, in which the narrator knows everything about everyone. Omniscient narrators may be intrusive, commenting on everything, or unintrusive, recounting the story objectively. In Kate Chopin's novel, *The Awakening,* the narrator could be considered intrusive when she notes: "Her marriage to Leonce Pontellier was purely an accident, in this respect resembling many other marriages which masquerade as the decrees of Fate." Conversely, the narrator in Ernest Hemingway's enigmatic short story "Hills Like White Elephants" is completely unintrusive, limiting his narration to descriptions of the scenery and repetition of the two characters' dialogue without offering any commentary.

possessive case

A **noun** or **pronoun** is in the possessive **case** (also called *genitive case*) when it shows possession or ownership.

> *New York City's* skyline
>
> *his* ideas

Use the possessive case before a **gerund.**

> The flight attendant insisted on *my* wearing a seat belt.
> The instructor noted *Mark's* arriving late to class.

Possessive Nouns

Singular nouns and plural nouns that do not end in -*s* are usually made possessive with an **apostrophe** and -*s*. Plural nouns ending in -*s* need only an apostrophe. Both singular and plural nouns may also be made possessive with the insertion of the word *of* before them.

the *student's* schedule	the *students'* schedules
the *women's* gym	the length *of* the term

Proper Nouns   Proper nouns that end in -*s* show the possessive either with an apostrophe or with both an apostrophe and an -*s*. Whichever you choose, be consistent.

	Dickens's novels	Los Lobos's songs
OR	Dickens' novels	Los Lobos' songs

In the names of places and institutions, the apostrophe is often omitted.

Harpers Ferry	Writers Book Club	Veterans Administration

Coordinate and Compound Nouns   Coordinate nouns show joint possession when only the last noun is in the possessive form.

> *Raymond and Debra's* first child

Coordinate nouns show individual possession when each noun is in the possessive form.

> *Thomas's* and *Silvio's* test results

To form the possessive of a compound noun or a single term composed of two or more words, add -'s to the last word only.

> the *vice-chancellor's* car
>
> my *mother-in-law's* furniture [can also be revised to *furniture of my mother-in-law*]
>
> the *Department of Energy's* budget

Possessive Pronouns

Personal pronouns have two forms in the possessive case: an adjective form (*my, your, his, her, its, our, their*) and a noun form (*mine, yours, his, hers, its, ours, theirs*).

> That is *her* house. [The adjective form precedes nouns or gerunds.]
>
> That house is *hers.* [The noun form takes the place of a noun.]

Note that possessive pronouns, unlike possessive nouns, do not use an apostrophe before the -s. (See also *its/it's.*)

One-syllable **indefinite pronouns** (*all, any, each, few, most, none,* and *some*) require *of* phrases to form the possessive case.

> Both cars were stored in the garage, but rust had ruined the surface *of each.*

Longer indefinite pronouns use the -'s form.

> *Everyone's* contribution is welcome.

possessive pronouns   (See **possessive case** and **pronouns.**)

post hoc fallacy   (See the discussion of false cause under **logic.**)

predicate adjectives

A predicate adjective is an **adjective** used after a **linking verb** to describe the **subject.** (See also **subject complements.**)

> The coffee is *hot.*

predicate nominatives

A predicate nominative is a **noun** or **noun clause** used after a **linking verb** to rename the **subject**. (See also **subject complements**.)

She is my *doctor.*

predicates

The predicate is the part of a sentence that makes an assertion about the **subject**. The *simple predicate* is the **verb** (including any **helping verbs**). The *complete predicate* is the simple predicate and any **modifiers, objects,** or **complements.**

Ana *has been making* [simple predicate] *tamales* [direct object] *all morning* [adverb phrase].

A *compound predicate* consists of two or more verbs with the same subject.

We *vacuumed* the carpet and *dusted* the furniture.

A *predicate nominative* is a noun or noun clause that follows a **linking verb** and renames the subject.

She is my *lawyer.* [noun]
His excuse was *that he had been sick.* [noun clause]

The predicate nominative is one kind of **subject complement**; the other is the **predicate adjective**, which is used after a linking verb to describe the subject.

Warren's car is *blue.*

(See also **agreement of subjects and verbs** and **faulty predication**.)

prefixes

A prefix is an element added in front of a root word that changes the word's meaning. Most prefixes are one syllable, but a few have two syllables.

*a*symmetrical	*not* symmetrical
*anti*aircraft	designed for defense *against* aircraft attack
*dis*honest	*not* honest
*in*active	*not* active
*pre*conceive	conceive (imagine) *before*
*re*write	write *again*
*super*sensitive	*very* sensitive
*un*happy	*not* happy

Hyphens after Prefixes

Most prefixes are written solid with the root word. Generally, **hyphens** are used only when the solid word might be ambiguous or awkward. The hyphen prevents confusion between two words.

reform ("to change or improve")	re-form ("to shape again")
recreation ("leisure activities")	re-creation ("reenactment")
release ("to let go")	re-lease ("to rent again")

A hyphen can also be used to separate an awkward repetition or combination of letters that might cause the reader to hesitate. Consult a dictionary if you are not sure whether a hyphen is necessary for a particular word.

anti-art	cross-index	re-elicit
anti-intellectual	cross-stitch	re-up

Use a hyphen if the prefix is a capital letter or number or if the root word begins with a capital letter.

A-frame	anti-Semitic	6-inch
T-shirt	pre-Columbian	9-iron

By convention, a few prefixes, including *all-*, *ex-*, and *self-*, are always followed by a hyphen.

all-star	ex-president	self-discipline

premises (See **logic.**)

prepositional phrases

A prepositional phrase consists of a **preposition** (such as *at, in, on, to*) followed by its **object** (a noun or pronoun) and any **modifiers** of the object.

> *After the argument,* Virginia fell asleep *on the tattered sofa.*

Prepositional phrases usually function as **adjectives** or **adverbs**.

> We ate lunch *in the cafeteria.* [adverb]

> Garbage *with a high paper content* has been turned into protein-rich animal food. [adjective]

Separating a prepositional phrase from the noun it modifies can cause ambiguity or awkwardness. (See also **misplaced modifiers.**)

> *in the gray suit, who is*
> The man standing by the drinking fountain, ~~in the gray suit~~ is our president.
>   ∧

For **sentence variety**, occasionally begin a sentence with a prepositional phrase. (Long introductory phrases should be set off from the main clause with a **comma**; short phrases may not need the comma.)

At the summit, the snow started coming down.

Include the gerund ending (*-ing*) when constructing prepositional phrases with verbs.

driving
The police fined Sak for ~~drive~~ the wrong way on a one-way street.
                            ∧

prepositions

A preposition links a **noun** or **pronoun** to another sentence element by expressing a relationship such as direction, time, or location. The preposition and its object (and any modifiers) form a **prepositional phrase**, which usually functions as an adjective or adverb.

COMMON PREPOSITIONS			
about	beneath	like	throughout
above	beside	near	till
across	between	of	toward
after	beyond	off	under
against	by	on	until
along	down	onto	up
among	during	out	upon
around	except	outside	with
as	for	over	within
at	from	past	without
before	in	regarding	
behind	inside	since	
below	into	through	

Phrasal Prepositions

Prepositions may be more than one word. The following list includes some of the most common phrasal prepositions.

according to	by means of	in front of	out of
along with	by reason of	in place of	up to
apart from	by way of	in regard to	with reference to
as for	due to	in spite of	with regard to
as regards	except for	instead of	with respect to
as to	in addition to	near to	with the exception of
because of	in case of	next to	

Problems with Prepositions

Faulty Ellipsis If two or more different prepositions are called for in a compound construction, do not omit any of them. (See also **idioms.**)

He was accustomed ^to^ and not distracted by the stunning view from his office window.

[Idiomatically, *accustomed* is followed by *to*, not *by*.]

In Titles Capitalize a preposition only if it is the first or last word in the title (unless you are following a documentation style that calls for capitalizing prepositions of four or five letters or more—see **Research Processes**). (See also **capital letters.**)

For Whom the Bell Tolls   *A Bell for Adano*   "This Way Out"

Idioms ESL dictionaries include **phrasal verbs** and idiomatic combinations of certain adjectives or verbs and prepositions. (See also **idioms.**)

P

If Spanish is your native language, take care not to use *for* with **infinitives** to express purpose.

I am studying ~~for~~ ^to^ pass my comprehensive exams.

OR

I am studying for my comprehensive exams.

present participle

The present **participle** of a **verb** is formed by adding *-ing* to the plain, or **infinitive**, form (*waiting, looking*). Used with a *be* verb (*am, are, is, was, were*), it expresses an action in progress.

Kristina is *revising* her essay.

The taxi driver was *waiting*.

Jimmy may be *going* to summer school. [Use *be* with the present participle after a **modal auxiliary**, such as *may*.]

The present participle can also be used as a **modifier** before a noun (a *parking* ticket) or in a **participial phrase** to express an action occurring at the same time as that expressed by the main verb.

Flashing its lights and *sounding* its siren, the ambulance tried to get through the traffic.

present perfect participle

The present perfect participle of a **verb** is formed with *having* and a **past participle**. In a **participial phrase**, it expresses an action that occurred before that of the main verb.

Having turned off the lights and *locked* the door, Stephen climbed the stairs to bed.

present perfect tense

The present perfect tense of a **verb** combines a form of *have* and the **past participle**. The action of the verb begins in the past and extends into the present. (See also **tense**.)

I *have lived* in Michigan since I was born. [The writer still lives in Michigan.]

She *has cut* her hair. [The effect of the haircut is still noticeable.]

present tense

The present tense of a **verb** expresses action that is happening now. The plain form of the verb is used in all **persons** except for third-person singular, to which an -s is added. (See also **tense**.)

I/you/we/they *look*.

He/she/it *looks*.

The present tense is also used to express habitual or recurring action and universal truths.

He *plays* the piano well.

Salt *is* a combination of sodium and chloride.

With an **adverb** or adverb phrase, the present tense can express the future.

The semester *ends tomorrow.*

The present tense is also used in writing about literature and fictional events. In this context, it is called the **literary present.**

> Ishmael *is* the lone survivor of Captain Ahab's pursuit of Moby Dick.

prewriting (See **Composing Processes**, pages 6–11.)

primary sources (See **Research Processes**, pages 28, 35–36.)

principal/principle

Principal as an **adjective** means "main or primary"; as a **noun,** *principal* means the "chief official in a school" or a "main participant in a court proceeding." *Principle,* a noun, means a "basic truth or belief."

> My *principal* objection is that it will be too expensive.
>
> He sent a letter to the *principal* of the high school.
>
> Mother Teresa was a person of unwavering *principles.*

problem-solution as a method of development

The problem-solution method of development is especially common in scientific, technical, and business writing. Typically, the writer states the problem at the outset and then discusses a possible remedy or remedies.

In his essay "The Art of Teaching Science," Lewis Thomas describes problems in the way science is taught and suggests reforms. Throughout the essay, Thomas uses the problem-solution method of organization. Here he uses the method to organize a single paragraph.

> I believe that the worst thing that has happened to science education is that the fun has gone out of it. A great many good students look at it as slogging work to be got through on the way to medical school. Others are turned off by the premedical students themselves, embattled and bleeding for grades and class standing. Very few recognize science as the high adventure it really is, the wildest of all explorations ever taken by human beings, the chance to glimpse things never seen before, the shrewdest maneuver for discovering how the world works. Instead, baffled early on, they are misled into thinking that bafflement is simply the result of not having learned all the facts. They should be told that everyone else is baffled as well—from the professor in his endowed chair down to the platoons of postdoctoral students in the laboratories all night. Every important scientific advance that has come in looking like an answer has turned, sooner or later—usually sooner—into a question. And the game is just beginning.

process explanation/analysis as a method of development

To make a process or a procedure clear, divide it into steps and present them in order. The following two paragraphs describe the stages of NREM (non–rapid eye movement) sleep.

> Scientists further divide NREM sleep into four separate stages. As people fall asleep, their muscles relax and their heart and breathing rates gradually decrease until they drift out of conscious awareness of the surrounding world into stage one sleep. Typically, about 15 minutes after falling asleep, people enter stage two, which can be distinguished from stage one by differences in the sleepers' EEG patterns. While people awakened from stage one will become alert almost immediately and scarcely realize they have fallen asleep, a person disturbed during stage two will usually take several seconds to become fully awake.
>
> Stage three—which, together with stage four, is known as deep sleep—begins about half an hour after people fall asleep. As sleepers pass through stage three to stage four, their EEG patterns change again as their brains begin to produce slow, rhythmic patterns known as delta waves. People disturbed during deep sleep have drifted so far from waking consciousness that they may take several minutes to awaken completely.
>
> —"Sleep" (*The Almanac of Science and Technology*, ed. Richard Golob and Eric Brus)

progressive verb forms

Progressive verb forms consist of a form of *be* and a **present participle**. Each **tense** has a progressive form to express a continuous action.

PRESENT PROGRESSIVE
I *am watching*
he/she/it *is watching*
you/we/they *are watching*

PAST PROGRESSIVE
I/he/she/it *was watching*
you/we/they *were watching*

FUTURE PROGRESSIVE
I/he/she/it/you/we/they *will be watching*

PRESENT PERFECT PROGRESSIVE
I/you/we/they *have been watching*
he/she/it *has been watching*

PAST PERFECT PROGRESSIVE
I/he/she/it/you/we/they *had been watching*

FUTURE PERFECT PROGRESSIVE
I/he/she/it/you/we/they *will have been watching*

Certain verbs that express a mental or emotional state rather than describe an action do not have a progressive form. Here are some of the verbs that do not have a progressive form.

belong	know	prefer
care	like	realize
doubt	love	recognize
envy	mean	remember
fear	mind	seem
forget	need	suppose
hate	own	understand
imagine	possess	want

pronoun reference

A **pronoun** should refer clearly to a particular noun or other **antecedent**. The audience should not have to guess which of two possible antecedents the writer intended.

                           a big
The caterers made ~~the~~ salad and delivered the dinner. ~~It was a big one.~~
                    ∧
[Was the dinner or the salad big?]

A pronoun's reference should be specific. Be especially careful to avoid vague or ambiguous reference with *this* or *which*.

                                                    an experience
He deals with people of various backgrounds in his work, *which* helps him in his
                                                         ∧

personal life.

[A noun representing the concept "dealing with people of various backgrounds" is added to give the pronoun *which* a clear antecedent.]

The reference should also be explicit, not hidden or implied.

                                                                       the
A high-lipid, low-carbohydrate diet is "ketogenic" because it favors ~~their~~ forma-
                                                                        ∧
of ketone bodies
tion.
    ∧
[The antecedent of *their* is merely implied (by "*ketogenic*") in the original version.]

(See also **agreement of pronouns and antecedents**.)

pronouns

A pronoun is used as a substitute for a **noun** or a noun phrase. There are eight types of pronouns: personal, demonstrative, relative, interrogative, indefinite, reflexive, intensive, and reciprocal. Most of these pronouns can also be used as adjectives when placed in front of a noun. (See also **agreement of pronouns and antecedents** and **pronoun reference.**)

Personal Pronouns

A **personal pronoun** relates to an individual or individuals. The first-person pronouns indicate the speaker or writer (*I, me, my, mine; we, us, our, ours*). The second-person pronouns indicate the individual addressed (*you, your, yours*). The third-person pronouns refer to the individual or thing written or spoken about (*he, him, his; she, her, hers; it, its; they, them, their, theirs*). (See also **person.**)

> *They* asked *us* if *she* was *our* aunt.
>
> *You* must remember to send *them* a card when *we* return.

Demonstrative Pronouns

A **demonstrative pronoun** identifies or singles out the **noun** it refers to. The demonstrative pronouns are *this, these, that,* and *those.*

> *This* is my son.
>
> *These* are my children.
>
> *That* is my bicycle.
>
> *Those* children are in sixth grade.

P

Relative Pronouns

The **relative pronouns** are *who, whom, whose, which, that,* and *what.* A relative pronoun connects a **dependent clause** to an **independent clause** and serves as part of the dependent clause (usually its subject or object).

> The personnel manager decided *who* would be hired.

That is used with restrictive clauses, and *which* can be used with either restrictive or nonrestrictive clauses, although some writers prefer to use *which* only with nonrestrictive clauses. (See also **restrictive and nonrestrictive elements.**)

> Families *that adopt babies from reputable agencies* are nearly always happy. [A restrictive clause is not set off with commas.]

> The school calendar, *which was distributed yesterday,* shows a reduced Christmas vacation. [A nonrestrictive clause is set off from the main clause with commas.]

Interrogative Pronouns

Interrogative pronouns (*who, whom, whose, what,* and *which*) are used to ask questions and to introduce interrogative sentences. The antecedent of an interrogative pronoun is usually in the expected answer.

> *What* is the trouble?
> *Which* of these is best?

Indefinite Pronouns

An **indefinite pronoun** names a general class of persons or things. Common indefinite pronouns include *all, another, any, anyone, both, each, either, everybody, few, many, more, most, neither, nobody, none, several, some,* and *somebody.*

> *Everybody* wanted to go on the bus, but only a *few* could be accommodated.

Reflexive and Intensive Pronouns

The reflexive and intensive pronouns are *myself, yourself, himself, herself, itself, oneself, ourselves, yourselves,* and *themselves.*

A **reflexive pronoun** usually functions as the object of a verb, a verbal, or a preposition and indicates that its antecedent is acting upon itself.

> She rehearsed it over and over to *herself.*

An **intensive pronoun** gives emphasis to its antecedent.

> Only you *yourself* can know the answer to that question.

Reciprocal Pronouns

A **reciprocal pronoun** expresses a mutual relationship between people or things. There are only two reciprocal pronouns: *each other* and *one another.* Use *each other* to refer to two persons or things. Use *one another* to refer to more than two.

> My grandparents are still very much in love with *each other.*

> The team members work well with *one another.*

Grammatical Properties of Pronouns

Pronouns have different forms to reflect **person, number,** and **case.**

| | | CASE | |
PERSON/NUMBER	*Subjective*	*Objective*	*Possessive*
1st-person singular	I	me	my, mine
2nd-person singular	you	you	your, yours
3rd-person singular	he	him	his
	she	her	her, hers
	it	it	its
1st-person plural	we	us	our, ours
2nd-person plural	you	you	your, yours
3rd-person plural	they	them	their, theirs
	who	whom	whose
	whoever	whomever	—

Case Pronouns can show the subjective, objective, or possessive case.

The **subjective case** (also called the *nominative case*) is used when the pronoun is the subject of a sentence or a clause or when the pronoun follows a **linking verb.**

> *He* is the leading modern philosopher.

> The leading modern philosopher is *he.*

The **objective case** (also called the *accusative case*) is used when the pronoun is the **object** of a **verb** or a **preposition.**

> The taxi took *us* to the station. [object of verb]

> The pianist played the song for *her.* [object of preposition]

The **possessive case** (also called the *genitive case*) is used when the pronoun expresses ownership. Possessive pronouns have an adjective form (*my, your, his, her, its, our, your,* and *their*) and a noun form (*mine, yours, his, hers, its, ours, yours,* and *theirs*).

> He took *his* [adjective form] notes with him.
> She kept *hers* [noun form] in *her* [adjective form] purse.

Gender   Third-person pronouns can be masculine (*he, him, his*), feminine (*she, her, hers*), or neuter (*it, its*). A pronoun must agree in **gender** with its antecedent. (See **agreement of pronouns and antecedents** and **nonsexist language.**)

Number   Pronouns can be singular (such as *I, he, she, it*) or plural (such as *we, you, they*). A pronoun must agree in number with its antecedent. (See **agreement of pronouns and antecedents** and **indefinite pronouns.**)

Person   First-person pronouns (*I, me, my, mine* and *we, us, our, ours*) refer to the speaker or speakers. Second-person pronouns (*you, your, yours*) refer to the person or people being addressed. Third-person pronouns (*he, him, his; she, her, hers; it, its; they, them, their, theirs*) refer to the person or thing being spoken of. (See **person** and **point of view.**)

pronunciation   (See **dictionaries.**)

proofreading   (See **Composing Processes**, pages 20–21.)

proper adjectives

Proper adjectives are derived from **proper nouns**; therefore, they should be capitalized.

PROPER NOUNS	PROPER ADJECTIVES
America	American
Denmark	Danish
Christ	Christian
Shakespeare	Shakespearean

proper nouns

A proper noun names a specific person, place, or thing and is always capitalized. (See also **capital letters.**)

PROPER NOUNS	COMMON NOUNS
Jane Jones	person
Chicago	city
Australia	country
General Electric	company
Tuesday	day
Declaration of Independence	document

(For the **case** and **number** of proper nouns, see **nouns.**)

An article is not used with singular proper nouns except the names of most large regions (*the* Antarctic, *the* West Coast, *the* Gobi Desert, but Antarctica), most large bodies of water (*the* Atlantic Ocean, *the* Gulf of Mexico, *the* Nile, but Lake Michigan), historical periods and events (*the* Bronze Age, *the* Renaissance, *the* Battle of Gettysburg), and a few idiomatic phrases (*the* University of Colorado). *The* is used with plural proper nouns (*the* United States, *the* Rockies, *the* Great Lakes, *the* Middle Ages).

punctuation

Punctuation refers to the standardized marks inserted in written material to clarify meaning and to separate structural units of words, phrases, clauses, and sentences. Punctuation marks serve many purposes, and most marks can be used for more than one purpose. For example, they may connect or separate sentence elements, they may enclose material, or they may end sentences.

apostrophe	'	parentheses	( )
brackets	[ ]	period	.
colon	:	question mark	?
comma	,	quotation marks	" "
dash	—	semicolon	;
exclamation point	!	slash	/
hyphen	-		

purpose

When you know the purpose of a writing task, you can focus and organize your material appropriately. In most writing situations, your purpose is either to inform or to persuade your audience. With your purpose in mind, you can determine the best **method of development**, the appropriate **tone**, and the necessary length and depth. (See also **Composing Processes** and **Research Processes.**)

question marks

Use a question mark to end a sentence that is a direct question.

> Where did you put the snow shovel?

Question marks may follow a series of questions within an interrogative sentence.

> What were the dates of the semester break? the holidays? the midterm exams?

When a directive or command is phrased as a question, a question mark is optional.

> Will you make sure that you have locked the door.
>
> Will you please telephone me collect if you plan to arrive later than June 10?

Retain the question mark in a title that is cited in a sentence.

> *Should Engineers Be Writers?* is the title of her book.

Do not use a question mark at the end of an indirect question.

> He asked me whether enrollment had increased this year.

With Quotation Marks

Whether the question mark goes inside or outside **quotation marks** depends on who is asking a question. If the person being quoted is asking the question, the question mark goes inside the quotation marks.

> Sandra asked, "When will we go?"

If the writer is asking the question, the question mark goes outside the quotation marks.

> Did she say, "I don't think the project should continue"?

quotation marks

The primary use of quotation marks (" ") is to enclose an exact repetition of someone else's spoken or written words (unless the **quotation** is long enough to be set off as a **block quotation**).

> The article stated, "There are still some scholars who believe that Shakespeare did not write his own plays."

Do not use quotation marks with indirect quotations—which are usually introduced by *that*. Indirect quotations are paraphrases of a speaker's words or ideas.

> The article suggested that some scholars still doubt that Shakespeare wrote the plays attributed to him.

(See also **paraphrasing.**)

When a quotation is divided, the interrupting phrase is set off, before and after, by **commas,** and quotation marks are used around each part of the quotation.

> "This money," he stated, "is erased from the public ledger."

Use single quotation marks (on a keyboard, use the **apostrophe** key) to enclose a quotation that appears within a quotation.

> In *Slaughterhouse Five* Kurt Vonnegut writes, "When I saw those freshly shaved faces [of the soldiers of World War II], it was a shock. 'My God, my God—' I said to myself, 'it's the Children's Crusade.'"

In **dialogue,** when a speaker has two or more consecutive paragraphs, quotation marks are used at the beginning of each paragraph but at the end of only the last paragraph. In the following example, the first of Rose's comments (part of her attempt to persuade her elderly mother to move to the County Home) is two paragraphs long. In the rest of the dialogue, the two speakers alternate paragraphs.

> Rose . . . said she had seen the trays coming up, with supper on them.
>
> "They go to the dining room if they're able, and if they're not they have trays in their rooms. I saw what they were having.
>
> "Roast beef, well done, mashed potatoes and green beans, the frozen not the canned kind. Or an omelette. You could have a mushroom omelette or a chicken omelette or a plain omelette, if you liked."
>
> "What was for dessert?"
>
> "Ice cream. You could have sauce on it."
>
> "What kind of sauce was there?"
>
> "Chocolate. Butterscotch. Walnut."
>
> "I can't eat walnuts."
>
> "There was marshmallow too."
>
> —ALICE MUNRO, "Spelling"

To Set off Words

Use quotation marks to set off a word used in a special or ironic sense.

> What chain of events caused the sinking of an "unsinkable" ship such as the *Titanic* on its maiden voyage?

Do not, however, set off slang or clichés with quotation marks. If the word or phrase is appropriate, use it without quotation marks. If it is not, find a better synonym or rewrite the sentence.

The speech was "~~food for thought.~~" *thought provoking.*

Although more commonly italicized (underlined), words spoken of as words may be put in quotation marks. Be consistent, however.

> "Angry" was too strong a word for how he felt.
>
> OR   *Angry* was too strong a word for how he felt.

To Set off Definitions

Quotation marks may also be used to set off a definition within a sentence.

> *Quote* is a verb meaning "to repeat or copy the words of another."

For Titles of Short Works

Use quotation marks to enclose titles of short works or parts of works, such as short stories, short poems, articles, essays, chapters of books, and songs. (Titles of longer works, such as books, long poems, periodicals, movies, and plays, are italicized or underlined; see also **italics**.)

> Did you see the article "No-Fault Insurance and Your Motorcycle" in last Sunday's *Journal*?

Do not enclose the title at the top of your paper in quotation marks (unless the title is a quotation).

With Other Punctuation

Commas and **periods** go inside closing quotation marks.

> "Reading *Space Technology* gives me the insider's view," he said, adding, "It's like having all the top officials sitting in my office for a bull session."

EXCEPTION: When parenthetical documentation follows the quoted material, the period goes after the final parenthesis. (See also **Research Processes**, pages 63, 100–03, 116–17.)

> W. H. Auden admired T. S. Eliot "for his conversational tone and for his acute inspection of cultural decay" (Ellmann and O'Clair 735).

Semicolons and **colons** always go outside closing quotation marks.

> He said, "I will pay the full amount"; this certainly surprised us.
>
> She has two favorite "sports": eating and sleeping.

The rule for all other **punctuation** (such as **question marks** and **exclamation points**) is that if the punctuation is a part of the material quoted, it goes inside the quotation marks; if the punctuation is not part of the material quoted, it goes outside the quotation marks.

quotations

A quotation is any material repeated from another source. The material borrowed may be words, sentences, ideas, illustrations, or facts. Whether the quotation is direct or indirect, the source should be acknowledged to avoid **plagiarism**. Furthermore, the source should not be misrepresented by taking the material out of context.

Direct Quotations

Direct word-for-word quotations are enclosed in **quotation marks** (except for long quotations, which are indented as **block quotations**; for more discussion of block quotations, see **Research Processes**, pages 88–89, 113, 132, and 148). Except in **dialogue**, where utterances only a word or two long may be punctuated as complete sentences, quotations of less than a sentence are normally incorporated into the text, in quotation marks, without any punctuation before them.

> Professor Zucker accused us of "a lazy trust in historical drift."

Quotations of a sentence or more are usually preceded by either a **comma** or a **colon**. A comma normally follows short **signal phrases**, such as *he said.*

> The investigative reporter said, "The war that began when World War II ended is over. But the dinosaurs of the Cold War still live among us. And the greatest of them remains hidden within the walls of the Pentagon."

A colon often follows an introductory **clause.**

> The investigative reporter made a chilling assertion: "The Pentagon has a secret stash—they call it the black budget—that costs us $100 million a day. This money is still being spent on the weapons to fight the Cold War, and World War III, and World War IV."

Indirect Quotations

An indirect quotation paraphrases the words or ideas of another and is not enclosed in quotation marks. Often, an indirect quotation follows the word *that* without any punctuation. (See also **paraphrasing**.)

> In a recent article, he claimed that the Pentagon had secret funds for weapons.

To convert a direct quotation to an indirect quotation, change the pronoun from the first person (*I*) to the third person (*he, she,* or *they*) or from the second person (*you*) to the first or third person, depending on the **point of view** of your paper.

CHANGE	"*I* came to the United States seven years ago," she said.
TO	She said that *she* came to the United States seven years ago. [first person changed to third person]
CHANGE	Ms. Alvarez said, "*You* have a beautiful garden."
TO	Ms. Alvarez told me that *I* had a beautiful garden. [second person changed to first person]
OR	Ms. Alvarez told Anthony that *he* had a beautiful garden. [second person changed to third person]

If the "reporting" verb (such as *say, state, tell,* or *ask*) is in the present **tense**, the verb tense of the quotation stays the same. If the reporting verb is in the past tense, the verb tense of the quotation is usually changed: The present tense is changed to the past; the present perfect or past tense is changed to the past perfect; and *can, will,* or *may* is changed to *could, would,* or *might.*

CHANGE	"I *live* in Chicago."
TO	Angelina *said* that she *lived* in Chicago. [present tense changed to past]
CHANGE	"I *have traveled* across the United States."
TO	Talib *said* that he *had traveled* across the United States. [present perfect changed to past perfect]
CHANGE	"You *can* come along."
TO	Anita *told* her little sister that she *could* come along. [*can* changed to *could*]

To turn a direct question into an indirect quotation, follow the preceding steps, but in addition, change the question to a statement. If the question takes a yes or no answer, connect it to the reporting clause with *whether*

Q

("She asked *whether* I could go"). If the question begins with *who, what, when, where, which, why,* or *how,* no other subordinator is necessary.

CHANGE   "*When* did you come to the United States?"

TO   She asked *when* I came to the United States.

Deletions or Omissions

Quoted material is often shortened or made to read smoothly in the new context by leaving out unnecessary words, phrases, or even longer portions. (Caution: Always take care that the quoted author's meaning is not distorted.) An omission from quoted material is indicated by three **ellipsis points**. If material at the end of a sentence is omitted, a period is added to the three ellipsis points.

> Thirty years ago, Newton Minow told television executives, "I invite you to sit down in front of your television set . . . and keep your eyes glued to that set until the station signs off. . . . You will observe a vast wasteland."

Ellipsis points are not necessary at the beginning of a quoted passage.

> He told them, "/ / / You will observe a vast wasteland."

Inserting Material into Quotations

Any material the writer inserts into a quotation—an explanation, clarification, or translation—is enclosed in **brackets.**

> Linguist Bill Bryson observes that most English speakers today "looking at a manuscript from the time of, say, the Venerable Bede [English theologian, A.D. 673–735] would be hard pressed to identify it as being in English."

Sometimes, the original material may have an obvious spelling error or grammar fault. You may insert the word *sic,* in brackets, after the incorrect material to show that the error was in the source.

> The advertisement for the U.S. history book promised a "forward" [sic] by the president.

Incorporating Quotations into Text

Quotations of four or fewer lines (according to MLA style), less than forty words (according to APA style), or one line of poetry or fewer than eight lines of prose (according to CMS style) are incorporated into the text and enclosed in quotation marks. (See also **Research Processes.**)

The critic Herbert Muschamp wrote perhaps the most compelling assessment of the new museum, avowing that "its monumental forms appear to be shaped not by architecture but by history. It is not a building about the historical past. It is about the historical present."

When incorporating lines of poetry into the text, indicate line breaks with a slash and retain the original capitalization. (See also **capital letters**.)

One of my favorite images from "The Love Song of J. Alfred Prufrock" reads, "I should have been a pair of ragged claws / Scuttling across the floors of silent seas."

Longer quotations are set off from the text and indented (these are known as **block quotations**). For more discussion of block quotations, see **Research Processes**, pages 88–89, 113, 132, and 148.

(See also **signal phrases**.)

quote/quotation

Quote is a **verb** meaning "to repeat or copy the words of another." *Quotation* is a **noun** that means "a passage quoted."

His remarks were so unintelligible that I cannot *quote* him.

He is one of those people who go around spouting *quotations.*

Q

raise/rise

Raise is a **transitive verb** and always takes an **object** (*raise* taxes), whereas *rise* is an **intransitive verb** and never takes an object (heat *rises*).

Designers have *raised* hemlines again this year.

Hemlines seem to *rise* one year and fall the next.

readers (See **audience**.)

real/really

Real is an **adjective** meaning "not artificial or fraudulent"; *really* is an **adverb** meaning "truly."

Are those *real* diamonds or cubic zirconia?

I *really* love your earrings.

Do not use *real* in place of *really* or *very*.

really

Everything she said offended somebody, so we concluded that she was ~~real~~

insensitive.

reason is because

Reason is because is incorrect. Use either *reason is that* or *because* only.

that

Enrollment has increased more than twenty percent. The *reason is* ~~because~~ our

recruiters have been more aggressive this year.

OR

Enrollment has increased more than twenty percent this year *because* our recruiters have been more aggressive.

reciprocal pronouns

The reciprocal pronouns, *each other* and *one another,* indicate a mutual relationship or an exchange. *Each other* is commonly used when referring to two people or things; *one another* is used with two or more.

My roommate and I wear *each other's* clothes.

The committee members work well with *one another.*

red herring (See **logic**.)

redundancy (See **conciseness/wordiness**.)

reference books (See **Research Processes**.)

reference of pronouns (See **pronoun reference**.)

references (bibliographical) (See **Research Processes**.)

reflexive pronouns

A reflexive pronoun ends with *-self* or *-selves: myself, yourself, himself, herself, itself, oneself, ourselves, yourselves, themselves*. The reflexive pronoun usually functions as the **object** of a **verb**, a **verbal**, or a **preposition** and indicates that its **antecedent** is both the receiver and the doer of the action.

> The lathe operator cut *himself*.

Pronouns ending with *-self* or *-selves* that are used to emphasize their antecedent are **intensive pronouns**.

> I collected the data *myself*.

Do not use a reflexive pronoun without an antecedent.

> Joe and ~~*myself*~~ worked all day on it.

> He gave it to my assistant and ~~*myself*~~.

relative pronouns

A relative pronoun connects a **dependent clause** to an **independent clause**. The relative pronouns are *that, what, whatever, which, who, whoever, whom, whomever,* and *whose*. A relative pronoun also replaces a **noun**. The italicized words in the following examples show the relative pronoun and the noun it replaces.

> The grades were sent to his *parents, who* immediately opened them.

> The scholarship went to *Deborah Harmann, whom* everyone respects as a scholar.

> The students' main *objection, which* can probably be overcome, is that the library closes too early.

> The *memo that* you received yesterday sets forth the most important points.

Although clear writing usually requires that a pronoun have an antecedent, sometimes *what* or *whatever* does not refer to a specific noun.

> We invited the committee to see *what* was being done about the poor lighting.

In general, use *who* (*whom, whose*) to refer to people and *which* and *that* to refer to animals and things. *That* may also be used to refer to an anonymous group of people ("I want to contribute to a group *that* saves dolphins").

That is used with restrictive clauses, and *which* can be used with either restrictive or nonrestrictive clauses, although some writers prefer to use it only with nonrestrictive clauses. (See also **restrictive and nonrestrictive elements.**)

> The economists' report, *which was distributed yesterday,* shows that inflation increased five percent last year. [nonrestrictive clause]
>
> Cars *that are driven on salted roads* are likely to develop body rust. [restrictive clause]

The relative pronoun can usually be omitted if it is not the **subject** of the dependent clause.

> I received the handcrafted ornament [that] I ordered.
>
> The teacher [whom] I like best is Ms. Caputo.

(See also *that/which/who* and *who/whom.*)

repetition

Repetition can be used to emphasize a feeling or idea. (See also **parallel structure.**)

> *Nature is* wild, *nature is* tame, *nature is* free, *nature is* bound; but, most of all, *nature is* magic.

Repetition can also be used to achieve **coherence.** Repeating a word or phrase in consecutive sentences or paragraphs helps to clarify ideas and move smoothly from one idea to another.

> *Keeping up with* the Joneses was *the goal* in the first half of the twentieth century. *Keeping up with* change was *the goal* in the second half.

Avoid useless or awkward repetition, however.

~~The new series of stamps issued by~~ T̲he U.S. Postal Service ~~is a~~ series of stamps *issued a new*

commemorating rock-and-roll stars.

research (See **Research Processes.**)

respective/respectively/respectfully

Respective is an **adjective** meaning "separate."

> The football players returned to their *respective* benches.

Respectively is an **adverb** meaning "separately" or "in the order given."

> Her parents, Hank and Deeny, were sixty and sixty-three, *respectively.*

Respectfully is an adverb meaning "with respect or deference."

> The old politician expected to be treated *respectfully.*

restrictive and nonrestrictive elements

Phrases and **clauses** may be either restrictive or nonrestrictive. A phrase or clause is nonrestrictive if it provides additional information about, but does not limit or restrict the meaning of, what it modifies. It is set off by **commas** to show that it is not essential to the sentence. Nonrestrictive clauses usually begin with the **relative pronoun** *which* or *who,* although they can also begin with *where* or other words.

> The compact disc, *which is often called the CD,* has virtually replaced records and tapes. [nonrestrictive clause]
>
> Jed Beatty, *who came to dinner last night,* is my closest friend. [nonrestrictive clause]
>
> Liberty Park, *where I first met Louise,* is now closed. [nonrestrictive clause]

A phrase or clause is restrictive if it does limit or restrict the meaning of what it modifies. A restrictive phrase or clause defines and identifies; the sentence would have a different meaning (or no meaning at all) without it. Restrictive elements, being essential for meaning, are not set off by commas. A restrictive clause can begin with *who, that,* or *which,* although some writers prefer to use *which* only for nonrestrictive clauses.

> The compact disc *that you gave me for my birthday* is missing. [restrictive clause]
>
> The student *who came to dinner last night* is Jed Beatty, my closest friend. [restrictive clause]
>
> The park *where I first met Louise* is now closed. [restrictive clause]

The same sentence can have two entirely different meanings depending on whether a modifying element is restrictive or nonrestrictive.

> He gave failing grades to all the students *who picketed the graduation ceremony.* [Restrictive clause; the sentence suggests that only students who had picketed received failing grades.]

R

He gave failing grades to all the students, *who picketed the graduation ceremony.* [Nonrestrictive; the sentence indicates that all the students received failing grades and then picketed the graduation ceremony.]

résumés

A résumé is essential to any job search because it shows at a glance what you have to offer to prospective employers. Résumés should be no more than one or two pages, depending on your experience, and they should include the following information:

1. Your name, address, and phone number
2. Your immediate and long-range job objectives
3. Your education and professional training
4. Your work experience, including your employers and your responsibilities
5. Your special skills and activities

Format of the Résumé

A number of different formats can be used. Whichever you choose, however, be sure that your résumé is attractive, well organized, easy to read, and free of errors. A computer is ideal for creating a résumé because it allows you to tailor the résumé to particular jobs and to update it easily.

A typical résumé organizes information under the following headings (which should be underlined, capitalized, or printed in bold type so that they stand out):

Employment Objective

Education

Employment Experience

Special Skills and Activities

References (optional)

Whether you list education or experience first depends on which is stronger in your background. If you are a recent graduate, list education first; if you have substantial job experience, list your employment history first.

The Heading Type your name, address, and telephone number at the top of the page. Include your fax number and e-mail address if you have these. Each line is usually centered. You may wish to print your name in capital letters or in bold type if you are using a computer.

Employment Objective List a long-term objective as well as a short-term objective. The objectives can be eliminated, though, if the job you are applying for is temporary or is not related to your career goals.

Education   For each college you have attended, list the years attended, the field of study, the degree received, and any academic honors earned. If appropriate (for your first job, for instance), also list the high school you attended, the city and state, and the years attended.

Employment Experience   If you have had little work experience, list all your jobs, full-time, part-time, and temporary. Otherwise, list only your full-time jobs. Begin with the most recent job and work backward to the earliest job that is suitable for inclusion. For each one, specify the job title, the name and address of the employer, and the dates you were employed. Briefly describe the tasks you performed. You may wish to give an expanded description of your accomplishments and duties performed for a job that is similar to the job you are currently seeking or for a job that you have held for a long time at the same company. List the promotions and pay increases you received, but do not give your present salary. If you have served in the military, list the dates, your duties, and your final rank.

Special Skills and Activities   Near the end of the résumé, list any skills you have or activities you have participated in that are relevant to the job you are applying for. These skills and activities may include computer experience, knowledge of a foreign language, hobbies, writing abilities, community service, and club memberships. Limit the material you provide in this category to items not included elsewhere that pertain to your employment objectives.

Personal Data   Employers cannot ask job applicants to supply certain personal information—such as age, sex, marital status, race, and religion—because of restrictions imposed by the federal government. Consequently, include your date of birth and your marital status only if you believe this information will help you get the job.

References   For this category, you may state, "Available upon request." Include the references only if it is traditional to do so in your field or if you need to fill a short page. Be sure to obtain permission from your reference sources before listing them on your résumé.

Figure R-1 (page 450) shows a sample résumé.

revising

The more natural a piece of writing seems, the more effort the writer has probably put into revising. Revising is so important that some writers say that writing *is* revising; they reinforce this point by calling their first drafts "zero drafts." For detailed help with the sequence of steps involved in revising, see **Composing Processes**, pages 13–17.

CAROL ANN WALKER
273 East Sixth Street
Bloomington, IN 47401
(913) 555-1212

Employment Objective	Position as financial research assistant, leading to a management position in corporate finance.
Education	B.B.A., Indiana University (expected June 2002) Major: Finance Minor: Computer Science Honors: Dean's List (G.P.A.: 3.88/4.00), Senior Honor Society, 2002
Employment Experience	First Bank, Research Department (Bloomington, IN) Intern research assistant: Developed computer model for long-range financial planning. (Summer 2001)
	Martin Financial Research Services (Bloomington, IN) Intern editorial assistant: Provided research assistance to staff. Developed a design concept for in-house financial audits. (Summer 2000)
	Various part-time jobs to finance education. (1997 to 1999)
Special Skills and Activities	Associate editor, Business School Alumni Newsletter Wrote two stories on financial planning with computer models, edited submissions, surveyed business periodicals for potential stories.
	President of Women's Transit Program Coordinated efforts to provide safe nighttime transportation between campus buildings.
	Amateur photographer Won several local awards.
References	Available upon request.

Figure R-1. Sample résumé.

rhetoric

According to *Webster's,* this word has three different, but related, meanings: (1) the study of the structure and style of writing and speaking; (2) the art of effective expression and the persuasive use of language; and (3) insincere or pretentious language. The first sense is the one with which this text is concerned.

rhetorical questions

A rhetorical question is a question to which no answer is expected. The question is often intended to focus the reader's attention; the writer then answers the question in the article or essay. For example, the answer to the question "Does advertising lower consumer prices?" might be a detailed explanation of advertising's effect.

The rhetorical question can be an effective **introduction,** and it is often used for a title. When you use a rhetorical question, however, be sure that it is not trivial or forced.

rhetorical situation

The rhetorical situation is the context for an act of writing. It includes five elements: the writer, the occasion, the audience, the topic, and the purpose. (See **Composing Processes,** pages 3–6.)

rise/raise   (See *raise/rise.*)

run-on sentences (fused sentences)

A run-on sentence (sometimes called a *fused sentence*) is two or more **independent clauses** without **punctuation** separating them. Run-on sentences can be corrected in any of the following ways:

- By making two sentences

The new chancellor instituted several new procedures ⟋ome were impractical.

- By joining the two clauses with a **semicolon** (if they are closely related)

The new chancellor instituted several new procedures; some were impractical.

- By joining the two clauses with a semicolon followed by a **conjunctive adverb**

however,
The new chancellor instituted several new procedures; some were impractical.
∧

- By joining the two clauses with a comma and a **coordinating conjunction**

          but

The new chancellor instituted several new procedures, some were impractical.

- By subordinating one clause to the other

          of which

The new chancellor instituted several new procedures, some were impractical.

(See also **comma splice.**)

R

says/goes/said

Says or *goes* is nonstandard usage for the past-tense verb *said*.

So then I ~~says~~, "Don't talk that way to me," and he ~~goes~~, "I'll talk however I want."
            said   *said*

search engine

A search engine is a computer program that searches Internet documents in its database for **keywords** and returns a list of links to documents where the keywords were found. Most search-engine databases are compiled by computer-robot programs called "spiders," in contrast to **subject directories**, whose databases are compiled by subject specialists. (For a list of search engines, see **Research Processes** pages 54–55.)

secondary sources (See **Research Processes**, page 36.)

semicolons

The semicolon links closely related **independent clauses** or other grammatically equal sentence elements that are not linked by a comma and coordinating conjunction.

Between Independent Clauses

If the relationship between the independent clauses is clear, often the semicolon is enough.

> No one applied for the position; the work was too difficult.

> I came; I saw; I conquered.

If the relationship between independent clauses needs to be clarified, use a semicolon plus a **conjunctive adverb** or other transitional word or phrase, such as *consequently, for example, furthermore, however, indeed, in fact, moreover, namely, that is, therefore*. (For a list of transitional words and phrases, see **transitions**.) You can also clarify the relationship between clauses by subordinating one clause to the other or by using a **comma** plus the appropriate **coordinating conjunction** (*and, but, for, nor, or, so, yet*).

> I was discouraged; however, I kept trying. [The relationship between the clauses is made clear by use of a semicolon plus the conjunctive adverb *however.*]

> Although I was discouraged, I kept trying. [The relationship between the clauses is made clear by subordinating the first clause to the second one with the subordinating conjunction *although.*]

S

I was discouraged, but I kept trying. [The relationship between the clauses is made clear by use of a comma plus the coordinating conjunction *but*.]

In a Series

Semicolons are often used instead of commas either (1) for clarity, to link a series of grammatically equal **phrases** or other sentence elements that contain **commas,** or (2) for emphasis, to link a series of grammatically equal elements in which the writer wants stronger pauses than commas would provide.

Among those present were Jean Smith, president of Alpha Chi Omega; Linda Smith, president of Alpha Sigma Alpha; and John Smith, president of Sigma Chi. [semicolons for clarity between grammatically equal phrases with internal commas]

It was they who started the war; who continued the fighting after their cause was lost; and who even now resist all efforts to make peace. [semicolons for emphasis to link a series of grammatically equal elements, in this case subordinate clauses]

Misuse of Semicolons

Elements joined by semicolons should be grammatically equal. Do not use a semicolon between a **dependent clause** and an independent clause.

No one applied for the position; even though it was heavily advertised.

Do not use a semicolon between a clause and a phrase.

Three types of parking areas are under consideration; a few covered structures for faculty, nearby lots for graduate students, and off-campus lots for undergraduates.

With Quotation Marks

The semicolon always appears outside closing **quotation marks.**

The attorney said, "You must be accurate"; the client said, "I will be."

sensual/sensuous

Both **adjectives** mean "appealing to or satisfying the senses." But *sensual,* unlike *sensuous,* has a sexual **connotation.**

Some people consider watching Madonna's performances a *sensual* experience.

The Thanksgiving feast was a *sensuous* delight.

sentence faults

Some types of sentence faults are due to problems with punctuation: **comma splices, run-on sentences,** and **sentence fragments.** Others are caused by structural problems: **dangling modifiers, faulty predication, misplaced modifiers, mixed constructions,** and **shifts.** (See also **agreement of subjects and verbs, agreement of pronouns and antecedents, parallel structure,** and **subordination.**)

sentence fragments

A sentence fragment is a part of a sentence that is punctuated as a complete sentence. It may lack a **subject,** a **predicate,** or both, or it may be a **dependent clause.** Most sentence fragments can be revised in one of three ways: (1) by changing the punctuation to attach the fragment to another sentence, (2) by adding the missing subject or other word, or (3) by changing the verb form from a **verbal** to a **finite verb.**

Missing Subject or Predicate

A missing subject is often the result of faulty punctuation of a compound predicate. Either add the subject or change the punctuation to incorporate the fragment into the preceding sentence.

He quit his job. And *he* cleared out his desk.

OR

He quit his job, *a* And cleared out his desk.

A missing or incomplete predicate is often the result of using a verbal instead of a finite verb. Usually, the best remedy is addition of a **helping verb.**

Sheila *is* waiting to see you.

Dependent Clauses

Although a dependent clause has a subject and a predicate, it cannot stand alone as a sentence because it begins with a **relative pronoun** (*that, which, who*) or a **subordinating conjunction** (such as *although, because, if, when,* or *while*). A dependent-clause fragment can be repunctuated and added to an independent clause, rewritten as a separate sentence, or rewritten as an

S

independent clause and linked to another independent clause with a comma and a coordinating conjunction.

Larry was late for class,/ ~~Because~~ he had forgotten to set the alarm clock.
(b inserted above, comma and caret)

The gas station attendant gave us directions to the beach. ~~Which~~ turned out to be all wrong.
(They inserted above)

OR

The gas station attendant gave us directions to the beach, but they turned out to be all wrong.

Phrases

Usually, a phrase can be attached to the preceding sentence with a simple change in capitalization and punctuation.

My advisor approved the project,/ *~~A~~fter much discussion.*
(a inserted above)

[prepositional phrase as fragment]

We reorganized the study group,/ *~~D~~istributing the workload more evenly.*
(, d inserted above)

[participial phrase as fragment]

The cleanup crew decided to take a break,/ *~~I~~t being midafternoon already.*
(, i inserted above)

[absolute phrase as fragment]

Explanatory phrases (beginning with expressions like *for example, such as,* and *that is*), lists, and **appositives** are common sources of sentence fragments.

The faculty wants additional benefits,/ ~~For example,~~ *the free use of university automobiles.*
(, such as inserted above)

[Change the punctuation and capitalization to attach the explanatory phrase to the preceding sentence.]

OR

The faculty wants additional benefits. One is the free use of university automobiles. [Turn the phrase into a complete sentence.]

I have so many things to do today : w /Washing, ironing, vacuuming, dusting, baking,

and doing dishes.

[Change the punctuation and capitalization to attach the list to the preceding sentence.]

These are my classmates , a /A fine group of people.

[Change the punctuation and capitalization to attach the appositive phrase to the preceding sentence.]

Intentional Fragments

Sentence fragments are sometimes employed intentionally for **emphasis** or effect, especially in fiction and in advertising copy. In the following example, the series of sentence fragments helps convey the fast pace, the frustration, and the anonymity of working in a restaurant.

> Then there was dinner. Drinks. Wine. Specifics as to the doneness of steaks or roasts. Complaints. I ordered *medium* rare. Is this crab really *fresh*? And heavy trays. The woman who managed the restaurant saw to it that waitresses and bus girls "shared" that labor, possibly out of some vaguely egalitarian sense that the trays were too heavy for any single group.
>
> —ALICE ADAMS, "By the Sea"

Intentional fragments should be used sparingly in formal writing, however, and they work only if the missing words are clearly implied by the context.

> In view of these facts, is automation really useful? *Or economical?* [The words missing from the second question—*is automation*—can be easily supplied from the context.]

sentences

A sentence is an independent unit of expression. A **simple sentence** contains a **subject** and a **predicate**, which may include **modifiers** and **complements**. For other types of sentences, see **sentence types**.

For pointers on writing effective sentences, see **ambiguity, choppy writing, clarity, conciseness/wordiness, dangling modifiers, emphasis, faulty predication, misplaced modifiers, mixed constructions, parallel structure, shifts,** and **subordination**.

sentence types

Sentences are classified in three ways: by *structure*, by *intention*, and by *stylistic use*. Classified by structure, sentences are simple, compound, complex, or compound-complex. According to intention, sentences are declarative, interrogative, imperative, or exclamatory. Finally, classified by stylistic use, sentences are cumulative or periodic.

By Structure

A **simple sentence** has one **independent clause**. The most basic simple sentence consists of a **subject** and a **predicate**.

> Birds [subject] chirp [predicate].
>
> The choral music [subject] began joyously [predicate].

A **compound sentence** has two or more independent clauses. The clauses may be joined by a **semicolon**, by a **comma** and a **coordinating conjunction**, or by a semicolon and a **conjunctive adverb** followed by a comma.

> Getting yourself that new silk jogging suit is not extravagance; it is self-improvement. [semicolon]
>
> The concert did not start until 9 p.m. on Saturday, *but* the fans started lining up on Friday morning. [comma and coordinating conjunction]
>
> Victor will call you on Friday night; *however,* call him on Thursday if you change your mind. [semicolon and conjunctive adverb followed by a comma]

A **complex sentence** has one independent clause and one or more **dependent clauses**.

> The iron will shut off automatically [independent clause] if it is left standing for more than five minutes [dependent clause].

A **compound-complex sentence** has two or more independent clauses and one or more dependent clauses.

> When I got to our house [dependent clause], I rushed into the yard and called out to her [independent clause], but no answer came [independent clause].
>
> —JAMAICA KINCAID, "The Circling Hand"

By Intention

A **declarative sentence** conveys information or makes a factual statement.

> Seaweed is a valuable source of iodine and vitamin C.

An **interrogative sentence** asks a direct question.

> Have you ever eaten seaweed?

An imperative sentence issues a command. (See also **imperative mood.**)

> Eat your seaweed.

An **exclamatory sentence** expresses a feeling, a fact, or an opinion emphatically.

> This tastes too salty!

By Stylistic Use

A **cumulative sentence** (also called a *loose sentence*) begins with the major point, which is followed by one or more subordinate **phrases** or **clauses.** It is the most typical sentence pattern.

> A single knoll rises out of the plain in Oklahoma, north and west of the Wichita range. [The subject, *knoll,* and predicate, *rises,* are followed by two prepositional phrases, a pair of adverbs, and another prepositional phrase.]
>
> —N. SCOTT MOMADAY, "The Way to Rainy Mountain"

A **periodic sentence** (also called a *climactic sentence*) delays the main idea until the end and presents subordinate ideas or modifiers first. This kind of sentence can lend **emphasis** to the main point or create suspense.

> In all geographical regions of the United States, people of all classes, all races, and all cultures are working together harmoniously. [The subject, *people,* is in the middle of the sentence; the verb, *are working,* is in a position of emphasis near the end.]
>
> And there, in the middle of the stream, shone the nugget of gold. [The periodic sentence has an inverted subject (*nugget*) and verb (*shone*) to create suspense.]

sentence variety

To make your writing clear and interesting, use a variety of **sentence types** and lengths. (See also **emphasis** and **subordination.**) In the paragraph that follows, all the sentences are in the basic subject-verb pattern, and they are all about the same length. Because no idea is emphasized, the purpose is not clear and the paragraph is boring.

> We drove back after the show over the viaduct across Bayley Yard. It is a huge Union Pacific switching center. We saw high floodlights far down the line. The floodlights made gold rivers of a hundred intertwining tracks. The tracks curved off into the glare and dazzling dark. Trains are one of the really good things the Industrial Revolution did. Trains are totally practical and totally romantic. But one train was on all those tracks.

In contrast, here is the paragraph as it was actually written.

> Driving back after the show over the viaduct across Bayley Yard, a huge Union Pacific switching center, we see high floodlights far down the line make gold rivers

of a hundred intertwining tracks curving off into the glare and dazzling dark. Trains are one of the really good things the Industrial Revolution did—totally practical and totally romantic. But on all those tracks, one train.

—URSULA LE GUIN, "Along the Platte"

The variety of **sentence types** and lengths in this paragraph helps clarify its purpose and make it interesting. In the long first sentence, the **dependent clauses** and **phrases** before and after the main clause (*we see*) paint a word picture of the massive web of railroad tracks. In the next sentence, the author expresses her affection for trains with a **simple sentence** followed by a summarizing phrase. In the last sentence, by omitting the verb (thus intentionally creating a **sentence fragment**) and putting the subject last, Le Guin gives maximum emphasis to the words *one train*.

Sentence Length

In general, as the preceding paragraph by Ursula Le Guin illustrates, short sentences (and, occasionally, intentional sentence fragments) are suited to emphatic, memorable statements. Long sentences are suited to detailed descriptions, explanations, and information in support of arguments.

Sentence length also influences pace. Short sentences carry the reader along quickly; long sentences require a more leisurely pace. To maintain the reader's interest, vary the length of your sentences.

You can sometimes create a longer sentence out of two or more short ones by turning them into dependent clauses or phrases.

CHANGE   The river is sixty miles long. It averages fifty yards in width. Its depth averages eight feet.

TO   The river is sixty miles long, an average of fifty yards wide and eight feet deep.

Sometimes two sentences can be turned into one by simply eliminating redundancy. (See also **conciseness/wordiness**.)

The window cleaner fainted/~~He collapsed~~ on the scaffolding.

A long sentence can sometimes be made shorter by reducing a clause to a phrase.

Fortunately, the tree ~~that was~~ *uprooted in the storm* fell on a vacant lot.

Needing   *Li*
~~Because Li needed~~ time to think, ~~he~~ went for a walk.
       ∧   ∧

Word Order

Word order can be used to create **emphasis** because words at the beginning or end of a sentence stand out more than words in the middle, and words in an unusual order stand out.

Vary the Beginning of the Sentence Occasionally, start a sentence with a modifying word, phrase, or clause rather than the subject, as expected.

> *Recently,* her grades have improved. [adverb]
>
> *Exhausted,* Martin slumped into a chair. [past participle]
>
> *In the morning,* I will finish typing my paper. [prepositional phrase]
>
> *To graduate in four years,* one must work hard and be lucky. [infinitive phrase]
>
> *Because the FDA has completed its research,* the drug may now go on the market. [adverb clause]

Invert the Subject and Verb Typically, the subject comes before the verb. As the following pairs of sentences show, changing the order can add emphasis. (See also **expletives** and **subordination**.)

> CHANGE Then the *event came* that we had been waiting for.
>
> TO Then *came* the *event* we had been waiting for.

> CHANGE So *many have* never *been* so willing.
>
> TO Never *have* so *many been* so willing.

Non-native speakers should have a good mastery of English before they attempt to use **inverted sentence order** because in English, unlike many other languages, word order signals grammatical relationships. Reversing the subject and the verb can create a sentence describing an illogical or impossible action ("A hot dog ate Saraya"); at other times it creates graceful and poetic English ("So sweetly sang the nightingale, I thought my heart would break").

sequence of tenses (See **tense**.)

set/sit (See *lay/lie, set/sit.*)

setting

Setting encompasses the place, the historical period, and the social milieu in which the action occurs in a drama or piece of fiction. Settings can be general, such as a city (St. Louis) or country (France), or they can be specific, such as the bedroom or the queen's court. The setting can also change within chapters or between acts or scenes as the characters move about. Setting is an important element of literature because authors use it to establish the atmosphere or mood of the piece.

sexist language (See **nonsexist language.**)

shall/will

Although traditionally *shall* was used to express the future tense with *I* and *we*, *will* is now generally accepted with all **persons.** *Shall* is commonly used today only in questions requesting an opinion or a preference rather than a prediction (compare "Shall we go?" to "Will we go?") and in statements expressing determination ("I shall return").

shifts

Careless shifts in **person, tense, voice, mood,** or discourse style can confuse the reader.

Shift in Person

Maintain a consistent **point of view** by writing in the same **person:** first person (*I, me*), second person (*you*), or third person (*he, she, they*).

> **Writers** should spend the morning hours on work requiring mental effort, for
> *their minds are*
> ~~your mind is~~ freshest in the morning.
> ⋀
>
> OR
>
> *You* should spend the morning hours on work requiring mental effort, for *your* mind is freshest in the morning.

Shift in Tense

The only legitimate shift in tense records a real change in time. When you choose a tense in which to tell a story or discuss an idea, stay with that tense.

> *cleaned*
> Before he *installed* the printed circuit, the technician ~~cleans~~ the contacts.
> ⋀

Shift in Voice

Avoid unnecessary shifts between **active** and **passive voice,** especially when such shifts change the subject of a clause or phrase.

During fall semester, Ms. McDonald worked to improve her spelling; in the spring
she greatly improved
semester, her punctuation ~~was greatly improved.~~
  ∧   ⊙

Shift in Mood

Do not shift needlessly from one **mood** to another—from imperative to indicative, for example.

Re-cap the tubes of paint, and ~~you should~~ clean the brushes.

Discourse Shift

Discourse may be either **direct** or **indirect**. Do not shift between the two within a sentence.

whether I
Jeff wanted to know where the skating rink was and could *I* give him a ride?
                                                    ∧   ⊙

[shift from indirect to direct discourse corrected]

OR

Jeff asked, "Where is the skating rink? Could you give me a ride?" [both direct discourse]

should have/should of

Should of is nonstandard for *should have*.

have
I *should ~~of~~* gone to work today.
      ∧

sic

Use *sic* (enclosed in **brackets**)—which is Latin for *thus*—to indicate that an obvious error in a **quotation** appeared in the original. Do not quote an error, however, unless you have reason to do so. You can usually paraphrase the original or quote only the part that is correct instead.

The sign above the window read "Sheespkin [sic] Covers."

In some documentation styles, the word is written in regular type: [sic]. In others, it is italicized or underlined: [*sic*] or [s̲i̲c̲].

sight/site/cite   (See *cite/site/sight.*)

signal phrases

To integrate a **quotation** or **paraphrase** from a source, you should use a signal phrase that includes the author's name (or a pronoun or descriptive phrase substituting for it). Signal phrases can provide context for the information from the source, or they can indicate the author's credentials. They also help the reader tell which ideas and words come from a source and which are yours; they are a good way to avoid **plagiarism.**

Signal phrases can appear at the beginning, in the middle, or at the end of a quotation or paraphrase. If the author's name is included in the signal phrase, the parenthetical citation needs to include only the page number (for MLA style) or the year and page number (for APA style). (See **Research Processes**, page 31, for examples of signal phrases.)

simile

A simile is a **figure of speech** that uses *like* or *as* to make a direct comparison of two essentially unlike things. (See also **analogy** and **metaphor**.)

> Constructing the bookcase is *like piecing together a jigsaw puzzle.*

simple predicates

A simple **predicate** is the **verb** of a sentence.

> She *gave* him flowers.

simple sentences

A simple sentence consists of one **independent clause**. The most basic simple sentence has only a **subject** and a **verb**.

> Snow fell.

The subject and the verb may be compounded.

> *Annuals, perennials, shrubs, and trees* are sold at nurseries. [compound subject]
>
> Gardeners *dig, hoe, plant, and weed.* [compound predicate]

The subject and the verb may be modified by words or phrases.

> The *newly purchased* car runs *very well.* [adverb and adjective modifying the subject; adverbs modifying the predicate]
>
> The brown horse *with the white stockings* is the winner. [prepositional phrase modifying the subject]
>
> The brown horse was the winner *of the race.* [prepositional phrase modifying the predicate]

The subject and verb may be inverted.

> Along came [verb] Sally [subject].

(See also **sentence types** and **sentence variety**.)

simple subjects

A simple **subject** is a **noun** or **pronoun** that names the doer of the action in a sentence.

> Wayne's *father* gave him a look.

single quotation marks

Use single quotation marks to set off a **quotation** within a quotation that is enclosed in double quotation marks. (See also **quotation marks**.)

> Going through her old notebooks, Joan Didion finds some of the entries are now meaningless. "What is this business about 'shopping, typing piece, dinner with E, depressed'?" she asks. "Shopping for what? Typing what piece? Who is E? Was this 'E' depressed, or was I depressed? Who cares?"

site/sight/cite   (See *cite/site/sight.*)

sit/set   (See *lay/lie, set/sit.*)

slang and neologisms

A neologism is a newly coined word or phrase or a new usage of an existing word or phrase. Slang is a very informal or colloquial neologism. Whereas many neologisms are created to describe developments in society and technology (recent examples include *AIDS, blog,* and *hacker*), slang is used primarily to establish identity as a member of a particular group (you might refer to a friend as a *dude* or *homey;* you might praise something by saying it is *phat* or *tight*).

Slang can be used in dialogue, but it is not appropriate in formal writing. Other neologisms may be appropriate, however, if they have been accepted as standard English (such as the first set of examples in the preceding paragraph). Do not set off slang words or neologisms with **quotation marks**. Be cautious about using neologisms that still seem trendy, and do not use neologisms that your readers are unlikely to have encountered. (See also **English, varieties of.**)

slanted evidence   (See **logic**.)

slashes

In informal writing, the slash (also called a *virgule* or *solidus*) can indicate alternative items (549-2278/2335), take the place of the word *per* (miles/hour), separate the numerator from the denominator in fractions (2/3, 3/4), and separate the day, month, and year in **dates** (12/29/87).

In formal writing, the slash is used only to indicate line breaks when quoting lines of poetry. Insert a space before and after the slash.

> The poet Audre Lorde writes: "The difference between poetry and rhetoric / is being / ready to kill / yourself / instead of your children."

so

As an **intensifier**, *so* is vague. In formal writing, either use another intensifier (such as *very*) or complete the thought with a *that* clause.

> That dress is ~~so~~ pretty. *very*

> She writes *so* fast. *that I cannot read her writing*

some/somewhat

Some is an **adjective** or **pronoun** meaning "an undetermined quantity" or "certain unspecified people." *Somewhat* is an **adverb** meaning "to some extent."

> Her writing has improved ~~some.~~ *somewhat*

some time/sometime/sometimes

Some time means "a duration of time."

> We waited for *some time* before calling your parents.

Sometime means "at an unknown or unspecified time."

> We will visit with you *sometime*.

Sometimes means "occasionally (at unspecified times)."

> He *sometimes* visits his mother.

sort of/kind of (See **kind of/sort of**.)

source materials (See **Research Processes**.)

source

A source is the written, spoken, or illustrated original from which words, ideas, and images are quoted or otherwise used. A *primary source* is the work of the original writer, speaker, or artist him or herself, for example, Plato's *Republic*. A secondary source is the original author's work rewritten or recast by someone else, for example, an article written by a later philosopher in which parts of Plato's *Republic* are quoted and discussed. It is extremely important for writers to acknowledge all sources used in their work by means of appropriate citations. (See **Research Processes**, pages 29–34.)

spatial method of development

In a spatial sequence, you describe something according to the physical arrangement of its features. Depending on the subject, you may describe the features from far to near, top to bottom, side to side, east to west, inside to outside—and there are other possibilities. The spatial method of development is commonly used in descriptions, such as this one of the view from the Panamint Mountains above Death Valley.

> I stand by the cairn on the summit of Telescope Peak, looking out on a cold, windy, and barren world. Rugged peaks fall off southward into the haze of the Mojave Desert; on the west is Panamint Valley, the Argus Range, more mountains, more valleys, and finally the Sierras, crowned with snow; to the north and northwest the Inyo and White mountains; below lies Death Valley—the chemical desert—and east of it the Black Mountains, the Funeral Mountains, the Amargosa Valley and farther mountains, wave after wave of wrinkled ridges standing up from the oceanic desert sea until vision gives out somewhere beyond the curving rim of the world's edge. A smudge hangs on the eastern horizon, suggesting the presence of Death Valley's counterpart and complement, the only city within 100 miles: Las Vegas: Glitter Gulch West.
>
> —EDWARD ABBEY, "Death Valley"

speaker (See **persona**.)

specific words (See **general words/specific words** and **abstract words/concrete words**.)

spelling

(*continued*)

Always proofread your writing for misspelling. (For tips on proofreading, see **Composing Processes**, pages 20–21.) If you are writing with a computer, use the spell checker, but do not rely on it alone; it cannot catch one word substituted for another (*there* instead of *their*) or a typo that is a word (*form* instead of *from*).

You can improve your spelling by learning a few basic rules (some of them follow) and by being alert for commonly misspelled words (some are listed in a section that follows). Mnemonic (pronounced knee-mahn′-ik) devices, or memory aids, can also help you remember frequently misspelled words. For example, the phrase "your princi*pal* is your *pal*" can help you decide whether to use *principle* or *principal*. But rules always have exceptions, and memories are fallible; whenever you doubt the spelling of a word, consult a **dictionary**.

ei versus *ie*

The best way to decide whether to spell a word with *ei* or *ie* is to apply the old rule "*i* before *e* except after *c* or when pronounced 'ay' as in *neighbor* and *weigh*."

i before *e*	believe, chief, grieve, niece, piece, thief
e before *i* after *c*	ceiling, conceive, deceive, receive
e before *i* pronounced "ay"	beige, eight, freight, sleigh

EXCEPTIONS: foreign, forfeit, height, leisure, seize, weird

Adding Prefixes

When you add a **prefix** (such as *dis-*, *mis-*, *re-*, or *un-*), do not change the spelling of the root word. (For guidelines about using a hyphen after a prefix, see **hyphens**.)

disagree	misspell	reelect (*or* re-elect)	unnecessary
dissolve	misstatement	realign	underrated

S

Adding Suffixes

Words That End with a Silent -e   If the suffix begins with a vowel, drop the
-*e*. EXCEPTION: If the -*e* is preceded by a soft *c* or *g*, retain the -*e* before
-*able*, -*ance*, or -*ous* to keep the *c* or *g* soft.

care, caring	dense, density
notice, noticeable	courage, courageous

If the suffix begins with a consonant, keep the -*e* unless it is preceded by a
vowel.

care, careful	dense, denseness
argue, argument	true, truly

EXCEPTIONS: judgment, acknowledgment, ninth, wholly

Words That End with a Consonant   Double the final consonant before a suffix that begins with a vowel if the consonant is preceded by a vowel and if
it ends a one-syllable word or a stressed syllable. Do not double the final
consonant if it is preceded by two vowels or if the stress is not on the syllable
ended by the consonant.

plan, planned   tip, tipping   omit, omitted   occur, occurrence

BUT   repeat, repeated [Two vowels precede the *t*.]
          refer, reference [Stress has moved to the first syllable.]

Forming Plurals

Nouns   For most nouns, add -*s* to the singular form.

year, years   friend, friends

Add -*es* to nouns ending in -*s*, -*z*, -*x*, -*ch*, and -*sh*.

box, boxes	business, businesses	church, churches
buzz, buzzes	wish, wishes	

Most nouns that end in a consonant plus -*y* are made plural by changing
the -*y* to -*ies*. Most nouns that end in a vowel plus -*y* are made plural by
adding -*s*.

delivery, deliveries   monkey, monkeys

Most nouns that end in a consonant plus -*o* are made plural by adding -*es*.
Most nouns that end in a vowel plus -*o* are made plural by adding -*s*.

tomato, tomatoes	zero, zeroes	(*but* auto, autos)
radio, radios	video, videos	

Most nouns that end in *-fe* are made plural by changing *-fe* to *-ves*.

life, lives   knife, knives

A few nouns become plural with a change in spelling rather than the addition of *-s*.

woman, women   mouse, mice   goose, geese

A few nouns do not change in the plural.

fish   sheep

Compound nouns usually form the plural in the main word.

son-in-law, sons-in-law   passerby, passersby

If you are not sure of the plural form of a word, look it up in a **dictionary**, which will show the plural if it is irregular.

Numbers, Letters, Symbols, and Words Used as Words   The plurals of numbers, letters, symbols, and words used as words can be formed with either *-'s* or *-s* (but be consistent). The **apostrophe** is necessary, however, to form plurals that might be misread with only an *-s*—for example, the plurals of lowercase letters, of abbreviations that end in a period, and of *A*, *I*, and *U* (each of which forms a word when *-s* is added). Note that letters, numbers, and words used as words are italicized (or underlined), but the apostrophe and the *-s* are not.

three *10*s (or *10*'s)   all *A*'s   *&*s (or *&*'s)
three *very*s   I.D.'s

Frequently Misspelled Words

The following words are often misspelled. When in doubt, consult this list.

A   absence
accept
accidentally
accommodate
accomplish
accuracy
achievement
acquaintance
acquire
across
address

adolescent
affect
against
all right
almost
a lot
although
altogether
always
amateur
among

analyze
annual
answer
apology
apparent
appearance
appropriate
approximately
arctic
argument
ascend

aspirin
assassination
association
athlete
athletics
attendance
audience
average
awkward

B bachelor
bargain
basically
beginning
believe
benefited
brilliant
Britain
bureaucracy
burglar
business

C cafeteria
calendar
candidate
category
ceiling
cemetery
certain
changeable
changing
characteristic
chief
chocolate
chosen
column
coming
commitment
committed
committee
comparative
competition
conceivable
condemn
conscience

conscientious
conscious
consistency
convenient
counterfeit
courteous
criticism
criticize
curiosity

D dealt
deceive
decision
definitely
dependent
descend
describe
description
desirable
despair
desperate
develop
dictionary
different
dilemma
dining
disagree
disappearance
disappoint
disastrous
discipline
disease
dissatisfied

E efficiency
eighth
eligible
eliminate
embarrass
emphasize
entirely
environment
equivalent
exaggerate
excellent

exercise
exhaust
existence
experience
explanation
extraordinary
extremely

F familiar
fascinate
February
finally
foreign
forty
fourth
friend

G gauge
government
grammar
grief
guaranteed
guard
guidance

H harass
height
heroes
humorous
hypocrisy

I illiterate
imaginary
immediately
incidentally
incredible
independent
indispensable
inevitable
infinite
innocence
intelligence
interest
interrupt
irrelevant
irresistible

S

K knowledge

L laboratory
   legitimate
   library
   license
   lightning
   literature
   loneliness
   lose

M maintenance
   maneuver
   marriage
   mathematics
   medicine
   miniature
   mischievous
   muscle

N necessary
   nickel
   niece
   ninety
   ninth
   noticeable
   nuclear
   nuisance

O occasion
   occur
   occurred
   occurrence
   optimistic
   original
   outrageous

P pamphlet
   parallel
   particular
   pastime
   performance
   physical
   physician
   pleasant
   poison
   possess

practically
prairie
precede
preference
preferred
prejudice
preparation
privilege
probably
proceed
professor
prominent
pronunciation
psychology
publicly
pumpkin
pursue

Q quantity
   quiet
   quite
   quizzes

R receipt
   receive
   recognize
   recommend
   reference
   referred
   regular
   repetition
   restaurant
   rhythm
   ridiculous
   roommate

S safety
   salary
   sandwich
   schedule
   secretary
   seize
   sense
   separate
   sergeant
   siege

similar
since
sincerely
skiing
sophomore
specimen
strength
strict
succeed
successful
summary
surprise

T temperature
   therefore
   thorough
   through
   tomorrow
   tragedy
   transferred
   tries
   truly
   Tuesday
   twelfth

U unanimous
   unnecessary
   until
   usually

V vacuum
   vegetable
   vengeance
   villain

W Wednesday
   weird
   where
   whether
   wintry
   withdrawal
   without
   woman
   wreck
   writing

Y yield

Homonyms and Frequently Confused Words

A common source of misspelling is words that are pronounced the same (or almost the same) but have different meanings and spellings. The pairs in the following list are some of those most often confused. (The pairs in bold italic type are discussed, with examples, in their own entry.)

A *accept* (to receive)
   except (other than)

   access (means of entry or use)
   excess (too much)

   adapt (to modify)
   adept (skillful)
   adopt (to choose)

   adverse (unfavorable)
   averse (unwilling)

   advice (suggestion)
   advise (to counsel)

   affect (to influence)
   effect (consequence)

   alley (narrow street)
   ally (friend)

   allude (to refer to indirectly)
   elude (to avoid)

   allusion (indirect reference)
   illusion (fantasy)

   already (before)
   all ready (prepared)

   altar (sacred platform)
   alter (to change)

   altogether (completely)
   all together (as a group)

   anyone (any person at all)
   any one (a single member of a
        group)

   are (plural form of verb *to be*)
   our (belonging to us)

   ascent (going up)
   assent (agreement, approval)

   awhile (for a short time)
   a while (a short time)

B bare (unclothed)
   bear (a large animal; to carry)

   board (piece of wood)
   bored (uninterested)

   born (given birth to)
   borne (carried)

   brake (to stop)
   break (to destroy)

   breath (air inhaled or exhaled)
   breathe (to inhale and exhale)

   buy (to purchase)
   by (near)

C *capital* (center of government)
   capitol (legislative building)

   carat (unit of weight for precious
        stones)
   caret (insertion mark)
   carrot (orange root vegetable)
   karat (unit of measure for gold)

   casual (informal)
   causal (related to the origin of)

   censor (to limit expression)
   censure (strong disapproval)

   choose (to select)
   chose (selected)

   cite (to refer to an authority)
   sight (view)
   site (location)

   climactic (related to a climax,
        a finish)
   climatic (related to the
        weather)

   cloth (fabric)
   clothe (to put clothing on)

S

coarse (rough)
course (route, program of study)

complement (to go with)
compliment (to flatter)

conscience (sense of right and wrong)
conscious (aware)

continual (repeated at intervals)
continuous (uninterrupted)

council (group of advisors)
counsel (advice; to advise)

currant (small berry)
current (recent; flow)

D dairy (place where milk products are processed)
diary (personal journal)

decent (proper)
descent (downward slope; ancestry)

desert (dry, sandy region; to abandon)
dessert (sweet dish at end of meal)

device (instrument)
devise (to invent)

die (to cease to live)
dye (to color)

discreet (cautious, modest)
discrete (disconnected)

dominate (to rule over or control)
dominant (controlling, most widespread)

dual (double)
duel (combat between two people or groups)

E *elicit* (to call for, to evoke)
illicit (illegal)

emigrate (to leave a place)
immigrate (to move to a place)

eminent (famous)
imminent (about to happen)
immanent (inherent)

envelop (to cover, to encircle)
envelope (paper container for a letter)

everyday (ordinary)
every day (each day)

explicit (expressed openly)
implicit (suggested)

F fair (just; an exhibition)
fare (fee)

farther (at greater physical distance)
further (additionally)

faze (to unnerve, to disconcert)
phase (stage of development)

flare (to break out, to extend)
flair (talent, aptitude)

foreword (front matter in a book)
forward (ahead)

formally (officially)
formerly (once)

forth (ahead)
fourth (one of four parts)

G gorilla (large ape)
guerrilla (resistance fighter)

grate (to shred; to irritate)
great (large, outstanding)

H hear (to sense with one's ears)
here (in this spot)

heard (past tense of verb *to hear*)
herd (group of animals)

heroine (female hero)
heroin (illegal drug)

hoarse (losing one's voice)
horse (four-legged animal)

hole (excavation, opening)
whole (complete)

human (person)
humane (kind, compassionate)

I   immoral (wicked)
    amoral (neither moral nor
        immoral)
    ingenious (clever)
    ingenuous (naïve)
    insure (to guarantee life or
        property)
    ensure (to make certain)
    assure (to promise or convince)
    its (belonging to it)
    it's (contraction of *it is*)

K   know (to understand, to be
        familiar with)
    no (opposite of *yes*)

L   *later* (at a future time)
    latter (the second of two
        mentioned)
    lead (metallic element; to direct,
        to guide)
    led (past tense of verb *to lead*)
    loose (unconfined, free)
    lose (to misplace)

M   manner (style)
    manor (mansion)
    marshal (military or judicial officer)
    martial (warlike)
    marital (relating to marriage)
    maybe (perhaps)
    may be (might be)
    meat (animal flesh)
    meet (to encounter)
    moral (ethical, principled)
    morale (spirits, motivation)

N   naval (relating to the navy)
    navel (belly button)

P   pair (two)
    pare (to shave, to peel)
    pear (fruit)
    passed (past tense of verb *to pass*)
    past (gone, finished)

patience (composure,
    perseverance)
patients (people receiving medical
    treatment)
peace (absence of war)
piece (part, component)
pedal (foot-operated lever)
peddle (to sell door to door)
persecute (to torment, to abuse)
prosecute (to bring to trial)
personal (individual, private)
personnel (staff)
perspective (viewpoint)
prospective (in the near future)
plain (simple, unadorned;
    grassland)
plane (airborne vehicle; to make
    level)
populace (population)
populous (full of people)
pray (to say a prayer)
prey (an animal hunted for
    food)
precede (to go before)
proceed (to continue)
predominant (having greatest
    importance)
predominate (to be in the
    majority)
prescribe (to instruct, to order
    the use of)
proscribe (to forbid)
presence (closeness; dignity)
presents (gifts)
principal (head of a school; most
    important)
principle (moral standard)
prophecy (prediction)
prophesy (to predict the future)

Q   quiet (still, not noisy)
    quite (almost)

S

R rain (precipitation)
rein (leather strap used to guide a horse)
reign (to rule)

raise (to elevate)
raze (to tear down)

right (correct; the opposite of *left*)
rite (ceremony)
write (to form words on paper)

road (street)
rode (past tense of verb *to ride*)

S scene (view)
seen (past tense of verb *to see*)

sense (meaning; awareness)
since (from then until now)
cents (units of money)

shown (past tense of verb *to show*)
shone (past tense of verb *to shine*)

stationary (not moving)
stationery (paper for correspondence)

straight (direct; not bent)
strait (channel; confined)

suit (matching jacket and trousers or skirt)
suite (group of rooms)

T *than* (conjunction used in comparisons)
then (at that time)

their (belonging to them)
there (at or in that place)
they're (contraction of *they are*)

thorough (complete)
through (across; finished)
threw (past tense of verb *to throw*)
through (across; finished)

to (preposition indicating direction)
too (also)
two (one plus one)

track (path, course)
tract (an expanse of land; a system of organs)

W waist (the middle of the body)
waste (garbage; to consume carelessly)

weak (not strong)
week (seven days)

wear (to cover oneself with clothing)
were (past tense of verb *to be*)
where (adverb or conjunction indicating place)

weather (atmospheric conditions)
whether (conjunction indicating an alternative)

which (relative pronoun)
witch (person with supernatural powers)

who's (contraction of *who is*)
whose (belonging to whom)

Y *your* (belonging to you)
you're (contraction of *you are*)

American English Spelling

People who first learned British or Canadian English need to take special care to use American English spelling when writing for an audience in the United States. The following list summarizes some of the most common differences between American English and British English spelling.

AMERICAN ENGLISH	BRITISH ENGLISH
center, fiber, theater	centre, fibre, theatre
color, honor, labor	colour, honour, labour
defense, offense	defence, offence
encyclopedia, medieval	encyclopaedia, mediaeval
enroll, fulfill	enrol, fulfil
civilization, organize	civilisation, organise

split infinitives

A split infinitive has an adverb or an adverbial phrase between the sign of the infinitive, *to,* and the **infinitive** itself. A modifier, especially a long one, between the two words can often be awkward; in most cases, it is preferable not to split an infinitive.

He planned *to* ~~as soon as possible~~ *complete* the forms. *as soon as possible*

Sometimes, however, splitting an infinitive is necessary to prevent awkwardness or ambiguity. Compare the following sentences.

He opened the envelope unexpectedly *to find* the missing papers. [*Unexpectedly* seems to modify *opened* rather than *find.*]

He opened the envelope *to find* unexpectedly the missing papers. [This sentence is awkward.]

He opened the envelope *to* unexpectedly *find* the missing papers. [In this case, splitting the infinitive is the least awkward way to modify *find.*]

squinting modifiers

A modifier squints when it can be interpreted as modifying either the sentence element before it or the one after it.

The mob that had gathered *immediately* stormed the jail. [Had the mob gathered immediately, or did it immediately storm the jail?]

A squinting modifier (which is a type of **misplaced modifier**) can sometimes be corrected simply by changing its position, but recasting the sentence is often the best solution.

The mob that had gathered stormed the jail immediately.

The mob that had immediately gathered stormed the jail.

A mob immediately gathered and stormed the jail.

(See also **dangling modifiers** and **misplaced modifiers**.)

S

standard English

Standard English is the language of business, industry, government, education, and the professions. (See also **English, varieties of.**)

stanza

A stanza in a poem often fulfills the same function as a **paragraph** in a work of prose: it is a series of lines related to the same concept or idea. A stanza may also be used to summarize, to emphasize a point, or to serve as a transition between two related stanzas.

strong verbs

Strong verbs are concrete and specific (such as *amble, caress, shriek*), and they make sentences more interesting and less wordy than weak verbs (such as *is, has, do*). (See also **abstract words/concrete words, conciseness/wordiness,** and **general words/specific words.**)

style   (See **informal and formal writing style.**)

style manuals   (See **Research Processes.**)

subject complements

A subject complement is a word or word group that describes or renames the **subject** of a sentence. It follows a **linking verb** in the **predicate**. When the subject complement is a **noun**, it is called a **predicate nominative**. When it is an **adjective**, it is called a **predicate adjective**.

> This milk tastes *sour.* [adjective]
> She is my *lawyer.* [noun]
> This book is *a best-selling historical novel.* [noun phrase]
> His excuse was *that he had been sick.* [noun clause]

subject directory

Subject directories are search tools with smaller and more selective databases than those of **search engines**. Their links are selected by librarians and subject experts rather than by computer programs. (For a list of subject directories, see **Research Processes,** pages 58–59.)

subject heading

Subject headings are the search terms used to search for books and periodical articles on a topic. The principal source for subject headings for books is the *Library of Congress Subject Headings* directory. Libraries use it to catalog their books. Indexes of periodical articles, such as the *Readers' Guide to Periodical Literature*, contain lists of subject headings that they use. (See **Research Processes**, pages 41–42.)

subjective case

The subjective case (also called the *nominative case*) is used to refer to the person or thing acting. **Subjects** of verbs and **subject complements** are in the subjective case.

> *She* called Jennifer. [subject.]
>
> It was *she* who wrote the article. [subject complement]

(See also **case** and **pronouns**.)

subjects (grammatical)

The subject of a **sentence** or a **clause** is a **noun** or noun substitute (such as a phrase or clause) that names the doer of the action or identifies what the **predicate** is about. (See also **agreement of subjects and verbs**.)

> *We* often study late. [pronoun as subject]
>
> *To err* is human. [verbal phrase as subject]
>
> *That he will come* is doubtful. [noun clause as subject]

A **simple subject** is a noun or pronoun; a **complete subject** consists of the simple subject plus its modifiers.

> *The pines that we planted* have grown several inches. [The simple subject is *pines*; the complete subject is italicized.]

In imperative sentences, the subject, *you,* is usually understood.

> [*You*] Go to the store.

A missing or implied subject can cause a lack of **clarity**. (See also **dangling modifiers** and **faulty predication**.)

> *it was*
> She knew smoking was bad for her health, but until scorned by many of her friends,
> ∧
>
> she indulged in it.
>
> [Does *scorned* refer to *smoking* or to *her*?]

S

A sentence that does not have a noun (or noun equivalent) as a subject should have a **pronoun** as subject.

It is
"Byzantium" was written in 1932. ~~Is~~ one of Yeats's later poems.
            ∧

Do not use a subject pronoun, however, if the sentence already has a noun as the subject.

Marie Curie ~~she~~ made immeasurable contributions to the field of chemistry.

subjunctive mood

The subjunctive mood expresses something that is contrary to fact, conditional, or hypothetical; it can also express a wish, a doubt, or a possibility. Except for *be,* **verbs** have a distinctive subjunctive form only in the third-person singular of the present tense; the *-s* is dropped (that he *write,* that she *see*).

> Gary insisted that he *take* charge of the project. [subjunctive]
>
> BUT He always *takes* charge. [indicative]
>
> If I *were* ready, I would leave on Wednesday. [subjunctive of form of *be*]
>
> BUT I *am* ready, and I will leave on Wednesday. [indicative of form of *be*]

subordinate clauses (See **dependent clauses,**)

subordinating conjunctions

Subordinating conjunctions connect **dependent clauses** to **independent clauses.** The most frequently used subordinating conjunctions are the following:

after	before	since	until
although	even if	so that	when
as	even though	than	where
as if	if	that	whereas
as long as	in order that	though	whether
because	rather than	unless	while

subordination

To make your meaning clear to your audience, subordinate less important ideas by expressing them as **dependent clauses** or as **phrases** or words. For example, notice how the **emphasis** can be changed in the sentence "The report was carefully illustrated, and it covered five typed pages."

> The report, *which covered five typed pages,* was carefully illustrated. [Expressing the length of the report in a dependent clause makes it less important than the fact that the report is illustrated.]

> The report, *covering five typed pages,* was carefully illustrated. [A phrase subordinates the information about length even more than a dependent clause does.]

> The *five-page* report was carefully illustrated. [Expressing the length as a single modifier subordinates it still more.]

> The carefully illustrated report *covered five pages.* [A phrase subordinates the fact that the report is illustrated; the length is emphasized in the independent clause.]

Word order can also be used to subordinate or emphasize ideas. Words at the beginnings and ends of sentences receive more emphasis than those in the middle do.

Subordination Faults

Do not subordinate the main idea of a sentence in a dependent clause or phrase. Changing which clause is dependent or independent can change the message of a sentence.

> Although the new computer system saves money, many staff members are unhappy with it. [Because the savings, a benefit, is subordinated to the staff's complaints, this sentence is arguing *against* the new computer system.]

> Although many staff members are unhappy with it, the new computer system saves money. [This sentence, which subordinates the staff's complaints, is arguing *for* the new computer system.]

Do not overdo subordination. Too long a string of dependent clauses can confuse the audience, especially if relative pronouns do not have clear antecedents.

> *is a failure of the circulation that*
> Shock,/~~which~~ often accompanies severe injuries, severe infections, hemorrhages,
>   ∧
>
> burns, heat exhaustion, heart attacks, food or chemical poisoning, and some
>
>   *It*
> strokes,~~is a failure of the circulation, which~~ is marked by a fall in blood pressure
>   ∧
>   *causing*
> that initially affects the skin (~~which explains~~ pallor) and later the kidneys and
>   ∧
>
> brain.

Do not put so much detail into a dependent clause that it overshadows the main clause.

Because the noise level ~~on a typical street~~ in New York City ~~on a weekday~~ is ~~as~~
                          extremely high,
~~loud as an alarm clock ringing three feet away,~~ New Yorkers often have hearing
                                                  ∧

problems.

suffixes

A suffix consists of one or more letters or syllables added to the end of a word to change its meaning or grammatical function.

walk [singular]	walks [plural]	walk*ed* [past tense]
courage [noun]	courag*eous* [adjective]	courageous*ness* [noun]
practical [adjective]	practical*ly* [adverb]	practical*ity* [noun]

Common Suffixes

ESL learners can benefit from familiarity with suffixes and their functions. The following lists give some of the more common ones.

Noun-Forming Suffixes

PEOPLE

-ant, -ent (defendant, resident)   *-ian* (librarian, technician)
-ator (legislator, operator)   *-ist* (cyclist, typist)
-ee (employee, referee)   *-or* (actor, vendor)
-er (baker, teacher)

OBJECTS, SUBSTANCES

-ade (lemonade)   *-ode* (cathode, electrode)
-ene (benzene)   *-one* (silicone)
-ide (fluoride, oxide)   *-ose* (glucose, sucrose)
-ine (caffeine)   *-um* (aluminum, platinum)

STATES, CONDITIONS, SITUATIONS

-acy (democracy, privacy)   *-asm* (enthusiasm)
-al (arrival, renewal)   *-ation* (aspiration, beautification)
-ance (clearance, tolerance) *-ence* (eloquence, magnificence)

-*ency* (emergency, fluency)
-*hood* (childhood, motherhood)
-*ion* (election, fusion)
-*ism* (extremism, patriotism)
-*itis* (arthritis, tonsillitis)
-*ity* (humanity, legality)
-*ization* (civilization, mobilization)

-*ment* (development, movement)
-*ness* (greatness, illness)
-*ship* (hardship, kinship)
-*th* (depth, warmth)
-*tude* (gratitude, magnitude)
-*ure* (departure, disclosure)

PLACES

-*ary*, -*ery* (aviary, monastery)
-*ory* (dormitory, observatory)

-*um* (asylum, museum)

Adjective-Forming Suffixes

-*able* (manageable, treatable)
-*al* (comical, sentimental)
-*ant* (dominant, radiant)
-*ary* (contrary, solitary)
-*atic* (dramatic, operatic)
-*en* (ashen, golden)
-*ern* (western)
-*esque* (grotesque, picturesque)

-*etic* (pathetic, phonetic)
-*ial* (circumstantial, social)
-*ible* (edible, responsible)
-*ic* (civic, comic, tragic)
-*ical* (mythical, practical)
-*ine* (feminine, masculine)
-*ish* (greenish, selfish)
-*y* (rainy, sandy)

Verb-Forming Suffixes

-*ate* (accentuate, evaluate)
-*efy*, -*ify* (liquefy, purify)

-*en* (harden, sharpen)
-*ize* (humanize, rationalize)

summarizing

One of the most valuable skills you can develop, both as a reader and as a writer, is the ability to summarize. The basic technique of skillful classroom note takers, summarizing boils down, in your own words, something you have read or heard, putting it in the briefest form consistent with your purpose. It is a useful way not only to remember but also to analyze material. As summaries are in your own words, you do not need to use **quotation marks** (except for any expressions retained word for word from the original source). However, you must be careful not to pass off as your own any ideas you have gained from others; always give proper credit to your source, to avoid **plagiarism**. The only exception is factual information that is **common** knowledge. The line between common knowledge and specialized knowledge or opinion is not always clear, however. The best advice is to give credit if you are in doubt. (See also **paraphrasing** and **Research Processes**.)

The following example shows a quoted passage and then a summary of it.

ORIGINAL TEXT

One of the major visual cues used by pilots in maintaining precision ground reference during low-level flight is that of object blur. We are acquainted with the object-blur phenomenon experienced when driving an automobile. Objects in the foreground appear to be rushing toward us while objects in the background appear to recede slightly. There is a point in the observer's line of sight, however, at which objects appear to stand still for a moment, before once again rushing toward him with increasing angular velocity. The distance from the observer to this point is sometimes referred to as the "blur threshold" range.

— WESLEY E. WOODSON and DONALD W. CONOVER,
Human Engineering Guide for Equipment Designers

SUMMARY

In *Human Engineering Guide for Equipment Designers*, Wesley E. Woodson and Donald W. Conover explain that low-flying pilots use object blur and especially the "blur threshold" range as important visual cues (210).

superlative degree

The superlative form of **adjectives** and **adverbs** (made with the suffix *-est* or the adverb *most*) compares a person or thing with two or more others. (See also **comparative degree**.)

supposed to/suppose to

Suppose to is nonstandard usage for *supposed to*.

Jeff was ~~suppose~~ *supposed* to be home by 3:00 p.m.

sweeping generalizations   (See **logic**.)

syllabication   (See **hyphens**.)

syllogism   (See **logic**.)

symbolism

Symbolism is the use of a concrete object to represent or remind us of something else, usually an abstraction. For example, the American flag is a symbol of patriotism; the swastika is a symbol of Nazism, bigotry, and racism. In literature, authors often use symbolism. For example, Nathaniel Hawthorne uses a snake as a symbol of Satan, pink ribbons to symbolize purity, and a scarlet *A* to represent the shame of adultery. (See also **figures of speech.**)

symbols (See **numbers and symbols.**)

synonyms

A synonym is a word that means nearly the same thing as another word. For example, *avoid, shun,* and *evade* are synonyms. Although their basic definitions are the same, they differ in connotation. All three words mean "to get away or stay away from someone or something." However, *avoid* connotes keeping away from something or someone considered dangerous or difficult; *shun* connotes deliberately keeping away as a policy; *evade* connotes skillful maneuvering to avoid capture, and it can also imply dishonesty or irresponsibility.

Although a **thesaurus** is the basic reference book for synonyms, it does not define words or give their connotations. For the meanings of unfamiliar synonyms, you must consult a dictionary. Especially helpful are dictionaries that compare synonyms of selected words. (See also **connotation/denotation** and **word choice.**)

syntax

Syntax is the way that words, **phrases,** and **clauses** are combined to form sentences. (See also **sentence types.**)

S

tables

Tables present sets of data in columns (vertical) and rows (horizontal). The data may be words, numbers, or a combination of both. The columns are identified with column heads, and the columns and rows compare data from side to side rather than from top to bottom. Similar items of the table should be consistent in form. Parallel items should be expressed in parallel fashion. Comparable numbers should have the same number of decimal places.

Writers choose visual aids according to what each type does best. For example, a graph is a good way to represent numerical trends, and a table is a good way to compare stages concisely.

Following is an example of a table showing the stages of cognitive development in children.

Table 1 Piaget's Four Stages of Cognitive Development

Stage	Description
Sensorimotor (birth–2 years)	Infants' awareness of their world is limited to their senses, and their reactions to general action patterns, e.g., sucking, grasping, through which they incorporate their experiences.
Preoperational (2–7 years)	Children can use symbols such as words and images to think about things, but confuse the way things appear with the way they must be.
Concrete operational (7–11 years)	Thinking becomes more flexible, allowing children to consider several dimensions to things simultaneously, realizing that though an object may look different, it has not necessarily changed (conservation).
Formal operational (11 years–adulthood)	Thinking becomes abstract, embracing thought itself; adolescents can consider things that are only possible, as well as those that are real.

—NANCY COBB, *Adolescence: Continuity, Change, and Diversity*

Give each table a brief descriptive title (as in the example here), and refer to the table in the text (for example, "As Table 1 shows, children go through four stages of cognitive development").

tag questions

A tag question is an afterthought or a request for confirmation that occurs at the end of a sentence. Set off a tag question from the rest of the sentence with a **comma**. Tag questions are seldom used in formal writing.

486

You're coming to my party, *aren't you?*

You did get the invitation, *didn't you?*

In English, tag questions do not have a fixed form but instead vary according to the subject and the verb of the independent clause. If the tag question were put in the **indicative mood,** it would be an answer. Note also that if the independent clause is stated positively, the tag question is negative; but if the independent clause is negative, the tag question is positive.

The fifty-five-mile-per-hour speed limit makes sense, *doesn't it?* [Answer: *It does.*]

Last year was not a good one for England's royal family, *was it?* [Answer: *It was not.*]

take/bring

Use *bring* to refer to something coming toward you; use *take* to indicate something moving away.

Bring that new magazine along when you come over.

Please *take* out the trash.

tense

The tense of a **verb** indicates the time of the action. English has six tenses: three simple, or basic, tenses (present, past, and future) and three **perfect tenses** (present perfect, past perfect, and future perfect). Each of the six tenses has a **progressive verb form** (which combines the appropriate tense of *be* and the **present participle**) that indicates ongoing action. The following list gives the conjugation of regular verbs in the indicative mood. (For variations from this list, see **irregular verbs** and **subjunctive mood.**)

TENSE		PROGRESSIVE FORM
Simple Tenses		
Present	I start	I am starting
Past	I started	I was starting
Future	I will start	I will be starting
Perfect Tenses		
Present Perfect	I have started	I have been starting
Past Perfect	I had started	I had been starting
Future Perfect	I will have started	I will have been starting

T

Simple Tenses

Present Tense The simple present tense indicates an action or event occurring in the present, without any indication of time duration.

I *see* the stop sign.

The present tense also expresses habitual or recurring action and universal truths.

I *pass* the paint shop every day on the way to work.

Water *boils* at 212°F.

With an adverb or adverb phrase, the present tense can express the future.

The semester *ends* tomorrow.

The present tense is also used in writing about literature and fictional events. (See also **literary present**.)

Ishmael *is* the lone survivor of Captain Ahab's pursuit of Moby Dick.

Past Tense The simple past tense indicates an action or event that took place in the past. The past tense is usually formed by adding *-d* or *-ed* to the root form of the verb. (See also **irregular verbs**.)

We *closed* the office early yesterday.

Future Tense The simple future tense indicates an action or event that will occur after the present. It uses the helping verb *will* (or *shall*) plus the main verb.

I *will finish* the job tomorrow.

Perfect Tenses

Perfect tenses, which combine a form of *have* and the **past participle**, describe an action or event lasting until or completed at the time of another action or event.

Present Perfect Tense The present perfect tense describes a past action or event that is connected to the present; it is often used to indicate an action that is not yet completed or a situation that is still evident. It combines a form of the helping verb *have* with the past participle of the main verb.

I *have started* to write my term paper, and I will be working on it for the rest of the month.

Past Perfect Tense The past perfect tense indicates a past event or action that preceded another past event or action. It combines *had* with the past participle of the main verb.

> I *had started* to read the newspaper when the lights went out.

Future Perfect Tense The future perfect tense indicates an action or event that will be completed at the time of or before another future action or event. It combines *will have* and the past participle of the main verb.

> I *will have finished* the research by the time the library closes.

The simple future is often used instead of the future perfect.

> Joy *will finish* her painting by next weekend. [simple future]
>
> OR
>
> Joy *will have finished* her painting by next weekend. [future perfect]

than/then

Than is a conjunction used in comparisons; *then* is an adverb indicating something next in order of time.

> I would rather watch the NBA playoffs *than* the Super Bowl.
> Lily went to class, *then* to a meeting, and *then* to work.

that

Avoid unnecessary repetition of *that*.

> I think *that* when this project is finished ~~that~~ you should write up the results.
>
> OR
>
> When this project is finished, I think you should write up the results.

However, do not delete *that* if it is necessary to prevent even temporary ambiguity.

> *that*
> Quarreling means trying to show ∧ the other person is in the wrong.

(See also **conciseness/wordiness** and **relative pronouns**.)

T

that/which/who

In general, *who* refers to people, and *that* and *which* refer to animals and things. *That* may also be used to refer to an anonymous group of people ("I want to contribute to a group *that* saves dolphins").

> Professor Thomas, *who* is retiring tomorrow, has taught at the university for forty years.
>
> The whale *that* swam into the river was successfully returned to the ocean.
>
> The jet stream, *which* is approximately eight miles above the earth, blows at an average of sixty-four miles per hour from the west.

That is used with restrictive clauses, and *which* can be used with either restrictive or nonrestrictive clauses, although some writers prefer to use it only with nonrestrictive clauses. (See also **restrictive and nonrestrictive elements.**)

> After Peggy left the restaurant, *which* is one of the best in New York, she came directly to my office. [nonrestrictive]
>
> A restaurant *that* has reasonable prices usually succeeds. [restrictive]

(See also **who/whom** and **relative pronouns.**)

theme

The theme of a piece of literature can usually be summarized in a sentence describing the message it intends to convey. The theme of Thomas Kenneally's novel *Schindler's List* could be described as "how compassion masquerading as greed helped to fool the Nazis." Theme should not be confused with **plot**, which pertains to how the sequence of events in a literary work is structured to convey the theme. Usually, the term *theme* is used in reference to **literary analysis**; **thesis** is the analogous term used in reference to essays, articles, and other nonfiction.

themselves/theirself/theirselves

Theirself and *theirselves* are nonstandard usage for *themselves*.

> Those messy children ought to be ashamed of ~~theirselves.~~
>   *themselves*

there/their/they're

There is an **expletive** or an **adverb**.

> *There* were more than 1,500 people at the conference. [expletive]
>
> More than 1,500 people were *there*. [adverb]

Their is the **possessive** form of *they.*

> Our children are expected to keep *their* rooms neat.

They're is a **contraction** of *they are.*

> If *they're* messy children, they'll be messy adults.

thesaurus

A thesaurus is a book of **synonyms** and **antonyms,** arranged by categories or in alphabetical order. It can help you find the right word and clarify your meaning. Never use an unfamiliar word, however, without looking it up first in a dictionary to find out its **connotations.** The following books are three of the most readily available thesauruses.

> Rodale, J. L. *The Synonym Finder.*
> Roget, Peter M. *Roget's International Thesaurus.*
> *Webster's Collegiate Thesaurus.*

thesis

If you can state in a sentence what you want your audience to know or believe when they have read your writing, you have determined your **thesis.** A carefully conceived thesis statement can be helpful both to the writer, in deciding what to include and how to organize the paper, and to the audience, in following the paper's logic. Too often, beginning writers have difficulty phrasing and focusing their thesis. The following examples illustrate typical problems and ways to revise them:

1. *The thesis is too general.* The following initial statement suggests potential comparison to all areas of all games. Such a thesis could barely be covered in a book, let alone an essay.

CHANGE	Baseball is a great game.
TO	Baseball is superior to other professional sports because of its unique demands for strategy and execution.

2. *The thesis is too broad.* Even though the field has been narrowed to professional sports and specific skills, this is still too much information to cover in an essay.

CHANGE	Baseball is superior to other professional sports because of its unique demands for strategy and execution.
TO	Professional baseball players are superior to pro football players because of their knowledge of strategy and fine motor skills.

T

3. *The thesis is an announcement.* Once you have narrowed your topic, make sure your thesis states an opinion.

CHANGE   I want to tell you about the 1995 World Series.

TO   The 1995 World Series was the best entertainment since the 1990 series.

4. *The thesis is not argumentative.* For argumentative papers, your thesis must be not only narrow and specific but also controversial.

CHANGE   The Cincinnati Reds were clearly the better team in the 1990 World Series.

TO   The Reds were able to win the 1990 World Series because they got rid of Pete Rose.

5. *The thesis is a fact.* Even if a fact is controversial, it must be stated as an opinion. Although the initial statement that follows might raise controversy, it is a fact, not an argument, that the Reds won.

CHANGE   The Cincinnati Reds were clearly the better team in the 1990 World Series.

TO   The Reds won the 1990 World Series because of superior pitching, not because of bad calls by the umpires.

Where should you state your thesis? Although the thesis statement is most often located in an essay's introduction, its placement depends in large part on your purpose and your audience. If you are writing a descriptive essay, the thesis may come as early as the end of the introduction or as late as the concluding paragraph. If you are answering an **essay examination** question, a thesis is most effective in the first line or first paragraph. However, for other kinds of papers, you may want to begin with an engaging **introduction** and save the thesis until the end of the first or second paragraph. If you are writing an argument, the placement of the thesis depends on your audience's point of view. If you know that readers are likely to disagree with your thesis, you may find it wise to defer stating it until after you have built up supporting evidence. Whatever your readers' stance, as a rule, the thesis should stand out clearly. Skilled writers sometimes imply their thesis throughout a paper but do not specifically state it; however, you should use this strategy sparingly: Unless you are careful, your audience may simply be baffled.

Wherever you state your thesis, you need to develop it in the body of the paper. Your **method of development**—how you organize the paper—will depend on your subject and purpose.

See also **Composing Processes.**

title page (See **Research Processes,** pages 87, 112–13, 131–32, 147.)

titles

Like a **thesis**, a good title can help you shape your paper and help your audience know what to expect. Ideally, a title should capture the reader's interest as well as provide focus. Here are two examples of such titles, followed by the beginnings of the essays they head:

The Purple Martin—Birds of Our Feather?

Darwinians or not, we know that sometimes people mimic the behavior of lower animals. People may act like snakes in the grass or wolves in sheep's clothing, may be as proud as peacocks, as dumb as turkeys, or as stubborn as mules.

I'm convinced, however, that there is another side of the coin: some animals act like people. Consider the purple martin, our largest swallow. Since childhood I've closely observed the lifestyle of the purple martin, and I am amazed at the many ways its behavior resembles ours. . . .

—BUCK STROBECK

Heat on the Hoof

As fuel costs continue to spiral upward, the householder must continue searching for a reasonable and effective means of heating an establishment. Solar, or "passive," heating and woodburning stoves are popular alternatives to oil- and coal-burning systems; however, no discussion of modern heating methods would be complete without mention of the horse.

Horses may be used in a variety of ways as heating units. All of these are simpler than existing mechanical methods, and surprisingly effective. The average 1,200-pound horse has a caloric production rate of 600 therms per minute, and double that if the horse is angry or unsettled. The fuel-calorie conversion rate is extremely favorable, being about one to eight, which means that the standard four-bedroom house, with snacking center and media room, can be heated by one healthy horse and eight bales of hay per week; an appealing statistic and a soothing prospect. . . .

—ROXANNA BARRY

The most important requirements for a title, however, are clarity and relevance. Avoid titles that are too broad or too long.

CHANGE   The Purple Martin—Our Domestic Wonder [too broad]
TO   The Purple Martin—Birds of Our Feather?

CHANGE   An Introduction to Making Music with the Irish Bagpipes [long]
TO   Learning the Irish Bagpipes

Sometimes the best title will not occur to you until late in the writing process, perhaps not even until you have finished revising and editing. However, if you can think of an appropriate title early on (you can always revise it later), you will find that it helps keep you on course as you write.

Titles should stand alone. Do not refer to your title in the opening sentence of your paper as if it were a part of the text:

CHANGE   Learning the Irish Bagpipes
                      It's not as difficult as you may think. Start by . . .

TO   Learning the Irish Bagpipes
                      Learning to play the Irish bagpipes is not as difficult as you may think. Start by . . .

See also **Composing Processes.** For information about format and capitalization of titles in research papers, see **Research Processes.**

to/too/two

To is used as a **preposition** or as the mark of an **infinitive.**

Send the grocery bill *to* the caterer. [preposition]

I wish *to* go. [mark of the infinitive]

Too is an **adverb** meaning "excessively" or "also."

The price was *too* high. ["excessively"]

I, *too,* thought it was high. ["also"]

Two is a number.

The farm is *two* miles out of town.

tone

Tone reflects the writer's attitude toward the subject and especially toward the audience. (See also **informal and formal writing style** and **English, varieties of.**) Familiar tone is used when you are writing to yourself or to someone you know well; it is characterized by use of **slang**, colloquial language, **sentence fragments**, and **contractions.** Informal tone is found in casual conversations, in the media, and in many contemporary novels, plays, and films. Formal tone is appropriate for most business and academic writing; it is characterized by avoidance of **colloquial** expressions and by careful adherence to grammatical rules and conventions. In the following excerpt, note the differences between the familiar tone of the joke and the formal tone of the paragraph that follows it.

A joke floating around the Internet:
Q: How many Internet contributors does it take to change a lightbulb?
A: What are you trying to say, you worthless, scumbag jerk?
Computer networks are increasingly hyped as a new medium of virtuous democratic and social discourse, the cyber-version of the Acropolis. A *Time* magazine

reviewer recently called the Internet "the ultimate salon" of conversation, and *The Utne Reader* is promising "electronic salons" to soothe the anomie and coarseness of contemporary life. Author Howard Rheingold has celebrated the "virtual community" as a source of solace and fraternity, and columnist David Broder has written paeans to the new spirit of civic participation allegedly found on computer networks.

—GARY CHAPMAN, "Flamers"

In literary works, the tone may also be comic, satirical, ironic, or tragic, depending on the atmosphere the author wants to create and the message he or she intends to convey through **word choice** and **figures of speech**. Here is an example from a memoir of satirical tone (and very informal style):

> There's a sore at the top of my nose between my eyebrows, gray and red and itching. Grandma says, Don't touch that sore and don't put water near it or it'll spread. If you broke your arm she'd say don't touch that with water it'll spread.
>
> —FRANK MCCOURT, *Angela's Ashes*

topic

The topic of a writing project is its subject, usefully narrowed. A topic, however, is not the same as a **thesis**, which is the particular position the writer is taking on the topic. For information on choosing and narrowing a topic, see **Composing Processes** and **Research Processes**.

topic sentences

A topic sentence reveals the main idea of a **paragraph**. Other sentences in the paragraph serve to clarify, develop, and illustrate that idea. Usually, the topic sentence is most effective when presented as the first sentence, but it may have any position in the paragraph. Furthermore, the topic sentence may actually be more than one sentence.

In the first paragraph of the example that follows, the topic sentence is the first sentence, stating the subject. However, a paragraph can also lead up to the topic sentence (or sentences, as in the second paragraph). When a topic sentence concludes a paragraph, it receives extra **emphasis** and can also serve as a summary or **conclusion**.

> *The fearsomeness mistakenly attributed to me in public places often has a perilous flavor.* The most frightening of these confusions occurred in the late 1970s and early 1980s when I worked as a journalist in Chicago. One day, rushing into the office of a magazine I was writing for with a deadline story in hand, I was mistaken for a burglar. The office manager called security and, with an ad hoc posse, pursued me through the labyrinthine halls, nearly to my editor's door. I had no way of proving who I was. I could only move briskly toward the company of someone who knew me.

T

Another time I was on assignment for a local paper and killing time before an interview. I entered a jewelry store on the city's affluent Near North Side. The proprietor excused herself and returned with an enormous red Doberman pinscher straining at the end of a leash. She stood, the dog extended toward me, silent to my questions, her eyes bulging nearly out of her head. I took a cursory look around, nodded, and bade her good night. Relatively speaking, however, I never fared as badly as another black male journalist. He went to nearby Waukegan, Illinois, a couple of summers ago to work on a story about a murderer who was born there. Mistaking the reporter for the killer, police hauled him from his car at gunpoint and but for his press credentials would probably have tried to book him. *Such episodes are not uncommon. Black men trade tales like this all the time.*

—BRENT STAPLES, "Just Walk on By: A Black Man Ponders His Power to Alter Public Space"

The topic sentence may also be placed near the middle of a paragraph, as in this example:

The British, in their splendid isolation, used to regard foreigners as either a comic turn or a sexual menace. To learn a European language—apart from the dead ones from which English had kindly borrowed—was, at best, to seek to acquire a sort of girl's-finishing-school ornament, at worst, to capitulate feebly to the enemy. *Things are slightly different now: an uneasy awareness is dawning that linguistic isolation is no longer possible, that the languages of these damned Europeans may have to be taken seriously if they persist in pretending not to understand English.* Unfortunately, many educated Europeans do understand English, sometimes better than the British, and are very ready to speak it to British tourists and write it to British business firms, thus soothing that uneasy awareness back into insular complacency. But, in their soberest moments, most Anglophones will admit that the attitude of "Let them learn our language, blast them" will not really do.

—ANTHONY BURGESS, *A Mouthful of Air*

Occasionally, a single topic sentence controls two or more paragraphs, or the controlling idea is implied rather than explicitly stated. However, in general, you are well advised to make topic sentences explicit.

toward/towards

Both *toward* and *towards* are acceptable, although *toward* is generally preferred in the United States. Use one or the other consistently in your writing.

transitions

Transitions link and clarify the relationship of what has been said and what will be said. They may link sentence parts, whole sentences, paragraphs, or larger units or sections. A transition may be made with a word, a phrase, a sentence, or even a paragraph. Clear transitions are essential to the **coherence** of paragraphs and of compositions.

Transitional Words and Phrases

The following two paragraphs illustrate how transitional expressions can clarify and smooth the movement from idea to idea. The first paragraph lacks transitional words and phrases; the second paragraph contains them (printed here in italics).

> People had always hoped to fly. Until 1903 it was only a dream. Some thought that human beings weren't meant to fly. The Wright brothers launched the world's first heavier-than-air flying machine. The airplane has become a part of our everyday life.

> People had always hoped to fly, *but* until 1903 it was only a dream. *Before that time,* some thought that human beings were not meant to fly. *However, in 1903* the Wright brothers launched the world's first heavier-than-air flying machine. *Since then,* the airplane has become a part of our everyday life.

COMMON TRANSITIONAL WORDS AND PHRASES

- *Addition and sequence:* again, also, besides, even more important, finally, first, further, furthermore, in addition, in the first place, last, likewise, moreover, next, second, then, third, too
- *Cause and effect:* accordingly, as a result, because, consequently, for, for this reason, hence, so, then, therefore, thus
- *Comparison:* also, in the same way, likewise, similarly
- *Contrast:* although, at the same time, but, conversely, even so, however, in contrast, nevertheless, nonetheless, notwithstanding, on the contrary, otherwise, still, yet
- *Example:* for example, for instance, in fact, indeed, of course, specifically, that is, to illustrate
- *Place:* above, adjacent to, below, beyond, farther on, here, nearby, on the other side, opposite to, there, to the south
- *Purpose:* for this purpose, for this reason, to this end, with this object
- *Summary or conclusion:* as I have said, consequently, in any event, in brief, in conclusion, in other words, in short, in summary, to sum up, on the whole, that is, therefore
- *Time:* after, afterward, at length, before, earlier, immediately, in the meantime, in the past, later, meanwhile, now, since, soon, then, until then, while

---

T

Repetition, Pronouns, and Parallel Structure

In addition to using transitional words and phrases, you can link sentences by using **pronouns,** by repeating key words or ideas, and by using phrases or clauses with **parallel structure.** Notice in the following selection the repetition of the pronoun *it,* which refers to the civil rights movement. Most of the sentences begin with the words "It gave us," and nearly all the sentences are parallel in structure: *it*—verb—indirect object—direct object. In addition, the chain of the related words *living, lives, life,* and *live* not only provides coherence but also emphasizes the ongoing legacy of the civil rights movement.

> If the Civil Rights Movement is "dead," and if it gave us nothing else, it gave us each other forever. It gave some of us bread, some of us shelter, some of us knowledge and pride, all of us comfort. It gave us our children, our husbands, our brothers, our fathers, as men reborn and with a purpose for living. It broke the pattern of black servitude in this country. It shattered the phony "promise" of white soap operas that sucked away so many pitiful lives. It gave us history and men far greater than Presidents. It gave us heroes, selfless men of courage and strength, for our little boys and girls to follow. It gave us hope for tomorrow. It called us to life.
>
> Because we live, it can never die.
>
> —ALICE WALKER, "The Civil Rights Movement: What Good Was It?"

Transitions between Paragraphs

All the means discussed previously for achieving transition between sentences—especially the repetition of key words or ideas—can be used for transition between paragraphs. However, longer transitional elements can be used as well. One technique is to begin a paragraph by summarizing the preceding paragraph, as is done in the italicized sentence at the beginning of the second paragraph that follows.

> From the very beginning of his illness, ever since he had first been to see the doctor, Ivan Ilych's life had been divided between two contrary and alternating moods: now it was despair and the expectation of this uncomprehended and terrible death, and now hope and an intently interpreted observation of the functioning of his organs. Now before his eyes there was only a kidney or an intestine that temporarily evaded its duty, and now only that incomprehensible and dreadful death from which it was impossible to escape.
>
> *These two states of mind had alternated from the very beginning of his illness,* but the further it progressed the more doubtful and fantastic became the conception of the kidney, the more real the sense of impending death.
>
> —LEO TOLSTOY, *The Death of Ivan Ilych*

Another technique for transition between paragraphs is to ask a question at the end of one paragraph and answer it at the beginning of the next. In the following selection, Pat Mora asks a question in two successive paragraphs and answers it in the third.

> Your mother tells me that you have begun writing poems and that you wonder exactly how I do it. *Do you perhaps wonder why I do it? Why would anyone sit alone and write when she could be talking to friends on the telephone, eating mint chocolate chip ice-cream in front of the television, or buying a new red sweater at the mall?*
>
> And, as you know, I like people. I like long, slow lunches with my friends. I like to dance. I'm no hermit, and I'm not shy. *So why do I sit with my tablet and pen and mutter to myself?*
>
> *There are many answers.* I write because I'm a reader. I want to give to others what writers have given me, a chance to hear the voice of people I will never meet. Alone, in private. And even if I meet these authors, I wouldn't hear what I hear along with the page, words carefully chosen, woven into a piece unlike any other, enjoyed by me in a way no other person will, in quite the same way, enjoy them. I suppose I'm saying that I love the privateness of writing and reading. It's delicious to curl into a book.
>
> —Pat Mora, "A Letter to Gabriela, a Young Writer"

transitive verbs

Transitive verbs are **verbs** that require a **direct object** to complete their meaning.

> Willa *sent* the package [direct object] yesterday.
>
> Marc *bought* two tickets [direct object] to the concert.

However, when a transitive verb is changed from the **active voice** to the **passive voice**, the direct object becomes the subject. (Note that only transitive verbs can be put in the passive voice.)

> The package was sent yesterday by Willa.
>
> Two tickets were bought by Marc.

trite language

Trite words, phrases, and ideas are ones used so often that they have become stale.

> ~~It may interest you to know that all the folks~~ here ~~are hale and hearty.~~ I should finish my report ~~quick as a wink.~~
>
> Everyone ... is well and having fun. early this week.

Trite language shows that little thought has gone into the writing and that the writer is relying instead on the words of others. (See also **buzzwords**, **cliché**, **conciseness/wordiness**, and **word choice**.)

try to/try and

Try to is the preferred form.

Please *try ~~and~~* finish the report on time.
                  to

typefaces

Word-processing programs on computers make it easy to use different typefaces and different sizes of type within a document (technically, each size in each typeface is known as a *font*). Resist the temptation to use more typefaces or sizes than are necessary. Using too many is distracting at best, confusing at worst. In fact, in all matters concerning document appearance, the simplest solution that will do the job is likely to be the best. Any physical element that calls attention to itself distracts the audience from your message.

In general, typefaces with serifs (the fine lines that finish the main strokes of the letters) are easier to read than sans serif faces (such as this), and roman type is easier to read than *italic type* (see **italics**). It is good advice, therefore, to confine sans serif type to uses such as headings and illustration labels (*callouts*) and to save italics for the particular uses set forth in the discussion of italics earlier in this book. Avoid altogether script faces (*such as this*).

Finally, be aware that different documentation styles may have rules about the use of typefaces. If you are expected to follow a particular style, such as MLA or APA style, see **Research Processes**.

T

underlining (See **italics**.)

understatement

To understate is to play down, usually for humorous or ironic effect. For example, in the movie *The Wizard of Oz,* after a tornado transports Dorothy and her dog, Toto, to the fantastical land of Oz, Dorothy's understated comment is "Toto, I've a feeling we're not in Kansas anymore." (See also **figures of speech**.)

uninterested/disinterested (See **disinterested/uninterested**.)

unity

Unity is singleness of purpose and treatment; a unified paragraph or paper has one central idea and does not digress into unrelated topics. In general, a unified **paragraph** should develop the idea expressed in the **topic sentence**, and a unified composition should develop the idea expressed in the **thesis** statement. As you revise, assess the unity of your composition and eliminate digressions. (See also **coherence**.)

As part of its mission to provide care for animals, the M.S.P.C.A. maintains three hospitals in the state, of which Angell is by far the largest. The society also runs eight animal shelters, publishes a bimonthly magazine called *Animals,* operates a pet cemetery, runs a law-enforcement division, and lobbies the government for the animal protection cause. ~~I've always had pets, but I had no idea that the society had its fingers in so many pies.~~ Even though Angell's interests run counter in some ways to the society's formal goal of *prevention* of cruelty (since the animals are treated after the injury or illness has occurred), the hospital is by far the most illustrious of the M.S.P.C.A.'s operations, and the most expensive. ~~I know I couldn't afford it for Muffy.~~

U

501

URL

A URL is a Uniform Resource Locator, the address used to reach a site on the **Internet**. A URL has at least two parts (up to the single slash) and sometimes more: protocol://domain name/folder/file.

http://www.mhhe.com/socscience/english/

Internet protocol for a Web site	Domain name of McGraw-Hill Higher Education Division	Folder with files about Social Science subdivisions	Folder with English files

Figure U-1. An annotated URL.

Usage

Usage is the choice we make among the various words and constructions available in our language. Usage problems occur with commonly confused words (such as *advice* and *advise*), with homonyms, or words that sound alike (such as *foreword* and *forward* or *principle* and *principal*), with commonly misspelled words (such as *altogether* and *all right*), and with **nonstandard English**, such as **colloquialisms** and **slang**. Words must always be spelled correctly, but the choice between standard and nonstandard English depends to some degree on what is most appropriate for the **audience**, subject, and **purpose** of a particular piece of writing.

The most common usage problems are listed below. They are discussed, with examples, in their own entries. See **spelling** for additional lists of commonly confused words and homonyms and for commonly misspelled words.

A a/an
above
accept/except
adapt/adopt/adept
adverse/averse
advice/advise
affect/effect
agree to/agree with
ain't
all right/alright
all together/altogether
almost/most
a lot/alot
already/all ready
a.m./p.m. (or A.M./P.M.)

among/between (see *between/among*)
amount/number
and/or
and etc.
ante-/anti-
anxious/eager
anyone/any one
anyways/anywheres
as
as/like
averse/adverse (see *adverse/averse*)
awful/awfully
awhile/a while

B   bad/badly
    because
    being as/being that
    beside/besides
    between/among
    between you and me
    bias/prejudice
    both . . . and
    bunch
    burst/bursted; bust/busted

C   can/may
    capital/capitol
    censor/censure
    chair/chairperson/chairman/
        chairwoman
    cite/site/sight
    committee
    compare/contrast
    complement/compliment
    consensus
    continual/continuous
    could have/could of
    criterion/criteria
    critique

D   data
    different from/different than
    differ from/differ with
    disinterested/uninterested
    due to/because of

E   each
    effect/affect (see *affect/effect*)
    e.g.
    either
    either . . . or
    elicit/illicit
    emigrate/immigrate
    eminent/imminent/immanent
    enthuse, enthused
    et al.
    etc.
    everybody/everyone
    everyday/every day
    explicit/implicit

F   farther/further
    female

few/a few
fewer/less
first/firstly
flammable/inflammable/
    nonflammable
foreword/forward
former/latter
further/farther (see *farther/
    further*)

G   good/well

H   had/had of
    had ought/hadn't ought
    half
    hanged/hung
    he/she, his/her
    healthful/healthy
    himself/hisself
    hopefully
    however

I   I
    i.e.
    if
    illegal/illicit
    immigrate/emigrate (see *emigrate/
        immigrate*)
    imminent/eminent/immanent (see
        eminent/imminent/immanent)
    implicit/explicit (see *explicit/
        implicit*)
    imply/infer
    in/into/in to
    incidentally/incidently
    incredible/incredulous
    infer/imply (see *imply/infer*)
    ingenious/ingenuous
    in order to
    input
    in regards to
    inside/inside of
    insure/ensure/assure
    irregardless/regardless
    is when/is where
    it
    its/it's

K   kind of/sort of

U

L later/latter
lay/lie, set/sit
lead/led
learn/teach
leave/let
lend/loan
less/fewer (see *fewer/less*)
liable/likely
lie/lay (see *lay/lie, set/sit*)
like/as (see *as/like*)
little/a little
loose/lose
lots

M male
man/mankind
may/can (see *can/may*)
maybe/may be
media/medium
Ms./Miss/Mrs.
must have/must of

N neither . . . nor
none
not only . . . but also
nowhere/nowheres

O off/off of
OK/O.K./okay
on account of/because of
only

P per
percent/per cent/percentage
persons/people
phenomena/phenomenon
plus
p.m./a.m. (see *a.m./p.m.*)
principal/principle

Q quote/quotation

R raise/rise
real/really
reason is because
respective/respectively/
respectfully
rise/raise (see *raise/rise*)

S says/goes/said
sensual/sensuous
set/sit (see *lay/lie, set/sit*)
shall/will
should have/should of
sic
sight/site/cite (see *cite/site/sight*)
sit/set (see *lay/lie, set/sit*)
so
some/somewhat
some time/sometime/sometimes
sort of/kind of (see *kind of/
sort of*)
supposed to/suppose to

T take/bring
than/then
that
that/which/who
themselves/theirself/theirselves
there/their/they're
to/too/two
toward/towards
try to/try and

U uninterested/disinterested (see
distinterested/uninterested)
use/utilize
used to/use to

V very

W wait for/wait on
well/good (see *good/well*)
where/that
where . . . at
whether/if
which/that/who (see
that/which/who)
who/whom
who's/whose
will/shall (see *shall/will*)
would have/would of

X X-ray

Y your/you're

use/utilize

Use is generally preferable to *utilize*.

When you are proofreading your papers, ~~utilize~~ *use* your English handbook.

used to/use to

Use to is nonstandard for *used to*.

She ~~use~~ *used* to be happy.

U

vague words

A vague word is one that is imprecise in the context in which it is used. Words such as *nice, important, good, bad, contact, thing,* and *fine* encompass such a broad range of meanings that they are vague in most contexts. In your writing, be concrete and specific. (See also **abstract words/concrete words** and **general words/specific words.**)

CHANGE	My poetry class was *useful;* we learned *a lot.*
TO	My *Modern American Poetry* class *taught* me to *understand modernism* and to *appreciate the work of Eliot, Stevens, and Crane.*

verbals

A verbal is a **verb** form that can function as a **noun**, an **adjective**, or an **adverb**. The three kinds of verbals are gerunds, participles, and infinitives.
A **gerund** is a verb form ending in *-ing* that is used as a noun.

Jogging is *exercising* that increases your heart rate.

A **participle** is a verb form that can be used as an adjective or in a **verb phrase**. The **present participle** of a verb usually ends in *-ing*. A regular **past participle** ends in *-ed,* and most irregular past participles end in *-en* (*forgotten*), *-n* (*risen*), or *-t* (*built*). (See also **irregular verbs.**)

That *exercising* equipment is expensive. [adjective]

They made a *determined* effort to exercise daily. [adjective]

He *had jogged* regularly before the accident; now, he *is exercising* at the gym. [verb phrases]

An **infinitive** is the plain form of the verb and is usually preceded by *to.* Infinitives can function as nouns, adjectives, or adverbs.

She likes *to jog.* [noun]

The problem is where *to run.* [adjective]

The weather helps *determine* how far to run. [adverb]

verb errors

Tenses

To express ongoing action that began in the past, use the **present perfect tense,** not the present or the present progressive.

have lived
We ~~live~~ in Vallejo since 1987.
  ∧

has worked
My sister ~~is working~~ for Bio-Tech for three years.

Do not use the present perfect tense to refer to actions that have been completed.

I ~~have~~ finished my exams two days ago.

Use the **present tense** to express habitual action that could continue indefinitely. Use the present **progressive form** to express ongoing action that will not continue indefinitely.

completes
The earth ~~is completing~~ one orbit around the sun in a year.

My brother is working in Saudi Arabia for three years.

Do not shift verb tenses in compound **predicates**.

listened
Whenever I felt sad, I sat by the river and ~~was listening~~ to the birds sing.

Helping Verbs

Include the **helping verb** in **perfect tenses** and in **progressive forms**.

has
Desktop publishing improved in recent years.

is
The market for information disks growing rapidly.

In verb phrases with helping verbs, use the plain form of the main verb.

learn
Where *did* you ~~*learned*~~ to speak English?

feel
Amelia *doesn't* ~~*feels*~~ well and is planning to go home early.

verb phrases

A verb phrase consists of a main **verb** preceded by one or more **helping verbs**.

He *is* [helping verb] *working* [main verb] hard this summer.
You *should* [helping verb] *go* [main verb].

V

verbs

A verb is a word or word group that expresses an action or a state of being.

> The child *darted* across the yard. [action]
>
> The baby *is* content now. [state of being]

A verb may also show the effect of an action on a subject.

> Margie *was touched* that Elden remembered her birthday.

A verb is one of the eight **parts of speech.**

Properties of Verbs

Verbs change form to indicate person, voice, number, tense, and mood. (See also **agreement of subjects and verbs.**)

Person indicates whether a verb refers to the speaker, the person spoken to, or the person (or thing) spoken about.

> I *see* [first person] a yellow tint, but he *sees* [third person] a yellow-green hue.
>
> I *am* [first person] convinced, and you *are* [second person] not convinced.

Voice indicates whether the subject of a verb acts or receives the action. If the subject acts, the verb is in the **active voice;** if it receives the action, the verb is in the **passive voice.**

> The aerosol bomb *propels* the liquid as a mist. [active voice]
>
> The liquid *is propelled* as a mist by the aerosol bomb. [passive voice]

Number indicates whether the subject of a verb is singular or plural.

> The car *was* in good operating condition. [singular]
>
> The cars *were* in good operating condition. [plural]

Tense indicates when an action took place. The six tenses—present, past, future, present perfect, past perfect, and future perfect—are all derived from the three principal parts of the verb: the infinitive, the past form, and the past participle. (See also **irregular verbs.**)

> I *believe.* [present, based on infinitive]
>
> I *believed.* [past]
>
> I *will believe.* [future, based on infinitive]
>
> I *have believed.* [present perfect, based on past participle]
>
> I *had believed.* [past perfect, based on past participle]
>
> I *will have believed.* [future perfect, based on past participle]

Each of the six tenses also has a **progressive form**, which indicates ongoing action and consists of the appropriate tense of *be* and the present participle (the *-ing* form) of the verb.

I *am writing.* [present progressive]

I *was writing.* [past progressive]

I *will be writing.* [future progressive]

I *have been writing.* [present perfect progressive]

I *had been writing.* [past perfect progressive]

I *will have been writing.* [future perfect progressive]

Mood indicates whether the verb is intended to make a statement or ask a question (**indicative mood**), to give a command (**imperative mood**), or to express a wish or a condition contrary to fact (**subjunctive mood**).

How *is* Kendra *doing* in spelling? Her test *was* correct. [indicative mood]

Install the wiring today. [imperative mood]

If I *were* you, I would postpone the trip. [subjunctive mood]

Transitive and Intransitive Verbs

A **transitive verb** requires a **direct object** to complete its meaning.

They *laid* the foundation on October 24. [*Foundation* is the direct object of the transitive verb *laid.*]

Only transitive verbs can be put into the **passive voice**. The direct object in the active voice becomes the subject in the passive voice.

The foundation *was laid* on October 24. [*Foundation* is the subject.]

An **intransitive verb** does not require an object to complete its meaning.

The audience *howled.*

Although intransitive verbs do not have an object, certain intransitive verbs, called **linking verbs,** may take a **subject complement**, which may be a noun (or pronoun) that renames the subject or an adjective that modifies it.

A calculator *is* a useful tool. [The noun *tool* renames *calculator.*]

The report *seems* complete. [The adjective *complete* describes *report.*]

Finite Verbs and Verbals

Finite verbs function as the verb of a clause or a sentence.

The telephone *rang,* and the secretary *answered* it.

V

Nonfinite verbs, or **verbals**, function as **nouns**, **adjectives**, or **adverbs**; they cannot function as the verb of a sentence. The three types of nonfinite verbs are gerunds, infinitives, and participles.

A **gerund** is the *-ing* form of a verb used as a noun.

Seeing is *believing*.

An **infinitive** is the root form of a verb (usually preceded by *to*) used as a noun, an adverb, or an adjective.

He hates *to complain*. [noun, direct object of *hates*]

These are the classes *to take*. [adjective modifying *classes*]

She was too tired *to study*. [adverb modifying *tired*]

A **participle** is a verb form that can function as part of a **verb phrase** (was *parking*, had *painted*) or as an adjective in front of a noun (a *parking* ticket, a *painted* fence), after a linking verb (as a **predicate adjective**), or in a **participial phrase** modifying a noun (the fence *painted* by Huck).

His *closing* statement was very *convincing*.

Wearing her new dress, Brenda waited nervously for the interview.

Helping Verbs and Modal Auxiliaries

A **helping verb** (sometimes called an *auxiliary verb*) is used in a **verb phrase** to help indicate **tense**, **mood**, **voice**, **person**, and **number**. The most common helping verbs are the various forms of *have* (*has*, *had*), *be* (*is*, *are*, *was*, and so on), and *do* (*did*, *does*).

I *am* going.

She *was* going.

He *has* gone.

Did they go?

The **modal auxiliaries** *can*, *could*, *may*, *might*, *must*, *ought*, *shall*, *should*, *will*, and *would* are used to express ability, probability, advice, wishes, or requests. They do not change form to indicate mood, voice, person, or number.

We *must* go. [indicative mood; active voice]

If you were to clean your room, you *would* be allowed to go out tonight. [subjunctive mood]

Let me know *should* I be needed. [imperative mood]

Smoking *should* not be allowed inside the building. [indicative mood; passive voice]

very

As an **intensifier**, *very* can be used for emphasis but should not be used unnecessarily.

> Bicycle manufacturers had a *very* good year: sales were up forty-three percent.

> Martha was ~~very~~ happy to hear the news.

visuals

The term *visuals* lumps together all illustrations, photographs, charts, graphs, or other pictures that are used to supplement, explain, or enhance written text. Carefully chosen visuals can add a great deal to a report, making ideas easier to understand and remember. (See **graphics**.)

voice (grammatical)

Voice in grammar is the property of **verbs** that shows whether **subjects** are acting or are acted upon. A verb in the **active voice** indicates that the subject is acting.

> Bruce Springsteen *wrote* the lyrics.

A verb in the **passive voice** indicates that the subject is acted upon or is the product of the action.

> The lyrics *were written* by Bruce Springsteen.

Both sentences in the examples say the same thing, but the **emphasis** is different. The first sentence emphasizes the doer of the action, Bruce Springsteen. The second sentence emphasizes the product of the action, the lyrics.

Active voice makes writing concise, clear, and vigorous. Consequently, use active voice generally for direct and effective writing. However, the passive voice is preferable when the doer of the action is irrelevant, when the doer is less important than the result or the recipient of the action, or when naming the doer would be impractical or undiplomatic.

> A plume of smoke *was seen* in the distance.
> Rita *was treated* to a birthday lunch by her colleagues.
> Taking photographs *is not permitted* during the performance.

Whether you use the passive or the active voice, avoid awkward shifts between the two voices.

> After Ms. McDonald *corrected* her misspelling, the paper *she retyped* ~~was retyped by her.~~

Sometimes, however, a shift in voice is appropriate. In the sentence "He *is widely viewed* as a liberal, but he *regards* himself as a conservative," the passive-to-active shift keeps the focus on the subject of the sentence, *he*. Putting both verbs in the active voice alters that consistent focus: "Many people *view* him as a liberal, but he *regards* himself as a conservative."

voice (in literary analysis) (See **persona**.)

voice (stylistic) (See **tone**.)

V

wait for/wait on

Wait on means "serve." *Wait for* means "await."

> Joe's feet ached after eight hours of *waiting on* tables.
>
> I will *wait for* your answer.

Web browser

A Web browser is software, such as Netscape Navigator or Internet Explorer, that gives you access to the **Internet**.

Web page (See **Web site**.)

Web site

A Web site, or Web page, is an interactive, graphical document on the **World Wide Web**. It is accessed at its **URL**.

well/good (See *good/well*.)

where/that

Do not substitute *where* for *that*.

> *that*
> I read in *Newsweek* ~~where~~ people send letters to the president's cat.
> ∧

where . . . at

Do not use *at* with *where*.

> *Where* is his office ~~at~~?

whether/if

Use *whether* in the statement of an alternative and *if* in a conditional statement.

> *If* the rains continue, the river may flood.
>
> We could not decide *whether* to go.

which/that/who (See *that/which/who*.)

W

513

who/whom

Use *who* as the **subject** of a verb or as a **subject complement**. Use *whom* as the **object** of a **verb**, a **verbal**, or a **preposition**. If the pronoun begins a **dependent clause**, its **case** is determined by its function in the clause, not by the clause's function in the sentence.

When in doubt about whether to use *who* or *whom*, mentally substitute a **personal pronoun**. If *he, she,* or *they* fits, use *who*.

> She is a research assistant *who* also likes to teach. [*She* also likes to teach.]

If *him, her,* or *them* fits, use *whom*.

> The new teaching assistant, *whom* I met yesterday, is also doing research. [I met *her* yesterday.]

Do not let an inserted clause—such as *you thought* in the following sentence—mislead you.

> *who*
> These are the men ~~whom~~ you thought were the architects.
>   ^

In this sentence, *who* is the subject of the predicate *were the architects;* it is not the object of the inserted clause *you thought.* To determine the correct case in a sentence with an interjected clause, mentally remove or relocate the inserted clause.

> These are the men *who* were the architects, you thought.

Some writers prefer to begin **clauses** and sentences with *who* instead of *whom* even when the objective case is appropriate, but others consider this usage ungrammatical, especially in formal contexts.

> *Who* [*Whom*] did the team choose as the most valuable player of the season?

who's/whose

Who's is a **contraction** of *who is;* it should generally be avoided in formal writing.

> *Who is*
> ~~Who's~~ scheduled to teach the Henry James seminar next semester?
> ^

Whose is the possessive form of *who.*

> *Whose* department will be affected by the budget cuts?

W

will/shall   (See *shall/will.*)

word choice

The right word is the one that means exactly what you want to say and has the level of formality appropriate for your audience and your purpose.

Entries that will help you be precise in your choice of words include **abstract words/concrete words, antonyms, buzzwords, cliché, connotation/denotation, dictionaries, euphemisms, figures of speech, general words/specific words, jargon, metaphor, simile, strong verbs, synonyms, thesaurus, trite language,** and **vague words.**

Entries that will help you choose words appropriate for your audience and purpose include **colloquial usage; English, varieties of; idioms; informal and formal writing style; nonsexist language; nonstandard English; slang and neologisms; standard English; tone;** and **usage.**

word division   (See **hyphens.**)

wordiness   (See **conciseness/wordiness.**)

working bibliography   (See **Research Processes,** pages 42–44.)

works cited   (See **Research Processes,** pages 60–153.)

World Wide Web (WWW)

The World Wide Web, the most popular and public part of the **Internet,** uses hypertext transfer protocol (http) for transmitting graphics and text. Web **URLs** begin with *http.*

would have/would of

Would of is nonstandard for *would have.*

> *have*
> If I'd known you were coming, I *would of* baked a cake.
> ∧

writing a draft   (See **Composing Processes,** pages 11–12.)

writing on a computer

Computers can help you record ideas quickly, rewrite and revise easily, and create clean and attractive final drafts. But the ease of making minor sentence-level changes may cause you to lose sight of the larger concerns of scope and organization. The following tips will help you take advantage of the benefits offered by computer technology.

W

Creating a First Draft

On a computer, you can easily save, change, rearrange, and delete material. To counter the temptation to interrupt the flow of ideas during **freewriting** or **brainstorming,** turn down the contrast on the screen and make the words invisible.

Computers lend themselves to developing outlines. You can arrange your freewriting ideas into an outline and then add material, such as research notes, under each topic.

As you work on various drafts, be cautious about permanently deleting anything. You may find that material you once thought irrelevant is useful when you develop the paper further. Rather than deleting unused material, paste it into a separate file. Use the save command frequently as you write, to prevent accidental deletions.

Even though corrections are easily made on a computer, do not spend too much time polishing the wording, spelling, and punctuation of the first draft—do the polishing after you have established the basic content and or-ganization. And do not let the finished look of a document printed by a com-puter tempt you to regard the first draft as the final draft.

Revising, Editing, and Proofreading

In addition to the ease with which computers allow you to rearrange, change, and delete material, they aid in revising, editing, and proofreading. A spell checker can locate spelling errors and typos—but it cannot take the place of careful proofreading because it cannot identify any error that forms a word, such as the misuse of *there* for *their.* Style and grammar checkers are less useful; they sometimes do not "understand" the text and suggest faulty "corrections."

You can use the Find command to look for empty words and phrases (such as *there is* or *the fact that*) and then delete them and reword the sentence. You can also develop a file of words you frequently misuse, overuse, or mis-spell and use the Find command to spot them.

Many writers prefer to read a printed copy of their entire draft rather than to read it fifteen to twenty lines at a time on the screen. Some writers like to make all their changes on paper and transfer them to the screen; other writ-ers simply note on paper where changes are needed and do the rewriting on the keyboard. Experiment to find the best combination for you. Whether you edit and proofread on paper or screen, however, print a copy of your doc-ument for **peer response** before you make final revisions.

Before you print out the final draft, make sure that you know the in-structor's preferences for manuscript format—for margins, space between lines, page numbers, and the like. (See **manuscript form** and **Research Processes.**)

X-ray

X-ray, usually capitalized, is always hyphenated as an **adjective** and **verb** and usually hyphenated as a **noun.** Whether you choose to use a capital or a lowercase *X* and whether you choose to hyphenate the noun, be sure to do so consistently.

portable *X-ray* unit [adjective]

The technician *X-rayed* the ankle. [verb]

X-rays and gamma rays [noun]

your/you're

Your is the possessive form of the personal pronoun *you; you're* is a **contraction** of *you are.*

If *you're* going to the seashore, be sure to wear *your* sweater.

zip codes (See **addresses, letters,** and **numbers and symbols.**)

Credits

ESL Index

E-1

Index

HOW TO USE THIS INDEX:
1. As in the handbook entries, alphabetizing in this index is letter by letter—that is, all spaces and punctuation are ignored in alphabetizing. In the subentries, prepositions and other clarifying words or phrases before key words are also ignored.
2. *See* and *See also* references are to index listings, not to entries in the body of the handbook.
3. Readers whose first language is not English should also see the ESL index, which precedes this main index and focuses on matters of special concern to speakers of English as a second language.

effect, and cause, as method of development, 10, 222, 373, 379, 402–03
e.g., 281
ei/ie (spelling), 468
either, 281
either . . . or, 281
either/or fallacy (bifurcation), 364
electronic databases. *See* databases (computer)
electronic mailing lists, 59–60
electronic newsgroups, 59–60
electronic sources, documenting
  APA style, 109–11
  CMS style, 122–23
  CSE style, 146
  MLA style, 72–84
elicit/illicit, 281
ellipsis points (ellipsis marks, points of suspension), 281–82, 414, 442. *See also* quotations
elliptical constructions, 282–83
  commas in, 237
  eliminating unnecessary repetition, 252–53
  like in, 203
e-mail, 283–84
  APA style for, 111
  CMS style for, 124, 128
  documenting, 76, 78, 111, 124, 128
  electronic newsgroups and mailing lists, 59
  MLA style for, 76, 78
  Netiquette for, 283–84
emigrate/immigrate, 284
eminent/imminent/immanent, 284
emotions of reader (*pathos*), appeal to, 197, 199, 413
emphasis, 19, 284–87
  active and passive voice for, 169, 511–12
  balancing sentences for, 286
  dashes for, 286
  exclamation point for, 286
  hyperbole for, 287
  intensifiers for, 287
  intentional sentence fragments for, 286, 457
  italics for, 287, 343
  in paragraphs, 284–85, 286
  parallel structure for, 286
  repetition for, 285, 446
  in sentences, 285–86
  sentence variety for, 459
  subordination, 481
  with words, 286–87

employment search. *See* job search
empty words and phrases, 251–52
enclosure notations, in letters, 355
encyclopedias, 38–39. *See also* sources, using
endings (conclusions), 12, 254–55
endnotes, 116–17
end punctuation (in sentences)
  ellipsis points, 281–82, 414, 442
  exclamation points, 293
  parentheses, 408–09
  periods, 414
  question marks, 437–40
  quotation marks, 437–40
English as a second language (ESL) dictionaries, 275
English, varieties of, 287–88. *See also* nonstandard English; standard English
ensure (insure/ensure/assure), 334
enthuse, enthused, 288
envelopes, for letters, 355
equivocation (fallacy), 364
ESL dictionaries, 275
essays, composing, 3–21
essay tests, 288–90
et al., 290
etc., 290–91
ethnic groups, capitalizing names of, 212
ethos (appeal to character of writer in argument), 291
etymology (word origin), 272–73
euphemisms, 291
evaluating sources, 44–46, 55–56
everybody/everyone, 291
everyday/every day, 292
everyone (everybody/everyone), 291
evidence, 292
  biased or suppressed, 365–66
exactness
  abstract words/concrete words, 168
  ambiguity, 190–91
  clarity, 18, 225
  conciseness/wordiness, 250–54. *See also* conciseness/wordiness
  connotation/denotation, 259
  defining terms, 265–66
  details, 271, 400–01
  dictionaries, 271, 400–01
  emphasis, 284–87
  general words/specific words, 18, 305
  subordination, 480–82

for emphasis, 446
wordiness and, 250–51
reports. *See* documentation (of sources);
 research processes; sources, using
reports, oral, 395–96
research papers, peer response for, 17. *See
 also* documentation (of sources); research
 processes; sources, using
research processes, 29–34
 central catalog, 51–54
 documentation styles
  APA style, 99–114
  CMS style, 114–38
  CSE style, 139–52
  MLA style, 61–98
 Internet documents, judging reliability of,
  55–56
 interviews in, 28, 335–36
 library research vs. Internet research,
  38–51
 listing subject headings or keywords,
  40–42, 346
 note taking, 34, 45–48
 online searches, 54–60, 175, 208, 372, 453
 overview of, 28–60
 periodicals, 48–51
 reference works, 38–41
 sources, evaluating, 44–46
 topic, deciding on, 5–6, 28, 29
 working bibliography, 29, 34, 41–44
respective/respectively/respectfully, 447
responsibilities, of research writers, 29–34
restrictive and nonrestrictive elements,
 447–48
 appositives, 231, 236, 456–57
 dependent clauses, 226, 268–70, 385
 that/which/who, 447–48
résumés, 448–49, 450
revising, 13–17, 22, 449, 516
 collaborating (peer response), 5, 15–17, 413
 conclusions (endings), 12, 254–55
 editing, 17–20, 23, 280, 300, 516
 introductions (openings), 13–14, 336–38
 large-scale concerns, 13–14
 paragraphs, 14
 small-scale concerns, 14
 titles, 14, 493–94
 See also Revision Symbols (back inside
  cover)
rhetorical questions, 451

rhetorical (writing) situation, 3–6, 451
rise (raise/rise), 444
rooms in buildings, capitalizing, 218
root forms of verbs. *See* infinitives
run-on (fused) sentences, 18, 451–52

S

said (says/goes/said), 453
salutations in letters, 217
same-meaning words. *See* synonyms
says/goes/said, 453
scanned images, 312–13
scientific terms
 capitalizing, 215
 italic or bold type for (CSE style), 148
sculpture, italics for titles of, 344
search(es)
 job, 352, 353, 356–57, 448–49, 450
 keyword, 346
 literature, 34–60
 online, 54–60, 175, 208, 372, 453
search engine(s), 41, 50, 54–58, 175, 307,
 372, 453, 478
seasons (lowercase for), 214
secondary (indirect) sources, 36
 APA documentation style for, 102
 CMS documentation style for, 130
 MLA documentation style for, 66
 See also sources, using
second-page headings, in letters, 354
second person (grammatical), 415, 421, 435
segmented bar graphs, 311
self-referential (reflexive) pronouns, 433, 445
semicolon(s), 436, 453–54
 colons vs., 232–33, 453
 commas vs., 234, 453–54
 with conjunctive adverbs, 236, 258
 between independent clauses, 453–54
 misuse of, 454
 with quotation marks, 454
 in series, 454
sensual/sensuous, 454
sentence beginnings
 capital letters for, 211, 216
 with coordinating conjunctions, 234
 expletives, 294–95
 with numbers, 391
sentence variety and, 461

U

REVISION SYMBOLS

The following symbols are commonly used by instructors in marking written work. Most of the symbols are keyed to pages where the problem is discussed.

ab or **abbr**
abbreviations, 158–67

adj   adjectives, 171–75

adv   adverbs, 176–79

agr   agreement, 180–88

appr   inappropriate word or phrase, 515

awk   awkward construction

cap   capital letters, 211–18

case   case, 218–22

cit   citation form, 63–67, 100–03, 115–26, 140

coh   coherence, 228–29

coord   coordination, 257–58

cs   comma splice, 239–40

d   diction (word choice), 515

dev   inadequate development, 372–73, 400–05

dm   dangling modifier, 263

emph   emphasis, 284–87

exact   inexact word choice, 259, 515

frag   sentence fragment, 455–57

fs   fused (run-on) sentence, 451–52

hyph   hyphen, 317–20

id   idiom, 321–22

inc   incomplete comparison, 325

ital   italics (underlining), 343–45

jarg   jargon, 346

lc   lowercase letters, 211–18

mixed   mixed construction, 375–76

mm   misplaced modifier, 373–75

ms   manuscript form, 86–98, 112–14, 131–38, 146–52, 368–69

nonst   nonstandard usage, 287–88, 384

num   faulty use of numbers, 390-92

pass   ineffective passive voice, 169, 411–12

pn agr   pronoun-antecedent agreement, 180–83, 194

ref   pronoun reference, 431

rep   repetition, 250–51, 446

ro   run-on (fused) sentence, 451–52

shift   inappropriate shift, 462–63

sp   spelling, 467–77

sub   subordination, 480–82